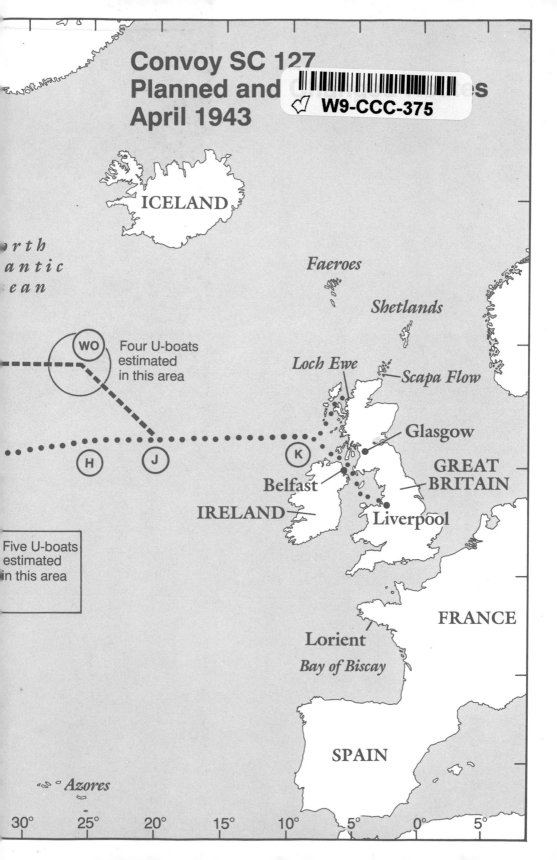

Convoy SC 127
Planned and ... es
April 1943

ICELAND

North
antic
ean

Faeroes

Shetlands

Loch Ewe

Scapa Flow

WO — Four U-boats estimated in this area

Glasgow

H

J

K

GREAT
BRITAIN

Belfast

IRELAND

Liverpool

Five U-boats
estimated
in this area

FRANCE

Lorient

Bay of Biscay

SPAIN

Azores

30° 25° 20° 15° 10° 5° 0° 5°

SEIZING
THE
ENIGMA

SEIZING THE ENIGMA

*The Race to Break
the German
U-Boat Codes,
1939–1943*

DAVID KAHN

HOUGHTON MIFFLIN COMPANY
BOSTON
1991

Library of Congress Cataloging-in-Publication Data

Kahn, David, 1930–
Seizing the enigma : the race to break the German U-boat
codes, 1939–1943 / David Kahn.
p.   cm.
"A Thomas Congdon book" — T.p. verso.
Includes bibliographical references and index.
ISBN 0-395-42739-8
1. World War, 1939–1945 — Cryptography.   2. World War,
1939–1945 — Naval operations, German.   3. World War,
1939–1945 — Naval operations — Submarine.   I. Title.
D810.C88K34   1991   90-25128
940.54′85 — dc20   CIP

Printed in the United States of America

A THOMAS CONGDON BOOK

Maps by Richard Cornett

Chapter 2 was published in *Military History Quarterly*,
2 (Winter 1990).

To
Miriam and Arthur
Louis and Barbara

Contents

List of Maps

Preface

This book recounts the secret history of World War II's Battle of the Atlantic. It exposes the chief hidden factor that helped the Allies win it: they intercepted, solved, and read the coded radio messages between Admiral Karl Dönitz, Hitler's commander of submarines, and his U-boats at sea. The solutions gave the British and Americans intelligence about the locations and movements of the U-boats, enabling the Allies to divert their convoys around wolfpacks and to sink subs. This was of fundamental importance because whoever won the Battle of the Atlantic would win the war. The struggle between Allied ships bringing supplies to Britain and German submarines seeking to sever that lifeline was the longest battle of the greatest war of all time, beginning on its first day and ending on its last. Winston Churchill has evoked its significance in words that, though familiar, still ring with high drama:

> The Battle of the Atlantic was the dominating factor all throughout the war. Never for one moment could we forget that everything happening elsewhere, on land, at sea, or in the air, depended ultimately on its outcome, and amid all other cares, we viewed its changing fortunes day by day with hope or apprehension. . . .
>
> Amid the torrent of violent events one anxiety reigned supreme. Battles might be won or lost, enterprises might succeed or miscarry, territories might be gained or quitted, but dominating all our power to carry on the war, or even keep ourselves alive, lay our mastery of the ocean routes and the free approach and entry to our ports.

The Germans used a cipher machine called the Enigma to put messages into secret form. Contrary to popular opinion formed since the 1974 publication of Group Captain F. W. Winterbotham's *The Ultra Secret,* however, the Enigma used by the German navy — unlike that used by the air force — generally withstood

British codebreaking for the first two years of the war. It was not until the British captured key documents from German warships that they were able to break the naval Enigma continuously. This book tells, for the first time, the story of those seizures and the role they played in helping win the Battle of the Atlantic.

The book differs in several other ways from earlier accounts of the Enigma. It depicts the codebreakers, especially those working on the naval Enigma, behind their closed doors and relates case histories of the role of the decodes in the defeat of the U-boats. It focuses upon personalities and rests as much as possible upon primary sources, namely documents and interviews. It shows how much of a "near-run thing" the cryptologic battle was and seeks to explain why the Allies won it. Finally, it weighs the effect of codebreaking on the war at sea.

I believe that this book tells an essentially complete story of the failures and successes of British codebreaking, thanks in large part to the magisterial history of British intelligence in World War II by Sir Harry Hinsley and his coauthors. Those three volumes are based upon primary sources, many of them not yet released to the public, and upon Hinsley's own wartime experiences evaluating German naval intercepts. In some areas, such as the circuitry and mechanism of the cryptanalytic testing machines called bombes, my descriptions are based on interviews and reconstructions. This and other portions of my text dealing with technical matters are not intended to provide detailed instruction in Enigma cryptanalysis, though they give, I hope, enough information for readers who wish to pursue the matter to carry through their own analyses. This material may seem dry, but to leave it out would obscure a main point of the book: the fearful difficulty of the work of the cryptanalysts, which could not succeed without outside help.

As much as possible, I have used cryptologically precise terminology. Thus I distinguish between codes (which, to oversimplify, work by words) and ciphers (which work by letters). I usually write "encipher" in connection with ciphers and "encode" with codes. But sometimes, for simplicity or rhythm or sound, I use "code" and its derivatives when "cipher" or even "key" (a setting of the wheels or plugs of the Enigma, for example) would be correct: "codes" in the subtitle, which stands for "keys," is an instance.

* * *

Among the many people who helped with this book I should like to thank first of all Tom Congdon, who has believed in it for many years and whose tough but sensitive editing improved the text. Robie Macauley of Houghton Mifflin had enough faith in the idea to contract for it. My agent, Max Becker, provided valuable moral support. John Sterling of Houghton Mifflin handled the publishing with energy and flair. Peg Anderson of that house did not a good, but a great job of copyediting, tightening and rearranging the text and suggesting improvements.

Others helped with the substance. Sir Harry Hinsley patiently answered torrents of questions. Dr. Jurgen Röhwer steered me right on the Battle of the Atlantic. Ralph Erskine generously shared his expertise on the naval Enigma. Dr. Cipher Deavours made complex cryptanalyses plain. Carl Ellison helped in this as well. Christine Kelly located many retired Royal Navy officers and men. My researchers Alexander Lesnoff-Caravaglia and Mary Z. Pain came up with what I needed in the Public Record Office. Ilan Berkner computed times of solution for messages. Franz Selinger provided names and addresses of crew members of the German weather ships. The late Patrick Beesly furnished information and encouragement.

Archivists and historians who greatly helped included John Taylor, Harry Rilley, Tim Mulligan, Bill Cunliffe, and Bob Wolfe at the National Archives, Dr. Dean Allard, Bernard Cavalcante, and Kathleen Lloyd at the U.S. Navy's Operational Archives, Dr. Hansjoseph Maierhofer and Dr. Manfred Kehrig at the Militärarchiv, and David Brown at the Naval Historical Branch of the Ministry of Defence.

Richard Cornett of *Newsday* drew fine maps, and Bob Newman of that newspaper helped with art matters. Karen Bacon and Rita Porzelt typed a hard-to-read manuscript. I thank my colleagues at *Newsday* for their help and understanding: Jim Lynn, Peg Finucane, the late Lou Renzulli, Marty Hollander, Judy Bender, Jim Klurfeld, Ilene Barth, Mark Howard, and Eileen McDermott.

My friends Edward S. Miller and Dr. Louis Kruh encouraged me. Bernie Bookbinder provided valuable emotional support. Dr. Zita Brandes's professional aid was indispensable. Others who helped include Dr. Robert N. Grant, Dr. Alec Douglas, and Gilbert Bloch, as well as all those who answered questions in interviews or in letters. Susanne Kahn discussed problems sympathetically; our sons Oliver and Michael reminded me of what really matters. My father, Jesse Kahn, offered advice, and together we remembered my mother, Florence Kahn, who died while the book was being written.

I am grateful to all for their help. The responsibility for errors lies with me, of course, and I shall appreciate any corrections that readers send.

Great Neck, New York
October 1990

SEIZING
THE
ENIGMA

One

A Staff School Memory

From under the ruffled waters of the springtime North Atlantic, the captain of the German submarine U-110 peered through his periscope at the oncoming convoy. He chose four ships in the second column as his targets, took aim, and, at 30-second intervals, fired three torpedoes from his bow tubes.

His intended victims were members of Convoy OB 318, lumbering west toward America to be refilled with supplies for wartime Britain. In the center of the front line of the warships that surrounded the convoy steamed Escort Group 3's flagship, the Royal Navy destroyer *Bulldog*. She was skippered by Commander A. J. (Joe) Baker-Cresswell, a fresh-faced, boyish-looking career officer, just turned forty.

Baker-Cresswell had fixed his midday position by shooting the sun with his sextant through the thickening clouds when, to his astonishment, he saw a column of water rise near the merchantman *Esmond*, which was leading the starboard column. For a moment he was incredulous. The convoy, southwest of Iceland, was only 300 miles from the Greenland coast; no submarine had ever attacked that far west. But his surprise did not stop him from swinging at once to starboard, in the direction from which he sensed the torpedo had come.

The local time was noon, the date, Friday, May 9, 1941. Great Britain and Nazi Germany had been at war for a year and a half. The United States was not yet involved, though that very day President Franklin D. Roosevelt's son James had said that the country was at war in all but name. Adolf Hitler's forces had overrun Poland, Denmark and Norway, Belgium, the Netherlands, and France.

But England, buoyed by Winston Churchill's trumpet-tongued defiance, had withstood the German threat. In the fall of 1940, Hitler abandoned his plan to invade Shakespeare's "sceptered isle . . . set in the silver sea." He had decided to force Britain to surrender instead. His bombs would destroy her war industry and the people's will to resist. His submarines would cut her lifelines and starve her.

And indeed, in the sea lanes between the British Isles and North America, U-boats were sinking American and Canadian ships supplying Britain, and the convoys' escort vessels were fighting off the U-boats. This was the Battle of the Atlantic, the only battle in World War II that lasted from the first day of that war to the last.

Paralleling this visible battle was an invisible one — the code war. British codebreakers were intercepting German radio messages and trying to crack German naval codes. The Allied naval commands used whatever information they could gather about U-boat movements to divert convoys and sink subs. Unlike the men in combat, the codebreakers did not face death, but they labored under intense pressure. The U-boat cipher was the most difficult of all the ciphers used by the Kriegsmarine, the German navy, and they had been unable to crack it. They were perfectly aware that their efforts would determine not only the fate of men and ships, but even how quickly the war would end.

The transatlantic convoy system was a great chain of waterborne buckets bringing food, military supplies, and raw materials to Britain and taking money-earning goods to her allies. OB 318 was a typical outward convoy — outward from Britain — the 318th in the OB series, which had begun sailing from Liverpool on September 7, 1939, four days after Britain declared war. The O in the designator meant "outward"; the B distinguished this series from the identically numbered OA convoys, which left from London. On average four OB convoys a month sailed for North America.

On April 25, 1941, seventeen of the many ships swinging at anchor in the Mersey River estuary at Liverpool were issued orders that would form them into the core of OB 318. Vessels at Welsh and Scottish harbors were ordered to rendezvous at certain times and places with the Liverpool group. During the week before the sailing, the masters of the vessels met with one another and with the senior officer of the warships escorting them to answer questions and to get acquainted.

Not all of the ships nominated for the convoy were ready on time, and an extra one joined, so in the end OB 318 consisted of thirty-eight vessels. They varied in size from a little trader of 890 tons to a passenger-cargo steamer, the *Ixion*, of 10,263. The loaded merchantmen carried clay, coal, chalk, wood, pulp, Scotch whisky. Sixteen had brought supplies to Britain but had been unable to find cargoes for their outboard voyage to America, so they were now in ballast, loaded with rock or sand for stability at sea. Most of the ships were heading for the United States or Canada, but some were destined for the Caribbean or South America. Their company markings had been painted over with gray, and most had a 4-inch gun at the stern as well as some lighter, dual-purpose (antiaircraft and low-angle) weapons. Though some of the vessels could steam at 12½ knots, the convoy was limited to the speed of its slowest ship, 9 knots. In practice, because of the difficulties of steaming in formation, that speed was reduced to about 8 knots.

The Liverpool core departed in the afternoon of Friday, May 2, and proceeded up the west coast of Britain, annexing the other elements along the way. At 10:15 P.M. on Sunday, the full group sailed out between the Butt of Lewis, the northernmost point of the Outer Hebrides, and the tall majestic cliffs of Cape Wrath, at the northwestern tip of Scotland, to pass into the long swells of the open Atlantic. Here the warships of Escort Group 7, which would accompany the convoy to the waters off Iceland, joined and took command, and here OB 318 assumed its ocean formation of nine short columns about 500 yards apart, with the ships in each column about 200 yards from those ahead and astern.

The next morning, as OB 318 swung west, the sky was clear and the weather warm. Overhead an airplane patrolled.

To defend against the U-boats the British had to know where they were. Asdic, the underwater sound-ranging system, could detect submerged submarines within a half mile on average. Radar could spot them on the surface 2 to 3 miles away if the weather was calm; the range dropped in rough seas. But both of these systems were little more than crude aiming devices. There was no way to locate the U-boats in time for ships and airplanes to concentrate against them. The few airplanes available could cover only a tiny fraction of the ocean, even when flying from British-occupied Iceland.

Radio intelligence was little better. At that time it relied chiefly on direction-finding: rotating a radio antenna until an enemy signal was heard most loudly, much as one turns a portable radio to get the best reception. The direction from which the signal came was its line of bearing. Two or more antennas took bearings on a signal from different places, the lines were drawn on a map, and the point at which they crossed gave the location of the transmitter. The direction-finders of the time were not precise, however. Although the margin of error averaged 25 miles, it could range up to 60 miles 500 to 1,000 miles offshore. Moreover, at that time ships did not have direction-finders. Thus the area from which a U-boat had radioed could be only generally fixed. The vagueness of direction-finding meant that the British could be directing a convoy straight at a U-boat infestation instead of past it. Besides, direction-finding told only where the U-boats were at that moment, not where their orders were directing them.

Only one source could provide more exact information in time for the convoys to detour around the U-boat groups. That source was the solution of coded German naval messages. And Britain had not then solved enough to help them. For the U-boat messages were well protected by the cryptographic armor of an electrical cipher machine called the Enigma, with which the Germans put radio messages into secret form.

The Enigma operator pressed the keys of a typewriter-like device as one does in hunt-and-peck typing. When a key was depressed, current flowed through a set of wired codewheels to illuminate an output letter on a glass panel. The output letters comprised the cryptogram of the original message. This was transmitted by radio to a U-boat. There the radioman—cipher clerk, using an identical machine identically set up, typed in the letters of the cryptogram. On the illuminable panel flashed the letters of the original German text.

Cracking the Enigma was the job of the British agency called the Government Code and Cypher School, or G.C.&C.S. (the name was a disguise). Formally a branch of the Foreign Office, G.C.&C.S. was housed at Bletchley Park, an estate in the town of Bletchley, some 50 miles northwest of London. Here more than a thousand people — mathematicians, linguists, chess champions, clerks — labored to read not only the Enigma messages of the Kriegsmarine but also messages enciphered in the Enigmas of the Luftwaffe, the army, the SS, and other German organizations, as well as nonmachine, or pencil-and-paper, cipher systems.

With the Luftwaffe's Enigma, which used a simpler keying system than the navy's, and with some of the Kriegsmarine hand ciphers, G.C.&C.S. often succeeded. These solutions were translated, supplemented by information from previous solutions, and forwarded to the armed forces. The output of G.C.&C.S.'s Naval Section — weather reports, reports of damage to German merchant shipping, local messages about the departure and return of U-boats, and data on troop transports — was sent via teleprinter to the Operational Intelligence Centre, a branch of the Naval Intelligence Division. The O.I.C. was bunkered in an almost windowless, forbidding concrete annex behind the Admiralty building off London's Trafalgar Square. Among its other duties, O.I.C. tracked the U-boats in the North Atlantic that were working to sever Britain's supply lines. But its intelligence was inadequate. Bletchley Park was unable to read the naval Enigma, which guarded the U-boats' orders, except on rare occasions. In the 613 days of war up to the moment when torpedoes struck the *Esmond,* Naval Section had solved less than 70 days' worth of Enigma messages. And most of those were too old to help. As an example, G.C.&C.S. had last teletyped a solved U-boat intercept to the O.I.C. two days before the U-110 attack — and that was of a message transmitted eleven days earlier.

The submarines were sinking more ships than Britain and the United States were building. And the sinkings were accelerating — from 126,000 tons in January 1941 to 249,000 tons in April. Rationing was beginning to hurt. In March 1941, two months before the attack on Convoy OB 318, meat rations were cut for the fourth time. Cheese rationing was begun in April. Butter and sugar had long been restricted, and fresh fruit and eggs were rapidly becoming a memory. It was said that people were beginning to think with their stomachs. Churchill had estimated that 31 million tons a year of nontanker imports were necessary to keep Britain's population healthy, her factories running, her armed forces fed, equipped, and fighting. In the first four months of 1941, the annualized rate was under 28 million tons.

The codebreakers understood that unless they could solve the naval Enigma and ascertain the U-boats' movements in advance, the British were in grave danger of losing the Battle of the Atlantic, with possibly fatal consequences for the nation. Different measures that might turn the tide, such as building more merchant ships or adding more escort vessels, would take a long time; solving the naval Enigma offered the only possibility of immediate aid. Naval Section urged itself on.

Other intelligence sources sometimes provided help. At 9:38 A.M. on Monday, May 5, the navy's Western Approaches Command, probably alerted by direction-finding, diverted Convoy OB 318 to the south of its planned track "to avoid possible U-boat threat." That afternoon, course was altered again, a little more to the south. The next day, as the convoy furrowed the calm sea in its painfully slow progress, airplanes patrolled above it; around teatime, a Sunderland flying boat lumbered overhead, then departed, leaving the convoy without air escort. That morning, the four merchantmen from Iceland that were to join OB 318 had sailed under the protection of three corvettes and an armed trawler, part of Escort Group 3. And the next morning, Wednesday, May 7, the destroyers that formed the powerful core of that group steamed out of Reykjavik harbor to protect OB 318; when it arrived, Escort Group 7 would return to Britain.

Escort Group 3's commander, Joe Baker-Cresswell, was born in London on February 2, 1901, while most of his family was watching the funeral procession of Queen Victoria. After attending Gresham's School in Norfolk, he joined the navy and served in a variety of ships, from submarine to battlewagon. He then attended the Naval Staff College in Greenwich. At the start of the war, he was on the Middle East Joint Planning Staff, but he wanted a command at sea. In London one day, as he entered the Admiralty to plead his case, he ran into Admiral Sir Percy Noble, commander in chief Western Approaches, under whom he had served earlier. He explained his wish. Noble said, "Leave it to me," and in January 1941 Baker-Cresswell was appointed commander of Escort Group 3, which he soon molded into an efficient force.

Baker-Cresswell tested various colors as camouflage in the northern Atlantic waters, found pale mauve the best in spring and summer and white the best in winter, and painted his ships those colors. He had blue and yellow squares painted around the tops of his ships' funnels — the color and pattern of the naval signal flag meaning "3." He flew his pennant from the *Bulldog*, an eleven-year-old, 1,360-ton destroyer whose original armament of guns and torpedo tubes had been reduced to enable her to carry more depth charges.

As Baker-Cresswell was heading south on May 7 with his three destroyers, the British intercepted a U-boat radio message. Although they could not read it, they recognized that it was a sighting report, from the characteristic Morse symbol that preceded it as prescribed by German radio regulations. The Admiralty apparently obtained only a single bearing on this transmission and was therefore able to determine only the line from which it originated and not the point. Thus, though the U-boat was telling of a convoy far to the east of OB 318, the Admiralty guessed that OB 318 was the one sighted. So at 3:04 P.M. on Wednesday, the Admiralty notified Escort Groups 3 and 7 of its suspicions and ordered the convoy to make an evasive turn to starboard and then to steer due west. This directed it straight at the U-94, which with the U-110 was one of the nine U-boats in the North Atlantic north of 55° north latitude (approximately the latitude of Belfast in Northern Ireland and of the middle of Labrador). The commander of the U-boats, Rear Admiral Karl Dönitz, had ordered six submarines to area AK on the Kriegsmarine's gridded chart of the world's oceans; the chart used pairs of letters to compress location specifications and to keep them secret. AK lay smack in the middle of the North Atlantic, athwart many of the convoy routes.

Baker-Cresswell arrived at the rendezvous point 150 miles south of Reykjavik (and within AK) a bit ahead of time. After a brief search, he found the convoy only 7 miles north of the rendezvous point and fifteen minutes early — much closer to plan than usual. It was about 4 P.M. A little later, the U-94, on the surface, spotted the convoy's funnel smoke.

She headed for the convoy as Escort Group 7 transferred responsibility for OB 318 to Baker-Cresswell. He arranged his destroyers forward and aft of the merchantmen, with his own *Bulldog* ahead of the starboard columns. The weather was fine; one of the merchant captains remarked that never in his long life had he known the Atlantic so calm so far north. At 7 P.M., the *Bulldog*'s asdic contacted an object 200 yards ahead, then lost it. Baker-Cresswell reversed his course and, knowing that U-boats liked to get between two convoy columns and fire torpedoes from fore and aft tubes, steamed back down between the seventh and eighth columns. He found nothing.

But the U-94 had submerged and sneaked between two other columns. Between 7:09 and 7:11, she fired three single shots from her bow tubes and one from her stern tube. The latter missed, but the bow torpedoes struck, almost simultaneously, the big British steamer *Ixion* and the Norwegian *Eastern Star*, a 5,600-tonner, both carrying Scotch whisky. The two ships burst into flames and began sinking. When the U-94's skipper came to periscope depth to see what he had done, a lookout on the sloop *Rochester* spotted the periscope in the smooth sea at almost the same time that the destroyer *Amazon* gained asdic contact. The *Bulldog* led the depth-bomb attack, which damaged the U-94's hydroplanes and some gauges. But despite a lengthy hunt, the submarine escaped. The crews of the sunk steamers were rescued, along with a number of cases of Vat 69 Scotch which were perhaps later issued to the seamen for medicinal purposes.

By 11 P.M. the convoy was back to its normal routine, as were the screening vessels, their watches broken only by the continuous pinging of the asdics and the periodic ringing of the zigzag clocks, which told the helmsman when to zig and when to zag to confuse the U-boats. Baker-Cresswell spent the next day, Thursday, in an unsuccessful search for the U-boat. He felt sure he had driven it off, and the Admiralty sent no more warnings.

In U-boat headquarters, however, Admiral Dönitz was planning another move. He knew that during the spring of 1941 the range of convoy protection had expanded to the west as the number of escort destroyers grew. He had consequently sent his submarines farther west to attack convoys where they were still unprotected. Dönitz estimated the limit of escort protection at between 25° and 30° west longitude. Thus, in the first eighteen months of the war, U-boats sank only eight Allied ships west of 25°, but in the next two months, March and April 1941, they sank twenty-four. Now, on Thursday, May 8, Dönitz moved some of his northern boats west. They joined the U-110, which had already arrived south of Iceland. Its commander was twenty-eight-year-old Lieutenant Fritz-Julius Lemp.

Lemp was one of the German navy's most successful U-boat commanders. A jaunty young man with pudgy cheeks, he had joined the navy in 1931 at age eighteen. At the outbreak of the war, he commanded the U-30, a three-year-old Type VIIA, the Kriegsmarine's principal operating submarine, known for its excellent performance.

On the very first day of the war with Britain, Lemp became the first U-boat captain to sink an enemy ship. But this opening of the Battle of the Atlantic harmed Germany more than it helped her. For Lemp had torpedoed the unarmed passenger liner *Athenia*, which he had apparently mistaken for an armed auxiliary cruiser. The loss of 118 lives and the apparent flouting of a Hague convention convinced Britain that Germany had resumed the unrestricted submarine warfare of World War I; consequently she at once initiated all measures against this aggression.

Lemp made eight cruises in the U-30. In August 1940, after an especially successful cruise, he was acclaimed for having put a torpedo into the battleship *Barham* and for having sunk, it was claimed, nine ships. (The actual number was six; U-boat captains, like fighter pilots, continually overestimated successes.) Dönitz, who seems to have had a soft spot for Lemp, awarded him the Knight's Cross to the Iron Cross.

In November, Lemp commissioned the U-110, one of the new large Atlantic Type IXB boats. The submarine, 252½ feet long and displacing 1,050 tons, could cruise for 12,400 miles. Top speed was 18.2 knots on the surface, 7.3 submerged. It carried twenty-two torpedoes, could submerge in about half a minute, and could dive to 330 feet.

Most of the enlisted men were new, having just come from their various training schools. Lemp brought two of his three officers with him from the U-30. The exception was his second in command, Lemp's cousin, who was not popular with the crew members. They regarded him as a Jonah because two of his ships had been sunk under him. With 4 officers, 15 noncoms, and 27 seamen, the crew totaled 46. Lemp made a good impression on the men. He was open, avoided spit and polish, and knew how to weld them together. He didn't throw his weight around, but it was clear that he was the boss. The Knight's Cross gained him automatic respect. The men believed they were serving under one of the best commanders in one of their country's most important forces.

Because of trouble in the U-110's diesels, she did not sail on her maiden war patrol until March 9, 1941. As she searched the vast wastes of the North Atlantic for prey, the seamen stood four-hour watches, the machinists six-hour. Though it was a scramble to eat and sleep in the four hours off, the watches were often boring. Excitement came only during the rare spurts of action. During her first cruise, the U-110 sank two ships. Lemp used the classic tactic of slipping between the first and second columns of a convoy at night, firing torpedoes from the bow at one column and from the stern at another, and then diving deep to avoid the expected attack.

One of Lemp's log entries reveals his thoughtless enthusiasm:

> 16.3 [1941] 0022. Tanker passes within 100 meters. . . . Stern shot. . . . Hit. Tanker flies in the air with a great flash and is atomized. . . . Night lit up like day by the light of the fires of exploding tankers. U-boat stays between tanker and destroyer 3,000 meters [2 miles] away in the middle of the convoy as if in a spotlight. Since destroyer turns toward U-boat with big bow wave, emergency dive.

During the depth-bomb attack that followed, Lemp showed his leadership. Often he would give an order just to let the crew hear the lack of anxiety in his voice. His calmness soothed the younger men. And the boat survived.

Another log entry a week later indicates his honesty and self-confidence. After missing three shots, the last at only 500 yards, "(1) Out of mistrust of torpedoes, (2) out of fury, I order an artillery attack." But one of the seamen had forgotten to remove the muzzle tampion from the 4.1-incher, and when the gun was fired, it exploded and damaged the U-boat. No longer able to dive fast, the U-110 was ordered back to Lorient, on the Atlantic coast of France, for repairs; after its return Dönitz visited the boat and awarded the Iron Cross to several crew members.

Following two weeks of repairs and furlough, the U-110 sailed again on April 15. The next day, Dönitz radioed the location of her operating area. He was hoping to concentrate the nine U-boats then in the North Atlantic against the convoys. Experience had shown that having one of the subs command the others on the spot did not work; the lead submarine sometimes had to submerge and so lost contact with the rest. Control had to be exercised from Dönitz's headquarters in France. This required constant radio communications, all enciphered in the Enigma machine. The responsibility for both ciphering and communicating fell on each U-boat's radiomen.

Of the four radiomen aboard the U-110, the most junior was Radioman Third Class Heinz Wilde. Open-faced and friendly, he had been a radio amateur as a teenager in Breslau before the war. A naval officer had come to one of his club's meetings in 1937 and persuaded many of the members to join the navy. Wilde entered on November 1, 1939. After basic training, he went to the naval communications school at Flensburg, close to the Danish border. Here he deepened his knowledge of radio, and here he was introduced to the Enigma cipher machine. The instructors boasted that the machine was the best and couldn't be solved. This emphasis on the machine's unparalleled cryptographic security, Wilde thought, led many students to think its physical security not so terribly important. Wilde, the best in his class, was assigned to U-boats; after specialized submarine training, including instruction in acoustic detection, he was assigned to the U-110.

There, in the closetlike radio room, he stood four-hour watches, chatting or reading a book and playing phonograph records over the loudspeaker system for the crew while listening for a signal through the whistlings, peepings, and static that filled his earphones. As soon as he heard the tone of the transmitter, he would turn down the phonograph, stop talking or reading, and begin taking down the Morse message. All messages were taken down, even those addressed to other U-boats; all were deciphered and given to the captain. The locations of other submarines and of convoys were entered on charts. Wilde never received more than four messages on a watch; sometimes none came in. To minimize the number of transmissions and to eliminate clues to its location, a U-boat did not signal receipt of a message. Garbled transmissions, which are difficult or impossible to decipher, were relatively rare; to ensure that important messages were not missed, U-boat headquarters repeated each one half an hour to an hour after the first transmission. During an action, the radioman worked the listening apparatus. This array of hydrophones gave the range and bearing of sound sources, such as torpedo explosions and attacking enemy warships; Wilde thought the data it yielded were imprecise.

On April 21, the day after the U-110 reached the waters west of Ireland where she would begin her patrol, Dönitz radioed her an attack location, AL58 on the Kriegsmarine grid, 400 miles west of Ireland's west coast. The next day, Dönitz ordered "Attack!" Three days later, Lemp sank a 2,500-ton ship steaming alone. He missed on April 28 with a single shot on a fishing trawler. Dönitz moved the U-110 south, then north, then west over the eastern Atlantic, perhaps on the basis of German codebreaking that told him where convoys might be.

On Thursday, May 8, Lemp saw smoke and the mast of a warship. Coming up on her starboard, he discovered that she was escorting a slow-moving convoy heading west at 7 or 8 knots. He transmitted a sighting report, which was intercepted by the British Admiralty. It determined the location of the transmitter by a direction-finding fix, then compared the location with its plot of convoys at sea. At 7:07 P.M., Greenwich mean time, the Admiralty warned OB 318 that it was being shadowed. The convoy altered course 30° to port, away from the U-110.

At about the same time, Dönitz ordered other U-boats to report their positions and directed Lemp to maintain contact with OB 318 and to attack if possible. But the convoy's turn away broke Lemp's contact until the listening apparatus again detected the convoy. However, Lemp was unable to take action because the moon was too bright. He decided to attack the next day, when two other U-boats were expected to be nearby. At 2:16 A.M. local time on Friday, May 9, he again reported the convoy's position; Dönitz ordered several U-boats to concentrate. A few hours later, the U-201, commanded by Lieutenant Adalbert Schnee, hove into sight. Using light blinkers to communicate, the two captains agreed to attack that day, Lemp first.

Early that morning, Baker-Cresswell came onto the bridge of the *Bulldog* to watch his group take up its day screening positions.

It was to be his last day with the convoy. His ship would leave late in the afternoon with sufficient fuel to return to Iceland. By that time the convoy could disperse; it would then be at about 34° west longitude, and no Axis submarine had ever sunk a ship that far west. His good feelings were reinforced by the arrival of his breakfast, wrapped in a napkin and served by his faithful steward. As the morning wore on and nothing happened, those feelings seemed to be justified.

But Lemp had moved into position to attack. From in front of the convoy and to starboard, at periscope depth, he fired three torpedoes at a diagonal distance of 800 yards, or half a mile, at three steamers. Just as Baker-Cresswell was preparing to exchange noon positions with the commodore of the convoy's merchantmen, he saw a spout of water on the *Esmond*'s starboard side. A few moments later, the *Bengore* was hit. Her stern rose almost to the vertical and the crated cargo on her deck cascaded into the sea. It looked, one witness said, like "a child pouring toys out of a box."

Baker-Cresswell, recovering from his astonishment, swung the *Bulldog* to starboard and raced to where he thought the U-boat might be, determined to destroy her. At the same time one of Escort Group 3's corvettes, the *Aubretia,* which had detected the incoming torpedoes on her asdic, increased speed and turned to starboard. Two minutes later she obtained an asdic contact, then lost it, so the captain stopped her engines to improve the reception. A minute later the *Aubretia* spotted a periscope dead ahead, about 800 yards away, traveling from port to starboard. She sped toward it and dropped a full pattern of depth charges, set to explode at 100 and 225 feet.

The crew of the U-110 heard these explosions and were shaken by the speed of the attack; they had thought they would have fifteen minutes to dive and get away. The explosions, however, were distant. The submarine continued in attack mode. A few minutes later, Lemp, at the periscope, turning his submarine for a stern shot, spotted a destroyer coming at him with great speed. "Down deep!" he ordered. The crew ran forward to speed the dive.

But no sooner had the vessel begun to tilt than at least a score of depth charges, dropped by the *Aubretia* and set to discharge at 150 and 385 feet, exploded very close to the submarine. They blew out the main electric motor switch, stopped the electric motors, shattered all depth meters, and started leaks in the oil bunkers; the submarine started to take water and sank even deeper. The plates that formed the deck of the control center, which normally butted one another, overlapped from the pressure. Wilde and others thought it was the end. Although they were frightened and felt helpless, nobody screamed or wept. Lemp, meanwhile, was trying to blow the tanks to get the boat to rise. Suddenly, the men felt her moving upward, perhaps pushed up by depth charges.

Her rise caused a patch of water on the surface to become disturbed, drawing the eyes of the men on the *Aubretia,* the *Bulldog,* and another destroyer, the *Broadway.* Then, at 12:35, the U-boat burst up from the seemingly vacant sea. Water streamed from her uppers, and she rolled in the slight swell. Inside, the crew members felt the motion and knew, to their great relief, that they were on the surface. Lemp, instead of releasing pressurized air through a valve, opened the hatch. A cloud of dust blew out. The crew was ordered to put on life vests and to get out. Ventilation ports and sea strainers were opened to let in water.

Baker-Cresswell saw red when the U-boat surfaced. She had just sunk two ships, and now this embodiment of all the evil he was fighting had appeared before him. Firing his heavy guns, he ordered 12 knots — suitable ramming speed. But as he saw the German crew boiling out of the conning tower, he realized that they were abandoning ship.

At that moment, there flashed into his mind a story he had heard at the Naval Staff College in Greenwich in the mid-1920s. It may have made an impression because it involved the father of a fellow student, Lieutenant Louis Mountbatten. During World War I, the Russians had salvaged a German codebook from a German cruiser that had grounded in the Baltic, the *Magdeburg.* They had delivered the code to Mountbatten's father, who was first sea lord, the head of the Royal Navy. The codebook had enabled the Admiralty to solve many German coded messages during the war, to great advantage.

As Baker-Cresswell saw the U-boat rocking on the surface of the ocean, he asked himself, "Is there a chance we can do another *Magdeburg?*" And he ordered full astern to stop the *Bulldog* from ramming the sub.

Two

The Wreck of the *Magdeburg*

O<small>N THE AFTERNOON</small> of August 24, 1914, a gray German warship steamed out of the East Prussian harbor of Memel toward the most fateful accident in the history of cryptology. She was the *Magdeburg,* a four-stacker, what the Germans called a small cruiser to differentiate the type from the larger light cruisers. She was new (three years old), well armed (twelve fast-firing 4-inch guns), fast (27.6 knots) — and unlucky. Her acceptance test had not gone well: her commissioning was delayed several months. She never participated, as was intended, in the fall 1912 naval maneuvers. Some equipment was still not in order when she was declared "ready for war" and when the ancient city of Magdeburg, southwest of Berlin, for which she was named, sponsored her in two days of festivities. One of her turbines gave trouble. And, unlike her sister ships, which got assignments suitable for cruisers, the *Magdeburg* became a torpedo test ship.

During one of her cruises in 1913, when she sailed to the Canary Islands off the northwestern shoulder of Africa to test the range of the naval radio station at Neumünster, her radio officer, a young lieutenant named Walther Bender, bought a puppy. Schuhmchen, the puppy, became a favorite of the crew. Later, in Kiel, whenever Bender spent the night ashore, Schuhmchen went down to the gangway in the morning as the launch shoved off from the dock to return to the *Magdeburg.* How did he know that Bender was aboard?

The *Magdeburg* was part of the Baltic Fleet. When war with Russia, France, and England broke out in August 1914, she dropped her test assignment and undertook more typical cruiser tasks. These were directed against the Russians, whose empire included the countries bordering the eastern Baltic: Finland, Estonia, Latvia, and Lithuania. In her first operation, the *Magdeburg* and another small cruiser, the *Augsburg,* arrived off Liepaja, Latvia's naval port, to lay mines. They gained an unexpected success: the Russians, thinking the appearance of the two ships portended a major fleet operation, blew up their own ammunition and coal dumps and scuttled ships in the harbor entrances. In the two ships' second and third operations, they shot up some lighthouses and a signal station and laid a minefield not far from the mouth of the eastern arm of the Baltic Sea, the Gulf of Finland, at whose farther end lay the Russian capital, St. Petersburg (now Leningrad).

A few days later, on August 23, the commander of a new flotilla ordered his vessels, which included the two cruisers, to assemble for operations. The *Magdeburg,* in Danzig, then a German port, went first to Memel, at the extreme east of Prussia, for some gunnery exercises meant to reassure the population, nervous because the border with Russia was not far from the city limits. The next afternoon the warship set out for the rendezvous, and early on the twenty-fifth it joined the *Augsburg,* three torpedo boats, a submarine, and three other warships off Hoburgen lighthouse on the scuthern tip of the Swedish island of Gotland. There the officers were told the plan. The ships were to slip by night behind a Russian minefield believed to protect the entrance to the Gulf of Finland and attack whatever Russian ships they found. At 8:30 A.M. that same day, the flotilla set out, moving northeast at the fairly high speed of 20 knots. The sailors aboard the *Magdeburg,* who suspected the presence of enemy armored cruisers, thought the assignment was a suicide mission.

By 5 P.M., in a calm sea, the air misty, the navigational plots of the *Magdeburg* and the *Augsburg* differed by a mile. But this raised no concern, since the *Magdeburg* was to follow the flagship by half a mile: if the *Augsburg* struck a mine, the *Magdeburg* could avoid hitting any herself.

Soon, however, fog — common in those waters in summer — rolled in. By 9 P.M., it was so thick that even with binoculars an officer on the bridge of the *Magdeburg* could not see the lookout on the stern. At 11 P.M., the *Augsburg,* intending to run along the supposed Russian minefield before swinging east to enter the Gulf of Finland, turned onto a course south-southeast ½ east — and

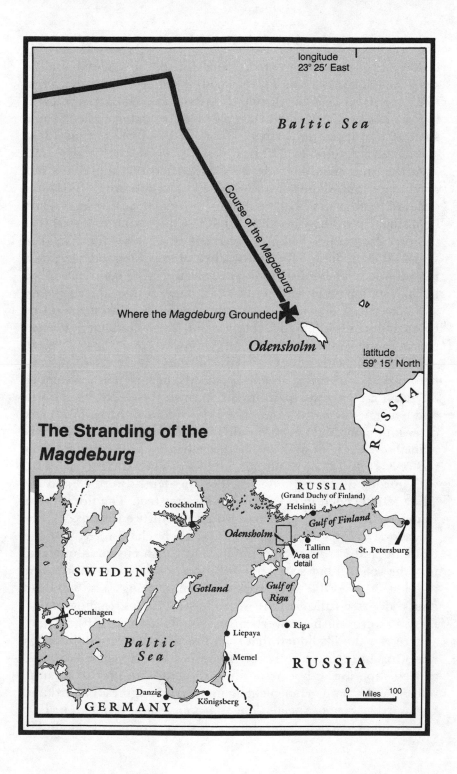

longitude
23° 25' East

Baltic Sea

Course of the Magdeburg

Where the *Magdeburg* Grounded

Odensholm

latitude
59° 15' North

RUSSIA

The Stranding of the
Magdeburg

RUSSIA
(Grand Duchy of Finland)

Stockholm

Helsinki

Gulf of Finland

Odensholm

Tallinn

Area of
detail

St. Petersburg

SWEDEN

Gotland

*Gulf of
Riga*

Riga

Liepaya

*Baltic
Sea*

Memel

RUSSIA

Danzig

Königsberg

GERMANY

Copenhagen

0   Miles   100

ordered the *Magdeburg* to do the same. She did so, maintaining the same speed, about 15 knots, that had kept her at the proper distance from the *Augsburg* during the afternoon. Her captain, Lieutenant Commander Richard Habenicht, had soundings taken. These showed the depth decreasing: 190 feet, 141 feet, and, at 12:30 A.M., now of August 26, 112 feet.

At the same time the radio shack reported that a message was coming in; four minutes later it was decoded and on the bridge. It ordered that course be altered to east-northeast ½ east. The helmsman spun the wheel and, at 12:37, just as he reported that the new course was being steered, still at 15 knots, the luckless vessel hit something. She bumped five or six times and, shuddering, stopped. The cruiser had run aground. As a consequence of her navigation error, which put her a mile south of the *Augsburg*, she had struck shallows 400 yards off the northwestern tip of Odensholm, a low, narrow, sandy island 2½ miles long at the entrance to the Gulf of Finland.

At once, Habenicht sought to free his ship. He reversed engines; he rocked her with various engine speeds; he assembled the entire 337-man crew on the quarterdeck to push the ship's stern down and her bow up and then went full speed astern; he had the crew carry munitions aft. The ship didn't budge. Soundings showed that at the bow, where the *Magdeburg* normally drew 16½ feet, the water was only 16 feet deep to port and 9 feet to starboard; at the stern, with normal draft just under 20 feet, the depths were 13 and 17. The vessel needed to rise between 3 and 7 feet. The tides of the Baltic, measured only in inches, would not suffice for this.

Habenicht let go the anchors and their chains. He had the drinking and washing water pumped out. Ash ejectors flung coal into the sea. All but sixty boxes of munitions were dumped over the side. All movable steel parts — the minelaying rails, bulkhead doors, doors on the forward turrets, steel cables, coaling equipment — were pushed overboard. The Germans' efforts were spurred by the likelihood that the officials on Odensholm, which was Russian territory with a lighthouse and a signal station, had alerted superior authorities at the major Russian port of Tallinn, only 50 miles away. Habenicht again ran the engines forward and backward at various speeds. The *Magdeburg* moved not an inch.

Habenicht worried that the cruiser's secret documents might fall into the hands of the Russians. In addition to the charts of German minefields and the ship's war diary, these included the main Imperial German Navy code and the cipher key used to encipher its codewords and thus provide another layer of secrecy. Bender, who was in charge of the destruction of these documents, brought the codebook that was in the steering room, together with its cipher key, to the stokehold and burned it. Sailors did the same for other secret documents. But two other codebooks — one on the bridge and one in the radio shack — as well as a cipher key were retained for communicating with rescuers and higher commands. A fourth lay hidden and apparently forgotten in a locker in Habenicht's cabin.

As dawn approached, the seabed and the stones on which the ship was lying became visible. At 8:30, with the fog lifting, the fast and powerful German torpedo boat V-26 appeared, attached a line, and tried to pull the *Magdeburg* off. She failed. Habenicht decided he might as well do some damage and fired some 120 shots at the lighthouse, chipping it, and at the signal station, setting it ablaze. By then the radio shack was reporting many signals from Russian ships; apparently they were on their way. Since all attempts to free the *Magdeburg* had failed, Habenicht regretfully concluded that he had to blow her up instead of letting her fall undamaged into enemy hands.

Charges were set fore and aft. The crew was to get off the ship and onto the V-26, which was to come alongside. Suddenly a shout rang through the ship. "The fuses are lit!" Habenicht had not ordered this; it had been done by mistake. The vessel would blow up in only four and a half minutes! In the tumult that ensued, Bender, the first radio officer, directed the second radio officer, Lieutenant Olff, to have the codebook and the cipher key from the radio shack brought to the V-26. On Olff's instructions, Radioman Second Class Neuhaus grabbed the codebook, and Radioman Third Class Kiehnert the cipher key papers. The bridge's codebook was in the hands of Radioman Second Class Szillat. The first officer, unable to find Habenicht as the seconds ticked away, ordered the crew members to the afterdeck, where the V-26 was to pick them up. He called for three cheers for the kaiser, had the two ship's boats lowered, and commanded, "All hands abandon ship!"

Upon hearing this, Szillat flung the codebook he was carrying over the side, toward the stern. It splashed into what he said was a "dark" place about 15 feet from the ship and immediately sank. Then he leaped overboard. Kiehnert, too, jumped into the water, holding the radio shack's cipher key. He was struck by men following him, and when he came to the surface, he noticed that he had lost the key. Then, at 9:10, the forward charge detonated. It split the vessel in half, tore open the fore part from near the bow to the second smokestack, and hurled huge pieces of steel into the air. They rained down upon the scores of men who were trying to swim to the V-26. Neuhaus, who had the radio shack's codebook, was seen in the water before the explosion but was missing later; no one knew what happened to the codebook he was carrying.

The V-26 picked up many of the swimming men, including Szillat and Kiehnert. For fear of being destroyed in the explosion of the *Magdeburg*'s after charge, the V-26 stayed away from the cruiser and did not rescue the men still aboard. The Russian ships, appeared and began to fire at the torpedo boat. One shell swept eight men overboard; another smashed into her starboard side, destroying the officers' wardroom and killing all who were in it, mainly wounded men from the *Magdeburg*. But the V-26 got away.

Habenicht appeared briefly on the *Magdeburg*'s bridge when he heard the cheers for the kaiser, then vanished again into the bowels of his cruiser. Along with a few others, he awaited his fate on the ship. Bender, his little dog, and a few dozen sailors, among them Neuhaus, swam to Odensholm, where they were taken prisoner. One of the Russian ships, the torpedo boat *Lejtenant Burakov*, sent a boat with armed men, led by its first officer, Lieutenant Galibin, to the *Magdeburg*. The crew members still on board offered no resistance and were taken prisoner. Habenicht, whom Galibin thought was "a true gentleman," offered the Russian his dagger, which Galibin courteously declined. The Germans on both the ship and the island were rowed to one of the Russian cruisers and were later sent to a prisoner-of-war camp in Siberia; on the way, the little dog Schuhmchen was taken from Bender. He was never seen again.

Galibin lowered the black, white, and red German naval war flag and raised the white czarist flag with its diagonal light blue cross. Then, revolver in hand, he searched the wreck of the *Magdeburg*. He found a locker in Habenicht's cabin and broke it open. Hidden deep within it was a German codebook, forgotten by all in the excitement of the catastrophe. Galibin removed it and, together with a packet of Bender's private letters and other documents, had it transferred to the *Lejtenant Burakov*. The Allies had come into possession of the key secret of the Imperial German Navy, the one that could give them access to many others.

Later, Russian divers supplemented Galibin's find. Using strong electric lights to inspect the stony seabed up to 30 feet from the stranded vessel, they found in the clear waters the codebook that Szillat had thrown overboard and the one that Neuhaus had lost in the water.

Recognizing the value of the codebooks and cipher keys to the British, the major naval power, the Russians loyally notified their ally of their find and said that they would give the British the documents if they would send a small warship "as most secure means" of getting them and the officers accompanying them to Britain. The Russians courteously set aside for the British the undamaged code, the one found in Habenicht's locker, which bore the serial number 151. They kept the waterlogged codes for themselves.

The task of taking codebook No. 151 to England was assigned to three naval officers, Captain Mikhail A. Bedrov, Commander Mikhail I. Smirnov, and Count Constantine Benckendorff. A cosmopolitan, mustachioed combat veteran of the Russo-Japanese War, Benckendorff was the son of the ambassador to Great Britain. He had served a year as a cipher clerk in the London Embassy. One Sunday morning in September he was on watch on the battleship *Poltava* in Tallinn roadstead, pacing the quarterdeck and listening to the sailors' choir chanting the Russian Orthodox mass, when a yeoman handed him an order to report immediately to the flag captain. On the flagship he was "amazed and delighted" to be told he would be going to London.

He was given the precious codebook in St. Petersburg. It was in a satchel with a large piece of lead sewn in to make it sink in case he had to throw it overboard and with a strap to carry it over his shoulder. This bag he took with him to Archangel, where he boarded a Russian volunteer fleet steamer. The vessel was to meet H.M.S. *Theseus* at Alexandrovsk (now Polyarnyy), a port near Murmansk, where the aging cruiser had arrived early in September. Owing to delays and misunderstandings, the *Theseus* and the steamer did not sail until October 1. After an uneventful crossing over the top of Norway, punctuated only by a few vague U-boat warnings, they arrived on October 10 in Scapa Flow, the great circular basin north of Scotland that served as one of the Royal Navy's chief bases; the Russian steamer went on alone, reaching the English port of Hull a couple of days later. After a slow night train ride, Benckendorff reached the Russian embassy at dawn. He greeted his parents, then routed out the naval attaché, and the two went, early on the morning of October 13, to the Admiralty. There, in one of the most significant moments in the long history of secret intelligence, they handed Winston Churchill, first lord of the Admiralty, a gift more precious than a dozen Fabergé eggs: the big, fat, blue-bound *Signalbuch der Kaiserlichen Marine.*

The *Signalbuch* went to the Admiralty's fledgling codebreaking agency. This had come into being, quite by chance, on the day Britain entered the war. Though individuals in the British army had solved cryptograms in the Boer War and on India's Northwest Frontier, the navy had never engaged in cryptanalysis and had made no preparations for it. But when hostilities formally commenced on August 4, 1914, radio stations of the Royal Navy, the post office, and the Marconi company began to pick up coded messages, apparently of German origin. These they forwarded to the Admiralty's Intelligence Division. Its director, Rear Admiral H. F. Oliver, recognized their potential and knew at once who might realize it: his good friend, the director of naval education, Sir Alfred Ewing. A short, thickset Scot, given to wearing mauve shirts with white wing collars and a dark blue bow tie with white polka dots, Ewing was a distinguished engineer. He had dealt with cables in Uruguay and had, a year or so before, described a cipher mechanism to Oliver. Oliver regarded him as of "very great brain power, in fact a man who stood out among clever men." Everyone thought naval education would not be much needed during the few months until victory was won. Oliver told Ewing he had no one to deal with the intercepts; would Ewing see if he could make anything of them? Grasping "at even the most unpromising chance of being useful," Ewing accepted at once.

To assist him, he called on some people whose abilities would be useful and who were discreet and available: faculty members, particularly instructors in German, at the Royal Naval Colleges at Dartmouth and Osborne, which were on vacation in August. One of the first volunteers was Alastair Denniston, thirty-three, a German master at Osborne. A short, quiet Scot, he had studied at Paris and Bonn and had helped win a bronze for Great Britain in field hockey as a member of the Scottish team in the 1908 Olympics in London. Like the others, Denniston was, in his own words, "singularly ignorant of cryptography."

He and his colleagues worked in Ewing's cramped office. They did little more than sort and file intercepts, learn to distinguish German naval messages from military ones, and discover that call signs such as POZ and KAY, the "names" of radio stations, were not the same as the coded texts of messages. But they made not a dent on the German naval messages.

A month later, the *Signalbuch* from the *Magdeburg arrived in Ewing's office.* But what seemed to be the answer to a cryptanalyst's prayer did not at first turn many of the coded messages into plain German. The book consisted essentially of hundreds of pages of columns of five-digit and three-letter groups standing opposite German words:

```
63940 OAT  Ohnmacht -ig
   41 OAU  Ohr, Ohren-
   42 OAÜ  Okkupation, Okkupations, -ieren
   43 OAV  Ökonomie -isch
   44 OAW  Oktant
   45 OAX  Oktober
```

This meant that *Oktober* would be encoded as OAX or 63945, and OAÜ (the Germans usually used the letters, not the numbers), would mean *Okkupation* or its derivatives. But attempts to reduce the intercepts to German by this straightforward method produced gibberish in most cases; the only messages that were solved were weather reports and messages to auxiliary vessels. To resolve the mystery, Ewing brought in the head of the Intelligence Division's German Section, Fleet Paymaster Charles J. E. Rotter, who had spent many leaves in Germany. He was installed in Ewing's secretary's office.

A break came when the *Handelsschiffsverkehrsbuch*, or *HVB*, another maritime code, seized from a merchantman off Melbourne, Australia, arrived at Ewing's office, along with a method for disguising the code's four-letter codewords. The letters of the code-words were replaced with other letters given in a list, or key. For example, the codeword for *Fregattenkapitän* (commander) was RABL; the key specified that the substitute for R was T, for A, L, and so forth, so that RABL would actually be transmitted as TLIN. This procedure is called superencipherment.

Rotter seems to have reasoned that the Germans were using the same system to encipher the codewords of the *Signalbuch*, so that OAO might become, for example, JVJ. Working with a succession of messages whose serial numbers the Germans had enciphered — "Their folly was greater than our stupidity," Alastair Denniston commented — Rotter by early November had discovered the key to the superencipherment, thus exposing the main messages of the High Seas Fleet.

This breakthrough suddenly gave the handful of cryptanalysts plenty to do. More cryptanalysts were taken on, and a new, larger workplace was found, Room 40 of the Old Building of the Admiralty. "Room 40" became the unofficial name for the codebreaking agency.

Early in December this thriving and fortunate agency got another lucky break. The third major codebook of the Imperial German Navy arrived in sodden condition in Ewing's office. The captain of the torpedo boat S-119 had thrown it and other papers overboard in a lead-lined chest when he encountered a British squadron off a Dutch island; a month and a half later a British fishing boat hauled it up in its trawl. Soon the new codebook, the *Verkehrsbuch,* a five-numeral code (*Kaiser* = 46786) used at sea by flag officers, was drying before Ewing's fire.

The new book too was used with a superencipherment, which was discovered the day the book arrived. Some days earlier the British had intercepted two almost identical German naval messages. One was encoded entirely in the *Magdeburg codebook* and so could be read by Room 40. A small part of the second was encoded in the newly found code. "It is never wise to mix your ciphers," Ewing remarked. "Like mixing your drinks, it may lead to self-betrayal." This did. The *Signalbuch* gave the meaning of the coded portion of the *Verkehrsbuch* message; these German words could be looked up in the *Verkehrsbuch* to find the basic codenumbers, and comparison of those with the superenciphered code-numbers of the message revealed the formula for conversion.

Thus, before the war was four months old, Britain had gained, mainly through means other than codebreaking, the ability to read the most secret intentions of its chief enemy's navy.

Nor did Britain's cryptologic gifts from the sea end there. Later in the war the Germans changed their codes, but divers recovered the new ones and their superencipherments from U-boats sunk in the shallow waters around Britain. One of the most successful of these divers was Shipwright E. C. Miller, a pale, wiry young diving instructor. His most remarkable characteristic was a sangfroid in facing horrors that would have frightened off many other men. Once he investigated a German submarine sunk off the Yorkshire coast. She was lying on her side, and Miller found no point of entry. He rigged charges and blew off the top of the conning tower. As the water cleared, he saw the head of a dead German seaman rise above the ragged rim of the conning tower as if peering out. That didn't stop Miller. In his bulky suit and spherical armored helmet, he clambered in. At once the imprisoned corpses crowded around him. He calmly tied them up with lanyards and pursued his exploration of the U-boat, stumbling through the narrow black passageway of the underwater tomb until, in a compartment aft of the officers' quarters, he found a strongbox. This contained one of the new codes and some of its superencipherment keys.

As the war progressed and the value of codebreaking became increasingly obvious, the staff of Room 40 swelled. Ewing recruited many members from Cambridge University, where he himself had been a professor of mechanical engineering, and from that university's King's College, of which he had been a fellow. Curiously, more of his recruits were classicists and linguists than mathematicians and scientists. One who proved most successful was a scholar of Greek named Alfred Dillwyn Knox, called Dillwyn.

He was the second of four sons of the Anglican bishop of Manchester. At Eton he became close friends with the future economist John Maynard Keynes. At King's he refused the homosexual advances of Lytton Strachey, the future author of *Eminent Victorians,* who had fallen in love with him.

"Did I tell you," Strachey wrote of Knox, "that he has a wonderful veil of ugliness that he is able to lower at any minute over his face? His method is, you see, to lure you on with his beauty, until at last, just as you step forward to seize a kiss, or whatever else you may want to seize, he lets down a veil, and you simply fall back disgusted. Isn't it a horrid trick?" Witty, clever, always ready with a new limerick, Knox played first-rate bridge with unorthodox moves that more often than not succeeded. But Keynes, who followed him to King's, said, "He has got one of the most confused brains I have ever come across. . . . He is quite abnormally untidy in his work and always forgets to write down the most necessary steps."

Knox, tall, thin, light of build, with full lips and a receding forehead, was elected a fellow of King's in 1909, and for a short time he tutored Harold Macmillan, the future prime minister. He worked with his own tutor, a classics scholar, in preparing an edition of the minor Greek dramatist Herodas, whose sketches had been discovered at Oxyrynchus in Egypt in 1889 on a roll of papyrus. The copyist of this manuscript, Knox wrote, was "constantly puzzled by the form of the letters which he was copying," was "prone to all the common errors of copyists," and made "stupid alterations." Knox and his tutor had to determine the correct meanings. The intense analysis and detailed reconstructions required by this kind of study are also needed in cryptanalysis, and when Knox was recruited for Room 40 early in 1915 at age thirty-one, he found codebreaking congenial.

He was followed to Room 40 by a younger friend from King's, Frank Birch. Birch was seen as "a many-sided human being — a rather dull historian, an acceptable drinking companion, a mysterious private personality, a brilliant talker and a born actor. In his impersonations, as in those of all great comedians, there was a frightening element." One of his best was of a classics tutor, who had only one eye and one hand; in Birch's pantomime, he took himself apart so thoroughly in his room each night that nothing was left of him at all. Birch, an Etonian and a keen yachtsman, had served at sea during the first part of the war. He and Knox shared a house at 14 Edith Grove in the Chelsea section of London, where Birch gave weekly musical parties; Knox chose those occasions to work all night at Room 40. Birch excelled less in codebreaking than in collating and explaining the results.

Room 40 was one of the Admiralty's deepest secrets. This secrecy, combined with the great human capacity for denial, worked its woes upon the Germans during the first year or so of the war.

They refused to believe that their codes had been jeopardized and their communications compromised. Neither direct evidence nor circumstantial persuaded them.

In reporting on the *Magdeburg* disaster, the admiral commanding the squadron in which the cruiser had served never mentioned that the codebook might have been lost. He restricted himself to the much less damaging statement that "the encipherment key to the codebook [was] not destroyed with certainty." The naval staff could not shut its eyes so tightly to the possible survival of the code, but it took the hint proffered by the admiral and concluded that "no serious consequences are feared here from the possible loss of the codebook." It merely ordered the printing of a new encipherment key.

A special investigation into the disposal of the *Magdeburg*'s secret documents likewise led to no overhaul of naval cryptography. The probe was ordered by the commander of the Baltic naval force, Prince Heinrich of Prussia, the kaiser's bearded younger brother. Heinrich had been viewed before the war as unqualified for high command, but in pursuit of code security, at least, he proved dogged and imaginative.

His investigation reached the disturbing judgment that the Russians had probably fished up some of the German charts from the sea, and "in the same way the Russians probably also got their hands on the cipher key that was lost in the water, and finally the possibility must also be considered that the Russians, by diving, got one of the codebooks out of the shallow, clear water." Heinrich proposed a new codebook and even urged mechanical encipherment. His proposals were ignored. In March 1915, a letter from a German naval officer who was a prisoner of war said in a veiled way that Britain possessed the German code. And in August the Germans captured and interrogated the very man, Lieutenant Galibin, who had found the codebook aboard the *Magdeburg* and heard from his lips that their enemy had their main code. The naval staff ignored it.

Meanwhile the navy determined that "the *Handelsschiffsverkehrs-buch* has fallen into enemy hands, probably by the seizure of the auxiliary hospital ship *Ophelia*." The reason was wrong — the *HVB* code had been taken in Australia — but the conclusion was right.

The reaction of the naval staff to all these indications of a serious problem was that of many another bureaucracy: tokenism. A new superencipherment key was put into effect on October 20, 1914, and was replaced three months and six months later, on January 20 and March 20. But the original codebooks continued in service.

The strong circumstantial logic of events should also have told the Germans that their coded messages were being read. In December 1914, when a German naval squadron raced for home after bombarding some English coastal towns, it encountered some British cruisers athwart its path and escaped only with the help of fortuitous fog and rain squalls. The following month, when another German force sallied from its North Sea ports on a sweep to find and destroy isolated warships or freighters, it met British battle cruisers. This time the Germans weren't so lucky. In a long-range heavy-gun battle that became known as the Battle of the Dogger Bank, the British sank one capital ship and greatly damaged two others. In March 1915, the new commander of the German High Seas Fleet planned a drive southward on the sixteenth but abandoned the plan when the weather grew bad. Nevertheless, German submarines and patrol ships reported that the British fleet had gone to sea on the sixteenth. On the twenty-ninth of that month German forces again left their harbors — and so did British. In the middle of April the British Grand Fleet sailed from Scapa Flow even before the Germans executed their planned sortie from their harbors — and returned to Scapa the day the Germans went home. On April 21, the two enemy forces again steamed out at the same time, as they did on May 17 and May 29.

By that time it had become clear to the high German commanders that the British knew in advance of all major German movements. They looked frantically for the cause, but they could think only of betrayal, of some hidden observer, of enemy submarines. They found nothing. The commander of the High Seas Fleet flatly rejected the possibility that the enemy was solving German naval messages.

As a consequence, tokenism triumphed again. The commander directed that superencipherment should not take place in the presence of subordinate personnel, who, being less trustworthy than officers, might betray it for money. He also instituted a new superencipherment. Still the codes were not changed.

* * *

What could possibly have engendered so self-destructive a denial of the evidence and enforced so dangerous an inertia? One probable reason was that few beliefs are as widespread or as firmly held as the belief in the unbreakability of one's own codes. In Germany this attitude may have been intensified by arrogance: were the codes not German? Second, the naval staff may have wanted to avoid the consequences of the enemy's possession of the codes. The staff would have to tell fellow officers that they had failed and would be transferred. Plans would have to be changed. Tactics and organizations, feared exposed, would have to be revised. And new codes would have to be compiled, printed, and distributed. Such a vast, costly, labor-intensive undertaking seemed out of the question for the *Signalbuch der Kaiserlichen Marine,* which measured 12 inches by 15 inches, was 6 inches thick, and had been issued so recently—in 1913.

A third likely reason was that the naval staff did not understand the capabilities of codebreaking. Such ignorance was not exclusive to Germany before World War I; Britain suffered from it as well. For years codebreaking had not provided information of any great value to either government. The isolated solutions of the Franco-Prussian and the Boer wars did not publicize the activity, and the lessons of Britain's eighteenth-century Decyphering Branch and of the Hanoverian, Saxon, and Prussian black chambers, all of which had closed three-quarters of a century before, had long been forgotten. Those allies of each country that had codebreaking units — Austria-Hungary on the one hand, France and Russia on the other — were reluctant at first to share this hard-won, easily lost source. The prewar German naval communicators, concentrating on getting their own messages through with the new technology of radio and congratulating themselves when they succeeded over ever greater distances, never dreamed that someone other than the person to whom they were sending might be hearing those messages. So far was such a consideration from their minds that when they themselves overheard Royal Navy transmissions, probably accidentally at first and later deliberately, they concerned themselves only with range, frequency, and call signs, not with content.

The fluctuations in reception seem to have led the Germans to believe that interception was too undependable for reliable intelligence. Regulations for the conduct of maneuvers even forbade gaining intelligence of the opposing forces by listening to their radio transmissions.

The situation began to change late in 1914, after the western front had calcified into a continuous line of trenches. Field telephones were used for communication, and the operators of the German Sixth Army's main radio station in Roubaix, in northern France some fifteen miles behind the front, found themselves with little to do. So they were assigned to listen to British radio communications, most of them naval, since neither army relied on radio very much. Most of the intercepts were in code or cipher, and some of these, using the simple system in which one letter invariantly replaces another, had been solved by some of the station's personnel. Many were messages from British minesweepers, and the Germans put some of their solutions to practical use. When a British minesweeper reported a particular channel swept clear, the Germans would send a U-boat to lay new mines, and sometimes the codebreakers would soon thereafter read a message that a trawler in that channel had been blown up.

Successes like these led the navy to set up its own intercept posts and eventually a main controlling unit at Neumünster in northern Germany. Wooden towers, 150 feet tall, jutted above the pine woods to snare British messages for the new B- and E-Dienst (Beobachtungs- und Entzifferungs-Dienst, or Observation and Cryptanalytic Service), under the command of Lieutenant Martin Braune, the founder and soul of German naval communications intelligence.

Their solutions of British cryptosystems eventually persuaded the Germans that their own systems could be broken. Gradually the naval staff began to improve its practices. It speeded up the changes in the superencipherment key for the *Signalbuch* and began preparing a replacement for the *HVB*. In practice, these steps proved inadequate. Another attempt, the *Allgemeines Funkspruchbuch* (General Radio Message Book), or *AFB*, much better constructed, went into service May 1, 1917. And a little while later a new code finally replaced the *Signalbuch*. From the time it first had reason to fear the loss of its main code, the navy had delayed three years in making that fundamental change. This delay ranked as one of the greatest communications security failures in history.

Until then.

Three

The Man, the Machine, the Choice

ON MONDAY, April 15, 1918, Germany's forces on the western front plunged forward in a supreme offensive intended to defeat France and Britain before America's strength could be brought to bear. "Great success" screamed a headline in a special edition of the *Berliner Lokal-Anzeiger*. And on that day a thirty-nine-year-old resident of the capital, writing from Hildegardstrasse 17, addressed a letter to the Imperial Germany Navy:

> Under file number Sch 52638 IX/42n I have applied for a patent for a cipher machine. The commercial exploitation is at present assigned to Certified Engineer E. Richard Ritter & Co. as representative. The firm takes the liberty of submitting the enclosed further details about the apparatus, which in my view may be of interest.

The machine, the writer pointed out,

> would avoid any repetition of the sequence of letters when the same letter is struck millions of times. . . . The solution of a telegram is also impossible if a machine falls into unauthorized hands, since it requires a prearranged key system.

The writer was Arthur Scherbius, an electrical engineer, who had invented a wholly new system of cryptography. He had done so independently of three other men in the United States, the Netherlands, and Sweden, who had conceived the same principle at about the same time. This was the principle of the rotor.

A rotor is a wired codewheel. Its body is a disk about the size of a hockey puck made of a nonconducting material such as hard rubber or bakelite. Evenly spaced around the circumference of the disk on both sides are electrical contacts, usually twenty-six, usually of brass. The contacts on one side are connected by wires through the body of the rotor to contacts of the opposite face in a random arrangement. If each contact represents a letter, the rotor embodies a cipher alphabet. An electrical impulse fired into the rotor at the input contact representing a given plaintext letter, say *a*, will emerge at an output contact representing a ciphertext letter, say, Q. The wiring is the heart, the basic secret, of the machine.

Electrical encipherment was, however, not revolutionary. What distinguished this system was the ability of the wired codewheel to rotate. Imagine one rotor placed between two fixed plates. Each plate has a circle of contacts spaced like those on the rotor. In Scherbius's machine, each contact on the input plate was connected to a key on a typewriter keyboard. Each contact on the output plate was connected to a flashlight bulb that illuminated a letter on a glass screen. Batteries provided the current.

Enciphering with a rotor machine consists of pressing the typewriter keys corresponding to the letters of the plaintext and noting the successive lit-up letters. These form the ciphertext. As each letter is enciphered, the electrical current passes through the input plate contact for that letter, enters the rotor at the rotor contact opposite, winds through the rotor, emerges at a different position on the other face, passes into the output plate, and goes to the bulb underneath the ciphertext letter.

If the rotor did not turn, each plaintext letter would always have the same ciphertext letter. But the pressing of a typewriter key pushes the rotor forward one space, ¹⁄₂₆th of a revolution, which gives each plaintext letter a different internal rotor path and thus a different ciphertext letter. For example, if a plaintext includes a double letter *r*, the first *r* might be replaced with Z and the second with M.

Suppose a plaintext consists solely of the letter *a*. The first 26 *a*'s will all have different ciphertext replacements as the rotor revolves. But the 27th will have the same ciphertext as the first because the rotor will have returned to its first position. So short a period — 26 letters — is a cryptographic weakness. However, the period can be lengthened, and the cipher simultaneously made more complex, by placing a second rotor, with wiring different from the first, next to the first and having it turn one space each time the first wheel completes a revolution. The continually varying positions of the two rotors will create different internal combined wiring until the first wheel has revolved 26 times, when the second rotor returns to its original position. The first wheel's 26 revolutions of 26 letters each means that 26×26, or 676 letters, will be enciphered through a different wiring maze. Only at the 677th will the internal maze be the same as for the first letter. (The alphabet, of course, has only 26 letters, and many of these will repeat in the ciphertext. But if the plaintext consisted only of *a*'s, the sequence of ciphertext letters would start to repeat only at the 677th *a*).

Using the same principle, more rotors can be added, each one lengthening the period by a factor of 26. Four rotors produce a period of 456,976 letters; five rotors, a period of 11,881,376.

To decipher a message in such a machine, the cipher clerk obviously needs to know the starting positions of the rotors. This crucial information, called the key, must be agreed upon by sender and receiver in advance of any communication between them. Often a key takes the form of a list of starting positions for each day in a month; the sheets of paper bearing this list are distributed by couriers to all the radio or telegraph stations that will encipher or decipher their communications with the same machine. A key can encompass other elements as well. If, for example, the rotors are removable, so that they can be inserted into the machine in varying orders, the key will specify the order of the rotors from left to right. Without the key the decipherer would not be able to read the message except by playing codebreaker.

The mechanism that Scherbius offered the navy in the spring of 1918 was a sample multirotor machine. His memorandum explained the rotor principle and then his chief point: the impracticability of the enemy's solving a message even if he had the machine:

> The key variation is so great that, without knowledge of the key, even with an available plaintext and ciphertext and with the possession of a machine, the key cannot be found, since it is impossible to run through 6 billion (seven rotors) or 100 trillion (thirteen rotors) keys [rotor starting positions]. If the examination of each telegram takes half a minute in a 24-hour workday, this would require 5.8 years with a simultaneous employment of 100 machines of seven rotors and 14.5 years for 1,000 machines of eight rotors.

He noted, correctly, that "it would only make sense to search for a key in this way when it is known that unknown cryptograms have the same key. And when the same key is maintained for a long time."

The naval staff examined Scherbius's machine and found that it afforded "good security, even if compromised." But it decided not to buy it "because with the present kind of naval cipher traffic, the use of machines is not worthwhile." Instead it recommended that the Foreign Office examine the machine to see if it were suitable for diplomatic correspondence. The price of a ten-rotor machine, measuring 12 by 5½ by 4¾ inches, with an attached typewriter to print the output, was 4,000 to 5,000 marks, or $1,600 to $2,000 (about $14,400 to $18,000 in 1991 dollars), and delivery time was eight weeks. This price, Scherbius said, could be reduced to 1,400 to 1,800 marks, or $560 to $720 ($5,000 to $6,500 in 1991 dollars), if a thousand machines were bought.

But the Foreign Office was not interested either. This may have discouraged Scherbius, but it did not defeat him. The cryptography bug had bitten him.

Scherbius was born on October 20, 1878, in Frankfurt-am-Main, the son of a small businessman. He graduated from that city's Oberrealschule, a type of secondary school that emphasized mathematics, natural sciences, and modern languages; most of its graduates went into engineering. After studying electricity for the 1901–02 winter semester at the Technical College in Munich, Scherbius matriculated May 13, 1902, at the Technical College in Hanover. He studied one or two courses at a time for several months, among them Electrical Installations and Factory Installations, and completed his studies in March 1903. The following year he finished his dissertation, "Proposal for the Construction of an Indirect Water Turbine Governor," which was accepted. At the age of twenty-five, he was granted a doctorate in engineering.

Scherbius worked for several of Germany's major electrical firms and for a large Swiss electrical firm. He made his first invention, a high-voltage drive motor designed to handle sudden changes of stress, for the Swiss company. In 1918, he and E. Richard Ritter, the certified engineer mentioned in his first letter to the navy, founded the firm of Scherbius & Ritter. As a partner in it, he continued to invent (electric pillows, ceramic heating parts, and asynchronous motors, among others), research (problems of high-tension direct current and temperature control), and publish. He wrote articles on such subjects as a shunt phase compensator and a ninety-one-page pamphlet on magnetic induction in closed coils. His name became enshrined in the field with the Scherbius principle for asynchronous motors.

It was probably World War I that made Scherbius succumb to the bacillus of cryptography. Yet that science was underdeveloped in German-speaking lands. The most recent comprehensive text in German dated from 1881, more than forty years before, and the author had had to publish it himself. The German and Austrian literature after that time consisted of a handful of scholarly historical articles and books, a few survey articles in scattered magazines, pamphlets telling how to shield love letters and telephone conversations from pryers, a booklet overview of elementary ciphers intended for businessmen, and studies of cable secrecy and codes. A few dozen cipher devices had been patented in Germany, Austria, and Switzerland, but they had merely mechanized systems that were hundreds of years old.

Perhaps the greatest activity, and that not very intense, was manifest in the publication in German of commercial codes. These thick books, sometimes produced privately for a firm, sometimes published for general sale, replaced business and personal phrases with codewords. "Do not exceed limit," for example, might become JIWUL. Their chief purpose was to economize on cable tolls. But they did provide some secrecy, they were constructed in the same way as many secret governmental codes, and they had the word "code" in their titles, all of which brought them into the purview of cryptology. The codewords, sometimes taken from real languages, sometimes made up, were always "pronounceable," because international telegraph regulations set lower rates for pronounceable codewords than for unpronounceable ones or for codenumbers.

Scherbius's first cryptographic device sought to maintain this economy while making these mostly nonsecret messages secret. It enciphered codenumbers into pronounceable codewords by replacing the successive digits alternately with vowels and consonants. One of the first cipher mechanisms to employ electricity, it passed the input impulses through "multiple switch boards which connect each arriving lead with one of the outgoing leads and which are adapted to interchange this connection with great facility of variation."

These switchboards formed the germ of the rotor. That concept may have come to Scherbius while he was at a concert, as his best ideas often did. He was said to be very musical, but his mind apparently wandered frequently from the melody, for he often jotted ideas and made calculations on his cuffs while the orchestra played. His first rotor enciphered numbers, presumably code-numbers, gaining security but losing pronounceability.

A rotor for letters followed, and it was this device that Scherbius submitted to the navy and the Foreign Office in the spring of 1918. That both rejected his machine did not diminish his confidence in it. He turned to the commercial market.

Scherbius & Ritter transferred the cipher patent rights to the Gewerkschaft Securitas. Though a *Gewerkschaft* was, in the German law of the time, a corporation for mining (and this one was indeed headed by a mining director), this one's name, Securitas, and the fact that it had also been granted the rights to the Dutch rotor patent suggests that it may have been established to funnel risk capital into cipher machines. On July 9, 1923, Securitas founded the Chiffriermaschinen Aktien-Gesellschaft (Cipher Machines Stock Corporation), which began operating in August 1923 at Steglitz-erstrasse 2, in central Berlin. Scherbius and Ritter sat on its board of directors.

The firm publicized its cipher machine — by now named the Enigma — as much as it could. It printed flyers and exhibited the Enigma at the 1923 congress of the International Postal Union. A number of articles about the machine appeared in German and foreign electrical and business publications. Many were illustrated with diagrams of rotors and photographs of the firm's ponderous printing version of the Enigma — a 15-inch-high monster with knobs and handles on its right side that weighed more than 100 pounds. This was being tested by the Deutsche Reichspost. Another version worked directly from and to punched teletypewriter tape.

Gradually the simpler version that indicated its output by illuminating letters, the "Glow Lamp" Enigma, became the most widely known and, eventually, the only one produced by the firm. It was much more compact than the printing version, standing only 4½ inches high, 10 inches wide, and 10¾ inches deep, and it weighed only 15 pounds. At the front stood three rows of typewriter keys. Behind them lay the three rows of circular windows for the output letters. In back of these and to the right was a switch allowing the operator to choose battery or house current. On the left, the tops of four rotors and four toothed thumb-wheels for setting them poked up through the closed lid of the machine. The lid also had little windows through which showed the letters on the rims of the rotors.

The mechanism incorporated three significant improvements by other people over the straightforward system described by Scherbius in his letter of 1918. Two came from Willi Korn, an engineer in Scherbius's employ, and one from Paul Bernstein, a Berliner.

Korn designed rotors that were removable. Previously their order left to right was fixed, but now the operator could put them into the machine in any order. This made possible Bernstein's improvement: a movable ring with indicator letters on it on each rotor. The ring rode the circumference of the rotor like a tire on a wheel; the ring could be turned to any position and locked in place with a pin. Previously, a particular indicator letter meant that the rotor was in a particular position; now the indicator letters bore no relation to the position of the rotor. The position of the alphabet ring on the rotor had to be known to the decipherer, so it became part of the key. In addition, Bernstein shifted from the rotor to the ring the notch or notches that caused the rotor to the left to move one space at a certain point or points in the rotor's revolution. This disjoined the rotor moves from the rotor encipherment, throwing up a further obstacle to solution.

Finally, Korn converted the leftmost of the four rotors into a reflector. Although it was called a rotor, it did not turn. It had contacts only on one face, and it sent the current that had come from the three normal rotors back through them along a different path before it illuminated an output letter. The reflector was sometimes called a half rotor because its wiring went from one contact on the side facing the three main rotors to another contact on the same side; it consequently had only thirteen connections instead of the twenty-six of the main rotors. The current's double traversing of the rotors meant that encipherment was like decipherment: if plaintext *a* became ciphertext X, plaintext *x* became ciphertext A. This reciprocity had the advantage of eliminating the need for any switch to shift from enciphering mode to deciphering and vice versa, thus precluding the error of enciphering a message in the deciphering mode. But it had the cryptanalytic disadvantage of yielding the knowledge of a second plaintext letter whenever a first was found. The double passage brought another advantage and disadvantage: it complicated the cryptosystem, but it meant that no letter could ever represent itself, a fact that might speed solutions by showing which possibilities could be rejected.

In 1924, the firm got the German post office to exchange Enigma-enciphered greetings with that year's congress of the International Postal Union. Later a book on cipher machines by an Austrian criminologist, Dr. Siegfried Türkel, gave the Enigma extensive coverage, including a detailed description of the various models, many photographs, and praise from the Austrian cryptanalyst and author Colonel Andreas Figl. But, no more than any other cipher-machine inventor of the time who had dreamed of getting rich by selling protection for businessmen's messages, no more than Alexander von Kryha or Edward H. Hebern or Arvid Damm, did Arthur Scherbius make money. By the end of 1924, his firm still had not paid dividends.

The situation, however, was changing. Behind the sandstone walls of the four-story headquarters of the Naval Command at Tirpitzufer 72–76, facing Berlin's tree-lined Landwehr Canal, the cryptologic branch that had turned Scherbius down in 1918 was reconsidering the security of German naval communications. The reason was the shocking discovery that the British had been reading coded German naval messages for much of World War I.

The first clue came from the fiery builder of Britain's Dreadnought navy, the retired first sea lord, Admiral of the Fleet Sir John Fisher. In his *Memories,* published in 1919, he wrote:

> The development of the wireless has been such that you can get the direction of one who speaks and go for him; so the German daren't open his mouth. But if he does, of course, the message is in cypher; and it's the elucidation of that cypher which is one of the crowning glories of the Admiralty work in the late war. In my time they never failed once in that elucidation.

Subsequent indications were even more specific. In 1923, the official history of the Royal Navy in the war revealed various in-

stances when intercepts had given the British an advantage. At the
same time a dramatic and authentic story drew the attention of all
to Britain's cryptanalysis.

In his best-selling *The World Crisis,* the first two volumes of which
were also published in 1923, Winston Churchill, who had been the
civilian head of the Royal Navy at the start of the war, revealed, in
his flamboyant style and with some poetic license as to facts, the
basis of Britain's codebreaking successes:

> At the beginning of September, 1914, the German light cruiser
> *Magdeburg* was wrecked in the Baltic. The body of a drowned Ger-
> man under-officer was picked up by the Russians a few hours later,
> and clasped in his bosom by arms rigid in death, were the cipher
> and signal books of the German Navy and the minutely squared
> maps of the North Sea and Heligoland Bight. On September 6 the
> Russian Naval Attaché came to see me. He had received a message
> from Petrograd telling him what had happened, and that the Rus-
> sian Admiralty with the aid of the cypher and signal books had been
> able to decode portions at least of the German naval messages. The
> Russians felt that as the leading naval Power, the British Admiralty
> ought to have these books and charts. If we would send a vessel to
> Alexandrov, the Russian officers in charge of the books would bring
> them to England. We lost no time in sending a ship, and late on an
> October afternoon Prince Louis [of Battenberg, first sea lord, whose
> name was later changed to Mountbatten] and I received from the
> hands of our loyal allies these sea-stained precious documents.

Churchill followed this with some colorfully told stories of how
solved German intercepts had enabled the British to fight better at
sea. Soon a volume of the official German naval history acknowledged that "the German fleet command, whose radio messages were
intercepted and deciphered by the English, played so to speak with
open cards against the British command."

Suddenly, the German navy saw that a mere change of codes
was no longer enough. It needed to fundamentally transform its
system of secret communications. It had to have a cryptosystem
that would not give away any secrets even if captured. Perhaps a
machine was the answer. They navy had been offered one half a
dozen years ago that promised security to messages whether or not
the machine was in the hands of the enemy. The staff had rejected
it as unsuitable, but now the navy saw things differently. It may
have examined other cipher machines on the market, such as the
wholly inadequate Kryha, but it turned back to Scherbius and began letting contracts.

By 1925, Chiffriermaschinen Aktien-Gesellschaft had started production of the first Enigma machines for the navy. They differed from the commercial model in several ways. The order of letters on the typewriter keyboard and on the illuminated panel was not the QWERT of the commercial version but alphabetical. The rotor wiring was different. Though only three rotors were used in the machine at one time, five were supplied, providing a greater choice of keys and therefore greater security. Since the reflecting rotor could not be turned, only three toothed thumbwheels instead of four projected above the cover. Instead of twenty-six contacts, the naval Enigma had twenty-nine, adding to the normal alphabet the three umlauted letters ä, ö, and ü, included because the codebook in which plaintext was to be encoded before encipherment by the Enigma had umlauted codewords.

This pre-encoding and the extra codewheels were only two of the ways in which the navy sought to increase the security of messages enciphered in its new machine. Another measure sought to preclude the navy's chief security concern: espionage. The navy required that only officers, whose honor presumably immunized them against the blandishments of money and women, could set rotor positions.

Another major security measure was aimed at blocking the only method that any German cryptanalyst could then conceive of for solving Enigma messages. Called superimposition, it would require having thirty or so messages, of which portions had been enciphered with the same succession of rotor positions; with very heavy traffic, this might happen. To avoid an accumulation of overlapping texts, the navy prescribed rotor starting positions that were far apart. These were listed in a booklet. The enciphering clerk would choose one and communicate it to the deciphering clerk by an indicator — a group of letters. The indicator was itself enciphered, and the randomness of the prescribed rotor starting positions eliminated the possibility of a cipher clerk's making up a starting position that was not random, such as XXX or LIL.

A final security measure assigned messages different grades of security — general, officer, staff — with successively more complex cryptosystems and keys held by fewer people.

By the start of 1926, all of these systems had been prepared and Scherbius's firm had delivered enough Enigmas for the navy to put the machine into service as its Funkschlüssel C (Radio Cipher C). The twenty-three-page manual for it, dated February 9, 1926, covered, in addition to a description of the machine and the method of enciphering and deciphering, such matters as how to test the bulbs and how to deal with ciphering errors.

The navy's satisfactory experience with the Enigma during its first year became known to the army's Chiffrierstelle, or Cipher Center. The officer in charge in 1926 and 1927 was Major Rudolf Schmidt, a World War I signals officer who had written the chapter on communications for a major study of the war. He and his cryptologists saw the merits of the Enigma. They made some changes to suit it better for army practice: twenty-six-contact rotors, only three rotors (perhaps to have less to carry in mobile warfare), a standard QWERT keyboard, and a system of message keys that required no booklet, only a set of keys that enabled the cipher operator to make up a different key for each message. On July 15, 1928, the Enigma went into the army's service.

That year a single Enigma cost 600 reichsmarks, or $144 ($900 in 1991 dollars); volume purchases may have reduced this price. But the firm's sales remained low. A few machines were sold to businesses, but the commercial market never materialized (nor did it for other cipher-machine makers). By the end of the decade the navy had bought no more than a couple of hundred machines, and the army about as many. Still, it was a start.

Then, one spring day in 1929, the team of a horse-drawn wagon that Scherbius was driving at his factory shied and smashed the wagon against a wall. Scherbius suffered severe internal injuries. On May 13, he died, only fifty years old. But his business survived.

By the mid-1930s the firm was manufacturing a variety of cryptographic machines. The army experimented with an eight-rotor printing version for a while. The most important change had come in 1930 with the army's addition of a plugboard on the front of its machine. This consisted of a plate with twenty-six sockets, each representing a letter, that could be connected with one another by short cables with jacks on the end. The sockets were connected by wires to the keyboard and to the lamps, so that the enciphering and deciphering current passed through the plugboard. It added an extra substitution that overlay the rotor substitution. If on the plugboard the C socket and the R socket were joined by a cable and if without the plugboard the cipher letter for a plaintext *e* was C, the plugboard would convert the C to R. If the plugboardless cipher letter was R, the plugboard would replace this with C. The army connected only six pairs of letters, meaning that twelve letters were enciphered through the plugboard, the others being enciphered only with the rotors. But even twelve encipherments increased the number of keys — and so, theoretically, the number of trials a cryptanalyst would have to make — by billions. The plugboard was an excellent improvement.

In 1935, Hitler denounced the Versailles treaty and began his enormous expansion of Germany's armed forces. They needed cipher machines, and they continued to buy Enigmas. Other agencies also purchased them: the railroad administration, the Abwehr (the military espionage service), and the Sicherheitsdienst, or SD (the Nazi party intelligence service).

During those rearmament years, both the army and the navy continually improved the Enigma and developed their systems of secret communication.

The navy alertly scanned the cryptologic horizons for new ideas. In the summer of 1930, for example, its cryptographers reported on a cipher machine devised by one Dr. Ruckhaber. "In its mechanical construction the method resembles in many points the not very successful Kryha system," they wrote. Its mechanism slipped or jumped and caused many enciphering errors. Its output letters were harder to read than those of an illuminating system. Changing its setting took longer than changing the Enigma's. It appeared easy to solve. The navy turned it down.

The Reichsmarine (its name was changed in 1935 to Kriegsmarine) developed its own cryptosystems, mostly for specialized uses. Some naval attachés held *Schlüssel A* (Code A), a code with a numerical superencipherment. The *Werftschlüssel* (Dockyard Cipher), a pencil-and-paper system, served shipyards and small ships. Early in 1939 the navy reworked and reissued the *Funkschlüssel H* (Radio Cipher H), which enciphered in pairs the letters of the nonsecret International Radio Telegraph Code. One edition, of 1,400 books in gray binding, served the merchant marine (Handelsmarine); the other, 800 in red, was for warships and naval posts. Shortly after war broke out, the navy prepared a *Wetterkurzschlüssel* (Short Weather Cipher) to abbreviate weather information so it could be transmitted "in the shortest possible time."

The Enigma remained the navy's basic and most widespread cryptosystem. And the navy proved itself not stiff-necked in continually evaluating it. In particular, it accepted the uncomfortable conclusions of a study by Lieutenant Henno Lucan, second radio officer of the battleship *Elsass,* that in neither physical nor cryptologic security did the Enigma meet modern requirements. At about the same time, the army proposed that the navy adopt the army version of the Enigma, with its twenty-six-contact rotors and with a plugboard, which the navy's lacked. The army gave two reasons: the plugboard had greatly improved security, and a single machine would make the services cryptographically compatible.

In February 1930, the chief of the Naval Command requested that the B-Dienst look into the army's proposal. The B-Dienst, successor to the codebreaking B- und E-Dienst of World War I, replied that the main questions to be answered were, did the army machine meet navy requirements and did the use of the same model in larger numbers imperil the navy's cryptographic security?

On June 21, the B-Dienst offered a positive judgment of the army machine, chiefly because "it offers considerably greater security." The improvement stemmed from the plugboard, which, the B-Dienst said, raised the number of possible enciphering circuits by 2 to 3 billion. This greatly outweighed the loss of 5,213 starting positions that the army machine's smaller rotor would entail. Several years passed before the navy's bureaucracy accepted this argument and before enough of the new machines and rotors were produced and distributed throughout the navy. Finally, in August 1934, the navy began using the army Enigma machine, with its plugboard and typewriter keyboard. But it sought an extra measure of security: each machine had a set, not of three rotors, like the army model, nor of five, like the earlier naval machine, but of seven. The instructions for the new machine — the *Funkschlüssel M* (Radio Cipher M, the M perhaps for Marine) — required that rotors I, II, and III serve for talking with the army, that IV and V stay in reserve, and that VI and VII be used when the navy wanted to send messages to itself. The navy improved the system early in 1939. It recalled rotors VI and VII of all its Enigmas and cut a second notch in the alphabet rings. Notches now stood next to H and U. Each notch caused the rotor to the left to move one space when the notch reached a certain point in its rotor's revolution. Rotors I to V and later the added rotor VIII each did this once in a revolution. When rotor VI or VII was used in the machine, its extra notch caused the rotor to the left to step twice in each revolution of VI or VII. Though this shortened the period, it also reduced the probability of a successful superimposition.

A few months later, the navy divided its cipher communications into two nets, one using a home waters key, one a foreign waters key. This lowered the volume of messages in each key and so lessened the chances for solution. In addition, the navy continued its three grades of messages. The general keys were widely held; enlisted men could handle them. Officer-grade messages used the same inner settings of the Enigma as the general grade but different plugboard settings, and if officer-grade messages were to be radioed, they were reenciphered with the general key. Staff-grade messages had their own inner settings and plugboard arrangement.

Paralleling these improvements in cryptographic security were those in physical and personnel security. On January 24, 1930, the Naval Command notified its four major units that "a surveillance of the machine and the rotor box [which held the rotors not in the machine], more comprehensive than before, especially on smaller vessels, is planned. . . . A sharp supervision of the personnel who have access to the machine is necessary." The Naval Command noted that it intended (as Lieutenant Lucan had proposed) to secure the machine with a lock instead of just a lead seal.

Subordinate units reported, as ordered, on the measures they were taking. The commander of the battleship *Hessen* said the machine was "housed in a specially prepared, lockable compartment of the cipher desk in the radio shack. . . . The rotor boxes are kept under a secret lock in the office of the radio officer." Captain Wilhelm Canaris of the battleship *Schlesien* urged keeping the lead seal. "If an unauthorized person succeeded despite all security measures in obtaining the key to this [proposed new] lock," Canaris wrote, "it would in that case be difficult, often impossible, to detect this unauthorized intervention." The commander of the Baltic Naval Station reiterated the regulation that only officers should change and set the rotors.

Personnel security was reinforced by the Defense Ministry's memoranda on espionage. Officers used these to instruct enlisted men on the need for secrecy and the dangers from foreign intelligence agencies. The memo of October 15, 1934, included a monitory tale about the Enigma.

> During a change of position in a field exercise, a noncommissioned officer and a private of a communications battalion left, through negligence, the cipher machine and a hand cipher in the field. The loss was noticed by them upon arrival in their new position, but the cryptographic material was not found in the place where it had been lost. A civilian had taken it and delivered it to the mayor of a neighboring village within half an hour.
>
> Both soldiers were sentenced to confinement in a fortress for negligent betrayal of military secrets, thereby endangering the security of the Reich.

The same memorandum included a frightening summation of persons sentenced in Nazi Germany for treason or betrayal of military secrets: 148 in all of 1933, 155 for just the first seven months of 1934.

One of those people may have been Radioman Second Class Egon Bress of the Fourth Torpedo Boat Half-Flotilla in Wilhelmshaven. His careless lifestyle raised suspicions, and an investigation showed that, though his correspondence consisted largely of erotic exchanges with young women, he had taken several hundred photographs of cryptographic documents — the *Allgemeines Funkspruchbuch (AFB)* code, several superencipherments, and a keying procedure for the Enigma, among others. The photos, which he had had developed at a drugstore, were found in the home of a barmaid. Bress was arrested on February 16, 1934.

At the same time that it was watching over these obvious aspects of security, the navy was also seeking to prevent cryptanalytic losses. It recognized that using the cryptosystems correctly was as important as having good systems — perhaps even more important. Navy cryptologists may not have remembered the time in 1916 when the British transmitted virtually the same message in three different codes, enabling the German codebreakers at Neumünster to expand its solution of all of them. But the lesson had sunk in: improper usage could jeopardize even the best system. So cryptologists monitored the navy's cryptographic operations. In some cases they merely warned of poor practices. After a radio exercise in

1932, for example, a reviewer cautioned that messages in a particular system "should not have time groups ending in 0 or 5" and that "the multiple representations [of geographical positions] were not sufficiently utilized." In other cases violators of the rules were punished.

On the evening of January 8, 1932, Radioman Kunert of the Baltic Naval Station at Kiel was encrypting a message. He first encoded it in a codebook, then enciphered the resultant groups with the Enigma. The cipher form of the time had three columns: one for the plaintext words, one for their four-letter codegroups, and one for the codegroups' four-letter Enigma encipherments. Regulations called for the twenty-line column of unenciphered codewords to be crossed out so that they would not be transmitted. But Kunert erroneously ran his pencil instead through the column of enciphered codewords. Around 10:30, he began to transmit his message, consisting of the unenciphered codewords, to the T-151, the command vessel of the Second Torpedo Boat Half-Flotilla, then at sea. When Kunert reached the twenty-ninth group, he spotted his mistake and stopped transmitting. He reported the situation to Radioman First Class Schmaland aboard the T-151.

On the assumption that the urgent message should suffer no delay, Schmaland directed Kunert to retransmit the message, giving the correct groups. This would give anyone listening both the unenciphered and the enciphered forms of an Enigma message. The monitors raged. Through this "entirely incomprehensible order" arose a radio violation "of the grossest sort. A better handhold for tackling the *Funkschlüssel C* [the 1926 naval Enigma] cannot be given to foreign cryptanalytic services. Thirty-six positions of the letter sequence were given to foreign cryptanalysis, which under certain circumstances could lead to further solutions." This was rather exaggerated, as the cryptologists half admitted later on. To avoid a repetition of this blunder, they proposed that "all radio personnel should be forcefully instructed . . . about such errors and how their consequences can endanger the security of national defense." Then, taking no chances, the navy changed keys.

In addition to moving against theft, betrayal, and accidental compromise, the navy sought to nullify the possibility of seizure of cryptographic material by enemy action. It did not fear capture of an Enigma alone — indeed, one memorandum stated specifically that "it is assumed in judging the security of the cryptosystem that the enemy has at his disposition the machine including all rotors" — because it believed that the great number of keys would not allow the correct key to be recovered in time to be useful. But it worried that seizure at the same time of the list of current machine settings and the booklet of indicators for the message keys would expose its messages to alien eyes for at least the duration of validity of the list and the booklet.

So the navy began to print its cryptographic documents in watersoluble ink. The ink was red; the paper, pink, was like blotting paper, intended to soak up water even if pressed tightly between book covers on a shelf. Of course, on a ship the danger existed that spray, rain, condensation, or spilled liquids would make the ink run and the document illegible. So the navy issued two copies of each document and urged that each one be enclosed in a protective envelope. The envelope, however, was not to be airtight but was to allow water to come in when submerged.

Finally, the navy provided a fallback system in case the enemy captured all four elements needed for a current reading of German cryptograms: a machine, a list of current settings, the booklet that listed the prescribed rotor starting positions and their indicators, and the bigram tables for enciphering the indicators. The method, to be memorized or written in an innocuous form, changed the rotor order and the ring positions, thus invalidating the captured documents. In the system's first implementation, the cipher clerk would add 3 to the key list's rotor number, so that when the key list said the rotor II was to go into the left-hand position, rotor V would be inserted instead. And the clerk would set the alphabet rings on the successive rotors respectively 4, 5, and 6 places farther down than the key list called for. Thus the key list's ring positions KYD would be set at ODJ. A cue word would institute these changes. The first was ALDEBARAN, the name of a star. The clerk was allowed to set this down in his notebook as "Aldebaran, R 3, L 456," in which R stood for "rotor" and L for "letter." All these measures complemented the basic complex keying system (see Appendix).

Thus, by the start of the war, the Kriegsmarine had in place an extremely well thought out cipher system. It sought to preclude the dangers of operators' stupidity and laziness, the capture of some documents, betrayal, and superimposition. It was content with its cryptographic systems. When the Monitoring Center that it had established at the start of 1939 to watch over its radio traffic submitted a report stating that communications should be held down as much as possible "because our cipher systems are to be viewed as not 100 percent secure," the Naval War Command agreed with the recommendation to limit communications but said that such conclusions as "not 100 percent secure" should not be drawn.

The excellence of the navy's cipher system played an important role in the ideas of one officer who had commanded a U-boat in 1918. He had adapted some World War I ideas on U-boat tactics that he thought would enable German submarines to choke off Britain's imports in the event of a new war. The attacks of isolated submarines on convoys had not succeeded in doing this in World War I; like others before him, the officer concluded that group attacks would be necessary. As he worked it out, the first U-boat to spot a convoy would radio its position and then maintain contact with the target. U-boat headquarters would centralize information about its own submarines and enemy vessels and instruct other U-boats to hasten to the convoy's expected position and join in a combined assault. These concerted tactics alone promised success, the officer believed.

He knew that this tactic would compel the U-boats to break a vital rule of the invisible arm: radio silence. But he felt that the value of coordination among U-boats outweighed the dangers of radio direction-finding by the enemy, and he further expected that the enemy's inability to solve either the coded sighting reports or his coded instructions to the U-boats would deprive the foe of the advance information needed to thwart the subs. The secrecy of these messages would result from the unbreakability of the German naval cipher machine. On the strength of the Enigma, then, turned the success of the wolfpack strategy of that officer, Commander Karl Dönitz.

Four

The Codebreaker and the Spy

THE BLACK ART of codebreaking gleamed golden in the 1920s and 1930s. Bespectacled men in guarded offices in Paris, London, Washington, Berlin — in every capital — read the intercepted secret messages of other powers. Hunched over their desks, they puzzled over the mumbo jumbo of five-letter codegroups in cablegrams, hesitantly wrote words in languages not their own in colored pencil between the lines of gibberish, erased them, tried others. They filled in the blanks of a partial solution with silent jubilation and had the completed text typed up for distribution to policy makers.

Everybody seemed to be reading everybody else's codes. France cracked the German and English codes. Germany read French, English, and Polish codes. Britain, whose postwar codebreaking agency was descended from Room 40, solved Soviet, French, and American codes. The United States broke the Japanese code; Italy, the British — among others in all of these cases. Usually, these were the minor codes of major powers or the major codes of minor powers. Less often were the major codes of the major powers broken — always with the exception of those of the United States, whose cryptograms were as transparent as a fish tank for any competent cryptanalyst.

Many of these countries had established cryptanalytic agencies to provide in peace the benefactions discovered in war. Yet one nation that had not learned codebreaking in World War I gained experience in its postwar struggle for existence, created an instant tradition of excellence, and advanced to an achievement that none of the great powers ever matched. This was Poland.

Shortly after her restoration as a state in November 1918, Poland had first resisted Soviet advances into what had been Polish territory before the first partition of the country in 1772, then had herself greedily moved into Soviet lands. In the seesaw struggle that raged from Kiev to Warsaw, codebreakers seemed to emerge in the Polish army fully formed. Their chief was Lieutenant Jan Kowalewski, a former chemical engineer who had always scored high on his mathematics examinations. At twenty-seven, he was a bear of a man whose good looks and sense of humor attracted many women. In 1919, when Kowalewski was on the army general staff, a friend asked him to take over the friend's duties for a fortnight while he went on leave to get married. The friend's work dealt with translating and evaluating intercepted telegrams. Kowalewski, who knew many European languages, had no difficulty with this. And when one day he found a Russian intercept in code on his desk, he determined to solve it. Within a few days he had done so. The message revealed information about the movement of some White Russian forces fighting the Reds in the Russian civil war — information of great interest to the Poles.

Kowalewski was directed to organize a radio intelligence service. Reluctantly, for he did not want to work in intelligence, he did so. He recruited mathematicians and brought in army officers to form a unit of a dozen men. He himself became passionate about the work. One day he ran about headquarters asking everybody for the words to a Russian folk song: it was evidently the key to a cipher. His unit very rapidly achieved remarkable successes. Many Russian cryptograms were solved the very day they were intercepted; most of the others were solved the next day.

In August 1920, with the Soviets at the gates of Warsaw, more than 400 solutions revealed to the Poles the enemy's organization, strength, locations, and plans. On August 20, for example, Kowalewski's unit read an operational order of Soviet General Mikhail N. Tukhachevsky, setting out the assignments of all his armies. Such intercepts were sent to the Polish commander, General Jozef Pilsudski. He used them to stop the Russians outside of the Polish capital and then to drive them back, preserving Poland's freedom and ending the Communists' dream of marching to Berlin to start turning Europe Red. Kowalewski received the high Polish order of Virtuti Militari. And though he soon left cryptology, the unit he had founded, the Biuro Szyfrów, or Cipher Bureau, remained in the Second Department (Intelligence) of the army general staff.

Among the bureau's functions was helping Poland move with surer knowledge in her difficult international situation. Punching the Soviet Union in the nose and settling the eastern boundary did not end the country's difficulties with her huge neighbor.

But the clamor from the west was louder. Germany, though defeated in World War I, claimed parts of Poland that had been German since the partitions. She was enraged by the Polish Corridor, which divided East Prussia from the rest of the nation and caused unending difficulties in trade, transportation, and communications. Some German leaders, inspired in part by historical precedent, urged the obliteration of the new Polish nation. Since the days of the Teutonic knights seven centuries earlier, Germans had pressed for a *Drang nach Osten*. And though Germany's army was only a third the size of Poland's, Germany believed herself to be, acted like, and was treated by all as a great power.

In the face of this situation, Poland, in February 1921, signed political and military agreements of mutual assistance with France. Poland gained the larger nation's support; France used Poland to make Germany worry about a two-front war. Poland clung tightly to the agreements through the 1920s as Germany rejected all attempts to accept the postwar borders with Poland, raised tariffs against that country, and thundered out ceaseless propaganda against her.

Self-preservation thus compelled Poland to keep her two dangerous neighbors under observation. One way was to read their messages. This work devolved upon the unit founded by Kowalewski and headed in the late 1920s by Franciszek Pokorny. It continued to solve Soviet cryptosystems, most of them hand ciphers or simple codes. And it cracked as well the Germany army field cipher, also a pencil-and-paper system. Then in 1926 the German cryptograms began to change.

In the naval messages, the indicators — the groups of letters that told the receiver's cipher clerk which keying variables were used — were different from the old ones. The frequency distribution of letters bore no resemblance to the older messages. Repeated groups of letters all but vanished. On July 15, 1928, Pokorny's cryptanalysts noticed similar changes in many messages of the German army. Perhaps the two German armed forces had converted to machine cryptography.

Pokorny assigned the analysis of these new messages to three

German specialists: Captain Maksymilian Ciężki, who had had to serve in the German army in World War I, Lieutenant Wiktor Michalowski, and a civilian, a Mr. Czajsner. They made little progress. They observed that the indicators for the new army messages consisted of six letters and that in all cryptograms of a single day in which the first indicator letter was, say, R, all the fourth indicator letters were, say, M. The second and fifth and the third and sixth letters likewise seemed to be related. But it was not clear what this meant. The cryptanalysts confirmed, perhaps from spies, perhaps from radiomen's chatter, that the cryptograms had been machine-enciphered. When they discovered that the machine was the Enigma, they purchased a commercial model. Experiment soon showed them that it could not decipher military messages. Beyond this, however, they were unable to learn anything. Statistical tests showed that there were not enough identically keyed messages for the standard superimposition form of solution to work. It appeared impossible to take even the first step in reconstructing the machine.

This was the situation in January 1929. But Pokorny and Ciężki were beginning to understand that cryptology was changing. For centuries nearly all cryptosystems had been linguistically based: elements of language, such as words or syllables or phrases, were replaced with codewords or codenumbers. Cryptanalysts thus had to be linguistically oriented: Dillwyn Knox was an archetype. After World War I, however, cryptography began to be mechanized. Increasingly, armed forces adopted cipher machines. And their basis is literal, or letters, not linguistic: a cipher machine will divide the *t* from the *h* in *the,* for example. While codes are books, cipher machines are like typewriters. Breaking their ciphers calls mainly for mathematical or mathematical-like knowledge. The generation of keys, the production of cipher alphabets, and other elements are ascertained through logical analysis, sometimes without recovering a single word of the plaintext.

To solve the Enigma, Pokorny and Ciężki sought mathematicians, particularly among students at the university at Poznán. Even though that city was not one of the centers of Polish mathematics, then perhaps the finest in the world, it was in the part of western Poland that had been German territory from 1793, the date of the second partition of Poland, to 1918; the Germans called the city

Posen. Many mathematics students there had grown up in the area, had attended German schools, and knew German. They thus would possess the mathematical skills necessary and the linguistic skills possibly helpful for attacking the Enigma. An instructor assembled a group with those qualifications for Pokorny and Ciężki, who invited them to join a class in cryptology. Some twenty accepted. Pledged to secrecy, they attended a night course once a week at the university's Mathematics Institute in the fake-medieval castle built by Kaiser Wilhelm II. The instructors — Ciężki, Pokorny, and a civilian cryptanalyst, engineer, and radio ham named Antoni Palluth — came from Warsaw, 200 miles away.

Palluth lectured first, on the basics of cryptology. Then Ciężki spoke on the German army field cipher that Warsaw had solved. It was not the Enigma but a pencil-and-paper system called a double transposition. It mixed the letters of the plaintext message rather than replacing them with other letters. The cryptanalyst's task was to unscramble them, to restore their original order. Ciężki assigned the students some actual intercepts to break. To help them, he told them that the messages dealt with winter quarters and bivouacs on training grounds.

Within a few hours, three students had solved the cryptograms. Gradually, as the test cryptograms became harder, more and more students dropped out of the course. And then one of the three who had solved the double transposition, Marian Rejewski, left — but not for lack of ability or interest. He had received his degree in mathematics and wanted to pursue studies in actuarial mathematics at one of the world centers for mathematics, the university at Göttingen.

Rejewski, a short, unprepossessing twenty-three-year-old, did not impress the other Polish mathematicians at Göttingen by his mind or his manner, by his looks or his personality. He had no close friends at the university, but he tagged along on the long walks that one of the Polish mathematicians, Henry Schaerf, liked to take. Rejewski's political views, in particular his opinion that the Jews should be expelled from Poland, seemed derived from newspaper articles on the program of the National Democratic Party. But he was not so rigid as not to listen to contrary positions. Schaerf thought him relatively immature in his mathematical work and saw in him no extraordinary ability, no flashes of brilliance.

For a year Rejewski studied applied mathematics, specializing in actuarial questions. He expected eventually to work in a relative's insurance firm. But upon his return home for the 1930 summer vacation, he found a letter offering him a teaching assistantship at Poznán. He accepted it and, with the depression rapidly making job prospects scarce, kept the position instead of returning to Göttingen. He wondered what had become of the cryptology course and soon learned that the other two students who had cracked the double transposition were now solving German cryptograms twelve hours a week in a basement office of the Poznán military command post in St. Martin's Street. Rejewski told one of them that he wouldn't mind working there as well. After an interview, he was hired. In mid-1931 the unit formally became an outpost of Warsaw's Biuro Szyfrów, or BS, which had been expanded by putting together several intercept and codebreaking units.

Ciężki, short, corpulent, jovial, now head of the bureau's fourth, or German, desk — BS-4 — had progressed no further in the solution of the Enigma than he had when Pokorny first presented the problem to him. In desperation, Ciężki called in a noted clairvoyant, but even his crystal ball could not reveal the mind of the machine. Ciężki's long-range plan, however, seemed hopeful; his three part-time mathematician cryptanalysts were showing promise. He offered them full-time jobs as cryptanalysts in Warsaw, and on September 1, 1932, Rejewski and his two younger colleagues, Jerzy Różycki and Henryk Zygalski, who had only recently graduated from the university, began work in a wing of the Saxon Palace, the general staff building on Saxon Square.

Ciężki did not think they were ready yet to attack the Enigma. He gave them instead as their first assignment the solution of a four-letter Reichsmarine code — a step up in difficulty from army hand ciphers but a big step away from the Enigma. The three began by making frequency counts of the code groups. Here Rejewski's actuarial studies found application, since much cryptanalysis rests on statistics. The trio noticed that many codegroups began with Y. Perhaps these groups represented the series of interrogatory words that begin in German (as in English), with *w*, a letter that, like *y*, stands at the end of the alphabet: *wer, was, wann* (who, what, when) and so on. One day, mulling this possibility, they noticed a short, six-group radiogram beginning YOPY that was answered with a four-group message. It appeared to be an exercise in which one operator had put a message into code and transmitted it to another, who had replied. Perhaps the first message was a question, the second its answer — probably, in view of its brevity, a year, with each codegroup representing a digit. The question would then be a query as to when something happened. Was it a battle? The birthdate of a famous man? The three quickly reasoned their way to the supposition that the six-letter message was *Wann wurde Friedrich der Grosse geboren?* (When was Frederick the Great born?) This guess proved correct and yielded as well the meanings of the four reply codegroups: 1, 7, 1, and 2. After making this first break, the three cryptanalysts merely expanded the solution. Their apprenticeship had ended.

The achievements of this young and relatively inexperienced cryptanalytic bureau equaled, curiously enough, those of one of the world's oldest. France's military cryptanalysts, whose work dated back decades before World War I, had had a remarkable history of success in cracking German military ciphers during the war. Some of their solutions had aided generals at crucial moments during the fighting. But by 1928 France had reduced the number of her army cryptanalysts to eight, and their capabilities were limited. They did not have the techniques needed to solve rotor machines. They dealt only with simple systems: the German army double transposition that Rejewski and the others had solved in their cryptology class, some German codes, a British code. The cryptanalysts and their superiors seemed content with that. The anti-German revanche that had spurred France to the forefront of cryptology after the defeat of 1871 had evaporated in the victory of 1918; the need for intelligence from codebreaking had declined now that France had shackled Germany with the restrictions of Versailles and possessed an army widely regarded as the best in the world. The attitude was the cryptologic equivalent of the Maginot Line.

But one French cryptologist, at least, was not content with his army's inadequate results. Gustave Bertrand had enlisted as a private in 1914, was wounded the next year in the Dardanelles, and was assigned after the war to the cipher section of the staff of French forces in Constantinople.

Cryptology attracted him. He served during the 1920s in the cipher sections of various headquarters and in 1929 was summoned to that of the army general staff. The poverty of the codebreakers' results may have led him to conclude that the coming generation of cipher machines would be solved not by pure cryptanalysis but only with the help of bought or stolen keys or descriptions. He proposed establishing a unit to purchase such information from traitors or to burglarize offices and examine and photograph the needed papers or mechanisms. On October 30, 1930, Bertrand, by now a captain, instituted the new Section D, for Décryptement et Interceptions, of the Service de Renseignements (Intelligence Service). Section D and the separate cryptanalytic section were both part of the army general staff's famous Deuxième Bureau (Second Bureau) for intelligence evaluation.

For almost two years, Section D yielded nothing of great value. With the approval of his chiefs, Bertrand contacted the intelligence services of countries keeping an anxious eye on a restive Germany: Poland and Czechoslovakia, with both of which France had military alliances, and Great Britain. They exchanged intercepts and direction-finding results, but no cryptanalytic results. Then Bertrand got a break.

In the summer of 1931, there arrived at the squalid offices of the Service de Renseignements, in a Ministry of War annex at 75 rue de l'Université on Paris's Left Bank, a letter dated July 1 and mailed from Prague. It stated that the writer had contacted the intelligence representative at the French embassy in Berlin on June 8 and had offered to sell documents of the highest importance. If the French were interested, they should contact him at Kaufhausgasse 2 in Basel, Switzerland, by October 1. If he had not heard from them by that date, he would go elsewhere. He listed two documents that he could deliver: the instructions for the use of the German army Enigma cipher machine and the instructions for setting its keys. The letter was signed Hans-Thilo Schmidt.

Paris contacted the Berlin embassy, and the Deuxième Bureau contact there, Maurice Dejean, confirmed that Schmidt had visited him. He added that Schmidt and his older brother, a lieutenant colonel, were both listed as being in the German Defense Ministry. This improved the chances that the approach was real and not a provocation.

The Service de Renseignements assigned the task of making the first contacts with Schmidt to its man Friday, who handled all sorts of details for the service — he could get train reservations that Cook's couldn't — but who specialized in recruitment and in the puchase of secret codes.

His codename was REX, he claimed to have been named von Koenig ("king" in his native German), his legal name was now Rodolphe Lemoine, but he had been born Rudolf Stallmann in Berlin on April 14, 1871. The son of a wealthy Berlin jeweler, he preferred travel — in France, Italy, England, Africa, Chile, and Argentina — to going into his father's business. Somewhere along the way he met and married a Frenchwoman, whose name he adopted; in 1900, he was naturalized as a French citizen. During World War I, in Spain, he developed a taste for spying, and in 1920 he came to Paris to work full-time for France's intelligence service. His pay came in the form of protection from the police in his shady dealings and of business concessions abroad that the French government awarded him. These activities he ran out of an office at 27 rue de Madrid in Paris's fancy eighth arrondissement.

Writing to the Basel address, REX arranged to meet Schmidt on November 1, 1931, at the Grand Hotel in Verviers, a town in eastern Belgium some 15 miles from the German border. There he learned much of the would-be spy's history.

Schmidt, then forty-four, had been born May 13, 1888, in Berlin, the second son of Professor Dr. Rudolf Schmidt and his wife, Johanna. The father, who was thirty-seven when Hans-Thilo was born, taught at the Charlotten school in Berlin. The first son, Rudolf, two years older than Hans-Thilo, had brought honor to the family when at twenty he was accepted into the army as a cadet. Hans-Thilo had had the standard college-preparatory classics education but then had studied business, with an emphasis on chemistry and technology. Both brothers had served in World War I. Rudolf distinguished himself in various signal corps posts, winning the Iron Cross, rising to captain, and ending the war in the general staff of the Fourth Army. Hans-Thilo, a lieutenant, likewise won the Iron Cross but had the bad luck to be gassed.

Rudolf was retained in the 100,000-man army that the Versailles treaty allowed Germany. Hans-Thilo started a soap factory, but in depression- and inflation-ridden postwar Germany, the business failed. By the mid-1920s, married and with two children, Hans-Thilo was desperate. He turned to his brother for help. Rudolf, who had no children and was close to his younger brother, prevailed upon a fellow signals officer to give Hans-Thilo a job. The officer was head of the Chiffrierstelle (Cipher Center), known as the ChiStelle, and he hired Hans-Thilo in part because Rudolf had been his predecessor. In fact, in one of the most exquisite ironies of intelligence history, Rudolf Schmidt, as head of the ChiStelle, had approved for army use the Enigma cipher machine that his brother was now proposing to betray! Hans-Thilo became a civilian clerk who distributed cipher material and supervised its destruction when it expired. He did his work well.

But he was embittered and rapidly grew more so. Despite his war record, his job paid poorly. His life seemed to be going nowhere. He was living in a furnished room at Lorenzstrasse 17 in west central Berlin, having sent his family to less expensive Bavaria to live with his in-laws. The contrast with his past was striking. His family had had enough money and high status: his mother was a baroness, his father a Professor Doktor — probably the highest nongovernmental standing a civilian could achieve in Germany. And the contrast with his brother's position was no better. Rudolf had not only been retained in the army, Germany's most prestigious institution, but had been promoted to lieutenant colonel and, after two assignments in divisional staffs, had been named chief of staff of the signal corps. Like thousands of others similarly disaffected, Hans-Thilo applied for membership in the Nazi party. But this did not immediately ameliorate his situation. And though a desire for more money and a sense of relative failure must trouble many men who hold state secrets, most do not betray their country. Hans-Thilo, from whatever motives, did.

REX learned much of this at Verviers. He sized up his man and examined the documents the spy brought with him. REX concluded that both the documents and the offer were genuine and directed Schmidt to return to the same place one week hence.

The Service de Renseignements, now persuaded that Schmidt would really spy for them, gave him, as they gave their other agents, a designation consisting of a group of letters. His was HE, which seems not to have borne any particular significance. In French, this pair is spoken *ahsh-AY*. This somewhat resembles the German word *Asche* (ash), which is sounded *AH-shuh* and which Schmidt himself later chose — with a premonitory shiver about the fate of most spies? — as his codename.

The rendezvous was set for November 8, 1931. The day before, REX, accompanied by the stout and sometimes difficult Gustave Bertrand and the Service de Renseignement's photographer, Bintz, arrived at the Grand Hotel, where REX had installed himself in princely fashion. Bertrand and Bintz had adjoining rooms with a bathroom between them: if it served as the camera studio, the shutter noise would not be heard in the hall. They spent part of the night adjusting the camera and their portable lights. The next morning they waited in their room for the call from REX. It came at 10 o'clock.

In a room filled with cigar smoke and with a radio playing music to deter eavesdropping, REX presented Schmidt to Bertrand. Schmidt, a whisky in his hand, smiled and bowed, heels together. Bertrand saw a man who wore a dark gray suit and down-at-the-heel shoes but who seemed to carry himself with assurance and to display the manners of a good upbringing. Bertrand was introduced as Monsieur Barsac. After some pleasantries, he examined the documents that Schmidt produced. They included an organization chart of the ChiStelle, an army hand cipher with its keys, a memorandum on poison gas, which Schmidt claimed to have obtained from his brother, and — most important — the two Enigma documents. The first was *Gebrauchsanweisung für die Chiffriermaschine Enigma*, the instructions for the use of the machine, numbered H.Dv.g.13 (for *Heeresdienstvorschrift geheim 13*, secret army service regulation 13). The other was the *Schlüsselanleitung für die Chiffriermaschine Enigma*, the directions for setting the keys on the machine, numbered H.Dv.g.14.

Bertrand could not conceal his pleasure, and Schmidt, seeing this, was radiant. REX and Bertrand agreed to pay him 10,000 marks, or $4,000 (about $27,500 in 1991 dollars). Bertrand took the documents and, running up the stairs two at a time, brought them to photographer Bintz. The two worked through lunch. About three, Bertrand brought the documents back to Schmidt, whom he found chatting with REX. The army officer, in his poor German, asked if Schmidt was pleased with the agreement.

"Jawohl, meine Herren. Besten Dank. Alles ist in Ordnung," Schmidt replied.

He bowed, took his money, and left.

Back in Paris, the elated Bertrand brought the documents to his friend Colonel Bassières, one of France's finest cryptanalysts, an amusing man with a limp who had honed his talents on German ciphers in World War I. Bassières accepted the papers, but he found that they provided only interesting generalities. H.Dv.g.13, warned, for example, "When putting the rotors on the shaft, be careful that the sides with the flat contact surfaces are always pointing to the side of the shaft that has a ring on its end." The keying instructions were more useful. They specified that the four elements of a complete key consisted of (1) the sequence in which the rotors were placed in the machine, given in roman numerals, such as III I II; (2) the setting of the alphabet ring on its rotor, given by a letter or its corresponding number, B or 2, for example; (3) the so-called basic setting of the rotors, specified by the letter or number of each rotor's alphabet ring that should appear in the rotor windows of the machine's lid at the start of the enciphering; and (4) the six plugboard connections, enciphering twelve letters, indicated by a pair of letters or numbers, such as A/O or 4/15.

This information seemed, however, to have little value in the absence of two critical elements not provided by the Schmidt documents: the wiring of the rotors and the actual keys in use on particular days. On Friday, November 20, two work weeks after he had given Bassières the documents, Bertrand went to him to learn how he had made out.

"Impossible to get anything useful from your documents," Bassières told him. "Too many things are lacking for us to reproduce the machine." He was referring primarily to the rotor wiring. "And even if we could, we would have to tie ourselves down to a monumental task of finding out the [daily] keys. We just don't have the means."

Hopeful that the British, with whom French intelligence had close relations, might do better, Bertrand immediately obtained permission to show them the documents. On Monday the twenty-third, he gave copies to the Paris representative of the British intelligence services, Commander Wilfred (Bill) Dunderdale. Three days later Dunderdale was back with the same judgment Bassières had rendered: the documents did not make it possible to solve Enigma messages.

Unwilling to give up without trying every avenue, Bertrand sought approval to give the information to France's ally Poland. Bertrand may have known, from a 1928 booklet describing Polish cryptanalytic successes in 1920, that the Poles had a good background in codebreaking. Approval was granted, and Bertrand himself was delegated to go to Warsaw. So that he would not be carrying anything compromising or risk losing the documents and so their secret, he sent photographs of the two booklets ahead by diplomatic pouch. He arrived Monday, December 7, 1931, and picked up the photos at the French embassy. At 9 A.M. the next day, he was in the office of the head of the Biuro Szyfrów, where he was warmly received. The chief, Major Gwido Langer, who had succeeded Pokorny, scanned Schmidt's offering, then exploded with joy. He ran out of the room and returned a few moments later with his boss, Colonel Stefan Mayer, the general staff's head of intelligence, and with Ciężki, head of BS-4. Mayer congratulated Bertrand warmly on his feat and asked for forty-eight hours to study the pamphlets.

At 4 P.M. on Thursday, Bertrand met Mayer and Langer in Mayer's office. This time the atmosphere was more temperate. The Poles explained that the documents showed that the machine had three rotors with movable alphabet rings on them and that the reflecting rotor did not turn during encipherment. The documents had further revealed the presence of the plugboard, which did not exist in the commercial Enigma. The Poles could not thank Bertrand enough. But, they explained, they did not know the rotor wiring, the rotor order, or the plugboard connections for a keying period. They did not know the alphabet ring positions on the rotors and therefore did not know the rotor positions for each message. All this could be determined by analysis, they said, but it would take much time. If Bertrand's informant could provide these details, and if the French could give the Poles specifics of their cryptanalytic progress on the basis of the new information, years of work could be saved.

Bertrand, embarrassed by his country's cryptanalytic ineffectualness, admitted that both French and English efforts on the Enigma had not produced as much as Langer presumed.

Langer sought to ease his chagrin. "You don't have the same

motivation as we do," he said generously. And on that note the two parted, with promises of further cooperation.

The next weekend, December 19 and 20, Bertrand and REX again met Schmidt in Verviers. The German had by then been admitted to the Nazi party with membership number 738,736. This demonstration of nationalistic orthodoxy did not keep him from delivering the keys that gave the daily settings for the machine for December 1931. Nor did it prevent him from meeting with Bertrand and REX three times during 1932: on May 8 in Verviers, on August 2 and 3 in Berlin, and on October 19 and 20 in Liège, Belgium. At each meeting, in addition to other information, Schmidt provided keys: for May, for September and October, and for November and December. Bertrand brought the keys to Warsaw.

The complexity of the Enigma problem led Ciężki to expand the plan he had instituted in 1929 of employing mathematicians to attack the new electromechanical forms of encipherment. The three young mathematicians he had brought to Warsaw from Poznán had gained experience in at least two different systems. Ciężki placed Marian Rejewski, the oldest and most apt, alone in a room on the third floor of the north wing of the general staff building, overlooking the tomb of Poland's Unknown Soldier. He gave Rejewski the photographs of the two instructional pamphlets from Schmidt and some obsolete key lists and in October 1932 assigned him in the greatest secrecy to solve the Enigma.

Rejewski read the stolen pamphlets and the few sheets of paper in the archives from earlier attempts and examined a curious equivalent of the commercial Enigma: a 2-foot-square frame with mobile vertical rods studded with nails that could be joined by multicolored threads to reproduce the wiring of the rotors. Then he picked up where his predecessors had left off: by analyzing the six-letter indicators with which each Enigma message started.

In these messages, all one day's indicators that had a particular letter, say, R, in the first position invariably had a certain letter, say, V, in the fourth position. The same held for the second and fifth and for the third and sixth positions. Rejewski saw that this pattern derived from the German keying method, which he knew from one of Schmidt's documents, H.Dv.g.14. The method utilized a three-letter key, say MGK, that was repeated: MGKMGK.

(The repetition assured the person receiving the message that the key had not been garbled in transmission. If the triads differed, the recipient could determine the right one in three trials.) The three letters were chosen at random by the cipher clerk for each message so that every cryptogram would have a different key. The recipient had to be told what this key was, but the information could not be transmitted in the clear and so was enciphered.

The instructions showed Rejewski that the clerk plugged in the six plugboard connections according to the key list. He inserted the rotors in the order given in the key list for that quarter of the year. He set each rotor's alphabet ring so that its spring-driven stud fit into the hole at a letter given in the key list for that day. Next he looked up that day's basic setting in the table of daily keys. He turned his rotors until the three letters given as the basic setting — say, PDX — appeared in the windows of the cover. He enciphered MGKMGK. Suppose that the six letters that lit up were OGKWZZ. This was his indicator, which he placed at the head of his message. He then turned his rotors until MGK appeared in the rotor windows. Only then did he begin enciphering the actual text of the message. This complicated procedure gave each message its own key and concealed that key in its transmission to the decipherer.

Now another cipher clerk in the same net that day might have chosen MIH as his message key. Since he would have the same plugboard connections, rotor order, alphabet ring positions, and rotor starting position as the first clerk, his two M's would be enciphered into the same letters as the two M's in MGKMGK, namely, O and W, even though the other letters differed. This relationship led Rejewski to build chains from the first and fourth letters of each indicator. If, for example, on a single day, two indicators were RTMGNU and GWAIZZ, Rejewski could string RG and GI together to make RGI. This constituted a chain — or at least the first links in one. Other indicators provided other links. Eventually each chain closed upon itself, returning to its first letter. Rejewski rapidly found that no single chain included all 26 letters, but that if he had enough indicators (usually around 60) all 26 would be included in other chains. The maximum of 26 was reached in only three ways, or cycles: two chains of 13; six chains of 10, 10, 2, 2, 1, and 1 letters each; and six chains of 9, 9, 3, 3, 1, and 1 letters each.

At this point, Rejewski's analysis branched into a path that differed fundamentally from all methods hitherto used in cryptanalytic attacks. In the past, cryptanalysts had depended upon statistics. Which letter was the most frequent? Which of several possible plaintexts was the most likely? Even the only known previous solution of a rotor machine, the dazzling 1924 success of American William F. Friedman in reconstructing the wiring of Edward Hebern's five-rotor machine, used a probabilistic and lower-algebraic approach. But Rejewski, for the first time in the history of cryptanalysis, utilized a higher-algebraic attack. He applied one of the first theorems taught in the theory of groups. In simplified form, the theorem states that if P and Q are permutations, then the permutation PQP^{-1} (read P, Q, P inverse) has the same cycle structure as the permutation Q. In the Enigma encipherment P could represent the plugboard input; P^{-1}, the plugboard output; and Q the total rotor encipherment. Group theory thus told Rejewski that his cycles depended only on the rotor setting and not on the plugboard encipherment. It told him, in other words, that the plugboard, in which the Germans placed great trust as enhancing the machine's security, could be ignored in at least part of the cryptanalysis.

The cycles Rejewski had discovered were produced by the substitutions generated by the six steps of the rightmost, or fast, rotor (the one that turned at the encipherment of each letter of the six letters of the key). Rejewski used the cycles to set up six huge equations that, if solved, would disclose the wiring of the fast rotor. The unknown terms of the equations were not simple ones like $3x$, but arrays of 26 elements. These elements consisted of Rejewski's quantification of the machine encipherment. If a rotor input contact was at the 12th position and the wire inside connected it to the output contact at the 20th position, the encipherment for that input position would be given the numerical value of 8. But for Rejewski, all 26 values, representing all 26 connections, were unknown.

Each of Rejewski's six equations had four complex terms. Three terms were unknown: the array of numbers representing the wiring of the fast rotor (which moved each time a letter was enciphered); the array of numbers representing the combined wiring of the middle and left rotors (which were assumed to be stationary, as they were in 21 cases out of 26) plus the reflector; and the connections of the six letter-pairs that were enciphered in the plugboard. (The plugboard could be ignored in the cycles but not in the eventual recovery of plaintext.) Rejewski assumed that he knew the fourth term, but in fact it was unknown. It represented the connections of the typewriter keys to the input plate that fed the current to the rightmost rotor. On the basis of the commercial Enigma that BS-4 had bought, Rejewski thought that these connections ran in keyboard order, from key Q to the first, or A, position on the input plate, from key W to input plate position B, from E to C, and so on. Finally, Rejewski introduced a permutation that would correct for the movement of the fast rotor as successive letters were enciphered.

He then tackled the equations. But the number of their unknowns overwhelmed him. It became clear to Ciężki, who visited him in his solitary office every day, that Rejewski was not going to succeed by himself. He would have to be given some of the material that Schmidt had supplied. Ciężki and Langer had thus far withheld this material, perhaps to make Polish cryptanalysis less dependent on gifts from France, which was just then cooling toward Poland's insistence on retaining the Corridor and on being superior in armed forces to Germany. On December 9, 1932, some six or eight weeks after Rejewski had started work, Ciężki gave him a copy of the daily keys for September and October 1932, which Schmidt had given REX in August and which Bertrand had brought to Warsaw in September.

The keys at once transformed one of the unknowns — the plugboard connections — into a known and simplified the rest of the equations. But they remained complex, and Rejewski continued to wrestle with them for several weeks. Then one day it struck him that his assumption for the wiring from the typewriter keys to the input plate could be wrong. Perhaps the wire from key Q ran to position Q rather than position A. He adjusted his equations. "The very first trial yielded a positive result. From my pencil, as if by magic, began to issue numbers designating the wiring in rotor N [the rightmost, or fast, rotor]," he wrote.

The twenty-seven-year-old cryptanalyst had uncovered part of the secret heart of the Enigma: the wiring of one rotor. This enabled him to lay the first Enigma solutions on Ciężki's desk at the end of December, as Christmas and New Year's lifted people's spirits in the Polish capital.

But these solutions comprised only a selected few, and further work was needed to complete the reconstruction of the machine. Here the Poles had a stroke of luck. The Germans changed the order of the rotors in the machine every three months, or quarter of a year. Fortunately, the keys that Schmidt had supplied straddled two different quarters: the third, for the September keys, and the fourth, for the October ones. This meant that in October the rotor in the right-hand position was different from the one in that position in September. Using the same technique as before, Rejewski determined the wiring on this rotor. After this, "finding the wiring in the third rotor, and especially in the reflecting rotor, now presented no great difficulties." Cleaning up the work — eliminating ambiguities to obtain completely correct information on wiring and rotor stepping — was greatly eased by a sample encipherment in one of the manuals that Schmidt had provided.

The solution was Rejewski's own stunning achievement, one that elevates him to the pantheon of the greatest cryptanalysts of all time. Much of the solution was due to his brilliance. Yet mathematics — even with Rejewski's extraordinary ability — had not sufficed. Pure analysis alone had not achieved a solution. The machine was too complex. Rejewski needed help from outside information, as he acknowledged:

> To this day, it is not known whether equation 3 [of the set of six equations with the arrays of 26 unknowns] is solvable. Admittedly, another approach to the reconstruction of the rotor wirings was found, in theory at any rate. But that approach is imperfect and laborious. . . . It requires the possession of messages from two days of identical or very similar settings of the rotors; therefore, finding the wiring of the rotors would depend on luck. In addition, it requires so many trials that it is not clear whether the director of the Cipher Bureau would have had enough patience to employ several workers for a long period without certain attainment of success, or whether he would have once more discontinued work on the Enigma. Hence the conclusion is that the intelligence material furnished to us should be regarded as having been decisive to the solution of the machine.

Britain and France also had these documents. Why had they not solved the Enigma?

They lacked mathematical cryptanalysts. Their cipher establishments, like generals still fighting the last war, saw no need to change the linguistic orientation that had brought them their successes of 1914–1918 and that was continuing to solve many diplomatic codes in the 1920s. France, for example, was breaking the codes of some ten countries. The cipher bureaus had no guarantee that an inexperienced mathematical cryptanalyst would succeed where experienced linguistic cryptanalysts had failed: Dillwyn Knox, a leading light of Britain's agency, had not broken the German Enigma despite great efforts. Though this agency had once considered training university mathematicians as reserve cryptanalysts, it had rejected the idea for fear that their indiscretions might reveal its codebreaking efforts. But Britain, at least, seemed justified in not expending more of its resources on the Enigma. The Admiralty maintained that Japan was Britain's chief threat, not Germany, where even that far-right exponent of revanche, Adolf Hitler, had written in *Mein Kampf* that to win England as an ally he would offer a "renunciation of a German war fleet."

In the end, what France and Britain lacked — and not only in cryptology — were vision and will. Poland had both. It was the great merit of Pokorny and Ciężki to have seen, before their counterparts in Europe's other cipher bureaus, the value of cryptanalysts with a strong mathematics background. And the great need to know what Germany was planning drove those cryptanalysts to extraordinary efforts. So Poland did what no other country had done — and what the Germans believed impossible.

But the work of Rejewski, that modern magus, was far from finished. It had, in fact, just begun.

Five
Racing German Changes

REJEWSKI'S GREAT SOLUTION had reproduced the Enigma and solved a few German messages. But it did not enable the Poles to read messages regularly. Indeed, the very concept of the Enigma, the reason for the machine's adoption, was that even if the enemy had a machine, he would not be able to obtain useful information from messages enciphered with it. So many keys were available, the thinking ran, that no cryptanalyst, or even team, would be able to find the right one before the messages had lost all military value. And the time it would take to solve an intercept was measured not in hours, not in days, but in years, in millennia.

Arthur Scherbius had enlarged the possible number of keys by proposing a machine with seven or even ten rotors. The German army had chosen instead to make the rotors changeable, to add alphabet rings, and to attach a plugboard. Their permutations raised the number of keys available to the astronomical figure of 10½ quadrillion. If 1,000 cryptanalysts, each with a captured or copied Enigma, each tested four keys a minute, all day, every day, the team would take 1.8 billion years to try them all. Since on average the codebreakers would reach plaintext halfway through, the typical solution would take them "only" 900 million years. For the Germans, this sufficed.

Rejewski thus faced a new and daunting task. Using Schmidt's keys, he had reconstructed the Enigma. Now, using the reconstruction, he had to find each message's key. And to decipher the German messages quickly enough to make current use of them, he obviously had to find a method other than exhaustive search.

For there were no flaws in the theory of the machine. It offered all the defenses that its inventor and proponents said it did; the

Germans' reasoning was impeccable, and their confidence was, in theory, not misplaced. But it was in practice. The ways in which men used the machine undermined its defenses. The army cryptographers' requirement that message keys be duplicated and then enciphered created relationships that vastly reduced the number of trials cryptanalysts would have to make to find the right key. Cipher clerks made up message keys, such as ZZZ, that were so easy to guess that the number of trials was reduced even more, and signal officers drafted stereotyped plaintexts, also easy to guess, that cut the number still further. The failure was not, as a later generation would say, in the hardware: it was a software problem.

Rejewski recognized this and struck at the same chink in Enigma's armor he had attacked at the start of his Enigma reconstruction: the doubling of the three-letter message key and its encipherment into a six-letter indicator.

But this time he had some help. "We can't have you solving these messages by yourself," Ciężki told him. "Now you'll work together with your colleagues again. They'll solve this material for the two months [for which Schmidt had supplied the keys], and I want you to think about how to go on from here." And so Rejewski's colleagues from Poznán, who had come to the Biuro Szyfrów with him, Henryk Zygalski, twenty-four, and Jerzy Różycki, twenty-three, were assigned to work with him in finding ways to recover the daily keys.

They were soon given replicas of the Enigma built by a small, specialized radio firm, one of whose founder-directors had served in the army from 1919 to 1922 with Ciężki. Another was Antoni Palluth, who had worked in BS-4 as a civilian cryptanalyst and had been one of the lecturers at the Poznán cryptology course. The firm was the Wytwornia Radiotechniczna AVA, or AVA Radio Manufacturing Company (the letters were from the radio call signs — TPAV and TPVA — of two of the four owners, all fanatic radio amateurs). From time to time the Biuro Szyfrów had given the little shop orders for highly advanced or very secret or particularly specialized equipment. So it was natural for the cryptologists to turn to AVA when they needed a copy of the Enigma. The firm took as its model the commercial Enigma that the army had bought years before and the photographs of the military Enigma from the booklets provided by Schmidt.

When the Enigma first went into army service, many cipher clerks used patterned keys such as AAA and RXR. Because several clerks sometimes chose the same key, identical encipherments resulted now and then. The Poles occasionally solved these by the classical method of superimposition, but this did not lead them to a general solution of the Enigma. For when the Germans recognized that repeated letters in their message keys were letting clerks create identical keys too often, they prohibited the use of keys with repeated letters. The Poles discovered this when superimposition stopped working.

With his new AVA machines and his new assistants, Rejewski returned to the six-letter indicators. If he had between sixty and a hundred intercepts from a single day, he could generate several chains of letters, as he had done in his original solution. He used these chains to construct tables of letters that enabled him to determine whether the first and second letters of the message key were the same at a particular setting of the alphabet rings. If he found that the letters were the same, he ruled out that setting, because repeated letters in the message key were forbidden. With enough messages, he could eliminate enough settings so that only the correct settings would be left. (Of course, if a German cipher clerk violated the regulations, the Poles might not solve any messages that day.)

But this work told the Polish cryptanalysts only the letters on the alphabet rings that showed through the windows of the Enigma's lid. They did not tell them which rotor was where. To ascertain this, they slid a grille — a sheet of paper with six narrow horizontal slots cut in it — with the first chain of letters written on it over tables of the cipher alphabets generated by each rotor. At each position of the grille, they sought pairs of letters. Six pairs on one table meant that they had found the correct rotor and its starting position. The tedium of this work was extreme. It took perhaps ten minutes to test just one setting of a rotor, and twenty-six settings had to be tested on all three rotors. Rejewski, Zygalski, and Różycki probably needed a whole morning to complete a test and find out which rotor was in the rightmost, or fast, position.

At first, the cryptanalysts had to repeat this process to determine the middle rotor. But they soon built up a catalogue that reduced this time to a few minutes.

They next had to find out where the alphabet rings had been set on the rotors. This was important because the rings carried the notches that stepped the rotor to the left. The cryptanalysts had two ways of determining this. One was to guess that a message began with *An* (German for "To") followed by an X as a word separator. One out of every five German army messages began this way, and good results would eliminate many ring positions on the fast rotor, leaving only the 26 × 26, or 676, positions of the other two rings to be discovered. For the four out of five messages in which *AnX* did not work, the cryptanalysts had to try all 17,756 positions one after another, sometimes rubbing their fingers raw and bloody on the gearlike setting wheels.

Now the cryptanalysts had ascertained three of the four keying elements: rotor order, rotor setting, ring setting. Still unknown were the plugboard substitutions. But these affected only twelve letters; a test decipherment at this point would produce a quasi-plaintext such as (to use an English example) *slarmlartsdmpaqmd*, which a cryptanalyst could determine meant *sparepartsdelayed*. This would tell him the plugboard connections. With this information the day's keys would be entirely reconstructed, that day's messages could be read in their totality and the work — painstaking, boring, grueling, but gloriously successful — could be completed, not in the 900 million years the Germans thought it would take, but in less than a day.

This unbelievable solution, which enabled the Poles to read many German cryptograms, swamped the cryptanalysts. They could not both recover the keys and then apply them each day to decipher the several dozen intercepts that the monitoring posts sent in. So in February 1933, the Biuro Szyfrów hired five or six clerks, swore them to secrecy, hastily trained them in deciphering Enigma messages, and set them to work around the clock using the AVA Enigmas to turn the intercepts into plain language. By mid-1934, a dozen Enigma replicas were available for message reading and for key recovery.

For a couple of years this work proceeded smoothly. Even the unexpected signing in January 1934 of the Declaration of Non-aggression and Understanding with the German government, by then headed by Adolf Hitler, did not decrease the flow of solutions. The cryptanalysts looked down from their offices at German visitors, such as the fat and bemedaled air minister Hermann Göring, laying wreaths at the tomb of Poland's Unknown Soldier, and smiled to themselves that he didn't know that they knew his secrets.

Then, in 1935, Hitler threw off the restrictions of the Versailles treaty and began to triple the size of his army. This expansion was soon reflected in an upsurge in military communications. The cryptographers of the ChiStelle knew that the more messages in a given key a cryptanalyst has, the easier it is to read them. So, on February 1, 1936, they required that the rotor order be changed not quarterly but monthly. This reduced by a third the number of messages sent using a particular order. In October, as rearmament further swelled the volume of messages, they changed the number of connections in the plugboard from a fixed six to a variable five to eight. And at the same time, they raised the tempo of the changes in rotor order from monthly to daily.

The Poles saw that they could not rest on their laurels. The race between codemaker and codebreaker had quickened from a pace that in ages past had been measured in centuries and more recently in decades to one that was measured in years or months.

By this time the cryptanalysts were working in a communications and radio intelligence installation newly built in an area that was relatively free of radio interference: the Kabacki woods some 6 miles south of Warsaw and half a mile east of the village of Pyry. The installation was enclosed by a high wall, several hundred yards long on each side. Within stood two brick buildings, the larger a garage and warehouse, the smaller a two-story bombproof radio station and cryptanalytic office. Trees screened the facility from the air. The three young cryptanalysts and their deciphering staff commuted in a dark blue official bus that left Warsaw's Theater Square near the general staff building every day at 7 A.M. and arrived twenty minutes later at the Pyry center.

They had plenty of work. The additional plugboard encipherments had caused solutions to plummet by some 40 percent, and the acceleration of the rotor order changes had greatly increased the cryptanalysts' workload. They fought back with new insights and with mechanization.

Sometimes they found in the day's harvest of six-letter indicators that a few Enigma operators had coincidentally chosen identical message keys out of the 17,756 possible keys. The cryptanalysts guessed that this happened because the operators had looked at the Enigma's typewriter keyboard and had selected patterns that merely looked random, such as QWE or the diagonal RFV. In those cases, instead of testing all 17,756 ring settings for the identical keys, the cryptanalysts had to try only some 30 or 40.

Mechanization saved more time. AVA built an electromechanical device that accelerated the recovery of rotor orders and settings. Called a cyclometer, it consisted of two linked sets of Enigma rotors. It served the Poles from 1936 to 1938, when, on September 15, the Germans changed their keying method. Rejewski soon found a way of determining the keys when the indicators in three messages fulfilled certain conditions. To speed this determination, he envisioned a device that consisted of three pairs of Enigmas. Each pair would have its rotors set at certain positions relative to one another based on the letters of the indicators. One pair would be testing the indicators of messages 1 and 2, another those of messages 1 and 3, and the third those of messages 2 and 3. The rotors of all three pairs would be driven through all their 17,756 positions looking for a three-way match. Such a match would reveal the rotor setting. It would not reveal the rotor order, however. So Rejewski proposed six machines to try all rotor orders at once.

His specifications were delivered to the AVA plant at Stepinska Street in the middle of October; less than a month later, the technicians under Palluth's direction had manufactured the necessary parts for the six machines. They were assembled in a room called the clock room — from the large clock over its black-curtained door — in the BS-4 offices in the Pyry facility. The machines worked perfectly. The parallel processing of the keys took a maximum of two hours, but often a possible solution was reached sooner. The machine would stop when it came to a possible solution; the cryptanalyst would read off the key and try it on one of the Enigma replicas. If the key produced plaintext, it was right; if it produced gibberish, the cryptanalyst restarted the machine to try again. The Poles called the machines *bomby,* or bombs, perhaps from the rounded ice cream sundae (a *bomba*) Różycki was eating when the idea was being discussed, perhaps from their time-bomb-like ticking, perhaps from the idea that they would destroy the German cryptograms.

One weakness of this method was that the indicator letter relationships could be changed by the plugboard. When five to eight plugs were used, the method still worked, but only about half the time. To avoid this problem, Henryk Zygalski devised a method that used sheets of cardboard about 2 feet square. Each Zygalski sheet was divided into 51×51 squares by a repeated alphabet (A . . . Z, A . . . Y) along the top and side. Each sheet recorded, for a given position of the fast rotor, the positions of the other two rotors that created certain indicator letter relationships; this was done by cutting a hole at the proper intersection. The four sheets would be aligned and stacked over a source of light; the holes through which light shone would indicate a possible rotor sequence and ring setting, without having to know the plugboard connections. It was therefore a powerful technique. But each sheet needed to have about a thousand holes cut into it at precise points, and 26 sheets were needed for each of the 6 rotor orders — a total of 156 sheets. So their preparation went more slowly than the manufacture of the *bomby*.

Nevertheless, the volume of Polish solutions of Enigma messages swelled in 1938 to its greatest ever. Most of the intercepts were of transmissions from the War Ministry in Berlin to German Military District I in East Prussia, bordering Poland to the north. They dealt with personnel transfers and postings and the buildup of the army. The head of the German desk of the intelligence branch of the Polish general staff incorporated the information from the twenty-odd intercepts he received each week into his briefings of the chief of the general staff, which took place two or three times a week early in 1938 and daily from June on.

During all these years, France's ace spy, Schmidt, met again and again with his handlers. After his six meetings in 1931 and 1932, he met eighteen more times with his French customers. Bertrand was present at all but three.

For him, the meetings began long before the actual contact with Schmidt. "Ah! Those departures from Paris, by taxi, at night, across the city, to get to the Gare du Nord or the Gare de l'Est [stations for rail lines to the north or to the east], among the neon lights and the often anxious thoughts, while I left all behind me — to find what ahead? And could ASCHE have been followed from Berlin?"

The circumstances of the meetings varied. Near the Czechoslovakian ski resort of Spindleruv Mlyn, Bertrand and another officer were astonished in September 1933 to see Schmidt get off a train in full Bavarian alpinist costume, complete with Tyrolean hat, suede shorts, and rucksack. He started hiking through the woods toward the Davidova Bouda hotel, a twenty-seven-room mountain chalet somewhat off the beaten track. The Frenchmen, guns loaded, followed. At the rendezvous, they discovered, to their pleased surprise, that the rucksack was filled with secret documents.

Schmidt was paid in reichsmarks in small and medium denominations placed in a small suitcase and deposited in the baggage room of a Berlin railroad station. The claim ticket was sent to him under a false name at general delivery, where he used a false identity card to pick it up. A postcard to his home notified him when the suitcase was ready.

The meetings from 1934 on took place in Switzerland, usually in Basel or Bern, except for one in Copenhagen in 1935 and one in Paris in August 1938. After his arrival in the City of Light, Schmidt drew the Enigma cipher keys for August and September out of a package of delicatessen food; he had given the package to the train conductor to put in a cool place, the conductor himself agreeing that the heat in the compartment would ruin the food. Schmidt expressed a desire to visit the Moulin Rouge nightclub in Montmartre, famous for its gorgeous seminude showgirls. Bertrand took him, accompanied by a young member of the French intelligence service, Paul Paillole. When Schmidt danced with one of the pretty women who hung around the club, Paillole was impressed by his unexpected grace and elegance. The two Frenchmen left Schmidt, in high good humor, drinking champagne with not one but two attractive women.

A few days later, Bertrand left for Warsaw, his twelfth trip delivering keys. But out of all this effort, the French were getting, they felt, no results. Bertrand had wondered about this situation as early as 1932. He had given the Poles the operating and keying instructions and one month's keys in 1931 and had personally delivered three months' worth of keys in two trips to Warsaw in 1932. As far as he knew, the documents had produced nothing of value. Was Schmidt feeding him phonies? Such things had happened before in espionage.

At the meeting at the Hotel d'Angleterre in Liège, Belgium, on October 29 and 30, 1932, Schmidt, after handing over a report on German maneuvers and the Enigma keys for November and December, had remarked to Bertrand, addressing him by his cover name: "Monsieur Barsac, I hope to be able to give you the daily keys every two or three months. With that you ought to be able to solve messages without too much trouble!"

Bertrand did not reply to Schmidt's comment, asking him instead, "Are you sure that the documents you have given us are those for the machine currently in service?"

When REX translated the question, Schmidt started. He frowned. He looked at Bertrand, then back at REX.

"I'm not a crook," he replied. "If you have such doubts, it's because your cryptographers are incompetent."

Another French intelligence officer present quickly turned the conversation to the prospect of food, and the matter rested there.

Bertrand asked the question because the French cryptanalysts had not been able to break the Enigma, even with the help of the Schmidt documents. Nor had the Poles reported any successes. Yet they seemed glad to have Schmidt's keys. Langer and Ciężki were friendly to Bertrand. They told him of their intercepts of German messages; they even invited him in 1938 to Pyry.

But they never told him of their reconstruction of the Enigma or showed him a single Enigma solution. Their discretion probably stemmed from a fear that any leak about their reading of German messages would degrade relations with Germany after the signing of the nonaggression declaration. Bertrand perhaps understood this aspect of Poland's delicate international situation, pressed as she was between two vengeful powers, just as he understood the need for a French ally in the east to threaten Germany from the rear. Apparently, his superiors also understood the situation. France had nothing to lose by supplying keys to the Poles, so Bertrand was allowed to continue doing so. Altogether the French gave the Biuro Szyfrów keys for thirty-eight months out of eighty-one. Surely the French hoped that eventually something would come out of it.

Astoundingly, however, none of these later contributions reached the Polish codebreakers. They were not given a single one of the keys that Bertrand delivered during those five years!

What made the superiors of the codebreakers deliberately with-hold documents that would have so lightened and accelerated their travails? The only answer that makes sense is that the chiefs wanted to develop a cryptanalytic capability that would function even if Schmidt quit or was caught, transferred, or turned, or if France, which was irritated at the Polish–German nonaggression pact, ceased supplying his data. Denying the cryptanalysts the keys in-deed reduced the volume of Polish intelligence — but increased its independence. And if the cryptanalysts failed to make progress, they could always be given the keys, as was done in 1932, when the bosses finally gave Rejewski the first keys that Schmidt had pro-vided. The withholding succeeded, and even better than the chiefs had hoped. For not only did the codebreakers resolve by pure analysis the fundamental problem of reconstructing the daily keys, not only did they keep up with the successive German security measures, but they continually improved their methods, thereby putting out more solutions faster.

This progress ended abruptly on December 15, 1938. On that day, the Enigma messages became unreadable. The Poles soon learned that the Germans had put into service two additional ro-tors. Though the Enigma still held only three rotors at a time, these were now chosen from a group of five instead of three, rais-ing the number of rotor choices and orders from six to sixty. And the wiring of the two new rotors was unknown.

Fortunately for the Poles, however, the nets of the Sicherheits-dienst, or SD, the Nazi party intelligence service, had not shifted over to a new indicators method that the army nets had begun to use on September 15. The SD messages enabled the Poles to use their old methods of determining the rotor order and rotor setting as well as the ring positions and the plugboard connections; with this knowledge, Rejewski could reconstruct the wiring of first one, then the other of the two new rotors, as he had done in 1932.

But the new number of rotor orders expanded the task the Poles faced by an order of magnitude. Instead of six *bomby*, they would need sixty, at a cost that was fifteen times the whole equipment budget of the Biuro Szyfrów for fiscal 1938–39. Instead of 156 Zygalski sheets, BS-4 would need 1,560 — and it had by then punched only 52. Nor was there any way out of this, for the Poles could no longer fall back on Schmidt's supply of Enigma keys. He had transferred on September 28, 1938, to a better job in another communications intelligence agency, Luftwaffe chief Göring's Forschungsamt. Though he still provided other information for money, he no longer had access to the Enigma keys.

The new situation overwhelmed the heroic capabilities of the Polish cryptanalysts. To make matters worse, on January 1, 1939, the number of plugboard connections rose to ten.

The head of the general staff's intelligence bureau proposed a meeting with the British and the French in hopes that they would have something to contribute. By chance Bertrand, in France, was then considering the same idea. The meeting took place on Monday and Tuesday, January 9 and 10, 1939, in the French intelligence service headquarters, which was housed in prefabricated structures huddled against the Invalides, the domed tomb of Napoleon; the Service de Renseignements had moved there in 1932. Present were Bertrand; a French cryptanalyst, Captain Henri Braquenié; Langer, the head of the Biuro Szyfrów; Ciężki, the head of BS-4; Alastair Denniston, the head of Britain's codebreakers, who had been one of the original members of Room 40; and two other Britons. The atmosphere was cordial, but no one revealed any solutions of the machine: the British and French because they had none, the Poles because they had been instructed to say nothing unless they got something in return. The conclusion of the conference was pessimistic:

> Reconstruction of the machine solely by the study of enciphered texts is proving itself practically impossible; this was, furthermore, the view of the German specialists who devoted themselves to the same task before putting their machine into service. . . . The labors undertaken [by the three nations] seem to have ended in an impasse from which only information from an agent will enable them to escape, so a technical questionnaire, as simple as possible, has been drawn up, to be given to an agent judged able to carry out such an assignment.

Two months later, Hitler, who had said at Munich that he wanted only the German-speaking parts of Czechoslovakia, occupied the rest of that country. The scales fell from the eyes of the British and the French. On March 30, Britain, seconded by France, guaranteed Poland "all support" in the event of an unprovoked attack by Germany and six days later signed a provisional treaty of assistance with Poland. On April 27, Germany, blaming that agreement, declared that its 1934 nonaggression agreement with Poland was "null and void." This declaration eliminated one of Poland's chief reasons for not revealing her cryptanalytic successes to France and Britain: fear that a leak would provoke Germany into denouncing the agreement, with all the bullying that might follow.

Then, in May, two developments impelled Poland to share the results of her codebreaking. First, in a secret agreement, France promised to advance with the bulk of her forces against Germany fifteen days after any German invasion of Poland, and Britain began military talks in Warsaw. Second, tension between Poland and Germany approached the breaking point. Hitler's anti-Polish speeches incited Germans in both countries; the fatal shooting of a German by someone in an official Polish car became a cause célèbre; Nazis marched in the Free City of Danzig, and Nazi propaganda minister Joseph Goebbels warned that no power on earth could prevent the return of that city to the Reich; Poles and Germans fought in Polish Silesia; bombs exploded in Polish homes; a German plane was downed over a Polish naval base; the Reich press reported attacks on Germans in Poland.

It was in this atmosphere that Langer, on June 30, telegraphed London and Paris. He said that something new had come up since the January meeting and invited the French and the British to another conference, this one in Warsaw.

On the morning of Monday, July 24, Bertrand and the cryptologist Braquenié arrived in Warsaw by the overnight Nordexpress, which linked Paris and Moscow. Three Britons flew in: Denniston, Dillwyn Knox, and Commander Humphrey Sandwith, the head of the section that had developed and controlled the Royal Navy's intercept and direction-finding stations. The French were put up at the Hotel Polonia, and the British at the Bristol, where Mayer, the head of intelligence, Langer, Ciężki, and the three young cryptologists entertained the visitors at lunch. The conversation, which dealt only with banalities, was, ironically, in German, the only common language of the Poles, the Englishmen, and Bertrand.

Later all the cryptologists traveled out to Pyry. Langer gave them a short tour of the cryptologic center and then took them into the cryptologists' office. On tables stood several objects under covers. When all had gathered around, Langer, without a word, removed the covers, revealing the Polish replicas of the Enigmas, which the French and British cryptologists recognized at once. They were utterly astonished.

"Where did you get these?" Bertrand asked.

"We made them ourselves," Langer replied.

The Britons examined a machine closely. Sandwith threw Langer an incredulous glance, and Langer repeated that the Polish cryptologists had built it. Knox, who was intimately familiar with the Enigma from his own work on it, asked the most questions.

One question was, what was the wiring from the keyboard to the first rotor? This problem, which Rejewski had solved in a flash of intuition, had frustrated Knox. He felt cheated when he was told that it was Q to Q, W to W, E to E, and so on. Denniston wanted to ring up the British embassy to have London send draftsmen and electricians to draw up the plans of the Polish machines so that they could be reproduced. Langer restrained him: more was to come.

In the next room, the foreign cryptologists saw six cupboards about four feet high: the *bomby*. Langer demonstrated how they worked. Rejewski answered questions, since the machines had been built to his design. Zygalski explained how his perforated sheets worked. The Poles described the various methods for recovering keys; they explained that for a long time, using the *bomby,* they had been able to find an Enigma key, under the right conditions, in two hours. Then the Germans had placed two additional rotors in service. Cryptanalysis now required ten times as much equipment as before if solutions were to be anywhere near current, and the Poles' capabilities had been outstripped. France and Britain had greater resources. Poland's sharing of her cryptanalytic knowledge with her two allies would enable them to continue solving the German cryptograms. This would be Poland's contribution to combating the common German menace.

The Britons and the French expressed their delighted thanks. Denniston again sought to telephone for the technicians. He could hardly believe his ears when Langer told him that the Poles had prepared two Enigma replicas for their visitors: one for the French, one for the British. These would be given to Bertrand for shipment under diplomatic seal to Paris and then for forwarding to Britain. The conference ended on Tuesday in an atmosphere of warmth, astonishment, gratitude, and anticipation.

A few days later, Langer, on his way to Britain, passed through Paris. Bertrand and one of his superiors took the Polish crypto-logic chief to lunch at Drouant, a classic Paris restaurant, where they feted him with champagne. "We owed him at least that!" said Bertrand. Soon afterward, the machines arrived. The equipment destined for Britain was packed into the largest diplomatic bags available at the embassy and placed under British diplomatic seal. The British intelligence liaison officer to the French, Dunderdale, and three assistants brought it to Paris's St. Lazare railroad station. Bertrand joined them on the boat train, the Golden Arrow. It was August 16. In Germany, troops were readying an attack on Poland. Captain Karl Dönitz, the submarine commander, had ordered his U-boats to their war stations at sea.

At Dover customs in England, Dunderdale ran into the French playwright Sacha Guitry and his wife, the actress Yvonne Printemps, on their way to the opening of a play of Guitry's in London. Dunderdale knew them by sight since they lived opposite him in Paris. Their luggage was voluminous, and Dunderdale made a deal with them: he would get it through customs duty-free if they would pretend that the bulky diplomatic baggage was theirs, to throw off the suspicions of any spies. The couple agreed and were waved through; the Enigma bags drew the attention of no German agents. That evening, the Golden Arrow pulled into London's Victoria Station near the end of the rush hour. The deputy chief of the British foreign intelligence service, Colonel Stewart Menzies, on his way to a reception, awaited them in black tie. "Accueil triomphal!" (Triumphal welcome), thought Bertrand. Menzies's men carted away the precious mechanism.

Once again, as in World War I, Britain had obtained the means for solving her adversary's messages through a gift from a loyal ally.

Six

Failure at Broadway Buildings

Early in 1919, profiting from the lessons of the Great War, the British cabinet had decided to establish a permanent code-breaking agency. The first lord of the Admiralty, who was both interested in intelligence and politically powerful, captured the agency for the navy, perhaps in part because it ran most of the intercept stations that provided the cryptanalysts with raw material. The director of naval intelligence, Captain Hugh (Quex) Sinclair, began by recruiting veterans of the navy's Room 40 and the army's M.I.1b. In particular, he brought in the two brightest lights of those bodies, Room 40's Dillwyn Knox, and M.I.1b's Oliver Strachey (the older brother of the Lytton Strachey who, years before, had tried to seduce Knox). Sinclair put Alastair Denniston in charge. Denniston, known because of his stature as "the little man" to his subordinates, was not the best administrator: one person spoke of him viciously "as possibly fit to manage a small sweet shop in the East End." But Denniston's dislike of hierarchy protected his individualistic cryptanalysts from the rigidities of bureaucracy. And his knowledge of the subject matter, his informality, and his willingness to delegate responsibility helped him build and sustain a secret government department of great value.

The new organization, which had the public function of securing the government's communications and the secret one of reading foreign governments' messages, was given the deliberately misleading name, proposed by a Foreign Office staffer, of Government Code & Cypher School. It officially came into being November 1, 1919, with 66 staffers — 29 professional and 37 clerical, 12 of these for constructing British codes. A year and a half later the new foreign secretary, Earl Curzon of Kedleston, who had long wanted control of codebreaking, took advantage of a political leak of some Soviet solutions and of the fact that the first lord of the Admiralty had been replaced by a man who had neither his political clout nor his understanding of intelligence and who was glad to reduce costs. By April 1921, G.C.&C.S. was under the practical control of the Foreign Office, and by April 1, 1922, under its formal control as well.

The next year the universally admired Quex Sinclair rose from director of naval intelligence to chief of the Secret Intelligence Service (S.I.S.) — "C," in the official hieroglyph. The Foreign Office agreed to let him assign G.C.&C.S. its work while it administered the agency. Soon after he took over, G.C.&C.S., which had been housed first behind the Charing Cross railroad station and next in distant quarters in Kensington, moved in 1925 into the third and fourth floors of the ten-story gray concrete Broadway Buildings. The office building, at 54 Broadway, a couple of blocks from Westminster Abbey, and housing as well the S.I.S., was a few hundred yards from the Foreign Office, which codebreakers visited an average of eight times a day, and only a little farther from the Admiralty. G.C.&C.S. expanded by 1935 to about 90 employees, 30 of them cryptologists, and by mid-1939 to 200, with 33 cryptologists. In addition, between 140 and 240 servicemen were intercepting foreign transmissions. Thus, by 1939, almost 500 persons worked in British cryptology at an annual salary cost of £100,000 (or about $3 million in 1991 dollars).

The armed services provided not only the intercept personnel but the intercept posts themselves. Economics compelled cooperation. The War Office handled the Middle East; the Admiralty, the Far East; the Air Ministry picked up what it could hear within the United Kingdom. The need to centralize interception, traffic analysis, and cryptanalysis under one roof largely withstood the centrifugal pulls of the different services to withdraw elements from G.C.&C.S. or establish their own duplicative bodies.

Like all agencies, G.C.&C.S. continually reorganized itself. Early in 1924 one of the more important of the Room 40 recruits, the prickly lawyer William F. (Nobby) Clarke, whose principal interest was naval cryptanalysis, was on vacation near Nice when a suicide in G.C.&C.S. opened up a senior assistant's slot. Denniston promoted one of his prewar friends who had been a subordinate of

Clarke's in Room 40 and whose work, Clarke thought, although good, had not been outstanding. Clarke was furious. Denniston explained upon Clarke's return that Sinclair had not chosen Clarke because Clarke was too busy on Admiralty assignments, among them lecturing to naval officers on cryptology to impress upon them the lessons of the war. The codebreaker protested violently that if his naval work was prejudicing any promotion, he wanted to be relieved of it. This put Denniston in a difficult position, as there was no one else capable of doing it. To Clarke's surprise, Sinclair invited him to a private lunch at his home.

> No junior [assistant] had ever had that pleasure, pleasure it was, for he was an excellent host [Clarke wrote]. I was the only guest, another change, and it was soon clear that I had been asked because he was anxious to hear my views. These I gave quite frankly and emphasized the importance of the naval side of our work and the vital necessity, in my opinion, of having a proper naval section; he listened, as he always did, most attentively, asking his usual searching questions and said he would think the matter over. Soon afterwards Denniston saw me, said the formation of a naval section had been decided on, that I was to be its head and that I would be promoted at once. This duly took place about the middle of 1924.

The Naval Section attacked the cryptosystems of foreign navies, while most of G.C.&C.S. concentrated on diplomatic solutions. In 1930, the Army Section was formed and, in 1936, the Air Section.

The most important cryptanalyst was Knox. In 1920, he had married a Room 40 assistant, Olive Roddam, and a year later, after selling most of his Great Western Railway stock, bought a damp, chilly, drafty house on 40 acres of woodland near High Wycombe, half an hour northwest of London. The cryptanalyst commuted to work by train, like his stockbroker neighbors, and in the coaches examined photographs of the papyrus rolls of the dramatist Herodas. In 1922, Cambridge University Press published the restored text of Herodas' mimes and their English translation, with Knox as editor and with notes by his former classics tutor. Much of the book's 465 pages consisted of densely printed commentary, mainly on Greek and Latin syntax and vocabulary. Because of the edition of Herodas and another contribution to classical scholarship, Knox was invited to become professor of Greek at Leeds University. But he turned it down, perhaps with regret.

He regarded his suburban neighbors with a certain cynicism: he was surprised at the prevalence of adultery when all the wives looked so much alike. But he played tennis with them, spinning the ball almost unreturnably. He bought a motorcycle for commuting as soon as he no longer had to study Herodas on the train; in 1931, he had the inevitable accident: he broke his leg, which left him with a slight limp. At about that time, frustrated by his work and yearning to return to Cambridge, he was kept from quitting by his wife's reminding him of his duty to educate his sons and of the national importance of his work. This he carried out in a chaotic office at Broadway Buildings at hours that defied Foreign Office routine: he arrived early in the morning and departed at 4 P.M. He seemed to live on black coffee and chocolate.

Knox and his colleagues enjoyed fair success in those glory years of codebreaking. With Strachey and Clarke, Knox focused at first on the all-important American codes. Most posed few obstacles, and those that did, such as a superenciphered code introduced after the end of World War I, were solved after not too great a delay. Knox also successfully tackled Hungarian codes. A former czarist cryptanalyst, E. C. Fetterlein, tall, stolid, whose index finger was adorned with a large ruby given him for his successes in the years before the overthrow of Nicholas II, read Soviet Communist cryptograms with great panache — until his work was nullified in 1927 by deliberate exposure of the intercepts for political reasons. G.C.&C.S. solved French, Italian, Japanese, and Spanish messages, among others. Every week it distributed between sixty and eighty intercepts, each identified by a six-figure number.

Against only one country's codes and ciphers did G.C.&C.S. fail: Germany. But it hardly seemed to matter. The former rival had been thoroughly defeated and all but stripped of her armed forces. The Admiralty, concerned more with Japan and America, had little interest in Britain's former enemy. Technical circumstances further inhibited G.C.&C.S.'s feeble efforts. The German Foreign Office was using the one-time pad, the only theoretically and practically unbreakable cipher. German army radio traffic was hard to intercept in the British Isles. And with almost no German navy at first, there were almost no naval messages to intercept. Moreover, though in 1924 the Reichsmarine was still using the *AFB* code — the edition that Room 40 had broken — the difference between wartime and peacetime vocabulary made it difficult to solve messages.

Later, as the German navy gradually revived, studies showed that it was using a machine to encipher messages that first had been encoded in *AFB*. This so discouraged G.C.&C.S. that it stopped intercepting German naval messages altogether. For a decade it ignored Reichsmarine traffic. It thus lost the contact that is vital for keeping up with the small modifications that individually can be mastered — as the Poles did with the Enigma keying changes — but that in combination raise too great an obstacle. The five-man Naval Section directed its energies instead to the traffic of the French, Italian, Japanese, Soviet, and American navies.

Then, in July 1936, Spanish General Francisco Franco, fed up with the republican government in Madrid, rose in insurrection. Within days, Fascist Italy and Nazi Germany began sending him weapons. Their troops followed. As the civil war in Spain widened, the Mediterranean swarmed with troop transports, merchant vessels, warships. The ether hummed with messages, many of them Italian. G.C.&C.S. had long ago reconstructed Italy's main naval code, in large part, Denniston remarked, "because of the delightful Italian habit of enciphering long political leaders [editorials] from the daily press." These solutions had enabled Britain to track the movements of Italian warships during dictator Benito Mussolini's invasion of Abyssinia in 1935, which threatened the Mideast bulwark of the very foundation of British power: India. Now the danger was more acute. Mussolini, hostile to Britain after her opposition to his aggression, was calling the Mediterranean *mare nostrum* and trying to make it an Italian lake. Just as his Ethiopian invasion had threatened British-controlled Egypt, the Spanish civil war imperiled Gibraltar, and Britain began to see that for the first time since 1798, she was threatened with being squeezed out of the Mediterranean.

It was in these circumstances that G.C.&C.S. realized that the Italian navy had introduced a cipher machine, soon identified as the commercial Enigma. Knox attacked the problem. The machine, including its rotor wiring, was known to G.C.&C.S., so it did not have to be reconstructed; only the daily keys had to be recovered. And since the commercial model lacked the plugboard of the military version, the problem was simplified. Knox used a technique that everyone who tried to solve rotor messages seems to have hit upon, one that has become known as *la méthode des bâtons*, the rod method, so called from the wooden rods onto which were glued strips of paper with the cipher alphabet of each rotor written on it.

Using the rod method, Knox succeeded in determining the keys for some messages and thus in reading other messages enciphered in that day's key. He then attacked the messages of the Franco forces and of the German forces in Spain, which used the commercial Enigma. By 1937, he had succeeded.

These successes, together with the rise in German naval traffic volume with the Kriegsmarine's arrival in some force in the Mediterranean, perhaps gave him hope that he might solve the German naval Enigma. G.C.&C.S. wanted to intercept lower-level messages in the hope of matching them to Enigma messages and so obtaining lengthy cribs, but lack of men and gear prevented this. And though Knox determined that the naval Enigma had a plugboard, he made no further progress.

The increase in international tension led to an important intelligence development within the Royal Navy. After Mussolini's aggression in 1935, the deputy chief of the naval staff, Admiral William James, became concerned about the ability of the Naval Intelligence Division to cope with an emergency. His concerns were exacerbated during the Spanish civil war by the lack of intelligence about foreign naval forces, particularly submarines, blockading the Republican-held areas. During the last two years of World War I, James had headed Room 40, technically Section 25 of the Naval Intelligence Division, and he knew that it was the lack of coordination between the intelligence and operations divisions that had enabled the German High Seas Fleet to escape at the Battle of Jutland. To avoid a recurrence of that flaw, James proposed a center for intelligence that would directly serve operations. The director of naval intelligence began to plan the expansion of the insignificant movements section of the intelligence division into such a unit. It would collect and evaluate all operational intelligence and disseminate what was needed to the fleet. He assigned the expansion to Paymaster Lieutenant Commander Norman Denning, a round-faced man in his thirties.

By June 1937, the nucleus of the unit had been formed. Its first task was to track Italian submarines, and one of its early experiences led to a fundamental rule in handling communications intelligence. G.C.&C.S. had sent the new body the gist of the solution of a message to two Italian submarines that Mussolini had placed at Franco's disposition. The message said that any merchant vessel attempting to break the blockade was to be sunk outside of Spanish waters. This appeared unbelievable in the political situation, and the Foreign Office questioned it. An investigation showed that the G.C.&C.S. evaluator had placed his own interpretation on a not too clear text. From that time forward, G.C.&C.S. provided only the originals of solutions to the Admiralty.

In February 1939, two months after Germany announced that she would build as much tonnage in submarines as the British had, the nucleus evolved into the Operational Intelligence Centre (O.I.C.) — Section 8 of the Naval Intelligence Division. To head it, the director of naval intelligence named a retired contemporary, a one-time watchkeeper in Room 40, a man widely regarded as impossible to rattle, Rear Admiral John W. (Jock) Clayton. The O.I.C. had four sections: Italy and Japan, submarines, direction-finding, and surface ships and outside liaison, headed by Denning. Liaison with G.C.&C.S. was ensured by the presence in O.I.C. of a small party from Naval Section under Commander M. G. Saunders. The intercept and direction-finding stations were administered and controlled not by O.I.C. but by a combined signals division–intelligence division group, DSD/NID 9, under Commander Humphrey Sandwith. He and Denning pressed successfully to increase the number of intercept stations. Denning, seeing which way the wind was blowing, had a map drawn with Berlin at the center to give him the German point of view. Similarly, G.C.&C.S.'s Naval Section, which in 1937 had begun attacking German naval traffic for the first time since 1928, started a German subsection in May 1938 on Quex Sinclair's recommendation. It consisted of an officer and a clerk, but no cryptanalysts for itself alone.

As the O.I.C. was coming into being, Sinclair, driven by a realization of the value of cryptanalytic information, the need for quiet in the work, the requirement for secrecy, and the likelihood of expansion in case of war, had a landed estate called Bletchley Park in the railroad junction town of Bletchley, some fifty miles northwest of London, purchased for G.C.&C.S. The estate consisted of a manor house greatly expanded in Victorian style in the 1870s by stockbroker Herbert S. Leon and the surrounding acres of landscaped grounds.

Since the house could not accommodate the hundred-odd employees, G.C.&C.S. built "huts" — long, narrow, peak-roofed, one-story wooden temporaries that huddled near the big house, which was headquarters. In July 1939, a few months after Britain had guaranteed to aid Poland in case of German aggression, a few weeks after Hitler and Mussolini had formalized the Axis, a few days after the Soviet Union had rejected a British-French proposal to block further Nazi aggression, Sinclair ordered G.C.&C.S. to move to Bletchley Park, later usually referred to as B.P.

Dillwyn Knox went to an office in former servants' quarters called the Cottage, a small, square, brick building. There he pursued his work on Enigma with the cipher machine given him by the Poles. But though they had shown that it was possible to climb this cryptologic Everest, many difficulties remained. In particular, the naval Enigma resisted solution. Its keying system and the navy's more careful use of it offered no handholds for the cryptanalysts.

A few weeks later, as German-Polish tensions rose, the German battlewagon *Schleswig-Holstein* visited Danzig. She was there purportedly for a twenty-fifth anniversary memorial service for the dead of the *Magdeburg*, who were buried in a Danzig cemetery. Early in the morning of September 1, 1939, she trained her 11-inch guns upon a Polish military depot 400 yards away. At 4:48 A.M., without warning, they fired the first shots of World War II. The depot's wooden buildings burst into flames. Moments later, hundreds of miles away, Hitler's armies crossed Poland's borders. Britain's guarantee went into effect. Two days later, the island kingdom, whose survival rested upon its ability to rule the sea, was at war — unable to read the main enemy's main naval cipher.

Seven

Phantoms

FIVE DAYS AFTER Hitler's armies invaded Poland, they surged to within forty miles of Warsaw. The Poles did not need their Daniels — their cryptanalysts — to read the handwriting on this wall. The army high command prepared to evacuate. The codebreakers burned papers and packed Enigma replicas, bombes, perforated sheets, and Polish cipher machines in heavy crates. On the night of September 5 they quit their offices for the Vilna railroad station. The evacuation train, leaving the next evening, took three days to cover the 125 miles to Brzesc (Brest), to the east of Warsaw. There Rejewski, Różycki, and Zygalski continued their journey by car. The codebreaking equipment was destroyed. The trio drove south, first in a mobile direction-finding vehicle with Major Ciężki and his family, later in a tiny car, with Rejewski bumping uncomfortably atop some batteries. After six days of detours, rain, and frantic searches for gasoline, the group, which included Colonel Langer, arrived at the tiny village of Kuty at the tip of the tongue of Poland that then protruded into neutral Rumania. The village, whose normal population was 400, was packed with a confused mass of soldiers, diplomats, bureaucrats, automobiles, and horse-drawn carts, all striving to squeeze onto the two-lane bridge over the Cheremosh River, which marked the border. The codebreakers crossed during the night of September 17.

The Rumanian authorities confined the military personnel but left the civilians on their own, so the three young cryptanalysts caught a train to Bucharest. At the French embassy, they received visas promptly when they mentioned Bertrand, who had begun to search for them the day they entered Rumania. Soon they were taking a succession of trains through Yugoslavia and Italy to France. They and a dozen other members of the Biuro Szyfrów arrived in Paris on October 1, some by special airplane, some by the Orient Express.

Five days later, the last of Poland's forces surrendered to Germany. The defeat demonstrated an elemental point about intelligence: unlike guns or morale, it is a secondary factor in war. All the Polish codebreaking, all the heartrending efforts and the heroic successes, had helped the Polish military not at all. Intelligence can work only through strength.

But France was strong, or was regarded as such, and on October 20 the fifteen Polish cryptanalysts resumed their war against Germany, working under Bertrand. He now headed the so-called Section d'Examen (Examination Section), which performed radio intercept, traffic analysis, and cryptanalysis, of the General Staff's Fifth Bureau, the mobilized form of the peacetime Service de Renseignements. As offices and billet for his section, Bertrand had requisitioned the Château de Vignolles, a large, three-story villa and associated outbuildings near the town of Gretz-Armainvilliers, some 25 miles northeast of Paris. The villa and its unit was called P.C. ("Poste de Commandement") Bruno. Attached to it as what Bertrand called his Z Team were the Poles, who enrolled in the Polish army in France, and, as his D Team, seven émigré Spanish Republican cryptanalysts, whom Bertrand had enlisted in the Foreign Legion. Several dozen French cryptanalysts and support personnel brought the section's total to seventy. Also present was Captain Kenneth Macfarlane, a British liaison officer, promptly nicknamed Pinky because of his rosy complexion; he had a direct teletypewriter line to Britain for exchanging results with Bletchley Park. The whole section ate meals together, and their differing tastes and temperaments led to sulks and arguments. Often, however, the problems were liquidated, so to speak, at the bar.

Rejewski and the others took up where they had left off. For weeks, the Enigma modifications of December 15, 1938, continued to defeat them. But toward the end of December 1939, assisted by a set of 1,560 Zygalski sheets that G.C.&C.S. had punched, P.C. Bruno recovered a German army key for October 28. A few weeks later, its solution of a Luftwaffe key for January 6, 1940, showed that the Wehrmacht had introduced no new procedures that would baffle the Allied cryptanalysts.

By that time Britain had achieved two remarkable breakthroughs that gave it the lead in Enigma cryptanalysis. These resulted from a shift in G.C.&C.S.'s thinking.

Toward the end of the 1930s, Alastair Denniston, the head of G.C.&C.S., had come to realize what the Poles had understood a decade earlier: that the shift to cipher machines required using mathematicians as cryptanalysts. So in the late summer of 1938, as British Prime Minister Neville Chamberlain flew repeatedly to Germany to appease Hitler, the British codebreaking agency held a series of courses in cryptology primarily for mathematicians. The move brought into the closed world of British communications intelligence the fresh thinking of a mathematician of world-historical importance.

Alan Turing was a prodigy, a genius. A tallish, dark-haired, powerfully built man of twenty-seven with sunken cheeks and deep-set blue eyes, he wore unpressed clothes, picked at the flesh around his fingernails until it bled, stammered, fell into long silences, rarely made eye contact, sidled through doors, ran long-distance races, and had, by the time he arrived at B.P., made two fundamental contributions to knowledge.

He had been born in London in 1912, the son of an English administrator in the Indian Civil Service and a mother who rejoined her husband when Alan was a year old, leaving him and his older brother to be raised by a retired army colonel and his wife on the south coast of England. Despite an undistinguished career at his public school, Sherborne, Turing was bright enough to win a mathematics scholarship to King's College, Cambridge. Upon his graduation, his brilliance was recognized by the college, which made him, at twenty-two, one of its forty-six fellows, enabling him to pursue his studies in mathematics.

That field was then in turmoil. A few years earlier, in 1931, the Czech mathematician Kurt Gödel had proved that contradictions would eventually arise in certain self-referential statements that would prevent some problems from being solved; mathematical knowledge would forever remain incomplete. Turing took this idea a step further in a paper published in 1936, when he was twenty-four. He began by envisioning a mechanism that could move to right or to left an infinitely long tape marked into squares and that could read and change or read and leave unchanged the blank or the mark — the 0 or the 1 — in each square. He demonstrated that this machine could compute anything that could be calculated. But then he proved that even this device could not tell whether the potentially solvable problems could be solved.

This remarkable paper had two results. It demonstrated that a fundamental problem in mathematics, the so-called *Entscheidungsproblem* — ascertaining whether certain problems could be solved — was not soluble. And, as became evident only later, the imagined device, eventually called a "universal Turing machine," was the idealization of general-purpose computers. Turing became, in other words, the intellectual father of the computer.

An American mathematician at Princeton had also been working on the *Entscheidungsproblem,* and Turing spent the academic years 1936–37 and 1937–38 at that university earning a doctorate. While there he frequently discussed ciphers, to which he had been attracted since he was a boy. He claimed to have found an answer to the question "What is the most general kind of code or cipher possible?" If he talked about cryptology at the King's College high table, he may have been recognized as a natural recruit by those Room 40 veterans who either were still fellows of or retained close ties with King's. This recognition perhaps led to an invitation to join the course in cryptology, which ran for a week or two at Broadway Buildings. Though many of the other students were mathematicians, a few linguists, including German scholars, also attended. The course may have been more than instructional. When the charming Oliver Strachey took the young men out and gave them a very good lunch at the Travellers Club, it struck one of them that the course sought as much to let the G.C.&C.S. hierarchs look over the recruits as to teach them cryptology.

Even though the war scare preceding the Munich pact in September had been followed by Chamberlain's promise of "peace for our time," G.C.&C.S. had Turing and others come down to London for a second course around Christmas of 1938. Afterward, he visited G.C.&C.S. every few weeks to help Knox, presumably in his attack on the Enigma.

In February 1939 G.C.&C.S. advertised for a "signals computer." A lean young Oxford graduate in mathematics applied. Peter Twinn hadn't the foggiest notion what the work entailed — and his interviewer talked all around it — but jobs were then hard to come by. Twinn was hired, together with another mathematician, J. C. T. Dryden, and in mid-February 1939 they reported to Broadway Buildings. When G.C.&C.S. moved to Bletchley Park in August, Twinn found himself working as a cryptanalyst side by side with Knox in the Cottage.

On September 3, Turing, in his room at Cambridge, heard Chamberlain intone on the wireless that the expiration of Britain's ultimatum to Hitler to withdraw his forces from Poland meant that Britain was at war with Germany. The next day, he reported to Bletchley, where he joined Knox, Twinn, and a Cambridge mathematician, John R. F. Jeffreys, in working on the Enigma. He found, as Twinn and Jeffreys had before him, that the continuing recovery of the Enigma keys was being achieved mainly by bright ideas, not by mathematics. It was, however, mathematicians who were having the ideas, thus at least partially vindicating Denniston's faith.

The most important breakthrough, an idea of Turing's, came late in 1939. It dealt with the Polish mechanism for testing for possible Enigma keys, the bombe, which the Poles had displayed to Knox at the July meeting in Warsaw but whose technical description had not arrived in England until August 16, just three weeks before Turing came to Bletchley. Turing was especially well equipped to work on this electromechanical device, for, though most of his work was theoretical, he was mechanically apt. He had once made an electric multiplier (for use in a cipher system he invented), machining and winding some of the relays himself, and had later designed a mechanism to answer a problem dealing with prime numbers, cutting some of the gears himself.

Turing had reached some of his most important conclusions by eliminating results that led to self-contradictions. If the *Entscheidungsproblem* can be solved, he had written, "then there is a general (mechanical) process for determining whether $U_n (M)$ is provable. By Lemmas 1 and 2, this implies that there is a process for determining whether M ever prints 0 and this is impossible, by §8. Hence the *Entscheidungsproblem* cannot be solved." He now applied the same sort of thinking to the Enigma.

He recognized that the Polish machine helped to identify keys by asking, in mathematical terms, whether the enciphered message keys of the cryptogram were consistent with the unknown basic setting that was wanted. The bombe actually did this by rejecting the thousands of inconsistencies and leaving the few noncontradictory situations to be tested to see whether their settings yielded German when applied to the intercepts. Turing advanced this testing method by a giant step.

A basic technique in cryptanalysis is that of the probable word. The cryptanalyst guesses that a particular word or phrase exists in the plaintext of a cryptogram — perhaps "enemy" or "attack" in a message transmitted after a military unit has been under assault — and employs it as a wedge to recover the full text and possibly the key of the cryptogram. The Poles had used this method in a limited area before they had bombes: to reduce the number of trials in finding the positions of the alphabet rings on the rotors, they assumed that the German military message they were attacking began with An, or "To," followed by the letter X, which separated words. Turing shifted the focus of this technique and endowed it with vast new power. He matched a probable word or phrase (longer than AnX) to a portion of an intercept and tested whether any rotor position allowed such an encipherment. He moved, in other words, from speeding the recovery of keys by finding noncontradictory links between the known and the assumed keys to speeding the recovery of keys by finding noncontradictory links between assumed plaintext and assumed keys.

His bombe did this by adding to the multiplicity of Enigma replicas a test register, a set of twenty-six relays. At each of the successive rotor positions the bombe was running through, this test register looked at the voltage at each of the twenty-six points equivalent to the output lights of the Enigma's illuminable panel. Two conditions — voltage appearing at all twenty-six points or at all but one — represented a noncontradiction between the assumed plaintext and the then position of the rotors. This position thus constituted a possible key, and clerks would see if it produced German plaintext. If it did not, the bombe would be restarted.

The work began with cryptanalysts imagining the possible plaintext of a message, which they called a crib. They made these guesses on the basis of their knowledge of German communications, gained through direction-finding, radiomen's chatter, service messages,

plaintext intercepts, solutions of simpler systems, captured documents, prisoner interrogations, and previous Enigma solutions that
used other principles. Suppose they learned that a Luftwaffe
headquarters sent a report every day at 4 P.M. to the general of
reconnaissance; they could guess that its messages started *Dem
General der Aufklaerungsflieger.* A navy communications outpost was
ordered to report every day to a central radio post the strength at
which the signal was being received. An army unit repeatedly
transmitted *Nichts zu melden* ("Nothing to report").

The crib would be set letter for letter above the ciphertext. The
cryptanalyst then sought a loop: letters in the assumed plaintext
and in the ciphertext that could be chained together, eventually
linking the first letter to the last. For example,

d e m g e n e r a l
W T E D L R O P G M

links the *m* in the upper line to the E below, one of the *e*'s above to
an L below, and an *l* above to an M below, thus forming the loop
M E L M. The bombe was set up in the basic position, with rotors
I, II, and III, in that order, set at A A A. (The ring positions were
ignored, and the cryptanalyst hoped that the middle rotor would
not step within the crib.) The plugboard positions were as unknown as the rotor order and position.

Voltage was then applied to the bombe position representing
one of the twenty-six possible plugboard substitutions for the first
letter of the crib. It went through the bombe's rotor array, into
and back out through the reflecting rotor, back through the rotor
array, then into the rotor array that was testing the second plain-
cipher pair of the loop and was advanced by the number of places
by which the first and second pairs differed in the text: the E-L
pair in the crib is two places further on than M-E, so the rightmost,
or fast, rotor of the second array has to be two clicks beyond the
fast rotor of the first array. The voltage emerged from this array
to pass through a third and then loop back into the first.

As it did so, the voltage passed through the test register. Suppose that the arrangement of rotors was correct and the choice of
plugboard substitutions was correct. The voltage would make a
single circuit through the rotors and show up at only one test
point — one of the two conditions for a correct match. The relay

would electromechanically interrupt the power to the bombe and stop it, enabling the cryptanalysts to ascertain this rotor position and use it to decipher the cryptogram to see if German plaintext appeared. Because of the plugboard, the test decipherment would include many cipher substitutes for plaintext letters, but it should retain enough of a German appearance to test its validity. The cryptanalyst would have to recover the plaintext by solution.

Suppose, however, that the arrangement of rotors was wrong. The voltage would pass through the first rotor array, come out at a letter that would not complete a loop, enter the second rotor at a nonloop point, pass through it, and emerge again at a nonloop letter that would send it into a third rotor array. The voltage would continue its errant course through the bombe's several rotor arrays — as many as letters in the crib — nearly always emerging at all twenty-six letters and putting voltage on all twenty-six relays of the test register. But this is not one of the patterns that would stop the machine. So the bombe would continue to run, searching for a position at which to stop. Suppose, finally, that the arrangement of rotors was correct but the choice of plugboard substitution was not. In this case, the voltage would spread out among the test pins, as in the case of an incorrect rotor arrangement, but would not be able to enter the one correct test pin. This would produce the second, more likely, correct condition, with voltage to all test relays except one, and the bombe would stop.

Turing's method had two advantages over the Poles'. It liberated the cryptanalysts from the need to find special conditions among the message keys, namely, the repeated letters in certain positions that the Polish cryptanalysts had called females. And it could look for help in the vast ranges of human endeavor distilled by messages, thus improving the chances that a message would be solved and increasing the volume of solutions.

But the method had not reached its full potential. A way of doing that was discovered totally unexpectedly by another Cambridge mathematician, Gordon Welchman. A chess player, but not a very good one, and a tennis player, even worse, he was a sturdily built man of thirty-four, of medium height with very pink cheeks, wavy hair, and dashing good looks. But he was austere and reserved and was regarded even by his friends as "a solemn old stick, without a great sense of humor." Welchman had attended Trinity College,

Cambridge, on a mathematics scholarship and after his 1928 graduation had taught mathematics at another Cambridge college, Sidney Sussex. He specialized in algebraic geometry.

Like Turing, Welchman had attended the introductory course in cryptology and had reported to Bletchley Park upon the outbreak of war. Denniston sent him to the Cottage, where he joined the group working on the Enigma under Knox. Welchman soon got the impression that Knox didn't like him — indeed, he soon concluded that Knox didn't like most people — and within a couple of weeks he had been exiled to another building, Elmers School, with another assignment. He was to study the externals of the intercepted German army messages — the radio frequencies on which they were sent, their call signs, message indicators, signatures, and addresses — to deduce what information he could from any patterns he found. To help with this, he was given a sheaf of solved Enigma intercepts.

Welchman quickly perceived that the traffic patterns reflected the organization of the German army. "The call signs came alive," he said, "as representing elements of those forces whose commanders at various echelons would have to send messages to each other. The use of different keys . . . suggested different command structures." He was independently inventing a form of intelligence called traffic analysis. He rapidly perceived the stereotyped nature of many of the addresses, text beginnings, and even whole messages, and wondered whether they could not be used as cribs. He was reinventing Turing's method of ascertaining a valid key. And, quickly spotting many of the same patterns and characteristics in the message indicators that Rejewski and his colleagues had found, he proposed using perforated sheets to narrow down the possible rotor orders and ring settings. He was reinventing the Zygalski sheets, which had, unknown to him, been adopted by G.C.&C.S. and named Jeffreys sheets after John Jeffreys, who was in charge of preparing them.

But Welchman, who had independently duplicated two of the most important ideas of Enigma cryptanalysis and one of the fundamentals of radio intelligence, was not doomed always to walk in the shadow of others. Before the war was three months old, his brilliance augmented the power of Turing's bombe and greatly accelerated the pace of Enigma solutions.

His method was based on the fact that Enigma substitutions were reciprocal. If plaintext r became ciphertext P at a particular rotor order and position and with particular plugboard connections, then plaintext p would become ciphertext R at the same setting. Welchman employed this principle to exploit the letters of a crib that did not form part of a loop. He set out, on a wooden board, a square array of 676 contacts lettered A to Z across the top and A to Z down the side. Then he connected by wires the contact in, say, row D and column F to the contact in row F and column D. All 676 contacts were thus wired. As a consequence, when the crib gave plaintext p and ciphertext R, the diagonal board automatically sent the voltage for ciphertext P and plaintext r through the rotor arrays. This reduced the number of erroneous stops.

Once Turing had sketched out the plan for his bombe, Commander Edward Travis, the bulldoglike deputy head of G.C.&C.S., began discussions with the British Tabulating Machine Company. The company named as its representative Harold (Doc) Keen, a friendly, talkative engineer who had often visited the International Business Machines Corporation in the United States. At one meeting, at the White Hart pub in Buckingham, Peter Twinn summarized the concept to Keen by saying that what was needed was a machine like forty Enigmas in a row. Keen also rapidly grasped Welchman's idea and incorporated the diagonal board into the British bombes. The main frame was about 4 feet wide and as tall as a man; it was supported on short legs that rolled on casters. Each bombe consisted of the equivalent of twelve Enigma machines (the two prototypes had only ten) plus a diagonal board. The face of each bombe was divided into six stacks of two horizontal rectangles; in each rectangle were mounted three wired wheels, each about 5 inches across. They emulated Enigma rotors but differed from them in that the current flowed not through them but across them: from an outer ring of contacts to an inner ring, both on the face plate of the bombe. Each vertical set of three rotors represented an Enigma with a different rotor choice and order. Five bombes would thus represent all sixty rotor possibilities. The wheels stepped as did the rotors, except that the lack of knowledge of the ring position introduced discrepancies that caused some accurate crib superimpositions to be rejected as not possible.

Behind the face of the bombe was the machinery that drove it, turning all the upper wheels together, all the middle wheels together and all the lower wheels together. The back of the bombe, which opened to give access to the mass of circuitry within, served as a frame for the diagonal board. Keen's two prototypes, built in part out of punched-card machinery, proved extremely flexible, largely because Keen's long experience with punched-card equipment had taught him that it was often used to perform tasks not envisioned when it was designed.

The first Turing bombe was installed in Bletchley Park's Hut 11 around the middle of 1940. Named AGNES, it became a prototype for machines superior to the sorters used by Germany for codebreaking.

The Government Code & Cypher School expanded rapidly, a phantom agency exercising apparently spectral powers. Its organization reflected that of the enemy whose cryptosystems were being read, because those cryptosystems varied according to the needs and usages of the services that employed them. Thus G.C.&C.S. Naval Section dealt with foreign naval intercepts, and other sections worked on foreign army, air force, and diplomatic intercepts. The military and naval sections each evolved into two parts: cryptanalysis, which cracked the cryptograms, and intelligence, which extracted information from the solved intercepts. These teams were soon known better by the number of their hut than by their formal organizational name.

The naval cryptanalysts, headed by Turing, worked in Hut 8. Seated at cheap wooden desks, they spent their time guessing at possible cribs, looking for loops, and testing them on the bombes; they did sums, drew diagrams, printed letters. They seldom spoke, though occasionally one might express some emotion in a reserved British way. Next to them in Hut 4 were the naval intelligence analysts, who translated and appended comments to the solved intercepts. Hut 3 housed the cryptanalysts solving the German army and air force intercepts; Hut 6, the analysts for these solutions.

The advances made by Turing and Welchman had left Knox far behind; he remained in the Cottage working on the Enigmas without plugboards used by the Italian navy and by Abwehr, the German high command's espionage service. The solutions that his little group produced were designated ISK, for Intelligence Service Knox.

Some of the higher positions of this growing organization were filled by Room 40 veterans summoned from their civilian occupations. Nigel de Grey, a solver of the Zimmermann telegram that helped bring the United States into World War I, a man barely five feet tall and given to wearing fawn-colored trousers, returned from the publishing world as a deputy director. Frank Adcock, a round-faced, secretive classics scholar at King's College with a way of telling a joke and then cocking his head while waiting for the laugh, returned in 1939. The pantomimist Frank Birch, forty-nine, also a fellow of King's, came back to head Naval Section. He had taught history at Cambridge from 1921 to 1928, where his histrionic gifts made his lectures extraordinarily vivid. He quit academe to act in and produce plays in London. Of medium height, with close-set eyes in a mobile face, he was a very good comic actor and very good company, very amusing — when he wasn't working.

As a boss he was less successful, some thought. Birch was a Prussian in his directing style, which didn't work very well at Bletchley. He never encouraged: if the cryptanalysts got stuck, he'd come in at once and demand, "What's wrong?" A poor judge of people, he played favorites. Knowing that he would probably be unable to get a knighthood because of wartime secrecy, he sought his reward in power: he liked results that he could display to the admirals. Once he admonished his cryptanalysts, "Don't tell Hut 3 [the army and air force cryptanalysts] about this." But although he was not the best leader of the 200 people eventually in his section, and although an element of ruthlessness and prejudice limited the number of his friends, he could be kind. After one of Knox's young women assistants had been married three days, Birch took her into the operations room. Just as her husband's convoy was being pointed out to her on the plot of the Atlantic, a U-boat symbol was put down next to it. Birch put his arm around her. "We'll send the whole navy," he said.

Many of the positions immediately beneath these senior levels, such as the heads of huts or the heads of shifts, were occupied by new recruits. Some came, as Turing did, through the King's College connection. Conel Hugh O'Donel Alexander, called Hugh, was a mathematician with a powerful intellect and extraordinary vitality. A former British boys' chess champion, he had gained first-class honors in mathematics at King's but not the star for exceptional distinction that he wanted. He attributed this to having played too much chess, which was probably an accurate assessment: he won the university championship his first year and every year after that but one. Nor did he succeed in becoming a fellow of King's. Instead he taught mathematics at Winchester, one of England's great public schools. Then, at the urging of his wife, a cosmopolitan, not to say Bohemian, Australian who had lived in Paris, he took a job in an elegant London's men's clothing store where the owner, a chess fanatic, maintained the London Chess Center. It was a ridiculous move, friends thought. As a member of the British chess team, Alexander was in Buenos Aires for a competition when war broke out. With mental visions of London in flames, he returned home. Early in 1940, he joined the team at Bletchley and was assigned to work in Hut 8, the naval cryptanalysts, under Turing.

Here he became a remarkable asset. His intellect was powerful — one of his coworkers later said that "Alexander was one of the most intelligent people I've known, and I've known a lot of intelligent people" — and his vitality extraordinary. A lively, talkative, enthusiastic person, he incorporated several contradictions. Though he worked in the solitary pursuit of mathematics, he dealt with people extremely well. He proved an excellent organizer and administrator though he was personally untidy: his desk was a mess, he dressed sloppily, his hair was all over. And though not good at most ball games, he played table tennis in an ungainly but effective way, rarely letting a ball get past him. He soon became Turing's chief assistant.

One of Alexander's great friends was Stuart Milner-Barry, the *Times*'s chess correspondent, who had preceded him as British boys' chess champion, had played chess with him at Cambridge, and had been a member of the team that went to Buenos Aires. When Milner-Barry arrived later at Bletchley, he was very glad to see his old friend. But it was through Welchman, not Alexander, that Milner-Barry got to B.P. He and Welchman were exact contemporaries at Trinity College, Cambridge, had later lived in Cambridge at the same time, and had played tennis together often. Soon after the war started, Welchman thought that Milner-Barry, a chess player, would do well as a cryptanalyst. So he recruited him. And shortly after Milner-Barry joined G.C.&C.S., he began recruiting others, driving his little blue Austin 7 to pick them up.

In other cases, chance and mystery played roles in obtaining people. Because Leonard Forster had gotten along better with his German master than his French at his public school, he specialized in the Teutonic tongue, took his degree in it at Cambridge, spent four years working and studying in German-speaking lands, and finally returned to Britain to instruct at Cambridge. One day in March 1939 he was summoned to a briefing in Broadway Buildings; he never found out how he came to be invited. He took the introductory course in cryptology that G.C.&C.S. gave and went to London a few times in the spring and summer to help solve a simple two-letter German code. When war came, he went straight to Bletchley, vanishing into an organization that was one of the great unseen fighters of the war.

But neither the recruiting of Britain's best brains, nor the remarkable breakthroughs of Turing and Welchman, nor the occasional solution of the Luftwaffe Enigma led to the cracking of the naval Enigma. Then, as sometimes happens in war, help came from an unexpected source.

Eight
The Rotors

IN THE FALL of 1939, soon after World War II had begun, Lieutenant Heinz Rottmann, a slender, energetic, twenty-five-year-old naval careerist, was summoned to the U-boat fleet. The summons came from the man who had captained the cruiser *Emden* during Rottmann's officer training cruise a few years earlier and who now commanded the entire U-boat fleet, Captain Karl Dönitz. He gave Rottmann his choice of the U-33 or the U-34. Rottmann chose the U-33, a three-year-old Type VIIA submarine because he knew her skipper, Hans von Dresky, from the *Emden* and because he liked her number.

Before Rottmann joined, the U-33 had sailed on an operational cruise — she had actually gone to sea in anticipation of hostilities and was in her patrol area when Dönitz instructed his U-boat captains to "commence hostilities against England at once." She had sunk three ships and, at her berth in Wilhelmshaven, had been given the highest mark of esteem to which the members of a U-boat crew could aspire: a visit from the Führer himself. Rottmann participated in the U-33's second cruise, in which she laid mines and sank some trawlers. Then the 700-ton, 212-foot-long submarine was returned to her builder, Germania Werft in Kiel, for an overhaul that included the replacement of a bad diesel.

Finally, in early February 1940, she was ready to sail again. At about 2 A.M. on the fourth, she was lying at a wharf in Wilhelmshaven's solidly frozen harbor, with sailors and longshoremen loading provisions and munitions, when she rapidly and unexpectedly listed 15 degrees to port and dipped by the bow. Water and ice poured through a torpedo hatch into the bow area. One of the seamen ran to the control area and blew all ballast tanks, thus pre-

venting greater problems. At about that time the engineer, Lieutenant Commander Friedrich Schilling, came on board. He concluded that the damage was minor and controllable and, in the
morning, when he reported the incident to the submarine's commander, Dresky ordered the vessel to depart on schedule.

At 8 A.M., Dönitz came to the dock to see the U-33 off. To the
newspaper reader, to the average German watching the newsreels
in the cinema, even to some members of the Kriegsmarine, a submarine was just the letter U followed by a number; the subs under
these impersonal designations seemed indistinguishable. But to
Dönitz, each number summoned up the face of the U-boat's commander, as well as her officers and crew. Each ship was an individual, with her own characteristics, temperament, and qualities. Dönitz
saw, rightly, that in addition to making operational decisions such
as where to concentrate his boats for the greatest effect, his chief
job was to inspire "his" crews, to make them want to do their best
for him in their dangerous tasks. So he went down to the harbors
to send them off and to greet them on their return. And the crew
of the U-33 did not forget that he had come on that wintry morning to wish them a successful cruise.

Of those forty-two men, only four were new. Most were regular
seamen; many had been together since the submarine's 1936
launching, and they had been forged into a team by sharing the
thrills and the fears of combat. Time had expunged any lingering
claustrophobia: they were used to being enclosed underwater. Morale was good — despite the captain. His first two patrols were successes, but Dresky, tall, with a thin beard and a pointed nose, was
not an inspiring leader. He was introspective, too serious, too quiet,
and not enough of a driver or daredevil to win the full respect of
his youthful, eager crew. Moreover, he hoped on this voyage to
sink one of Britain's giant ocean liners, the *Queen Mary* or the *Queen
Elizabeth,* or some capital ship of the Royal Navy, as Günther Prien
had sunk the *Royal Oak* in Scapa Flow four months earlier; he felt
that his destiny depended on how well he did. The sense of fate
constrained his command. And his men smelled it.

Their baleful feelings grew when the U-33 had difficulty getting
out of the harbor. Heavy pack ice forced her back several times.
Not until an icebreaker and a freighter preceded her did the U-33
succeed in passing the bar. It was an inauspicious beginning.

Once out in the tumbling, windy North Sea, the crew discovered the cause of the earlier listing: water had come in through two holes, one the size of a thumb hole in the port torpedo tube, the other a quarter-inch accidental drill hole in a copper pipe. The leaks were stopped with a wooden wedge and with rubber until the U-33 reached Heligoland, the cliff-sided German island and naval station in the North Sea. There she lay over for several days owing to thick fog, and the holes were sealed better. But the repairs were not properly completed, and this intensified the crew's foreboding: they could not forget the three days they had spent on the bottom repairing a diesel during the first cruise.

Finally, at 4:30 in the wintry afternoon of Wednesday, February 7, the U-33 cast off from a tug that had towed her out to sea and began her third war patrol. She moved on the surface in the darkness at 12 to 15 knots; with the coming of daylight, she settled to the bottom, even though she was still within the vast German minefield that protected the north German ports from the Royal Navy. When night fell, she surfaced and headed northwestward, engines running strongly at 85 percent of capacity. Once, to the east of Scotland, her lookouts' hearts stopped as they spotted several destroyers, almost certainly British. But the warships did not see the low profile of the submarine, and she continued undisturbed. She curved north around Scotland, taking the Fair Isle Passage between the Orkneys and the Shetlands. Three or four times her lookouts warned of aircraft, but again the submarine was not sighted.

On the morning of Sunday, February 11, she headed south into the entrance of the North Channel, which divides northern Ireland from Scotland. The channel swarmed with ships, both illuminated and darkened; lighthouse beacons swept over the waters. As it grew light — around 9 A.M. in those northern latitudes at that time of year — Dresky put the U-33 on the bottom in 200 feet of water. He planned to surface at darkness and to race at top speed as close as possible to the entrance to the Firth of Clyde, one of Britain's busiest estuaries and the home of the nation's most important shipbuilders. There he would again settle at daylight, surface at night to sow the mines the U-33 was carrying, and then get back to the open Atlantic before dawn.

It was cold and damp in the boat. The heating, not very strong in any case, was rarely turned on because it used up precious electricity. The sailors could see their breath when they spoke. Condensation ran down the bulkheads. But the men were well dressed. Their shoes had thick cork soles; they wore heavy underwear, and the elastic cuffs of their leather jackets and pants gripped wrists and ankles to retain body heat.

The day passed slowly. Little could be done for fear of making too much noise. Finally, night brought the tedious Sunday to a close, and Dresky put his plan into operation. On the surface of the black waters, visibility was about half a mile. Around 2 A.M. of February 12, the U-33 passed a huge shape, probably a heavy cruiser at anchor. The lookouts did not spot her. Below decks Schilling, the engineer, checked the machinery. Everything seemed *in Ordnung:* batteries at 161 volts at 30 degrees centigrade with 34 millimeters of acid. At 4 o'clock, he climbed to the conning tower. Dresky told him of the cruiser they had passed and said, almost as if it were a joke, that just now a destroyer was speeding toward them.

It was not a destroyer but a minesweeper, H.M.S. *Gleaner,* which had been on night patrol at the 15-mile-wide entrance to the Firth of Clyde. Under instructions to watch along the 25-fathom contour, her captain, Lieutenant Commander Hugh P. Price of the Royal Navy, a hydrographer, sailed a right triangle, one apex of which was near the rocky islet Ailsa Craig, which rises abruptly 1,100 feet from the sea to a conical summit. At 2:50 A.M., as the vessel was steaming on the due-south leg of the triangle, the seaman listening on the hydrophone reported hearing a strong sound from slightly off the *Gleaner*'s starboard bow. The officer on watch brought the 4-inch gun and the depth charges to the ready, altered course toward the object, which had moved to off the port bow at a range of almost 2 miles, and called Price.

On the bridge, Price heard strong hydrophone noises that sounded *tonk, tonk, tonk, tonk* at a rate of about two a second. He swung toward the moving object and increased speed to 16 knots. At 3:16 the range increased slightly, but thereafter it decreased. He swung his vessel to bring his searchlight to bear.

Aboard the U-boat, just after Schilling saw the shadow of the surface vessel, he and Dresky went below. "Prepare to dive" rang out. The U-33 submerged. A moment later Price, observing that the target bearing was rapidly drawing aft, had the searchlight switched on. He spotted something that looked white — possibly spray from the submarine — but it disappeared almost at once.

The light was seen aboard the U-boat, which had apparently then not gone entirely under. After she submerged totally, the crew heard each beat of the ship's screw passing overhead from starboard stern to port bow. Price knew he was passing over the target, but trouble with the depth charges led him to wait until he could fire a pattern instead of dropping the charges haphazardly. In the submarine, Dresky ordered a dive to 125 feet, but the vessel had reached only 80 feet when the *Gleaner*, which had circled around and made contact again at 3:53, fired a pattern of four depth charges that exploded at 150 feet, not far from the U-33.

The detonations shook the U-boat. Its lights went out. With the booms, the crew members ducked their heads and hunched their shoulders. The emergency lighting came on but could barely penetrate the dust, thick as fog, that the explosions had kicked up. None of the men screamed; no one cried; no one dirtied his pants. Their earlier attacks had toughened them, and their comradeship sustained them. From all parts of the vessel then came the reports of damage. The rudder and diving plane indicators had failed. All depth indicators were broken. There were two leaks. The starboard electric motor was sparking. The gauges of the rear electrical control panel were burned out. The gyro compass had reversed itself. A welded seam had torn. But all in all, the damage was not great. The crew began to replace the broken light bulbs. Dresky ordered the crew to put on their escape apparatus, then: "Absolute silence in the boat. Put her on the bottom!" And the U-33 settled to the sea floor. The men took off their shoes and spoke only in whispers.

On the *Gleaner*, the shock of the explosions briefly extinguished lights and caused her to lose contact with the submarine. The reloading party was having difficulty because the ship canted from side to side as Price turned her in giant figure 8's to remain over the target. At 4:12 he fired another pattern. In the U-boat, extra machine parts were flung from their holders. More bulbs failed. Both diesel exhausts began to leak. Dresky asked Schilling what they should do; the engineer proposed trying to sneak away under water. When Schilling started the pumps to force water out of the ballast tanks to increase buoyancy, however, Dresky ordered them stopped because they made too much noise. But the submarine, with 2 tons of negative buoyancy, could not free herself from the bottom by her propellers alone.

At around 4:40, the *Gleaner* approached for another attack. Schilling started the pumps, apparently thinking there was little to lose, but Dresky canceled the order. Five more depth charges rocked the submarine. The men remained unshaken. Lieutenant Johannes Becker, the second watch officer, sipped a beer in the torpedo room. "Water coming in!" was reported from astern. Rottmann went back to investigate. In the diesel room, the machinists were sitting on the equipment so their feet would not get cold. They looked at Rottmann's face when he came in to get a clue as to the condition of the boat. He put on a neutral expression so as not to frighten them. He need not have worried. Many seemed to have the same feeling that Machinist Ernst Masanek had about himself: "Don't worry. You'll get out of it all right." Rottmann reported that only a connection between two internal tanks had been torn and that water was running into the bilges.

Dresky then ordered Schilling to get the submarine off the bottom. There was no point in awaiting the next attack and the next and the next. But once the submarine was moving, then what? The man at the helm said that escape was not possible, that all they could do was save the crew. Schilling pointed out that traveling submerged in those narrow and shallow waters, which were streaming at 6 knots, was extraordinarily difficult. Dresky agreed and concluded that surface travel offered the best chance of escaping. He began preparing for this, ordering the first watch officer to ready the mines for discharge and the second watch officer, Becker, to prepare the secret materials for destruction.

The most secret item was the Enigma cipher machine. Becker knew that the rotors were its heart and that the machine, if recovered by the British, would have little value without them. So he took the three in the machine and the five others in their wooden box and distributed them among a few crew members, including Rottmann, Lieutenant Karl Vietor, and Machinist First Class Fritz Kumpf. He instructed them to drop the rotors into the sea as soon as they went overboard. Meanwhile the crew members prepared themselves for immersion in the frigid water by dressing in as many layers of clothing as possible. This would tend to hold the water that was warmed by their bodies near them and prevent their being chilled by cold water flushing past their skin. Rottmann put on, over his underwear, his pullover and service trousers, a coverall, a leather jacket, leather pants, fur pants, and his escape apparatus.

The effort to lift the vessel began. With two-thirds of the compressed air supply gone, Dresky ordered the unorthodox maneuver of blowing the water out of one of the torpedo tanks, then, "Surface!" and "Air in all tanks!"

A few moments later, the submarine breached. At 5:22 she was caught in the glare of the *Gleaner*'s searchlight but then was lost when the light failed, owing to broken arc carbons. Price substituted the 10-inch signaling lamps and spotted the U-boat again. The *Gleaner* fired five rounds from the 4-inch gun and turned to ram. Dresky, who had emerged onto the conning tower, saw that the British ship was only a few hundred yards away and shouted down into his boat: "Abandon ship! Blow her up! Report [the situation] by radio!" Schilling shouted that the diesel engines were still working, but Dresky repeated his order. As the crew members clambered out, Schilling opened the main induction flappers, heard with satisfaction the crackle of the fuse for the scuttling charge, and opened the vents of torpedo tubes 1 and 2. But he could open the latter's vent only part way. Someone called to him from above. He went to the conning tower and reported what was going on to Dresky, who came down, tried to open the vent of tube 2 without much success, and soon climbed back up. Schilling then went to the rear control room and opened both outboard valves until a heavy stream of water flowed over his feet. Satisfied, he went out, noticing that the main vent valves in the main control room were already under water.

On the surface, Price saw the crew tumbling out of the U-33 holding up their hands in surrender, so he had the wheel put hard to starboard and all engines put full astern. The *Gleaner* stopped parallel to the U-boat about 200 yards away. Suddenly a shower of sparks erupted from the conning tower: the explosive had apparently set off some signal rockets and some of the smaller munitions; the heavier munitions were already flooded. The crew abandoned the submarine, which almost immediately sank by the bow at an angle of 40 degrees.

As the stern disappeared, Dresky led the floating men in three cheers for the U-33. It was 5:30 A.M.

The water was bitter cold and choppy; the night was black. Rott-mann pulled his three rotors from his pocket and let them sink into the sea. Vietor did the same with his two. Dresky ordered, "Stay together as much as possible." Schilling, swimming in a large group of crew members, was often asked whether they would be rescued. As the minutes and quarter hours passed, he repeatedly told the men "They're on the way. Stick it out and keep swim-ming." His pod kept getting smaller as men vanished. Meanwhile the *Gleaner* had lowered boats and moved slowly into the center of the largest group of survivors. Suddenly Schilling saw a search-light nearby and then the side of a ship and a manila line, to which he clung before losing consciousness. He and the others had been in the water almost two hours. Only the many layers of their cloth-ing had saved them. The *Gleaner* and other vessels picked up four officers and seventeen men. Dresky did not survive, and his body was never recovered. He had met his doom.

Rottmann was picked up by a cutter, which took him to the *Gleaner*. He passed out, then woke up in a bathtub filled with warm water. The bearded Royal Navy ensign who was guarding him gave him pants and shoes. They spoke in German, and Rottmann asked whether he could visit his crew to see who was alive. The officer took him to a room in which a clump of men was sitting on the deck, each with a blanket, and shivering. On seeing Rottmann, Kumpf, the seaman who had been given three rotors to drop into the water, said, "Herr Oberleutnant!" and tried to rise to report in a proper way. But Rottmann put his hand on his shoulder and told him to stay down.

"Herr Oberleutnant," Kumpf resumed, "I forgot to throw the wheels away." Rottmann went over to the bulkhead where Kumpf's leather pants were hanging in the hope of finding the rotors so he could himself surreptitiously get rid of them. He squeezed the pants. They were empty. The British had gotten the wired codewheels.

Nine

Royal Flags Wave Kings Above

THE ROTORS that some alert British sailor had removed from Kumpf's leather pants went to Bletchley. Two turned out to be hitherto unknown naval rotors: VI and VII. Though in theory their wiring could have been reconstructed, their capture speeded the work of the Hut 8 cryptanalysts. Later they obtained rotor VIII from another naval capture. But even possession of a full set of rotors, together with a copy of the regulations for the use of the naval Enigma recovered from the U-13 in June 1940, did not make possible regular, or even frequent, solution of German naval cryptograms. And the U-boat war was increasing in intensity.

For, as the usage regulations booklet showed, the Kriegsmarine keying system excluded the weak points in the Luftwaffe Enigma that the clever men of Bletchley had found and exploited, coining a vocabulary of colorful specialized terms as they did so. A "crab" was the simultaneous turning of two rotors, and a "lobster," naturally, was when all three moved together. A "crash" occurred when the same letter stood in the same position in both a crib and a cryptogram, as *der* and DBV — an impossibility in an Enigma encipherment. The cryptanalysts of the Luftwaffe Enigma coined the term "cillies" — either the name of the girlfriend of an Enigma cipher clerk used as as a key or just a burlesque of "sillies" — for some of the foolish things that Enigma operators persisted in doing, despite regulations to the contrary. One was to use as message keys a sequence from their keyboard, such as QWE or NBV, or the first three letters of a girlfriend's name, or an obscene word. Another form of cilly occurred when a lazy encipherer chose as his message key the position that the rotors were in at the end of the encipherment of the previous message. Once the later message was solved, the cryptanalysts had merely to count the number of letters in the earlier message and turn the rotors backward that number of places to obtain the message key of the earlier message. Other cillies were the "nearness" and the JABJAB, so named from the indicator setting in which it was first seen.

Yet another shortcut to solution was called the Herivel tip. John Herivel, an undergraduate in mathematics at Trinity, had been recruited by Gordon Welchman. He was fascinated by physics and by the way physicists made their great discoveries; he wanted to do the same for the Enigma. So each night he would return to his digs, figuratively put his feet up, and think about how the system could be broken. One day in February 1940 a "happy brainwave" suddenly came into his head. Suppose, he thought, an Enigma operator was lazy. In setting a key, he would hold a rotor with his thumb, grasp the spring for the alphabet-ring pin, rotate the ring until the key letter faced him, then release the spring to lock the ring in place. He would then slide the rotor onto the axle and repeat the process with the next two rotors. When the assembly was put into the Enigma, the three key letters would still be approximately facing the operator and would be close to the letters showing through the apertures when the lid was closed. The lazy operator would not turn the rotors but would use those letters for his message key.

If the cryptanalysts thought an operator was following this procedure, they would have many fewer probable ring settings to try. Herivel's colleagues thought the idea was brilliant. But it remained only a hypothesis until the Germans invaded France on May 10, when the German cipher clerks were under such pressure, because of the volume of communications, that they did not follow all their instructions in detail. Herivel arrived at work that day to see people clustered around his colleague David Rees. They were breaking the Luftwaffe Enigma using the Herivel tip. Welchman said to Herivel, "You won't be forgotten!"

More help came from two characteristics of German cryptographic procedure. The air force never used the same rotor in the same position two days in a row, except perhaps from one keying period to the next. This knowledge reduced the number of rotor orders that the bombes had to test. Moreover, the Germans never connected two consecutive letters on the plugboard — never A with

B, for example. This enabled the British to add to the bombes a circuit called the CSKO, which, using the German term for "plug," *stecker,* stood for "consecutive stecker knock-out."

Another aid to solution came, paradoxically, from a German complication. Rotors I to V differed in the point at which the notch cut in the alphabet ring caused the rotor to the left to move one space. Rotor I, for example, kicked its neighbor when it (rotor I) stepped to ring position R (from ring position Q) during the course of encipherment. Rotor II gave its kick when moving to F, III to W, IV to K, and V to A. The Germans thought that this would create a more irregular movement, and in a way they were right. But the British cryptanalysts soon saw that the discovery that a rotor had moved could, if they knew the ring position of its neighbor to the right, identify that neighbor. (This is an interesting example of a complication that defeats itself. Had all the notches been cut at the same letter, cryptanalysts would not have been able easily to identify the rotor at a particular location — a point the Kriegsmarine recognized when it notched the rings at the same letters in rotors VI, VII, and VIII.) Because the different movement points were so important, Bletchley devised a mnemonic for them that made no sense but that stuck in the minds of the defenders of the monarchy: "Royal Flags Wave Kings Above."

With tricks like these, and with the standard analyses of keys and cribs, Bletchley began on May 22, 1940, to regularly read the Luftwaffe's general Enigma key, called RED by G.C.&C.S., apparently from Gordon Welchman's using a red pencil to underline discriminants and other data when he was first working on intercepts. Excitement mounted in Hut 3 as, day after day after day, RED fell before the British onslaught. To Dennis Babbage, a tall, slow-speaking algebraic geometer from Cambridge (who was, so far as he knew, no relation to Charles Babbage, the nineteenth-century father of the computer), the moment was unforgettable. "It was marvelous weather, the world crashing about our ears, France about to fall, England about to be invaded — and we made our first break into Enigma. It was exhilarating!"

By then, Britain had long had little need of the Poles' help. Indeed, during the phony war, from December 1939 to June 1940, the British with their greater resources had produced 83 percent of the solutions. Together, P.C. Bruno and Bletchley Park broke more than a hundred keys used on about a hundred days to read several thousand messages. These provided the Allies with such insights into German activities as that in a message of June 13: "Concerning directive of the 2nd Air Fleet for 14 June 1940: 1. Fourth Army attacks on 14 June 1940 over the Seine towards the southwest. Left wing on Chartres . . ."

But the cryptanalytic successes could not, by themselves, produce military ones. As in the campaign in Poland, strength was needed to turn intelligence into victory. And France, for whatever reason, lacked it. On June 14, Paris fell, and on that day P.C. Bruno ceased to exist. The Poles and the Spaniards were evacuated to Oran, thence to the Villa Kouba, south of Algiers, and eventually back to the part of France not occupied by the Germans. In another villa, the Château des Fouzes, outside Uzès, a Roman town in the south of France, they rejoined the French cryptanalysts, still under Bertrand, to form a codebreaking unit that continued to solve Enigma messages and to radio the keys to Britain (enciphering them, subtly enough, in Enigma.)

Here they worked somehow undisturbed for two years until, in November 1942, the Germans overran all of France. Most of the cryptanalysts escaped. But some key people were left in occupied Europe. REX, whose activities were known to German counterintelligence, was questioned; he cracked and disclosed the identity and treason of Schmidt, who was arrested and interrogated before he was shot in July 1943. But since neither man knew of the Polish work, much less of its success, they could not betray it. REX also told of his contacts with Bertrand, who was arrested in the white-domed basilica of Sacré Coeur in Paris. The Germans sought to get the officer to act as a double agent and find out, among other things, what German ciphers the British were reading. Instead Bertrand escaped, eventually getting to England. Ciężki and Langer were seized while trying to cross from France to Spain. Their prewar functions were known, and they were questioned specifically about Polish success with machine ciphers. But they convinced their interrogators, whom they suspected were German cryptologists, that the complications introduced into the Enigma encipherment before the war had made solution impossible. (It may have been what the questioners wanted to hear.) In Poland, the longtime chief secretary of the Biuro Szyfrów spoke only of superficial clerical matters when questioned about its work. Others — AVA technicians, Pyry deciphering clerks — never talked about the cryptanalysis. The secret of the Enigma solution was safe.

The cryptanalysts who escaped — all except Różycki, who drowned when his ship, the *Lamoricière*, went down in a storm — reached England in 1943 after harrowing trips. The Poles reaped the customary reward of the innovator whose efforts have benefited others: exclusion. The British kept Rejewski and the others from any work on the Enigma, assigning them instead to a signals company of the Polish forces in exile, where they solved low-level ciphers. It was not one of Britain's finest hours.

The success with RED, which ran virtually unbroken from May 1940 to the end of the war, had little technical effect on Bletchley's work with the naval Enigma: the keying systems were too different. But that success did have a strong psychological effect: it encouraged Naval Section. If the German air force Enigma could be solved, perhaps the German navy Enigma could be as well. A solution was badly needed. Germany was building more and more U-boats, and they were sinking more and more ships. Bletchley's hope was further kept up by the bits and pieces of German cryptography that dribbled in from time to time.

On the blustery morning of April 26, 1940, the British destroyer *Arrow* was returning to Britain. She had just carried men and supplies to Norway as part of the fight against the German invaders. At 6:50 A.M., three hours out and 60 miles northwest of the central Norwegian port of Ålesund, she sighted a trawler to the south and approached her. The trawler was flying a Dutch flag and had the Dutch colors and the word "Holland" painted on her side. She stopped when ordered but did not reply to other signals. The *Arrow*'s skipper decided to board her despite an extremely rough sea. As the *Arrow* was about to launch her boat, the trawler, about 300 yards to port, suddenly raced full ahead, swung to starboard, ran up the Kriegsmarine flag, and rammed the destroyer, holing her port side in the engine room about 4 feet above the waterline. The trawler's crew jumped overboard, and the *Arrow* fired sixty-one rounds, hitting the trawler eight times. But it took the cruiser *Birmingham*'s bigger guns to sink the trawler, with four salvos.

Upon reporting the sinking, the *Birmingham* was instructed to search in the vicinity for other ships. The *Birmingham* replied that the trawler was apparently only laying mines, but she followed orders. By then, the two warships had been joined by two other destroyers, the *Griffin* and the *Acheron*. At 9:55 A.M. they took station 4 miles to either side of the *Arrow* and headed approximately southwest at 15 knots. About 10:15 the *Arrow* sighted what appeared to be a trawler and ordered the *Griffin* to investigate.

With her men at action stations, the *Griffin* closed with the other ship at 25 knots. Like the first trawler, this one was flying Dutch colors and had the Dutch flag of red, white, and light blue stripes painted on her sides. She wore the name *Polares* and "Holland" on her sides, and on her stern was a registration number from IJmuiden, a Dutch port. She stopped when ordered to do so, putting up no fight, despite her two torpedo tubes, which suggested that she was not just a fishing vessel. The *Griffin* sent over an armed boarding party in a whaler. While it was struggling in the strong breeze and choppy seas, a member of the trawler crew threw overboard two canvas bags. One sank at once; the other floated. As soon as the boarding party realized the trawler was German, a prize crew was dispatched. The bag had by this time floated near the destroyer, but it could not be grappled. It was on the point of sinking when Gunner F. H. W. T. Foord of the prize crew jumped over the side of the whaler with a heaving line and caught hold of the bag. While he was being hauled back aboard in the rough water, the line parted and he went under. He came up still clutching the bag. Another line was thrown to him. He held this for a moment with one hand but could not hang on and went under yet again. Finally he managed to pass a bowline under his arms and was hauled aboard, saving the bag. The vessel, the former *Julius Pickenpack*, a 394-tonner built in Hamburg nine years before and converted to a disguised attack ship, was taken in tow.

The bag proved to contain documents, among which were, in addition to key tables for non-Enigma systems, notes comprising Enigma keys for April 23, 24, 25, and 26. These found their way to Bletchley Park. Foord's courage and alertness made possible the first break into naval Enigma. The slips of paper enabled Hut 8 to read some naval Enigma messages retrospectively in May for six days in April. But though this success expanded Naval Section's knowledge of the Kriegsmarine's signals organization, it neither affected naval operations nor made further naval Enigma solutions possible.

With the naval Enigma apparently impregnable, Hut 8 attacked simpler-appearing German navy cryptograms, hoping to produce at least some solutions. The characteristics of the cryptograms led the analysts to think that they were enciphered in hand systems: ciphers that employed only letter tables and pencil and paper. One system succumbed almost at once. This was Radio Cipher H, used by merchant ships controlled by the German navy. A bigraphic system, it was solved the month the war broke out by Dr. W. H. Bruford, a professor of German who had learned cryptanalysis in Room 40. Radio Cipher H rarely carried messages of significance. But in April 1940, when its reading was becoming current, a solution by two of Bruford's acolytes was sent to the Admiralty to show what Naval Section could do. The message merely gave Oxelösund, Sweden, as the destination of a German freighter of moderate tonnage. But the solution caused a stir because it dented the pessimism that reigned in high quarters about the possibility of solving any German naval signals in time for them to be of use. It did not dispel all doubts, however, for a few months later, with the naval Enigma still unbroken and a new high-grade hand system, the Dockyard Cipher, likewise unsolved, Denniston, the head of G.C.&C.S., remarked mournfully to Birch, "You know, the Germans don't mean you to read their stuff, and I don't suppose you ever will."

Like Radio Cipher H, the Dockyard system also replaced pairs of plaintext letters with pairs of ciphertext letters. But it used one of twenty tables that were changed every other month; later thirty tables were used and were changed monthly. Its cryptograms consisted of five-letter groups, easily distinguishable from the four-letter groups of Enigma cryptograms. Soon after Denniston made his pessimistic remark, a captured document yielded a crib to Dockyard. It enabled the hand-cipher unit of Naval Section to achieve its first solution in that system; subsequent solutions were derived from frequency analysis and probable words. The Dockyard Cipher proved to be used more widely than its name implied:

it served not only for messages to and from shipyards and their associated vessels and posts but also for messages to and from many smaller vessels, such as patrol boats and auxiliaries. At G.C.&C.S., seven cryptanalysts, the best of them a woman named Ruth Briggs, worked on it, rotating around the clock, aided by seven women who filled in the cipher tables as the cryptanalysts pulled out the bigram equivalences during their solutions. A certain Teutonic rigidity helped the cryptanalysts. Cipher regulations called for Dockyard plaintexts to end with a word of padding and gave as examples *Wassereimer, Fernsprecher, Kleiderschrank* ("water pail," "telephone," "clothes closet"). The young signalmen often used these very words as padding, varying them from time to time with *Rosengarten.* For the Bletchley cryptanalysts, Dockyard began to serve mainly as a source of cribs to Enigma cryptograms in cases where the Germans radioed virtually the same content both to vessels that had no Enigma and to those that had it. In Bletchley's colorful jargon, such cribs were called "kisses."

Naval Section exploited another form of radio intelligence called traffic analysis — in this case a study of the flow and volume of German naval communications. It worked from direction-finding and the external indicators of messages, such as addressees and radio frequencies, to build up a picture of the communications organization and of its normal activity. The analysts looked for any deviation from these norms, which might reflect some unusual activity. Gordon Welchman had made a similar study for German army messages.

Unlike cryptanalysis, which can explicitly reveal the intentions of an enemy in his own words, traffic analysis rests almost entirely upon inferences. A radio circuit normally quiescent springs to life. Does this mean that the squadron it serves is preparing for a sortie — or only that some disciplinary problem has arisen? These possibilities may be distinguished by the priority level and the length of the messages, but such indicators seem insubstantial and thin, and thus second-rate to someone who is not intimate with them.

Perhaps that was one reason Naval Section had assigned its traffic analysis to a very young man, a new recruit with no standing, given to wearing longish hair and corduroy trousers. In fact, having been plucked from university before he had completed his studies, he was technically still an undergraduate.

Francis Harry Hinsley, called Harry, had been recruited when Denniston sent a letter to the heads of about ten Oxford and Cambridge colleges asking them to recommend half a dozen of their best students for war work. Denniston realized that G.C.&C.S. needed able young generalists in addition to mathematicians and linguists. Hinsley, who had grown up in Walsall, a town eight miles northwest of Birmingham, had gotten into St. John's College, Cambridge, on a history scholarship, having chosen both the field and the school because the schoolmaster at Queen Mary's Grammar School in Walsall was a St. John's historian. Hinsley had been at Cambridge for two years and had just taken first-class honors in Part I of the history tripos when, on a morning in October 1939, he was summoned to an interview in the third court of St. John's with Denniston and two other G.C.&C.S. officials.

"We understand you've been abroad a lot," one of them said. Hinsley had spent his summer vacations from 1937 to 1939 with pen pals in Germany to learn that language, staying, for example, with a German family in Koblenz. Denniston and the others asked no penetrating questions, no questions about security or whether Hinsley was a Marxist, only such matters as whether he preferred government service to being conscripted. Their decision rested in part simply on liking his face and on the fact that the master of the college had recommended him; the old-boys method of recruiting — which failed so miserably with Kim Philby, Guy Burgess, Donald Maclean, and Anthony Blunt, all of whom were Communists — succeeded brilliantly with Hinsley and about twenty other Oxford and Cambridge undergraduates. He was hired into the Foreign Office at £150 a year; he was not told what work he would be doing but only to present himself on a certain day at London's Euston Station, when he would receive further instructions.

At breakfast on the day of his departure, he repeated these directives to the St. John's medieval history don. The don, who had himself been recruited by G.C.&C.S., realized that Hinsley was bound for the same destination and drove him there that day. At Bletchley Park, Hinsley learned what the work was about. Told that G.C.&C.S. needed men in both the air and naval sections, he chose the naval and was sent to the section chief, Frank Birch.

Naval Section had only started to accumulate information. Birch gave Hinsley lists of intercepts and told him to see what he could make of them. For each message, the lists gave the call signs of the sender and the addressee, its time of origin, the radio frequency of the transmission, the time of interception, and the number of cipher groups in the message. By examining and comparing these lists, together with intercepts of radio operators' chatter and service messages requesting retransmissions because of some error or other, plus direction-finding fixes on transmitters, Hinsley learned a great deal about German naval signals. He figured out the locations of the fixed transmitters ashore and tracked the movements of those aboard ship, saw which stations "talked" to which, and gained a feel for the normal message lengths and the traffic volume on each link. He did well in this rather mechanical work, from whose results he and others in Naval Section gradually sketched out the structure of the Kriegsmarine signal system and, by implication, of the Kriegsmarine organization. Then they identified the call signs of individual ships. Naval Section hoped eventually to warn when some potentially threatening enemy activity was afoot. Hinsley's familiarity with the German system made him the person to report any such activity to the Admiralty.

But the Admiralty's Operational Intelligence Centre paid little attention to this inferential evidence. On April 7, 1940, for example, Hinsley telephoned it to say that German naval radio activity had been heard in the waters west of Denmark and in the exit from the Baltic — activity that was unprecedented since the start of the war. This was G.C.&C.S.'s first substantial contribution to naval intelligence, but O.I.C. essentially ignored it. Clayton, the conservative head of O.I.C., and Denning, a deputy, had never met Hinsley; he was but a youthful voice on the telephone to them. He was, moreover, a civilian, with no experience of naval matters. They had built up no trust in him; they had had no experience with traffic analysis and had gained no confidence in it. Two days later, it turned out that the communications volume represented German warships and troopships sailing toward Denmark and Norway, which Germany was invading. This confirmation of Hinsley's traffic analysis did not, however, convince O.I.C. It took a catastrophe two months later to change its attitude.

The Allied front in France was collapsing when the British decided to bring their forces home from Norway. Their attempt to repel the German invasion had failed. But they were still fighting fiercely near the end of May, when the Germans ordered three cruisers to aid a German garrison isolated at Narvik in northern Norway. To alert German naval commands to this sortie, a flurry of communications swept up the coast of occupied Norway. The British overheard them, and Hinsley reported to the O.I.C. about it. That unit duly recorded that "from a study of German W/T [wireless telegraphy] traffic . . . there would appear to be a movement of certain enemy ships, class and type unknown, from the Baltic to the Skagerrak," the strait between Denmark and Norway. But the O.I.C. took no action. On June 4 the German flotilla sailed. It consisted of the *Gneisenau,* the *Scharnhorst,* the *Admiral Hipper,* and six support vessels. On Friday, June 7, Hinsley warned that the German warships might take "offensive action." The O.I.C. noted this but otherwise ignored it. As a consequence, the Admiralty issued no warning to its forces at sea.

The next day, the British aircraft carrier *Glorious,* with two destroyers as escorts, was steaming toward Scapa Flow with men and planes rescued from Norway. Built as a cruiser in 1916 and converted to a carrier in 1930, the *Glorious* was commanded by Captain Guy D'Oyly-Hughes, a man undoubtedly brave, undoubtedly energetic, but whose inept leadership had greatly reduced morale aboard his ship. The ship was carrying seven Hurricane fighters and ten Gladiator biplane fighters that had been flown aboard in a dramatic rescue operation: it was the first time that Hurricanes had landed on a carrier, a risk taken because the planes and their crews were badly needed in Britain to defend against the expected German air onslaught.

The day was clear and warm; visibility was excellent. The sea was calm except for a long swell from the northwest. There was little wind. Lassitude seemed to claim the ship. When one of the pilots commented about the warheads being removed from the torpedoes, the chief torpedo instructor said with a happy smile that they were getting "a lap ahead" to go on leave. The laxness led to carelessness. Though the *Glorious* carried no radar, D'Oyly-Hughes had not sent a lookout aloft to the crow's nest and had not flown patrols. In the afternoon, the carrier was zigzagging at 17 knots around a mean course of 250 degrees.

Suddenly, four fountains of water sprang up on the ship's starboard side. A sharp-eyed midshipman in the foretop of the *Scharn-*

horst had, a while before, spotted a puff of smoke from the carrier at a range of twenty-eight miles. The *Scharnhorst* and the *Gneisenau* tracked it until they discerned the *Glorious*. At 4:32 the *Scharnhorst* opened fire with the 11-inch guns of her two forward turrets.

"The first salvo arrived 20 yards on the starboard side," said one of the British aviators. "On the horizon were two little bits of smoke. I thought, this is extraordinary! I thought I'd go up to the bridge to see how they fought a naval action. The second salvo arrived just as I stepped on the flight deck. It wrote off the ladder I had just come up! There was a damned great hole in the flight deck."

The German ships' excellent optical range finders and outstanding gunnery soon had their shells hitting the *Glorious* and the destroyers again and again. Fires broke out in the hangars. Airplanes blazed. Men died. One airplane fitter was hit in the chest with a heavy fragment of black smoking shell. He fell flat on his back, exclaimed, "Oh my wife and children!" and died. A shell struck the bridge, destroying it and killing D'Oyly-Hughes and others but leaving the action helmsman immediately below unhurt, though he was now in the open and the body of the navigating officer lay in halves on either side of him. Shells tore into the carrier almost continuously. Corpses lay about, looking more like rag bundles than men.

The *Glorious* was listing 15 to 20 degrees to starboard and was burning out of control from stem to stern when the order was given to abandon ship. She sank at 6:10 P.M. in an enormous flurry of spray and foam. Both destroyers were also sent to the bottom. Many of the men who had survived their ships' destruction were dying in the water, some of them crying out for their mothers and for God to help them. The killed and missing for the three ships totaled 1,519, including most of the badly needed air crews. Only thirty-nine men survived.

The disaster taught a terrible lesson. The O.I.C. realized that had it listened to Hinsley and urged the Admiralty to warn its forces about the German ships, Britain might not have suffered its awful loss. Clayton and Denning brought him down to the Admiralty, where he stayed for three weeks during the Blitz (the German air raids on London) getting to know the personnel at O.I.C. and letting them get to know him. Hinsley had won their confidence.

Thus when, at the end of January 1941, G.C.&C.S.'s traffic

analysis revealed that heavy German warships were about to sortie from the Baltic, and when an attaché report confirmed the presence of battle cruisers in Danish waters, the Admiralty took action: major elements of the Home Fleet stood out from Scapa Flow to catch and destroy them. It was not the fault of G.C.&C.S. or of O.I.C. that the Germans brilliantly evaded the Royal Navy and later sank more than twenty ships in a two-month sortie.

The growing closeness between the codebreakers and the intelligence agency was further exemplified by the establishment of an assistant directorship of the O.I.C. to supervise the action taken by the Naval Intelligence Division on radio intelligence. The post was filled by Captain Jasper Haines, a tall, gray-haired officer so handsome that many of the young women in Naval Section regarded his regular visits to Bletchley Park from O.I.C., where he was based, as occasions — and woe to the boss who didn't find some excuse to keep Haines around a little longer. Haines supplemented the day-to-day contacts between London and Bletchley.

But the naval Enigma still could not be read. Seeing no chance of analyzing the machine, the British began to consider ways of capturing keys. Some vague discussions took place during the summer, but the first clear proposal came from the assistant to the director of naval intelligence, an imaginative civilian who later became world famous as the creator of superspy James Bond. In a note of September 12, 1940, to his chief, Ian Fleming wrote:

> D.N.I.
> I suggest we obtain the loot by the following means:
> 1. Obtain from Air Ministry an air-worthy German bomber.
> 2. Pick a tough crew of five, including a pilot, W/T [wireless telegraph] operator and word-perfect German speaker. Dress them in German Air Force uniform, add blood and bandages to suit.
> 3. Crash plane in the Channel after making S.O.S. to rescue service in P/L [plain language].
> 4. Once aboard rescue boat, shoot German crew, dump overboard, bring rescue boat back to English port.
> In order to increase the chances of capturing an R. or M. [*Räumboot*, a small minesweeper; *Minensuchboot*, a large minesweeper] with its richer booty, the crash might be staged in mid-Channel. The Germans would presumably employ one of this type for the longer and more hazardous journey.

Clayton supported the idea, and Fleming produced a more detailed plan. The bomber would take off shortly before dawn as one of the big London raids was ending. It would try to spot an isolated small minesweeper, cut an engine, emit smoke, drop fast, and pancake into the water. Fleming drew up a list of the personnel and material required, including a pilot who was "tough, bachelor, able to swim." In case word got out that a German boat had been brought into an English port, Fleming proposed to put out a cover story that the capture was done "for a lark by a group of young hotheads who thought the war was too tame and wanted to have a go at the Germans. They had stolen plane and equipment and had expected to get into trouble when they got back."

Frank Birch, the head of Naval Section, liked the plan, which he called "very ingenious," in part because it would not give away British cryptanalytic efforts if it failed. He provided a three-page memorandum of "Activities of German Naval Units in the Channel."

The plan was approved and given the codename Operation RUTHLESS. Fleming assembled the needed men. The director of naval intelligence, Rear Admiral John H. Godfrey, scrounged a bomber from the Air Ministry. A twin-engine Heinkel 111, shot down during a raid on the Firth of Forth, had crash-landed on the moors not far from Edinburgh without great damage. The British restored it to flyability. Group Captain H. J. Wilson, in charge of evaluating captured German aircraft, flew it to the Royal Aircraft Establishment in Farnborough, southwest of London.

A few months later, Wilson was visited by some naval intelligence officers. They explained the plot, referring to the capture not of cipher documents but of secret radio equipment. The plan — which, they assured him, had the blessing of Churchill himself and would guarantee a decoration for the pilot — had elaborated: Spitfires would mock-attack the bomber. Wilson pointed out that the crash landing in the rough autumn seas would unquestionably collapse the Heinkel's all-acrylic Perspex nose, would probably sink the plane almost at once, and would almost certainly seriously injure the crew. He asked how these shaken-up, soaked, cold crewmen could leap from their dinghy to intimidate the crew of the rescue vessel and capture it. He himself declined the navy's offer to participate, saying he preferred to work on successful operations than to win a posthumous Victoria Cross.

The intelligence officers were disappointed at his reaction but did not give up. When they advertised for men for a suicide mission, a love-sick pilot volunteered. Wilson reinforced the Heinkel's nose and found a way to inject oil into the exhaust to simulate an engine fire. All that the airmen could do had been done. In October, Fleming went to Dover to await his chance. None came. Air reconnaissance found no suitable German ships operating at night, and radio reconnaissance likewise found nothing. On the sixteenth, the Dover command postponed RUTHLESS but suggested trying it at Portsmouth. Four days later Birch wrote:

> Turing and Twinn came to me like undertakers cheated of a nice corpse two days ago, all in a stew about the cancellation of Operation Ruthless. The burden of their song was the importance of a pinch. Did the authorities realise that . . . there was very little hope, if any, of their deciphering current, or even approximately current, Enigma . . . at all.

Fleming replied that the value of a pinch was fully recognized and that RUTHLESS was still fully laid on. The navy awaited favorable circumstances. But they never materialized, and the plan faded away.

Thus the crisis with the naval Enigma continued. Pressure on the cryptanalysts increased. Churchill told the Commons on November 4, 1940, that "the recent recrudescence of U-boat sinkings in the Atlantic approaches to our islands" was "more serious than the air raids" of the Blitz. That same month, banana imports were stopped; the next month, the meat ration was ordered reduced. No cryptanalyst could envision a way of cracking the naval Enigma and reading the U-boat messages so as to steer the convoys bringing supplies to Britain out of harm's way.

Still, though Hut 8 had had little success throughout 1940, and despite the increasing strain, the atmosphere in the group was not disheartened but industrious. Then, early in 1941, another clue to the naval Enigma arrived, as tantalizing as it was helpful.

Ten

In the Locked Drawer of the *Krebs*

THE CENTRAL ACTOR was a blue-eyed baronet, Lieutenant Sir Marshall George Clitheroe Warmington, signals officer aboard the destroyer *Somali*. The son and grandson of London barristers, Warmington had been brought up in Great Missenden, Buckinghamshire, and educated at Charterhouse, one of England's better public schools. He wanted to join the cavalry, but his father vetoed that, and in 1928 he found himself in the Navy on the H.M.S. *Erebus*, a training ship. Warmington felt that this converted World War I monitor exceeded its name by being not just an anteroom to hell but hell itself. The future officers ate and slept and worked in a gunroom in which they couldn't stand upright. When the showers were working, they either scalded or froze those standing under them. Though the *Erebus* was docked at Devonport, the men were allowed ashore only twice a week, and then they had to be back by 7:30 P.M. The experience was rather squalid, but it was apt: the whole Navy, Warmington thought later, was rather squalid at the time.

This inauguration was followed by tours in the Mediterranean and in the Home Fleet, by study at Greenwich and Portsmouth, and then by long months of patrol under the broiling Red Sea sun. His ships, the *Penzance* and the *Hastings,* were supposed to be stopping the Arab slave trade, but they never did: the slave traders simply avoided them. Their real purpose was to show the flag. So the ships sailed from Aden near the mouth of the Red Sea to Malta in the middle of the Mediterranean, calling at Jedda and Port Sudan, nosing into the Gulf of Aqaba, passing British and French Somaliland. The tedium of idleness and of four-hour watches on the bridge was broken only by a bit of gunnery practice and some fishing from the motorboat. In August 1935, upon his father's death, Warmington succeeded him as third baronet, becoming a member of the lowest hereditary order, whose members, not peers, are addressed in society as "Sir." In the navy, however, all of the officers addressed one another by last name alone.

In December 1935, Warmington returned to Portsmouth for a year-long course in communications, or signals, as the Royal Navy called it. He liked the field, but the course was "jolly hard work": Morse code training twice each day to reach at least twenty-five words per minute, visual flag signals, wireless technique and technology, the communications aspects of maneuvering the fleet, codes and ciphers. Warmington then served for a couple of years as a signals officer for a submarine flotilla. After the war began, he was transferred to the staff of the forces that helped evacuate the tattered British forces from Dunkirk after Hitler's blitzkrieg smashed France. Then, to his pleasure, he was assigned to the *Somali*.

She was a member of the newest, largest class of destroyers in the Royal Navy. Earlier classes had been small, handy vessels with good torpedo armament, but the building by Italy and Japan of large fast destroyers with heavy gun armament, and indications that Germany might do the same, led the Admiralty to design a counterforce. The new ships, almost half again as big as the older ones, would double the number of the older classes' guns but halve their torpedo armament — a revolutionary design that some criticized as being more like that of a small cruiser than of a big destroyer. When a drawing was submitted to the Board of Admiralty for approval, one of the sea lords criticized the straight stem and penciled in a slight curve. This "proud nostril curve" in the profile of the bow distinguished the new class, which was called Tribal because its members bore the names of native tribes, many of the British Empire: *Zulu, Ashanti, Sikh, Cossack, Tartar, Maori*.

The keels of six Tribals were laid down in 1936. They displaced 1,959 tons and carried eight 4.7-inch guns, each of which hurled a 50-pound shell 10 miles, and four torpedoes in tubes. The vessels were not armored. Their speed was excellent, a little above 35 knots. The normal wartime complement was around 220, but some Tribals were fitted out as flotilla leaders with accommodations for the additional men and officers needed to command the eight vessels.

One such leader was the *Somali,* named for the Hamitic herders and fisher folk of the Horn of Africa. Launched in August 1938, the *Somali* was the first Home Fleet Tribal to be completed. After the others were commissioned, the *Somali*'s captain became the leader of the Home Fleet's Sixth Destroyer Flotilla; in Royal Navy parlance he was the "Captain (D)." The *Somali* became the first Royal Navy vessel to capture a prize at sea in World War II when, two hours after war was declared, she seized the *Hannah Böge* of Hamburg, which was carrying wood pulp from Canada. Later she engaged in operations in Norwegian waters, including the bombardment of Narvik. Soon thereafter Warmington joined the crew.

During the winter of 1940–41 some days were spent in practice with the guns or with the asdic gear for detecting and locating submarines or in antisubmarine exercises. Other days the destroyers screened heavier warships that were searching for a German raider or merchantman. Lookouts on both sides of the bridge scanned the horizon through their heavy 8×41 binoculars for five minutes, then were relieved by others for five minutes, and so on for one hour, after which both pairs were relieved. Visibility was often poor: during one five-day period the lookouts could see more than 10 miles for a total of only five hours. Many times, fog and mist reduced visibility to a mile or less. The strain, the chill of the North Atlantic, the days of four-hour watches, the wet — all wearied the men. But in some rare but lovely moments, the sea was calm and moonlit, and the lookouts could see out to the very rim of the horizon.

Then, early in 1941, orders came that broke the tiresome routine of training exercises and North Sea sweeps. The *Somali* was going to lead four other Tribals and two troop carriers on a commando raid on German-occupied Norway.

The raid had several specific objectives. One was to destroy herring- and cod-oil factories that were providing the Germans with valuable nutriments, in particular Vitamin A, it was said. Another was to perfect interservice cooperation in amphibious operations. Still other objectives were to arrest quislings (Norwegians collaborating with the occupiers), capture Germans, and evacuate Norwegians who wanted to fight for the Norwegian government in exile in London. An important purpose was to tie down large enemy forces by keeping realistic the threat of attacks anywhere along the Norwegian coast. Britain's leaders also perhaps entertained the hopes that a success might boost British morale: a raid was practically the only offensive action that Britain could take in those days when she stood alone against a continent overrun by Nazi forces. Finally, the British would be glad for any documents that they might seize.

Preparations for the raid began late in February. The naval commander was Captain Clifford Caslon, commanding officer simultaneously of the *Somali* and the Sixth Destroyer Flotilla. More a staff officer than a sailor, he was very efficient. He could wiggle his ears, and his officers soon learned that when he laid them flat against his head he was angry. Nevertheless, Warmington regarded Caslon as rather tender-hearted.

Anchored at the great naval base of Scapa Flow, the *Somali* and four other Tribals awaited the commandos. The 500-man detachment, supported by engineers and Norwegian volunteers, arrived in the early afternoon of February 22. For a week, the naval and military officers went over the plans for the raid in minute detail. Warmington arranged for shore-to-ship communications, instructing the sailors in the use of the commandos' radio sets. The occupants of the landing craft and their crews got to know one another. With preparations completed, the little task force of destroyers and troopships, now codenamed REBEL, got under way. At one minute after midnight, on Saturday, March 1, it passed the antisubmarine booms and the blockships and headed north.

The target was the Lofoten Islands. This archipelago lies above the Arctic Circle just south of where the Norwegian coast turns east to top off Europe. From north to south the strip of mountainous islands angles away from the cliff-sided coastline, leaving a bay, Vestfjord, in the shape of an inverted V. Scattered near its apex were the fishing towns with the fish-oil factories. Around the tip of the southwesternmost large island swirled the Maelstrom. Though this was not the giant fatal whirlpool of legend, with Edgar Allan Poe's "smooth, shining, and jet-black wall of water," its powerful currents did endanger ships. Indeed, strong currents and strong winds made sailing difficult and dangerous throughout the Lofotens.

Task force REBEL, after refueling in the Faeroes, reached what it called Point P, some 600 miles north of Scapa, at 1:30 A.M. on Monday, and turned almost due east for the 320-mile march to Point Q, at the mouth of Vestfjord. The weather favored the trip: the winds were gentle and the sea moderate to flat. The sky was overcast with low clouds, and snow showers reduced the chances of detection. The daily German meteorological flight did not spot the ships. Occasional breaks in the cloud cover permitted astronomical position fixes, which were confirmed by radio bearings taken on signals emitted by the Royal Navy submarine *Sunfish*, stationed near Point Q. REBEL passed Point Q a little after midnight on March 4, swung northeast, and moved up Vestfjord. At 4:30 A.M. the task force reached Point C, on the west side of the inverted V. Fifteen minutes later the light had grown strong enough for the lookouts to see the coastline. The wind was a light breeze, the sea calm, the temperature in the low twenties.

The previous morning a German weather flight had spotted a northbound force of one cruiser and five destroyers off the waist of Norway, some 200 miles south of where REBEL then was. The Kriegsmarine's Admiral Polar Coast had ordered "increased watchfulness" for all coastal observation stations, patrol boats, and batteries. But coastal navigation lights were not extinguished.

By between 5:30 and 6 A.M., the Royal Navy ships heading for three of the ports to be attacked had reached their stations. The *Somali*, another destroyer, and one of the troop carriers continued on to the fourth and most northeasterly of the ports. They crept by the 921-foot-high hump of the island of Skraaven, to their left. Only then, in the twilight, were they seen by lookouts there. The Germans raised the alarm. The commandant of the Narvik Sea Defense Zone was warned. Coastal batteries were alerted. The Luftwaffe was asked to send bombers. A minesweeping unit that was about to go to sea was stopped. Navigation lights were belatedly turned off. Messages came in about the other destroyers. The harbor captain of Svolvaer, the principal port of the Lofotens, reported, "Destroyer in harbor; we're leaving." But he was captured anyway, and the Luftwaffe never arrived.

Aboard the troop carriers, the commandos readied their equipment and climbed into their landing craft. They were to go ashore at 6:45. At 6:10, after assuring himself that the troop carrier that the *Somali* and another destroyer were escorting had almost reached its position for the attack, Caslon swung the *Somali* around and headed south to check on the activity at the other ports. Again she had to pass mile-long Skraaven, this time on her starboard. Once past the island, she could look over the water toward Svolvaer. And coming from that direction she saw, at about 6:20, a whaling trawler that had been converted into a patrol vessel by the mounting of a small gun in her bows and a heavy machine gun aft. It was the *Krebs* ("shrimp" in Norwegian, "crab" in German), commanded by Lieutenant Hans Kapfinger. Her usual function was probably to prevent Norwegians from sailing from the Lofotens to the Shetlands, where they could escape the occupation and join the fight against the Germans. But now, summoned by the alert, she was bravely coming out to do battle with the vastly superior forces that had invaded her domain. Caslon trained his guns on the little ship, then a little under 2 miles distant, and opened fire.

His first shots were high and did little damage. Then, with what Warmington thought was "all the guts in the world," the *Krebs* fired back at the British warship. None of her three rounds struck the *Somali*, but one holed a flag flying from the destroyer's forearm, which angered Caslon. His next three shots devastated the trawler. One detonated the ready ammunition; one burst in the wheelhouse; the third exploded in the boiler room. Smoke issued from the vessel, which appeared to have gone out of control. The *Somali* ceased fire. Survivors were seen in the water, and the destroyer went to rescue them.

The *Somali*'s No. 1, or executive officer, the second in command, was Lieutenant Henry A. Stuart-Menteth, a career officer of the Royal Navy. His former destroyer, the *Hunter,* had been sunk in 1940 during the Norwegian campaign; Stuart-Menteth had been wounded in the leg in the action and was unconscious when the Germans pulled him from the water. He didn't know where he was when he came to in a hospital, but the pictures of Hitler quickly brought him to his senses. Still, he remained grateful to the Germans for having saved his life — and for leaving him behind when they temporarily quit Narvik in the face of British attacks. Now, seeing the Germans swimming in the icy Vestfjord waters and watching one man in particular struggle, he reminded himself, "They hauled me out." He clambered down the net thrown over the ship's side and pulled the man aboard.

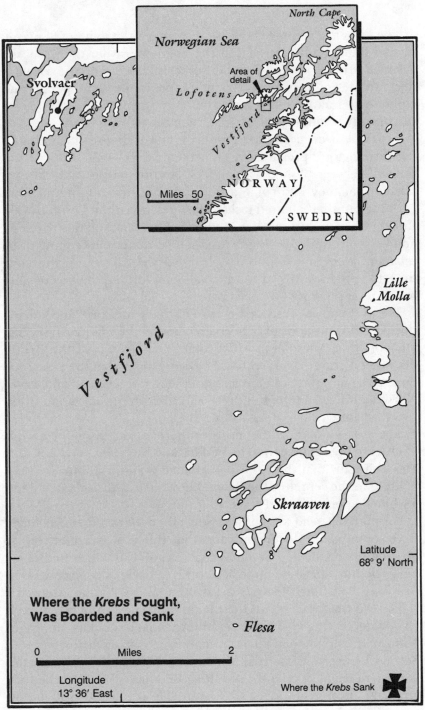

North Cape

Norwegian Sea

Area of
detail

Lofotens

Vestfjord

0 Miles 50

N O R W A Y

S W E D E N

Svolvaer

Lille
. Molla

V e s t f j o r d

Skraaven

Latitude
68° 9′ North

Where the *Krebs* Fought,
Was Boarded and Sank

0   Miles   2

· *Flesa*

Longitude
13° 36′ East

Where the *Krebs* Sank

The *Krebs* had stranded on a low, flat, rocky islet south of Skraaven named Flesa. So the *Somali* left the helpless trawler there. As she steamed off, a wounded German stoker climbed onto the trawler's deck. In the engine room he burned some of the secret papers and cipher material. Unable to help the two petty officers and two sailors who lay wounded above deck, he jumped onto Flesa.

At 7:10 Caslon permitted radio communications, which, thanks to Warmington's preparations, functioned excellently. Contact was immediately established with all four landing parties, and they reported that they had come ashore without opposition and were carrying out their allotted tasks. They destroyed the Lofotens Cod Boiling Plant and the Moller Medicinal Oil Plant and destroyed oil and kerosene tanks, setting fire to their contents and sending great pillars of black smoke into the clear Norwegian sky. At the same time, the other destroyers and naval demolition parties were sinking ships and taking Germans prisoner.

The cod run in Vestfjord from February to April, and during this period thousands of fishermen come to the islands. They had left port that Tuesday morning before the extent of the British operation became clear, and as they came to see that the attack was directed against the Germans and not them, they cheered and waved Norwegian flags on the hundreds of little fishing smacks and puffers that dotted the waters around the ports.

The *Somali* stood off the most southerly of the ports for a while to observe operations, then turned back to Svolvaer. As she passed Flesa, she saw that the *Krebs* had refloated and, still burning, was drifting to the center of the fjord. The *Somali* approached and saw a white flag being waved.

Warmington, who was on the bridge, thought that the *Krebs* might have some useful documents and that this was a rare chance to board an enemy ship. He knew that Caslon was concerned about being tied down, so he appealed to his superior's compassion: he proposed boarding the *Krebs* to save the sailors. Caslon assented.

To save time and retain the maximum freedom of movement, Caslon decided against lowering his own boat or coming alongside. Instead he summoned the commandos' Norwegian interpreter. Second Lieutenant Leonard M. Harper-Gow, a tall, imposing former member of Scotland's Ayrshire Yeomanry, had learned the language during summers in Norway. He was below, sulking because he had not been allowed ashore for the action; the communications were excellent and it was better for him to be at sea and mobile than fixed on land. Topside, he hailed a Norwegian fishing boat with "Halloo! Halloo!" When it came alongside, he explained what he wanted it to do. The skipper agreed, and at 9:10 Warmington, Harper-Gow, and another officer, Major A. R. Aslett, were ferried over to the *Krebs*.

She was still smoldering. In the wreckage of the wheelhouse, they found four or five bodies, including that of the captain, Kapfinger, next to the wheel. Five sailors cowered on deck; two were badly wounded, one having lost a lot of muscle in his arm, the other hit in the head.

Aslett flourished his service revolver and Warmington his own cocked Belgian pistol (the navy did not issue regulation handguns). The five men offered no resistance. Warmington put his pistol into the duffel coat he was wearing and hastily looked around. He found no signal books or codebooks and no cipher devices; evidently they had been jettisoned before the *Somali*'s shell struck the wheelhouse. He did find a pair of binoculars, which he liberated. Harper-Gow kept Kapfinger's cap; someone pinched the range finder. The *Krebs* was still burning below, and no one could enter the engine room or the forepeak. But in the captain's cabin Warmington found the Kriegsmarine's gridded chart of European waters from Iceland to Norway, some personal papers, and a variety of documents, some of which appeared to be secret. All these he swept up. The other two Britons grabbed other papers. Then, in going through the drawers, Warmington found one locked.

"If it's locked," he said to himself, "there must be something there."

He pulled out his pistol to shoot the lock off, as he had seen it done in movies. He cocked the gun, aimed it at the lock, looked away, and pulled the trigger. The gun fired; the lock fell apart. Warmington pulled open the drawer. Inside was a wooden box about 9 by 5 by 3 inches. He took it out and opened it. There, unharmed, lay two black disks about the size of hockey pucks, with electrical contacts and letters around the circumference and an indented flange. He had never seen anything like that before — the Royal Navy used codebooks and he knew nothing of the Enigma machine — but he recognized that they had to be for ciphering. He closed the box and looked about the cabin a bit more.

He did not have time to search the wireless office before the

Somali flashed for them to return. They had been aboard the *Krebs* for forty-five minutes, and Caslon may have been worried about air attacks. Warmington handed the charts and other papers to Aslett but kept the rotor box as the three officers got the five prisoners onto the Norwegian vessel that had ferried them over. The *Somali* rewarded the Norwegian fishermen with cigarettes and food. Once back on the *Somali*, Warmington gave the box to Caslon, who glanced at the rotors, understood what they were, and sent the box directly to his sea cabin, the room just beneath the bridge where destroyer captains spent most of their time at sea when not on the bridge. Warmington never saw the box again: Caslon was very security-minded. Aslett gave Caslon the papers the three had collected.

As the action on land continued, the *Somali* sought to sink the *Krebs*. It was not easy. Whalers were built very sturdily to withstand the ice of the northern seas. Twice the destroyer steamed past the *Krebs* and dropped depth charges near her; the charges shook the British warship and sent her cutlery flying but left the *Krebs* undisturbed. Then the *Somali* fired a broadside: the *Krebs* rocked but stayed afloat. The gunfire finally took effect, and at 10:30 the *Krebs* sank, taking with her the eighteen bodies of her twenty-four-man crew.

By this time the commandos were reembarking. They had sunk 10 ships, destroyed 18 fish-meal and oil factories, and set afire 800,000 gallons of oil. They took with them 12 quislings and 213 German servicemen, civilians, policemen, and merchant mariners. A Norwegian trawler escaped to the Faeroes. At 1:30 P.M., the destroyers and the troop carriers assembled and, in day cruising order, set course at best speed down Vestfjord, leaving a pall of smoke over the scene of the day's operations. At 4 P.M., Caslon radioed the success of the mission to the Admiralty, but said nothing about the cipher wheels or the other documents.

As it turned out, these included nothing less than the Enigma key tables for February: the inner and outer settings and the plugboard setting. Upon his return to Scapa, Caslon forwarded everything to the director of naval intelligence. From there the cipher material went to Bletchley Park.

Eleven

Kisses

DESPITE THE DRAMA of their recovery, the rotors that Lieutenant Warmington had gotten did not help Hut 8; it already had them. What did help were the February Enigma keys, registry number 1566, indicator HAU, that had been scooped up from the *Krebs*. When the keys arrived on Wednesday, March 12, Alan Turing receipted for them and immediately put them to work.

The volume of solutions jumped at once. On March 12, Naval Section teletyped ten messages to O.I.C.; on the thirteenth, thirty-four. The volume remained at that level or higher for almost a week, as Hut 8 read much of the Home Waters back traffic for February. The number of messages teletyped to O.I.C. declined thereafter, but within five weeks Hut 8 had read the back traffic for all of February. The knowledge gained from these solutions helped the cryptanalysts crack, between April 22 and May 26, all of the naval Enigma traffic for April. Later they read, with delays reduced to only about a week, much of the May traffic. Though this did not have much immediate effect on the sea war, it provided information for a series of events that did. And by showing that the naval Enigma could be broken, it led G.C.&C.S. to bring in more people as cryptanalysts on that problem.

Turing recruited his friend Shaun Wylie, whom he knew from Princeton, where both had obtained doctorates in mathematics. Wylie, another member of Hut 8 said, "had a very exact logical mind. When he understood anything, he seemed to understand it completely. . . . Shaun was a perfect gentleman who never lost his temper except on purpose, and was an extremely good listener. I used to believe that he wouldn't interrupt a conversation even to mention that the war was over." An international hockey player and a first-rate teacher, Wylie eventually became president of the Bletchley Park dramatic club and a winner of the unarmed combat competition of the local battalion of the Home Guard. He never mentioned any of his accomplishments.

The coworker who made these observations came to Bletchley six months after Wylie. He was Irving John Good, a short, wiry Cambridge mathematician who had been born Isidor Jacob Gudak, the son of a London shopkeeper. At Cambridge he had won the prestigious Smith mathematics prize and, placed on the draft-deferred list for scientific work, was doing postdoctoral work in his field, unhappy that it was not war work. One day the university employment office summoned him for an interview. As he was walking to the appointment, a friend told him to wear his scarf inside his coat, not outside, so he would look less like an undergraduate. The scarf may have helped, but more important was that one of the three Bletchley men who interviewed him was Hugh Alexander, with whom he had played chess. Good always suspected that he was taken on because he played chess well. When he reported to Bletchley, Alexander met him at the railroad station. As they walked, he told Good about the Enigma in a sensational conversation that Good would never forget. He was pleased and excited to realize that his work would be of immense importance to the war effort.

In Hut 8, his first assignment was to read a badly typed, very technical, very hard-to-follow description of the Enigma and how the cryptanalysts were attacking it. Presently he asked Turing, "How on earth did we get the wiring of the rotors?" Turing, who was seated at a table with his friend Joan Clarke, replied briefly, "Perhaps the Poles."

"Perhaps a pinch?" Good suggested.

"Something like that," said Turing, and Good saw that he should not ask any more questions.

G.C.&C.S. was wise — or desperate — enough to enlist women as cryptanalysts as well as clerks. Before the war Hilary Brett-Smith had been teaching Anglo-Saxon at various Oxford colleges; the students thought the subject was boring, and she enjoyed converting them by explaining such things as why English speakers today say "foot" and "feet" but not "book" and "beek." She was casting about for some war work when one day, just after the evacuation from Dunkirk, a mathematician whom she had known from the Dragon School, a private grammar school in Oxford, who was now at Bletchley, urged her to go there and work, though he couldn't tell her what the work was. Since the Foreign Office paid more than the War Office and was regarded as rather grand to work for, Brett-Smith accepted. And because of the gender ambiguousness of "Hilary," some clerk somewhere assumed she was a man and allotted her a man's salary. When she was recruited it seemed likely, because of her linguistic background, that she would work on making the many card listings of foreign technical terms and names; but in fact she began in Hut 8, working with Turing and Twinn and chess expert Harry Golombek.

One of the most intuitive of the cryptanalysts was Mavis Lever, who was eighteen when she arrived at Bletchley. She was sent there because she had studied German at London University. Assigned to work with Knox at the Cottage, she received her introduction to his arcane labors with the greeting, "Hello! We're breaking machines! Have you a pencil? Well, here you are." It was Lever who discovered that the baffling hexagram STGOCH did not stand for "St. Goch," a place or sanctified soul that none of the pundits had been able to find in any gazetteer or catalogue of religious names; nor was it an error for "St. Roch," a town in France, but instead was an abbreviation for "Santiago, Chile." It was also she who sensed something strange in an Italian Enigma intercept, realized after a moment that the message had not a single *l* in it and, knowing that the Enigma never replaced a plaintext letter with the same letter, concluded that the message was a dummy whose plaintext consisted entirely of *l*'s. She used this to reconstruct the key. Lever was a member of the team whose solution of Italian naval Enigma messages led the British to their victory over the Italian fleet at Cape Matapan — a victory that made the British masters of the eastern Mediterranean. After the battle Rear Admiral Godfrey, the director of naval intelligence, rang Naval Section and asked to speak to Knox. When told he was at home, Godfrey said, "Tell Dilly we have won a great victory in the Med and it is entirely due to him and his girls."

Few of the women at Bletchley reached such high levels. Most served in indispensable clerical positions as typists, filers, or decipherers of messages once the cryptanalysts had found the key. Many were subdebutantes or postdebutantes — daughters of earls who wanted to do their bit to win the war. Though the work was sometimes boring, they did not complain: many of them would never have had jobs in peacetime, and they loved working. They were extremely security-conscious and did not discuss what they were doing with chums outside B.P. One day the king visited. He saw a young woman who was a friend of his daughter, Princess Elizabeth, and asked her what she was doing there. "I can't tell you, sir," she replied. Like the others, she took her responsibilities very seriously indeed.

Bletchley Park was by now working at peak energy, if not yet at peak strength. Its workers, both the old-timers and the newcomers, were billeted in pubs and cottages in a radius of a dozen miles or so around the Park. Harry Hinsley shared half a cottage with two other Oxbridge types; a farmer and his wife and a cleaning girl lived in the other half and kept them tidy. Alan Turing lived at the Crown Inn at Shenley Brook End, a hamlet 3 miles to the north. He bicycled to work each day, but many of the thousand-odd staffers were brought to their jobs by buses, which made three circuits a day to cover all shifts. The workers ate together in a mess hall. Bletchley was not military and hence rather democratic. Uniforms were worn rarely; rank was sought mainly for greater pay or recognition, but it seldom affected relations among individuals because they knew the war work would not determine their futures. At a time when beards were rare in the general population, they were not uncommon at B.P. The inmates recognized what an odd collection they were. As one worker observed, "To work there, you needn't be mad, but it does help!"

In good weather the Bletchleyites sat on the lawn, walked, or played tennis or rounders or croquet. During these games, the journalist Malcolm Muggeridge, temporarily assigned there, observed that the players assumed

> the quasi-serious manner dons affect when engaged in activities likely to be regarded as frivolous or insignificant in comparison with their weightier studies. Thus they would dispute some point about the game with the same fervour as they might the question of free will or determinism, or whether the world began with a big bang or a process of continuing creation. Shaking their heads ponderously,

sucking air noisily into their noses between words [they would say], "I thought mine was the surer stroke," or: "I can assert without fear of contradiction that my right foot was already . . ."

In the evening, for those not working the night shift, the Bletchley Park Recreational Club offered rooms for coffee, newspapers, the radio, and quiet, as well as a library, a drama group, a musical society, bridge, chess, dances twice a week, badminton, and fencing. Groups, often quite talented, put on plays, revues, concerts, even operas. Romances flourished. Muggeridge wrote: "The females, too, were mostly donnish; either dons' molls, with solemnly pretty faces, studiously amorous or amorously studious, according to their temperaments or the exigencies of the occasion; or themselves academics, grey, untidy, rough and hairy and spluttering." Many women met men who became their husbands. Hilary Brett-Smith moved into the other half of the cottage Harry Hinsley was living in and came to feel that he needed a woman to buy him socks when they wore out. They married, and so did a great many others.

Hut 8's cryptanalytic section was divided into two groups. One group worked in an oblong room with three wooden tables, two chairs at each, and a rack for wide sheets of paper that were prepared in Banbury, a town just north of Oxford. The cryptanalysts called the procedure performed on intercepts in this room using the sheets "banburismus." It attacked intercepts for which no cribs could be envisioned.

The sheets were of heavy white paper about 10 inches from top to bottom. Printed on each were dozens of vertical A-to-Z alphabets side by side. The sheets varied in width from 2 to 5 feet, the narrower sheets being used for the shorter German intercepts. The young civilian women assigned to Hut 8, working from the "red forms," or intercepts on pink paper, punched out, in the successive alphabets of a sheet, the successive letters of an intercept. They did this twice on a sheet for a single intercept, then repeated the procedure with other intercepts of the day. Next they placed a sheet on one of the tables, with its dark surface, and laid another sheet on top of it, aligning the first alphabets above one another. Here and there dark spots appeared where two punched holes, representing the same letter, coincided. They counted the number of spots, then slid the top sheet one place to the right and counted the number of spots that appeared then. The women continued this procedure, later shifting the top sheet to the left, until all the statistically valid positions had been tabulated.

Few spots at a position represented only the coincidences that chance might produce. This was the case with most positions for most pairs of messages. Many spots, however, could mean that the two messages had been enciphered with the same rotors at the same positions. If the messages were long enough, and if several were found to have key overlaps, statistical analysis could sometimes show, on the basis of the number of spots, where this synchronization of the rotors had been ended by the middle rotor's being turned one place by the rightmost rotor. Analysis could sometimes determine the ring position of this rotor. And since each of the rotors I through V had the notch in its alphabet ring in a distinctive place — at R in rotor I, at F in rotor II, and so on (Royal Flags Wave Kings Above) — counting from the starting ring position could show where the notch was and so identify the rotor. (This did not work, of course, for rotors VI, VII, and VIII, because the navy had notched all of those rotors at H and U.) Knowing which rotor was in the rightmost position cut down on the number of trials the bombes would have to make, thereby saving precious bombe time and so speeding solutions.

The statistical determination of where the synchronization ended used a method developed by the eighteenth-century English mathematician Thomas Bayes. Turing took it a step further by inventing units in which the Bayesian calculation could be made. Basing his terminology on the cryptanalytic procedure, he defined a "ban" as a bit of evidence that would make a hypothesis ten times more likely than otherwise. He considered that a deciban, or a tenth of a ban, was about the smallest change in weight of evidence that is "directly perceptible to human intuition." So "deciban" became another of the singular terms used at Bletchley. A later refinement into half decibans, or HDBs, led to the cryptanalysts' talking to one another about "hudubs." Another technique, for improving the scoring of long repeats, was sarcastically called "romsing," for "resources of modern science."

Hugh Alexander was the champ at banburismus. He had a better feel than the others for the overlaps and the end of the synchronization and the figuring of the ring positions. But others sometimes had their lucky shots: once Good found a twenty-two-letter repeat, making the others rather jealous. Good liked the work. As he pondered letter chains, alphabets, probabilities, he was concentrating as if he were playing chess. The problems were hard enough to keep him absorbed but not so hard as to make him want to give up. Above all, the importance of the task motivated him.

The banburismus room was mostly quiet. There was little talk. And the feeling in it was good. The members got along well with one another; quarrels were rare. Workers often arrived ten to fifteen minutes early for their shifts so their colleagues would not have to work overtime. Those who were leaving would explain that they had found some chains of letters or some alphabets to enable those arriving to pick up the work, primarily the identification of ring positions. The cryptanalysts slid strips of paper with letter chains under alphabets to see if anything matched or looked good. In view of the Enigma's reciprocal substitution, they would reject an alphabet or a chain that produced an R, say, against an R — a "crash." They examined sheets of paper with the banburismus scores on them. Curiously enough, they rarely looked at the actual intercepts.

Banburismus was not used in cases where cribs were available. This was the job of the other part of Hut 8. Assumed plaintexts were set against cryptograms that were thought to be their ciphertexts, chains of letters were derived to generate possible bombe starting positions, called menus, and the possible keys were tested to see whether they revealed plaintext. The technique called for linguistic skills: Wylie, who had had a classical education before becoming a mathematician, and Brett-Smith, the Anglo-Saxonist, worked in the crib room.

By early 1941, most cribs came from "kisses" — identical messages transmitted in two cryptosystems, one of which G.C.&C.S. could read. Hut 4, which handled non-Enigma naval systems, was then reading the German navy's Dockyard Cipher currently. Among the more important messages it carried were those dealing with new mines discovered in a channel that had previously been swept clear. This information had to be reported to all vessels using the channel. But since auxiliary support vessels, smaller patrol boats, and minesweepers carried Dockyard but not Enigma, while combat U-boats carried Enigma but not Dockyard, the same information was transmitted in two cryptosystems. Often the two plaintexts were identical, since the drafter of the message did not know of the danger of this situation, and the communicators either did not care about it or refused to change the wording. When one of the Dockyard cryptanalysts in Hut 4, such as Christopher Morris, saw a solution that looked as if it might serve as a crib for an Enigma message, he carried it next door to Hut 8, where the codebreakers there sought to fit it to a cryptogram. And not infrequently it worked.

Indeed, so valuable was this technique that when kisses were needed, the British would sometimes sow mines anew in the channels that the Germans had swept and so provoke a flurry of messages that such and such a route was closed between two specified points — messages enciphered in both readable Dockyard and unreadable Enigma. The British called this technique "gardening."

Once, for example, the Admiralty messaged the Air Ministry that "special planting of willow is urgently required." Two days later, the British harvested from the airways a German "most immediate" message. Perhaps with the help of a Dockyard kiss, G.C.&C.S. solved it within three days. The message was, "Squares BF2927 and 2928 [off the north Brittany coast] closed owing to danger of mines."

Despite the help of kisses, solutions remained irregular. On April 30, 1941, for example, Bletchley teleprinted to the Admiralty's Operational Intelligence Centre eighteen messages: eleven general naval and seven U-boat messages. They were the first solutions to be sent in a week, and all of them were at least twelve days old.

The paucity of solutions meant that the O.I.C.'s Submarine Tracking Room had to obtain much of its information on U-boat locations from direction-finding, or DF. The DF section was headed by retired Lieutenant Commander Peter Kemp, who had lost a leg in a submarine in the late 1920s. When war threatened, he was called up for intelligence duty. Feeding him his data were eight direction-finding posts, from the Shetlands through Wick and Cupar in Scotland; Scarborough, Winchester, Lydd, and Land's End in England; and Gibraltar; later stations were added at Chelmsford, in Iceland, and eventually on the Azores. All were connected to Scarborough, the oldest intercept station, halfway up England's east coast. When Scarborough heard a U-boat radio message, it notified the other stations through direct landlines to take bearings on it. The stations reported these bearings to Kemp's section in the Admiralty, which took up a quarter of the Submarine Tracking Room.

Here Kemp had rigged an ingenious device that avoided the constant penciling in and erasing of successive bearings on charts. On a sloping board he pasted a chart of Britain and the North Atlantic. On its frame were scales indicating the bearings, in degrees, from each station. He drilled holes through the position of each direction-finding station and threaded a black string through each. On one end of the string was a pin; on the other, a weight. When a bearing from a station came in, Kemp or his watch leader pulled up the string and stuck the pin into the station's scale at the proper bearing. He did the same for the bearings from other stations. The area where the strings converged marked the location of the transmitter. This was a fix.

Every bearing, and consequently every fix, had a margin of error. How great it was depended upon cold fronts at sea, electrical storms, the different groundings of the DF posts, their weather, the height of the ionosphere, the experience of the DF operator. At the better stations the operators erred in their bearings usually by no more than plus or minus 3 degrees. In general, with half a dozen bearings, DF could locate a submarine within 25 miles. If this fix was close to a convoy, Kemp would have a signal sent to the convoy escort to warn him of the proximate danger.

At the time that Kemp's unit was supplying a substantial portion of the intelligence the O.I.C. was receiving, that agency was undergoing a significant change in personnel in its Submarine Tracking Room. The room's first head was a paymaster commander who had tracked U-boats for Room 40 in World War I: Ernest W. C. Thring. He set the tone of caution and skepticism so essential to accurate intelligence. When it was claimed, often hotly, that a U-boat had been sunk, he remained cool. "He lay skeptically at the center of his web," wrote one who observed him, "unimpressed by oil, unpersuaded by a corpse floating, according a reluctant 'probable' to what others might regard as overwhelming circumstantial evidence."

But as no signs of a breakthrough appeared in the Battle of the Atlantic, dissatisfaction grew with Thring's conservatism. He believed that guessing a submarine's future movements was too dangerous. Moreover, he was over sixty and disinclined to accept that both Britons and Germans might be using methods different from those of the previous war; he was difficult with coworkers, and his health was declining. In January 1941 Thring was replaced by his assistant.

The move was revolutionary: the assistant was not a career officer but a thirty-seven-year-old barrister appointed a temporary commander in the Royal Naval Volunteer Reserve; for the hidebound navy to appoint a civilian to such a critical department was unprecedented. But those who sought the change knew their man.

Rodger Winn had worked under Thring since August 1939. He was of medium height, broad, with powerful shoulders but a twisted back and a limp, the consequences of childhood poliomyelitis, which had kept him from realizing his ambition to join the navy. In the Submarine Tracking Room he often rested his hands on the edge of a table to take some of the weight off his legs. He was hardworking, intellectually honest, and pleasant to deal with, in part because of his good sense of humor and the many stories he told about his legal experiences. He was also hard-driving, intolerant of laziness or stupidity and, like Thring, inflexible in his standards of evidence. But above all he was willing to forecast U-boat movements. He felt that if he beat the law of averages by only 1 percent, he was ahead of the game in terms of Allied lives and ships saved and U-boats sunk.

Soon after Winn took over, the whole Operational Intelligence Centre moved from the subbasement of the Admiralty to the so-called Citadel, a modern, bombproof concrete bunker at the rear of the Admiralty. The Submarine Tracking Room, deep within the bowels of the Citadel, was dominated by a huge table, about seven feet square, brilliantly illuminated by overhead lights. On the table lay a map of the North Atlantic, dotted with pins and markers indicating Allied convoys and German U-boats. Stuck to the walls of the room were graphs of sinkings and of the construction of ships by the Allies. On a side table was spread the German naval grid, with its map of the vast ocean spaces marked off into lettered rectangles, each subdivided into numbered squares. Here Winn and his half-dozen assistants assembled information from air and sea sightings of submarines, from sinkings, agents' reports, direction-finding, and aerial photographs, and from intercepts teleprinted from Hut 8, their most important source. They collated these varied data to determine the number and location of U-boats at sea and, if possible, their identity, all to generate the U-boat plot.

The work involved an incredible mass of detail. Bits of seemingly contradictory information had to be reduced to their common germ of truth. Other bits had to be fitted into an overall pattern. Recollections of earlier references to a submarine or to an episode similar to the one at hand had to be summoned. Winn and his staff had to have intimate knowledge of convoys and U-boats, sources, and situations to make sense of it all and to recommend actions.

A little while after the flamboyant, abrasive Admiral Sir Max Horton took over as commander in chief Western Approaches, the man who largely ran the Battle of the Atlantic, he attacked Winn at a meeting of the antisubmarine warfare committee for an inadequate evaluation. Winn replied that if Horton would give him half an hour, he would lay out all the intelligence available to him at the time. When Horton arrived, he was confronted with a pile of varied intelligence reports. "It's all yours, sir," said Winn, "and" — slipping in a needle — "your chief of staff in Liverpool is in a devil of a hurry for the answer." Horton settled down to intense study. After a while, however, he turned to Winn and confessed that most of it was outside his province. With a smile, he extended his hand and said, "Goodbye, Rodger. I leave it to you." And thereafter he did.

Winn provided his information to the Operations and Anti-Submarine Warfare divisions, but he dealt most intimately with the Trade Division's Movements Section, which controlled convoys and ordered their reroutings. This section, just across a corridor, was headed by Commander Richard A. Hall, son of a famous World War I naval intelligence chief. He, like Winn, could hold strong views about what was happening at sea. One officer said of Hall and Winn, "If those two ever stop bickering, we shall lose the war."

* * *

By the spring of 1941, with the volume of solutions low and delays lengthy, an occasional sighting by a British ship or airplane or an actual attack on a convoy comprised virtually the only information the O.I.C. had about the location and movements of German submarines. Though its Submarine Tracking Room could tally the number of U-boats on patrol fairly accurately, it did not know — and direction-finding could not tell it — where Dönitz was sending them. So it could do little more than guess where the convoys should be routed to steer them around the wolf packs. And the number of U-boats increased by a third from January to April 1941.

Churchill expressed his concern in a broadcast to the nation. After paying homage to the shipwrights, the longshoremen, the minesweepers, and the merchant seamen "who go out in all weathers and in the teeth of all dangers to fight for the life of their native land," he declared, "Still, when you think how easy it is to sink ships at sea and how hard it is to build them and protect them, and when you remember that we have never less than two thousand ships afloat and three or four hundred in the danger zone; when you think of the great armies we are maintaining and reinforcing in the [Near] East, and of the worldwide traffic we have to carry on — when you remember all this, can you wonder that it is the Battle of the Atlantic which holds the first place in the thoughts of those upon whom rests the responsibility for procuring the victory?"

Goaded by this and by mounting ship losses, with direction-finding inadequate, with the need for codebreaking intensifying, Harry Hinsley, the long-haired undergraduate who had become one of the chief analysts of Hut 8's output, had an idea.

Twelve

A Trawler Surprised

Germany thirsted for weather information. She needed it for the air operations that supported her blitzkriegs, for the massive bombardments that were to bring Britain to her knees, for the planned invasion of Britain. But she was at a disadvantage. Weather moves from west to east, and for Germany to observe the phenomena that would determine the weather over Britain and Europe a few days later, she had to penetrate the North Atlantic, an area long dominated by British sea power.

Germany began this penetration with three airplanes in April 1940, after the occupation of Denmark and Norway, and soon expanded to a full weather reconnaissance squadron. But airplanes could not furnish repeated observations from one place, as ground stations or ships could. Spot reports of air pressure, temperature, humidity, and wind, at one point at sea level and at another, say, 300 miles away at 5,000 feet, could not take the place of twice-daily reports of several factors from various heights plus measurements of water temperature and sea conditions day after day, in bad weather and good, and farther west than German planes could reach. Moreover, the data obtained in flight were often imprecise: the crews sometimes estimated the direction of a light surface wind by firing a burst from the forward machine gun and observing which way the spray drifted.

By the summer of 1940, with the Battle of Britain in full force, the Germans were using ships for weather observation. On July 23, the *Adolf Vinnen* was positioned north of Iceland. Three weeks later, the *Hinrich Freese* sailed to relieve her. On September 14, the *Sachsen* sailed as a replacement for two stations on Greenland that the British had closed. She was commanded by Captain Otto Kraul, an experienced whaler.

The demand for weather information continued to grow. The Naval War Staff had declared that an "augmented weather reporting service is necessary" for Operation SEALION — the invasion of Britain — and that it was to be provided by weather buoys, U-boats, and fishing vessels. U-boat Command objected, saying that its submarines should not be endangered by such secondary missions and should be used exclusively in their primary function: to sink enemy ships. But the war staff overruled it, and U-boats were required to transmit regular weather reports.

These, however, could not be fully satisfactory. In the first place, they were transmitted from each U-boat's operating area, not from the weather factories in the northern and western Atlantic. In the second place, they lacked the regularity of reports from a ship in a single location. Even the subsequent postponement of SEALION did not end the need for weather information; it would be needed for the raids on British shipping that German surface forces were to undertake.

In the middle of November 1940, however, the navy found itself facing a crisis in weather ships. Three vessels that it had obtained for that purpose proved inadequate. And two of the four northern weather-reporting ships had been sunk. At 1:10 A.M. on October 24, the signal station at the Stadlandet headland on the coast of occupied Norway reported cannon fire and searchlight beams out at sea; the *Adolf Vinnen* had been sunk by a British submarine, survivors said. On November 16, the *Hinrich Freese,* visiting the German meteorological station on the Arctic island of Jan Mayen, radioed frantically: "Am being chased by enemy vessels." Nothing further was heard, even when she was ordered to report, and the navy concluded that she had been lost. Then an accident took the *Sachsen* out of service for a while, leaving only one weather ship operating in the north.

Now greatly pressured, the navy obtained, on November 23, four fishing vessels for use as weather ships. They had the capacity to be rebuilt for cruises longer than the three weeks or so that sufficed for fishing. One of them was the fourteen-year-old, steam-powered, 139-foot-long *München,* named for the lively capital of Bavaria. She had to be fitted out with additional water tanks, reserve fuel bunkers, more space for provisions, room for three or four more men, and radios. The *Sachsen* was mentioned as a norm:

she carried a 150-watt transmitter, a 40-watt portable transmitter, two portable receivers, one panoramic receiver, and one broadcast receiver. The *München* was worked on at the Seebeck dockyard in Bremerhaven, which estimated six weeks for the job. Her sand ballast was replaced by poured concrete. Marine engineers thought at first that the vessel should be strengthened for the ice. But Kraul advised that this was not necessary if the *München* did not plan to seek shelter in estuaries where she might be frozen in. This advice reduced the time needed for rebuilding.

The high command of the navy declared specifically that weather ships were not warships but auxiliary vessels belonging to the train of the Kriegsmarine. As a consequence, the original civilian crews were retained. But some new personnel, such as the weather observers and some of the radiomen, were members of the navy. They wore mufti but were given armbands saying "Deutsche Wehrmacht" that they were to wear in case of enemy contact. Despite the noncombatant nature of the weather ships, the navy acquiesced in the proposal made by the Naval Group Command North after it lost the *Adolf Vinnen* and the *Hinrich Freese*: that the weather ships be armed for self-protection. But because of the haste to get the ships to sea, the *München* had time only to have a machine gun installed. The vessels were equipped with cipher systems for communicating the results of their observations to Germany.

One was the *Wetterkurzschlüssel,* or Short Weather Cipher. This booklet, issued in October 1940, was printed on absorbent pink paper in water-soluble ink. Its 21 pages consisted mostly of tables. Each table condensed weather observations and locations into a single letter. These substitutions reduced the time it took to transmit a message from minutes to seconds, decreasing congestion on German radio circuits as well as the chance of enemy interception and direction-finding. The observer aboard ship converted his measurements into these letters in the order prescribed (see the Appendix for an example). He then added his ship's two-letter signature. The time of the observation was presumed to be within an hour of the radioing of the message.

The Germans knew that the meaning of these messages would quickly be ascertained by British meteorological cryptanalysts, donating valuable information to Britain. To prevent this, and to maintain security in general, the Germans enciphered their abbreviated weather messages in the Enigma. Each weather ship thus carried an Enigma and its associated manuals and key lists. The latter specified the Enigma settings that were to be used each day for a month throughout the German navy; sometimes two or even three months' worth of keys had to be carried, depending on the length and dates of a cruise. The keys specified the three rotors to be placed in the machine in left-to-right order, the position of the alphabet rings on each rotor, the setting of the three rotors, and the plugboard connections. Also included were the indicators book, which listed the three-letter message-grade indicators that, when tapped out on a set-up Enigma, yielded the message key — the position to which the rotors were turned at the start of the encipherment of a nonweather message — and the bigram tables.

Weather messages abbreviated this procedure. The Short Weather Cipher listed twenty-six three-letter groups that served as ready-made message keys. Each was represented by a letter: EDM, for example, by A. The encipherer chose one of these positions, say, that represented by Q. Then, with the rotor order and alphabet ring position specified in the current Enigma keying document, he turned the rotors until the three letters that Q represented appeared in the windows in the machine's lid. Then he enciphered his Short Weather Cipher text; MZNFPED plus, say, MR as signature, might become TVUOIGMVX. The encipherer prefixed the key indicator Q to this and, in front of that, a WW, meaning *Wetterkurzspruch* or "short weather message." The radioman, who was also the encipherer, would tap this out on a specified frequency in 15 to 20 seconds. He sent it "blind" — not addressed to any station. But any station that received the message was to acknowledge receipt. If the ship received no confirmation, she repeated her transmission fifteen minutes later on a different frequency. The main weather stations became Norddeich, for weather ships operating south of Iceland, and Kootwijk, in the Netherlands, for those north of Iceland; more often than not, however, other stations replied. The receiving station deciphered the message using Enigma, added a time group, and teletyped the Short Weather Cipher letters to the navy's weather central, which reconverted them into the original data.

One of the major determinants of Europe's weather is the polar front: the boundary between the warm moist air of the south and

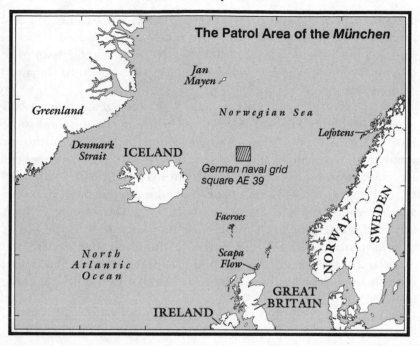

the cold dry air of the Arctic. Another is the North Atlantic Drift, the remnants of the Gulf Stream. To determine their locations and movements, the Germans favored two observation areas. One was some 300 miles east and slightly north of Iceland, a watery square 54 miles on a side designated as AE 39 on the Kriegsmarine grid. The other was the square AB 72, in the Norwegian Sea some 550 miles northeast of Iceland. Its southernmost boundary was at 71° north latitude, the parallel that cuts the North Cape, the northernmost point of Europe. The weather ships worked these areas for three to five weeks, excluding the time required to go to and return from their stations. The *Coburg*, for example, sailed on February 10, 1941, and returned on March 28; the *Ostmark* left port on April 2 and returned on May 6.

While the *Ostmark* was still at sea, the *München* received orders to relieve her. This was to be the *München*'s second cruise and the second time she had replaced the *Ostmark* in AE 39. And conditions would be better than on the first cruise, which had put the vessel in the freezing North Atlantic from the middle of February to the middle of March. She sailed in the evening twilight of Thursday, May 1, from Trondheim, the fortified seaport in whose ancient cathedral kings of Norway are crowned, steaming slowly in the gathering darkness down the wide fjord. She had 40 miles to go to reach its mouth, and another 30 until, after passing the chains of islands that paralleled the coast, she rocked to the swell of the open sea.

Her crew of about twenty consisted of some seamen who had worked on her as a fishing trawler and who ran the ship and some navy sailors who had been assigned to her for weather, radio, or weapons duties. One of them was the young weather observer Fritz Rebelein, who had been plucked from his barracks in Wilhelmshaven apparently at random to be trained in meteorological observation. Another was draftee Heinrich Wiggeshof, not yet 20. A ham radio operator in peacetime, he had been sent to the navy's communications school at Flensburg and then assigned to the *München* for his first duty afloat. Both had completed the first cruise, but this time Rebelein had a premonition that he would not come back.

Once the *München* had reached her assigned square east of Iceland, Rebelein and the other observers took measurements twice a day. They encoded the results in the Short Weather Cipher and gave them to one of the radiomen. He enciphered this in the Enigma, for which he, like all Kriegsmarine vessels in the Atlantic, had the Home Waters cipher net keys for May. And because the *München*'s replacement might be delayed, or the ship for some other reason might have to stay at sea longer than the scheduled twenty-five days, she also carried the keys for June.

The Germans were not the only ones paying attention to the weather ships. The solutions of naval Enigma traffic made possible by the documents from the *Krebs* included messages from the weather ships and acknowledgments of their reception. The messages often told of the weather ships' movements to and from their stations.

In his little office in Hut 4, Harry Hinsley, who analyzed the cryptanalysts' output especially for trends and for information on specialized (nontactical) matters, read these intercepts along with all the others. One day in the spring of 1941, a "passing thought" brought to his consciousness something that had remained beneath the surface of his mind: the weather messages were enciphered in Enigma. He asked himself whether the Germans would be so foolish as to put the cipher machine used for the whole German navy and its accompanying key documents on an isolated, vulnerable weather ship. But then, in a "mad moment," he concluded, "Good God, this must be right!" It further dawned on him that if the weather ships were out at sea for a long time, they had to carry Enigma keys for several months. Perhaps with Ian Fleming's unfulfilled idea of seizing cipher documents from a lured-out air-sea rescue boat and the success of the *Krebs* episode in the back of his mind, Hinsley thought of capturing Enigma papers from a weather ship.

The young intelligence officer discussed his idea with Clive Loehnis, Bletchley's liaison with the Admiralty, particularly its Operational Intelligence Centre. The O.I.C. was impressed by the idea, but it recognized the chief risk. If a weather ship radioed that it was being boarded, the Germans would probably change the keys, perhaps including the rotor wirings, and possibly even abandon the Enigma for another system. On the other hand, the O.I.C. and B.P. observed that, despite the destruction of two weather ships through British action, the Germans had not seemed to fear that their cryptographic documents had been compromised and had left their systems in place. Perhaps their complacency would continue. So the O.I.C. and B.P. concluded that the prize was worth the risk. Even if no cryptographic papers were captured, the Germans would be deprived of a source of weather reports. In addition, Hinsley knew, there were two weather ships on northern stations at a time, doubling the chances for capturing cipher documents and wiping out German weather ship information.

This clinched it for the intelligence types. With these arguments in hand, they approached Captain Haines, assistant director of the O.I.C. for radio intelligence. Operational questions like these came first to him. No doubt after satisfying himself of the necessity of such a "pinch" and the possibility of its succeeding, he discussed it with operational officers of the Admiralty. They concluded that such a seizure, while tricky, was not impossible.

Perhaps under the supervision of the director of the Operations Division (Home), Captain Ralph Edwards, Haines planned the attack. He determined the forces, the time of day, and the angle of approach that gave the best chance of success. He studied the three-page report on German weather ships that Hinsley had compiled on April 26, 1941, from various sources. The report made clear to any naval officer the isolation of the weather ships. Perhaps from later intercepts, the British concluded that the *München* was to sail May 1 to relieve the *Ostmark* in grid square AE 39, east of Iceland.

The same source may have revealed the presence of the other weather ship that Hinsley knew about, perhaps the *Sachsen*, in the other preferred observation area, AB 72. Edwards figured that seven ships would be needed to search the grid square. Since AE 39 extended about 1° of latitude from north to south, or 69 statute miles, and since ships would be able to stay in sight of one another at a spacing of 10 miles, seven ships would adequately sweep the area. Presumably one warship, quickly reinforced by others, could swiftly capture a surprised and lightly armed weather ship.

So it was decided. Edwards detached three cruisers and four destroyers from the Home Fleet for the assignment. In command of the forces was Vice Admiral Lancelot E. Holland, a gunnery specialist, head of the Eighteenth Cruiser Squadron. A short, slim man with sharp features and nearly white hair, Holland, intensely ambitious, was regarded as one of the most competent senior officers in the service. He flew his flag from the *Edinburgh*; the other two cruisers were the *Birmingham* and the *Manchester,* both armed with twelve 6-inch guns and capable of speeds greater than 30 knots. Also aboard the *Edinburgh* was Haines, who knew what the cryptanalysts needed and was assigned to search for it aboard the seized vessel.

The destroyers were the *Nestor* and three of the large, fast, and tested Tribals: the *Eskimo,* the *Bedouin,* and the *Somali.* All three had, barely two months before, participated in the Lofotens raid, in which the *Somali* had sunk the *Krebs* and captured Enigma rotors and keys. Now they and the cruisers, together with the other gray warships of the Home Fleet, held in readiness as a strategic force at Scapa Flow, tugged impatiently at their anchor chains.

On Monday, May 5, the seven ships raised anchor and steamed out of the basin. The destroyers took one route, the cruisers another to their rendezvous next morning north of the Faeroes. That afternoon the flotilla practiced a battle action. The *Manchester* acted as an enemy pocket battleship, with the *Nestor* laying a smoke screen to help it escape. During much of the day the force pretended to cover for some minelaying west of the Faeroes. At 3 A.M. on Wednesday, May 7, the group altered course from north-northwest to southeast. This was to disguise its intentions in case it was seen by that morning's German meteorological flight. At 6 A.M., the flotilla again altered course, this time to a little east of north. It was heading for its starting position for the sweep, which it reached a little after noon. At 12:55 Holland turned his ships east and eight minutes later spaced them at 10-mile intervals along a north–south line a little bit west of AE 39. Visibility was only 7 or 8 miles, which made it a little harder for the ships to remain in contact but enabled them to approach the weather ship more closely before being detected.

They steamed at 17 knots for two and a half hours, then Holland increased speed to 20. The sky was clear, the sea, slightly ruffled by a light breeze, calm. The temperature stood around freezing. The sun declined slowly on its shallow oblique to the sea. At 4 P.M., the *Birmingham* sent up an observer aircraft. Its pilot and the lookouts on all ships strained their eyes for the trawler's smoke or for the needle of her mast above the horizon. Aboard the *Somali*, the physician, Surgeon-Lieutenant Dr. M. G. Low, retired to the wardroom to read *Country Gentleman* while awaiting the action.

Suddenly, a few minutes after 5 P.M., someone aboard the *Edinburgh* saw smoke off the starboard bow between *Edinburgh*'s course and *Somali*'s. At about the same time the man who had shot open the locked drawer on the *Krebs*, Lieutenant Warmington, on the bridge of the *Somali*, spotted the smoke. The rattlers sounded action stations. Low threw down his magazine and ran out on deck. He, too, saw the smoke. The *Somali* increased speed to her maximum 32 knots and raced toward the ship that appeared to rise above the horizon.

Aboard the *München*, Radioman Wiggeshof was transmitting a weather report when the cry rang out, "Mastheads on the horizon!" The little ship put on way and ran. The crew began rushing about. The wireless noncom came into the radio shack, grabbed the Enigma machine, put it and the current keys into a canvas bag with a lead bottom, added papers and instruments that Rebelein brought up from below, and slung it overboard. At 5:28, Wiggeshof transmitted on 7769 kilocycles, in the clear, "Werde gejagt" (Being chased).

By then the *München* had emitted a dense white smoke screen and was dodging to and fro trying to stay behind it. On the *Somali*, Low felt a pang of sympathy for the little ship and her crew, suddenly seeing the bow waves of a flotilla of enemy warships heading toward her.

When she was about 3 miles from the weather ship, the *Somali* opened fire with her 4.7-inch guns. The *Eskimo* followed. The *München*, with only a machine gun, did not return the fire. None of the British shells struck her, but, rumbling over the trawler and sending up towers of water next to her, they had the desired effect: the crew members were seen abandoning ship in two boats. Not all escaped that way, however. Some of the lifeboats could not be dropped to the water, and Wiggeshof, as soon as he had transmitted his warning signal, drew on another pair of pants and jumped overboard. Others remained on deck.

The trawler's crew made no attempt to scuttle, in part because some of the seacocks had been cemented in when the sand ballast was replaced by concrete. The impression gained aboard the *Edinburgh* that the *München* was settling rapidly by the stern proved to be an optical illusion. The *Somali* readied her boarding party: Warmington; the second in command, Henry Stuart-Menteth, now a commander; and two seamen. She sped to the trawler at top speed, reversing to full speed astern to come to a thumping stop alongside. The boarding party, revolvers at the ready, jumped down from the destroyer onto the deck of the weather ship. One of the seamen shot himself in the toe with his pistol as he landed. Stuart-Menteth was nervous that the Germans had set explosives, but the party found none when it searched the ship. She was intact.

Warmington went to the radio shack, where he picked up a few bits of paper. He found nothing he thought worth taking; the Germans had apparently thrown everything valuable overboard. Haines came over from the *Edinburgh* with the prize crew. He seemed to know just what he was looking for and that some cipher documents were kept in officers' quarters separate from cipher documents in the radio shack. So he didn't bother with that room but disappeared into the depths of the ship, apparently looking for something specific. Within a few moments he seemed to have found it, for he emerged from below carrying papers.

The *Edinburgh* and the *Somali*, meanwhile, were picking up the enemy crew. "What's the name of that ship?" Captain Caslon bellowed down to Low, who spoke German. "Wie heisst deine Schiff?" shouted Low to the Germans. "*München*," they replied. Wiggeshof had lost consciousness in the 35-degree water; the next thing he knew, a British seaman was slapping his face and asking whether he wanted tea or coffee. Wiggeshof, who had never in his life had tea, must have nodded his head at the wrong time because the sailor brought him a steaming mug of it.

After about twenty minutes the boarding party returned to the *Somali,* and the prize crew took over. By 6:45, an hour and a half after the trawler's smoke had first been sighted, the *München,* escorted by the *Somali,* was on her way to a British port. Haines, meanwhile, transferred to the destroyer *Nestor,* which at 11:45 was ordered to bring him and his papers to Scapa.

Upon his arrival in Bletchley on Saturday, May 10, Haines turned over to Peter Twinn the Short Weather Cipher and the inner and outer Enigma settings for the home water keys for June. Holland had called them "rather undistinguished documents," but they bore within them seeds of great power.

That their weather ship with its documents might have been seized seemed never to cross the Germans' minds. They had received Wiggeshof's frantic signal about being chased, and the Naval War Staff concluded two days later, when the *München* failed to respond to a request to report her position, that she had been lost. The Germans picked up the intentionally misleading British official communique: "One of our patrols operating in northern waters encountered the *München,* a German armed trawler. Fire was opened, and the crew of the *München* then abandoned and scuttled their ship. They were subsequently rescued and made prisoner." But though the German navy duly noted this in several war diaries, nothing was said of the possibility that secret documents had been captured, and no changes in German naval cipher procedure were ordered.

How could they not have thought about this? How could they have not taken ordinary precautions? In the first place, the previous losses of weather ships had led to no dire consequences. Second, the Naval Group Command North was getting ready for its role in Hitler's vast ideological attack on the Soviet Union, less than seven weeks away. The group had to lay thousands of mines in the

Baltic before the assault began and had to keep track of Soviet warships. It had to escort freighters carrying nickel from Finland, ward off raids like that on the Lofotens, protect U-boat departures — all duties linked to Norway's being what Hitler called his "zone of destiny" in the war, and it would not be wise to fail the Führer. Finally, the high command had larger concerns. Only three weeks before the *München* was captured, Hitler and Admiral Erich Raeder, the head of the navy, discussed the perennial problem of the United States' hindrance of the U-boat war and the newer issue of Japan's planned attack on Britain's major Asian base at Singapore.

In these realms of high strategy, it was easy to forget a single trawler, one of many tiny specks on the chart of the North Atlantic, doing a secondary job. Her fate was seen as insignificant in a struggle in which ships were sunk daily and many men died. For all these reasons, the Kriegsmarine ignored the loss of the *München*. Wrongly.

Thirteen

The Staff School Memory

TWO DAYS AFTER the *München* was captured, and on the other side of Iceland, Fritz-Julius Lemp's U-110 was forced to the surface by the attacks of Joe Baker-Cresswell's Escort Group 3. As the submarine broke water, Baker-Cresswell ordered the heavy guns of his ship, the *Bulldog*, to open up on the U-boat. Then, intending to ram, he swung the *Bulldog* to port and called for 12 knots.

In the submarine, Lemp ordered the crew to put on diving vests and abandon ship. Discipline held. There was no panic, no jostling to be the first out. The young radioman, Heinz Wilde, forgot temporarily that his diving vest was in the radio room, then remembered, got it, and put it on. His brain was half on automatic after the overwhelming terror he had felt under the depth-bomb attack of moments before, when he thought his boat would go down and his life would end. So he got his cap and put it on but left his camera behind. Lemp opened the conning tower hatch, and someone else opened the forward hatch. The first men emerged from the conning tower.

Baker-Cresswell, recalling the story of the codebook recovered from the *Magdeburg*, ordered his ship full speed astern and his guns to cease firing.

The former order worked better than the latter. Within a couple hundred yards, the *Bulldog* had halted. It was harder to get the gunners to stop firing. The heavy weapons — the 4.7-inch, the 3-inch, the pom-poms — indeed ceased. But from behind Baker-Cresswell "a dreadful noise" shattered his ears: one of his officers was firing the Lewis submachine gun, something the officer had always wanted to do. As the Germans poured out of the conning tower and the forward hatch, the British sailors, perhaps fearing that the enemy was about to man the cannon on the forward deck, continued to fire their small arms; guns on the other British warships, by now in a circle around the U-boat, also shot at her. Some of the Germans were killed. Those who seemed about to serve the cannon scattered and dove into the water. The dots of heads littered the ocean. Some moved; some had arms that flailed the water; some were motionless. Then one of the other destroyers, the four-stacker *Broadway*, raced toward the submarine, apparently trying to ram her and thereby unwittingly end Baker-Cresswell's plan to salvage the codebooks. He grabbed a megaphone. "Keep clear!" he shouted at her. But would she hear? He ordered a signalman to flash the message to the *Broadway*. But would she see it? Could she stop in time?

The crew members still inside the U-boat heard the shooting and sensed or were told that the first men to emerge had been shot. This decreased whatever urgency there may have been to get out. Silence fell over the crew. Wilde wondered whether he should even climb out. Suddenly, as the *Broadway* raced toward the U-110, Lemp shouted, "Out! Out! The destroyer is going to ram us."

Wilde knew that if capture threatened, the boat's secret documents, including the cipher material, were to be destroyed. But the submarine's rise to the surface had been so swift and unanticipated, especially in face of the expectation moments earlier that the vessel would go down, that no preparations had been made to wreck the Enigma and soak its keys, printed in water-soluble ink. None of his three superiors in the boat's radio service had taken any steps to throw the machine or its papers overboard or otherwise render it useless to an enemy. And he had been indoctrinated with the belief that the machine was cryptographically so secure that even capture would not compromise its secrets. Still under the impress of the terror of death, he was not able to react calmly. And now, with the captain's shout raising in him the new fear that thousands of tons of steel were about to smash into his frail vessel and do what the depth bombs had failed to do, all thoughts of cipher machines vanished from his brain.

Wilde climbed up the ladder in the conning tower, went out onto the bridge, heard Lemp order, "Overboard!" and jumped 15 feet into the Atlantic. As he went down, he never thought about whether the water was cold or even that it was wet, only that it was a beautiful turquoise color. Still descending, he turned on the oxygen flask of his diving vest. It brought him up. His cap was floating next to him and, still in a trancelike state, he reached over and put it on. He saw others swimming in a group. The cook, next to him, said, "I'm swimming to a destroyer." Then the group of men, to keep their spirits up, began to sing one of the songs Wilde had played over and over on the submarine's loudspeaker system: "*Im Leben Geht Alles Vorüber*" (In life all things come to an end).

The *Broadway*, meanwhile, continued speeding toward the submarine. She did not intend to ram. Her plan was to drop two depth charges under the U-boat set to explode at about 100 feet to damage the sub so that she could not dive again and to encourage her crew to abandon ship. But the firing of the *Broadway*'s 4-inch guns had cracked her bridge windows so extensively that they were almost opaque, and her captain did not realize that he was on a collision course. He dropped his depth charges and at the last moment turned away, but the stern of the submarine, whose port motor had been running slowly, swung toward the destroyer. As the *Broadway* passed by, the U-boat's after hydroplane sliced open the destroyer's port forward fuel tank. Oil spilled into the water.

By then Baker-Cresswell had enforced his cease-fire order and, with his ship drifting only a hundred yards from the U-boat, was ready to realize his idea of boarding her. No plans had ever been made for the possibility of boarding a U-boat, so no training or drill had ever been carried out for it.

"Organize boarding party instantly," Baker-Cresswell said to his second in command, Lieutenant John Aitken. "The sub-lieutenant will be in charge."

The sub-lieutenant was David E. Balme, who in joining the navy had followed a long family tradition. Balme, just twenty, with a mischievous look and a twinkle in his eye, was once characterized as a type who made girls happy when he came ashore. He had studied at the Dartmouth naval school and sailed on training cruises in the Mediterranean and was serving aboard a destroyer as a midshipman when the war began. He liked the life and the responsibility, and in February 1941 he joined the *Bulldog*.

Someone hailed him: "Hey, you, sub! Away you go!" He reported to the bridge.

Baker-Cresswell instructed him. "Your job is to secure all important papers, ciphers, charts — anything that you can find." Balme armed himself with a huge service revolver — as dangerous to him as to the enemy, he thought — and the eight ratings (enlisted men) with rifles, revolvers, hand grenades, and gas masks (in case sea water had evolved poisonous chlorine gas from the batteries). The ship lowered the 27-foot, five-oared whaler off its port side into the water. It was 12:45 P.M., Friday, May 9, 1941.

The *Bulldog* was lying to the windward of the U-boat, and a heavy swell was running. It would have been safer to row around the submarine and come up on her leeward side, but this would have taken more time, so Balme made directly for her. Suddenly Baker-Cresswell saw two men who appeared to be manning her forward gun. He gave the order to open fire with the Lewis gun, and the two men appeared to be hit. Within moments, the U-110's whole crew seemed to have jumped or fallen into the water. They were picked up by the *Broadway* and the corvette *Aubretia* and promptly hustled below, so they were unable to see anything outside.

As the whaler approached the submarine, no fire came from her, so Balme grew confident that no one was in the conning tower. He could see the numerous holes in the conning tower made by the *Bulldog*'s 3-inch gun and pom-poms. The bowman in the whaler leaped onto the U-boat with the light line, and Balme and the others followed, clambering onto the slippery hull. Soon one of the ocean swells carried the whaler onto the U-boat, jamming it between the conning tower and the steel guard rails. The pounding of the waves soon broke it up. Balme felt it was almost suicidal for an inexperienced man to climb down the conning tower of a submarine with one hand holding a weapon. So he holstered his revolver. The sailors balanced themselves on the narrow, rocking deck, carrying their unwieldy weapons and trying not to accidentally shoot themselves or one another.

Balme climbed part way up the conning tower and entered through an opening on the starboard side. At his feet he saw a closed hatch. The boat had indeed appeared to be deserted, but if the hatch was closed, perhaps someone was aboard after all. For who would carefully close a hatch after abandoning a vessel under attack? And if the submarine was to be scuttled, wouldn't its captain want the hatch to remain open, to let water in and air out more quickly? Cautiously Balme turned the wheel that held the hatch screwed down, released a clip, and watched the hatch spring open. He saw the lower conning tower, empty, with a similar hatch at the bottom, also closed. The same question arose: Was the submarine really deserted? If not, anyone in the control room just beneath that second hatch would be able to shoot Balme before he could fire back. The sub-lieutenant briefly considered dropping a grenade inside. But that would defeat the purpose of the boarding. He was there to do a job. He went down the ladder and opened the second hatch.

More than a bit scared, and feeling very vulnerable, he climbed down into the control room. All the lights were on. Everything was silent except for the hiss of air escaping and the rumbles of distant depth charges. Hatches forward and aft were open. A large metal splinter from a conning tower hit lay on the deck. The control room was deserted — but were crew members lurking nearby, ready to kill their enemies? Would scuttling charges soon go off? Would the depth charges detonate them? Was sea water pouring in somewhere?

None of these things seemed to be happening, and no German appeared. Balme called the rest of the boarding party down into the submarine. As it became evident that no one was on the boat and no chlorine had been produced, they put down their weapons and their gas masks and looked around a little more carefully.

The submarine had clearly been abandoned in great haste. A plate of shrimps lay in the radio room. Books and gear were strewn about. The first quick examination took about five minutes. Balme ordered his party to send up all useful documents and equipment. He had signalman William Pollock wigwag a message that the boat was abandoned and appeared seaworthy and towable and that he was collecting gear. He ordered all books sent up except obviously recreational ones, so he recovered some general navigational texts in addition to the log books, signal books, and charts with heavy black lines showing the swept channels through minefields. The men passed these out of the ship by means of a human chain.

Baker-Cresswell watched nervously from the *Bulldog*, fearful that the men might drop into the sea the documents for which he had risked violating the Admiralty's basic instructions to escort commanders: "The safe and timely arrival of the convoy is the primary object, and nothing relieves the escort commander of his responsibility in this respect." In one anxious moment, he saw Able Seaman Claude Wileman stagger from the conning tower protecting an armful of documents with his body. He moved in spurts, hurrying a few paces, then holding on to the guard rail as a sea rocked the boat, then moving on. Once a wave all but covered him. He emerged, soaked but safe, and with the documents. Nor did any of the other seamen who maneuvered so carefully on the U-boat's narrow hull lose anything. They put their treasures into a motorized whaler from the *Broadway* that had replaced the *Bulldog*'s smashed boat.

Meanwhile the telegraphist in the party, Allen O. Long, went to the radio room. It had apparently served as the boat's office, for he found pay books and general correspondence as well as signal logs. He saw also the two compact high-frequency transmitters and the two receivers, a Telefunken and a civilian broadcasting receiver; he noted their settings. He also considered that the sets seemed far less complicated, far more compact than the Royal Navy's. And there Long saw as well a device that looked like a typewriter. It was still plugged in, drawing its current from the boat's power supply and not its own batteries, and appeared to have been in use when the U-boat was abandoned. Long pressed the keys. But the results seemed "peculiar" — pressing an *a* did not light up an A on the illuminated panel. It was not, therefore, just a special form of typewriter. Balme examined it as well. He hadn't thought of cipher machines before, but he recognized it for what it was and understood that it was useful. It was bolted to the table. Long unscrewed the bolts by hand and passed the machine out of the submarine via the human chain to the *Broadway*'s whaler, which took it, and the documents, to the *Bulldog*.

Two boatloads of equipment went over, and Baker-Cresswell was pleased to see that the German papers printed in water-soluble ink had lost only small portions of their text. Balme also passed up half a dozen sextants, which he regarded as of superb quality, far superior to those supplied by the Admiralty, and nine of ten Super Zeiss binoculars. The tenth was not handed in, Balme later finding it by far the best binoculars he had ever used.

The minutes turned into hours as Balme continued to scour the ship. Among the officers' belongings he found some wallets, slips of paper, cameras, a movie camera. In the radio room there was writing paper with well-printed letterheads and envelopes, ordinary books, cards, dice, and what he called "the usual art studies."

He was impressed by the U-boat. She was "new and a fine ship both in the strength of the hull, in the fittings and instruments and general interior construction. . . . Spotlessly clean throughout. Ward Room finished off in light varnished woodwork and all cupboards were numbered with corresponding keys to fit. . . . Plenty of tinned ham, corned beef and three sacks of potatoes in control room; also luxuries such as beer, cigars, Players cigarettes (German printing on packets). . . . Magnificent galley. . . ."

The *Aubrietia* and the *Broadway* picked up survivors while the *Bulldog*'s engineer officer went over to see whether the U-boat was seaworthy and to stop the port motor from its slow turning. He concluded that the vessel was able to stay afloat, and he slowed the motor by shifting what he presumed to be the central rheostat to the off position, but the shaft did not stop revolving. Nor did various other adjustments of the rheostat succeed in stopping it. And after a time the boat seemed to be a little more down by the stern than when he had come aboard.

Meanwhile, Baker-Cresswell was reporting that he had captured a U-boat, that she appeared to be taking water, that he had no one who could read German to fix her, and finally that he was taking her in tow to bring her to Scapa. But just as he started to attach a 3½-inch cable, and while the boarding party was aboard the submarine, news came that two ships of the convoy, which by now had steamed out of sight in the decreasing visibility, had been torpedoed. The submarine that had done this was being attacked by the ships of Escort Group 3 that had remained with the convoy. Soon the *Broadway* and the *Aubrietia* obtained an asdic contact with a presumed submarine and began dropping depth charges. Then lookouts on Baker-Cresswell's own *Bulldog* shouted that they had seen a periscope. Baker-Cresswell slipped the tow to the U-boat and searched for the new submarine, with no success.

Gradually the excitement subsided, and the *Bulldog* resumed the tow. The U-boat seemed to keep turning to starboard, perhaps a consequence of the slow turning of her port motor. But this, though a nuisance, did not prevent the *Bulldog* from increasing speed to 4 knots. Baker-Cresswell ordered all watertight hatches and doors to be closed on the submarine and the boarding crew to rejoin his ship. At 6:30 all were back, and the towing speed was increased to 6 knots. By 7 the next morning, however, the wind had become a strong breeze of up to 30 miles per hour and blowing from slightly south of west as the *Bulldog* headed northeast in a lumpy sea. It proved impossible to hold this course, so Baker-Cresswell let the submarine head downwind, a position in which she seemed comfortable, and kept the towing wire taut. Suddenly, at 11 A.M., the U-110, which had been settling by the stern, started to sink more rapidly. Soon her bow reared to the vertical. Baker-Cresswell had the towing line cut with an ax, and the submarine slid beneath the surface.

It was a terrible moment for Baker-Cresswell, who had badly wanted to bring his prize into port. He felt that the U-boat, having withstood so many shocks, should be able to stand the 400-mile tow to Iceland, then Scapa. But his disappointment was ameliorated when he examined the two packing cases of material from the boat that had been stored in his cabin. Of the many books and documents, he thought that the Kriegsmarine grid of the seas of the world was the most valuable. But he recognized the Enigma as "a typewriter for ciphering," and he consoled himself for his disappointment about the submarine: "At least I've got the cipher." It was what he had hoped for: a World War II *Magdeburg*.

His satisfaction increased soon after his arrival at Scapa Flow. Bletchley sent two men with a single briefcase to examine what he had captured and to bring back the most important items. They were stunned at the quantity and ecstatic over the quality. "I never thought we'd get any of this," one of them gloated to Balme. They dried off some of the documents and photographed the most important items, in case their plane crashed as they were bringing the originals back to Bletchley. They had special containers made because they had so much to take. On May 13 they gave the codebreakers of Hut 8 an unbelievable trove of cryptographic treasure: key tables not only for general-grade Enigma messages but also for officer-grade, the procedures for enciphering officer-grade and staff-grade messages, the indicators book, one of the books — codenamed BACH ("brook") — for enciphering the indicator bigrams, the directions for the cue-word system for changing settings in case the originals were compromised or feared so, and the U-boat Short Signal Book.

The value of these documents and those from the *München* was shown dramatically. On May 21, before the June keys took effect, Hut 4 was teleprinting translations to the O.I.C. with an average elapsed time from interception of eleven days. Luck or ability lowered this average to thirty-four hours on May 28. But then no translations were sent for the next three days, suggesting that no intercepts could be solved. When the seized keys came into force, however, the interception-to-teleprint time fell sharply. A German cryptogram intercepted at 18 minutes after midnight on June 1 was forwarded to Hut 8, deciphered there, translated in Hut 4, and sent to the O.I.C. by 4:58 A.M. And for the rest of the month, except for a few aberrations, the interception-to-teleprint time averaged around six hours. Thanks to the captures of the *München* and the U-110, the British were reading German naval messages practically as fast as the Germans themselves. But how long could this situation last?

Fourteen

"All This Rubbish?"

Even the remarkable successes of the two seizures — the *München* planned, the U-110 a windfall — did not slake the needs of Naval Section. When the captured keys expired, the cryptanalysts would face delays of forty-eight hours in solutions. They enjoyed none of the shortcuts to solution, such as cillies, that the cryptanalysts of the Luftwaffe Enigma did, and almost all of their cribs had to be run on bombes, which were in very short supply. Yet they had to try to stay current. Harry Hinsley reluctantly concluded that another operation, similar to that against the *München*, would have to be mounted.

He scanned the patrol rhythms and positions of the several isolated weather ships and concluded that the *Lauenburg* offered the most fruitful target. On June 19, he wrote that she had departed Trondheim during the night of May 27–28 to take over from the *Sachsen*, which had been on station for more than six weeks. "Evidence of her predecessor's patrol suggests that *Lauenburg* intends to be out after the end of June," he wrote. The "evidence of a tendency to overstocking with cypher material ... suggests that *Lauenburg*, leaving in the last few days of May, will be carrying keys both for June and July."

According to the ship's intercepted weather reports, she was working much farther to the northeast in the Norwegian Sea than the *München* had: along 72° north sliding between 1° and 4° west, within the German naval grid square AB 72, an area used by previous weather ships.

For the German need for meteorological data from the Atlantic could not abate until Hitler's forces had conquered Britain. The Kriegsmarine continued to convert fishing trawlers to mobile observation platforms. The *Lauenburg* was one of the newest — only three years old — a 136-foot-long motor-driven fishing vessel of 344 tons. She bore the proud name of the capital, 30 miles up the Elbe River from Hamburg, of an ancient former duchy.

Retained as her captain when she entered naval service was Hinrich Gewald, fifty-eight. Corpulent, stolid, taciturn, he had always lived in the East Frisian village of Westrhauderfehn, on the flat German fenland not far from the Dutch border, a region that sent many of its sons to sea. He spoke the Plattdeutsch dialect, some of whose words are more like English than high German: German *dass* ("that") became *dat*, *Schiff* ("ship") became *Schipp*, *gross* ("big," "great") became *grot*.

Like his father before him, Gewald became a fishing captain. In 1926 he gained a modicum of fame when he was mentioned in a book about fishing by Adrian Mohr, who had sailed aboard Gewald's boat the *Dortmund*. It was probably the captain's ability to navigate well in the far north, which poses special problems, his prowess in sailing among icebergs, and his World War I naval experience that commended him to the navy to continue to command the *Lauenburg*.

His crew of twenty-two men included three petty officers and three sailors from the navy, among them Georg Klarman, twenty, who manned the 3.7-centimeter gun. The others manned guns, worked the radio, and made the weather observations. Many of the nonnaval crew members had, like their captain, served aboard civilian fishing vessels. The baker, Kurt Braun, born twenty-four years before in the East Prussian seacoast town of Frauenburg, had sailed aboard several other fishing vessels before coming to the *Lauenburg*. Morale was good aboard the ship, though its members had not shared the common experiences that weld a bunch of individuals into a team.

Such were the vessel, the master, and the crew that sailed from Trondheim on May 25 (not on the twenty-seventh, as Hinsley had estimated). They reached their observation position within a few days. It was the *Lauenburg*'s first patrol, but she soon settled into her daily routine. The crew stood watch. Braun baked fresh bread daily. Lookouts watched for icebergs and other dangers, such as enemy ships. The meteorologists transmitted their observations

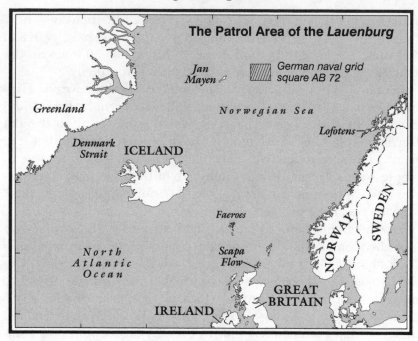

twice a day, between 6 and 6:40 A.M. and between 2:10 and 2:20 P.M., to the big radio station at Kootwijk, in central Holland. At 6:41 A.M. (British time) on June 27, she transmitted her first condensed weather report, prefixed with the required WW, on 12,040 kilocycles. The second, with the same prefix and on the same frequency, went at 2:11 P.M. — apparently the favored time, since for at least three days in a row she radioed at that same minute.

From time to time Captain Gewald shifted the *Lauenburg*'s position. Between June 6 and 19 she moved west along the 72nd parallel from 1° to 4° west longitude, occasionally slipping up to the 73rd parallel. At that latitude, more than 300 miles north of the Arctic Circle, and at that season, only days before the summer solstice, the sun turned incessantly about the ship, never setting, merely dipping in the north. At times, brash and growlers and full-sized icebergs covered the sea. To the west and north, the *Lauenburg*'s crew could sometimes see the edge of the permanent ice pack, a low white line glinting on the horizon. The sailors did not spend all their time working. Some caught seals, some read the books that had been brought aboard for their entertainment; some looked at the pornographic postcards they had slipped under their pillows.

Hinsley's memorandum of June 19 about the *Lauenburg*, with its implied recommendation that the ship be the target of the next operation to seize cipher material, went to the Admiralty, perhaps via Captain Haines, the liaison officer. The concept passed rapidly through the normal channels of the Plans and Operations divisions, and soon orders were issued that a task force be created to board the *Lauenburg* and grab the secret documents. To make sure that no important documents aboard the target vessel were overlooked and to scan the captured papers not only for cryptographic documents but for any others that might be of value, B.P. assigned one of its staff, Royal Naval Volunteer Reserve Lieutenant Allon Bacon, to sail with the task force.

Bacon was a member of naval intelligence's Section 8G, which liaised between the Naval Section of B.P. and the Admiralty; he dealt particularly with captured documents. A yachtsman who had made his money in the City, London's financial district, he was a friend of Commander Malcolm Saunders, the head of 8G. Before the war, he and Saunders had sailed his yacht to Kiel with a couple of Royal Navy radio operators belowdecks and had intercepted enough Kriegsmarine traffic to give British cryptanalysts more depth for an attack on some cryptosystem. Rangy, dark-haired, round-faced, and very handsome, he knew some German and something about the sea and got on well with naval officers; because of this ability, and because of his job specialty and his intelligence and resourcefulness, he was picked for the *Lauenburg* operation.

The head of the Home Fleet assigned the task to the commander of the Tenth Cruiser Squadron, Rear Admiral H. M. Burrough, sailing in the *Nigeria,* and gave him another cruiser and three destroyers with which to accomplish it. Two were powerful Tribals — the *Tartar* and the *Bedouin* — and one an even newer vessel, the *Jupiter,* on which Bacon sailed. But a collision with another ship caused the second cruiser to return to base, so only three destroyers and the *Nigeria* participated. All were at Scapa Flow. Burrough met with the captains of the destroyers and agreed on a plan of action, including procedures for boarding. At 10 P.M. on Wednesday, June 25, they cleared the antisubmarine booms of Scapa and set course for the Faeroe Islands, to the northwest.

At Skaalefiord, the flotilla topped up with fuel while command-ing officers and the heads of the boarding teams held final confer-ences. At 9:30 P.M. on Thursday, Burrough took his force out into the North Atlantic in rapidly declining visibility. He headed north at 21 knots, passing to the east of Britain's main Faeroes–Iceland minefield. As he approached the island of Jan Mayen, a forecast of fog and ice impelled him to pass to the south and east instead of the west and north to reach the trawler's reported posi-tion. This position was now at 73° north latitude, 4° west longitude, or some 300 miles to the northeast of Jan Mayen. The flotilla swung around the island and steamed north toward its unsuspecting target.

The *Tartar*'s skipper, Commander Lionel P. (Kim) Skipwith, had come aboard early in 1940. In his mid-thirties, Skipwith was an experienced destroyer commander: the *Tartar* was his seventh command. He was rather an individualist. For relaxation he em-broidered. He painted the wood in his cabin canary yellow and its deck a pale green — a refreshing change from the expanse of gray outside. A craftsman, he once modeled the *Tartar* beautifully in wood. He hated the Germans: during attacks on U-boats, he would sometimes stick one finger in the air to signal the gunners "Get me one dead German" as evidence of success if the sub surfaced.

Despite this, he was reasonable. Once he warned the chief gun-ner's mate that his gunners were striking matches at night. The mate replied that it was cold and they had to smoke, whereupon Skipwith gave permission for the mate to put a coil of slow match — a fuse that burned a yard every eight hours — in a bucket for them to light their cigarettes with. Perhaps for acts like this, perhaps for a tendency to bend the rules to get things done right, his men adored him. The chief gunner's mate, an experienced career sailor, thought him the finest captain he had ever served under.

He captained a vessel that was called "Lucky Tartar" by her flo-tilla mates because of her eerie success in avoiding damage. Dur-ing the German invasion of Norway, the *Tartar* came out un-scathed during air attacks that sank or damaged other British vessels. A year later, during the *Bismarck* chase, she escaped untouched when Luftwaffe bombing sank a sister ship. But she spent much time based at Scapa Flow as part of the Home Fleet, to block any movement of German naval forces into the Atlantic. And Scapa was awful. The wind never stopped. Ships constantly dragged their anchors. In winter it was never light, in summer never dark. There was nothing to do ashore except to walk or fish or — for the ratings — drink beer in a club. When other ships came in, the officers sometimes went over to visit with their friends. Occasionally movies were shown. Skipwith once mentioned that he hadn't been ashore for 100 days and a young officer rashly told him that he had him beat because he hadn't been on land for 101; the next day the officer, realizing that prudence was better than valor when it came to his commanding officer, yielded the record to Skipwith: he went to one of the islands around the harbor and took a walk for twenty minutes.

The *Tartar* also put in months of patrolling, "basically hammering back and forth in this unfriendly sea," an officer said, speaking of months of "gales endured on the open bridge." It was "very dull, soul-destroying" work. Soon the *Tartar* had established two records: she was the first destroyer to spend 200 days at sea in World War II, and she was the first to have run 100,000 nautical miles since the beginning of the war. This comforted the crew members but little. Thought one:

> You don't know what it was like, what with the cold and the wet and all. Sometimes, every time you jumped out of your hammock you'd land in water up to your knees. You were cold and wet and tired and hungry and scared and sick. You were always being thrown about. Sometimes you couldn't stand upright for weeks on end. It was awful. And you'd think, "I'll never go back to this." And when you were on leave, at home, and it was almost up, you'd think of your mates, and you'd think, "I can't let them down" — and you'd go back.

The raid on the *Lauenburg* was a change from the routine. "It was a welcome relief to be doing a particular thing," one officer said. The men did not know their target's name, or the secret purpose of the attack, only that they were going after a trawler.

After skirting Jan Mayen, the four-ship flotilla turned due north at 2:40 A.M. on Saturday, June 28. A few hours later, it swung to northeast by east. At 11:15, the *Nigeria*, the flagship, tested its close-range weapons; the *Tartar* tested her antiaircraft pom-poms.

Burrough, meanwhile, reconsidered his plans. He had intended a sweep from west to east, like the one that had worked so well with the *München*. But the position of a fog bank, and the presence of icebergs, meant that this course would require the ships to steam through the ice in thick fog. So Burrough decided instead on a south–north sweep, hugging the fog bank to port. At 12:08 P.M. he ordered the ships to form a line abreast west to east, guiding on the *Nigeria*, in this order: *Jupiter, Nigeria*, the *Bedouin, Tartar*. They were to spread out to the limit of visibility or to asdic range, whichever was greater. They were to close toward the *Nigeria* when fog was sighted ahead and to open out in clear spaces. If they did not find the trawler by the completion of the search — a time to be specified later — the *Nigeria* would signal a new course and speed and then start a new search. Burrough ordered that when the trawler was sighted, the shells fired should not be high-explosive but practice ones set to burst above the target, as these would persuade her crew to abandon ship while not endangering the precious documents that the British were working so hard to obtain. When Skipwith told the chief gunner's mate, Thomas R. Kelly, a wiry, intelligent hand, that "I would like you to fire at the ship but not hit her," Kelly cheekily replied, "Christ, that should be easy."

All the ships had boarding parties made up, with the men given belts and pistols and trained for the job. The *Tartar*'s was composed of some ten tough former merchant seamen who enjoyed a fight and who were under the command of an officer, with Kelly as second in command.

At 1:50 P.M., the *Nigeria* altered course to due north. The destroyers followed. At 2:02 Burrough signaled the flotilla to "Spread as previously ordered" and to steer "Course 000 [due north] speed 18 knots" until the first sweep was to end, at 9:30. At 2:15, the destroyers spread out to visibility range — some 6 or 7 miles at the time — and the search began.

Aboard the *Tartar*, Skipwith posted lookouts on the bridge and in the crow's nest. He announced to his ship's company, "We're looking for a weather ship that's giving the German bombers information to bomb your homes. So keep your eyes skinned for it." The gunnery control officer, Lieutenant Henry Durrell, a former merchant service officer, offered a pound to the first member of the crew to spot the trawler. He was himself perched in the director tower, a housing high up on the mast for the range finder, and so had a good chance to win his own bet.

A dim sun shone; the air was calm except for an occasional puff; the sea was smooth. The sub-lieutenant, Ludovic Kennedy, was struck by the incredible clarity of the light and by the metallic look of the water in the Arctic world, different, he felt, from anywhere else. The sky had an icy cast. Patches of fog blew in from the west, hampering visibility, and large bergs and growlers hindered the search.

At 4:11 P.M., the *Bedouin* obtained a radio direction-finding bearing of north by east on a transmission made by the unsuspecting trawler. The flotilla kept steaming north. The lookouts swung their heavy binoculars back and forth across their quadrants, arms growing weary, eyes growing tired as they scanned the horizon in hopes of seeing the top of the trawler's mast. At 5:08 the Admiralty reported that one of its direction-finding stations — at Cupar, in Scotland, some 10 miles west of St. Andrews and almost directly on the meridian of 3° west longitude — had heard the trawler's transmission on a bearing of due north, which would have put the *Lauenburg* not at 4° west, as previously reported, but at 3°. But at the *Lauenburg*'s latitude, 73° north, the distance between 3° and 4° west is only 17.6 nautical miles, and this difference, at Cupar's distance of 760 miles, was well within the margin of error of radio direction-finding. So Burrough did not alter course.

Two hours later, at 6:50, with the sun a little south of west and low on the horizon, the *Nigeria* suddenly swung to starboard, due east, perhaps because of fog blowing in from the west. Soon the *Tartar* recognized this change of course and turned as well. At this moment, "Shorty" Allgood, the leading seaman, whose job was to train the director tower on the enemy, sang out. "There's something behind that iceberg, sir!" he cried. The lookouts peered ahead. A dark blob with a mast emerged from behind one of the bergs. It was 6:59. The blob was bearing just to the left of dead ahead, at a range of 10 miles.

It soon proved to be the trawler. The *Lauenburg* was then 2 miles north of her announced position of 73° north and a little more than 13 miles east of her announced position of 4° west; the *Tartar*, being on the east of the patrol line, was the first to spot her.

On orders, the *Tartar* crew jumped from defense stations to action stations. Skipwith ordered full speed ahead. In the wheel-house, the quartermasters at the port and starboard telegraphs rang the engine room. The ship vibrated more strongly to the increased power. White water thrashed at her stern. The *Tartar* spurted ahead. Seven minutes later she signaled, "Possible two trawlers bearing 358° ahead." The *Bedouin,* too, increased to full speed. Two minutes after the *Tartar*'s message, she had spotted the trawler. She and the *Tartar* raced for the prize.

The *Lauenburg*'s crew had been fearing some unpleasantness ever since the radio operator had reported transmissions so strong that they could have come only from nearby vessels. He also may have determined their bearing using the ship's direction-finder. Braun and Klarman were on deck when one of the lookouts raised an alarm: he had seen the mast of a warship behind an iceberg to the south. At once Captain Gewald turned the *Lauenburg* to the north and pushed her to her top speed of about 12 knots. The British ships chased her at far greater speed.

On the *Tartar,* Chief Gunner's Mate Kelly prepared to follow Skipwith's admonition to fire at the ship but not hit her. He gave high-altitude practice shells, with a dollop of black powder to make a puff, to the two forward twin 4.7-inch guns of his A and B turrets. He worked out the range and the time for these to explode 75 feet above the ship. He set the shells' 206 fuse — the latest model, with a dial like a clock on which the time from firing to detonation could be set.

The destroyers soon determined the direction of the *Lauenburg*'s flight, and at 7:01 the *Bedouin* signaled, "Enemy's course 360°," or due north. Two minutes later she opened fire, and a minute after that the *Tartar* did.

At the same time, the *Tartar*'s radioman, listening on the *Lauenburg*'s usual frequency of 12,040 kilocycles, heard the trawler broadcast the international radio call CT, meaning "You should not come alongside." The call stopped almost immediately — not that the British would have heeded it anyway. The *Nigeria* began firing her 6-inch guns. The shells from all these ships exploded above or splashed ahead and to both sides of the *Lauenburg* 50 to 100 yards from her, as she steamed frantically away from the onrushing British. The *Tartar* closed in.

Aboard the *Lauenburg,* the sight of three gray warships racing

Britain's target: an Enigma cipher machine of the German navy. The Enigma put German messages radioed to U-boats into secret form; an identical machine, identically set up, reconverted the ciphertext to plaintext in the submarines.

How the Germans set up an Enigma machine for enciphering messages.

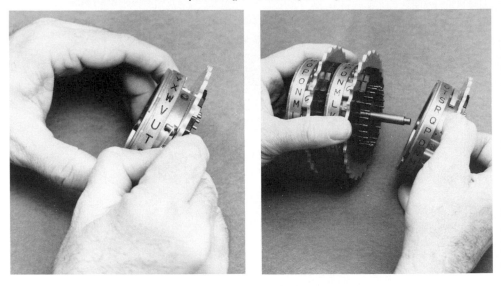

From the eight rotors available, the three specified by the key list for current use are chosen. *Above, left:* The alphabet ring on each rotor is turned to the position given in the key list and locked into place with a pin on a leaf spring. *Above, right:* The three current rotors are assembled on the shaft from left to right in the order given in the key list. *Below:* The rotors are inserted into the machine.

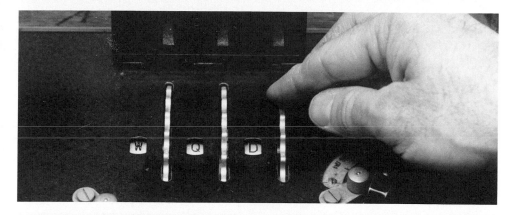

Top: The jacks on each end of several short cables are plugged into the sockets specified by the key list of a plugboard on the front of the machine. *Middle:* The rotors are turned until the letters specified by the key list appear in the windows of the Enigma's lid. *Bottom:* When the machine has been set up, encipherment begins. Each plaintext letter of the German message is pressed on the keyboard, and the letters that light up on the illuminable panel are written down. This is the ciphertext. After the entire message has been put into cipher, the cryptogram is radioed from headquarters to a U-boat or from a U-boat to headquarters.

Russian sailors look at the wreck of the *Magdeburg*, partly blown up near the island of Odensholm in August 1914.

Arthur Scherbius, the inventor of the Enigma.

Hans-Thilo Schmidt, the spy who revealed some secrets of the Enigma.

A. Dillwyn Knox, who made some progress in the attempt to solve the Enigma.

Marian Rejewski, the Polish mathematician who solved the Enigma.

The U-33 and some of her crew members.

The Führer greets von Dresky, skipper of the U-33.

Fish-oil tanks burn during the British commando raid on the Lofotens, March 1941.

The *Krebs* just before the British boarded her during the Lofotens raid and seized Enigma keys and rotors.

The ice-encrusted gun and the crew of the ill-fated U-110.

Sub-Lieutenant David Balme of the *Bulldog*, who boarded the U-110.

Radioman and Enigma machine operator Heinz Wilde of the U-110.

Four key members of the British codebreaking agency: *Top, left:* Edward Travis, its head from 1942 on. *Top, right:* Harry Hinsley, who evaluated solved German intercepts. *Bottom, left:* Hugh Alexander, head of the cryptanalysts of German navy messages. *Bottom, right:* Gordon Welchman, whose device accelerated cryptanalysis.

Codebreakers play rounders on the lawn of Bletchley Park. In the background is the main house.

Codebreakers watch a rounders match at Bletchley Park. Fifth from left, standing, is George McVittie, head of meteorological cryptanalysis. Standing at right is A. G. Denniston, then head of B.P.

Above: The boarding party of the *Tartar* musters on her forecastle as the British destroyer approaches the German weather ship *Lauenburg. Left:* The boarding party seizes all the papers it can find, including cryptographic keys, from the *Lauenburg.*

Right: The crew of the weather ship, blindfolded, is taken aboard the *Tartar.*
Below: The *Tartar* sinks the *Lauenburg* with gunfire.

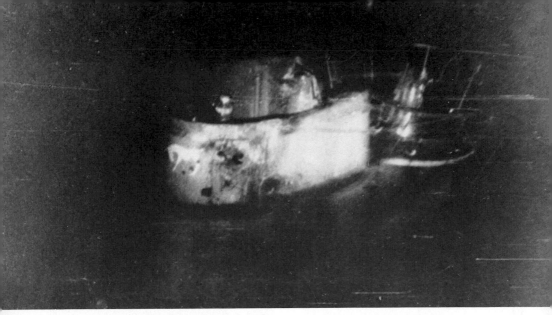

The conning tower of the U-559 emerges from the sea, its white
donkey emblem picked out by the searchlight of the destroyer *Petard*.

Antony Fasson, who lost his life getting
cipher documents from the U-559.

Admiral Karl Dönitz, commander of
U-boats.

The giant wall plot of the North Atlantic, which showed the positions of convoys, escorts, and U-boats, in the headquarters of Western Approaches Command in Liverpool. The circles showed areas to be avoided by Allied U-boat hunters because of the presence of Allied submarines.

A high-speed U.S. Navy mechanism, called a bombe, that tested for possible Enigma solutions.

Commander Kenneth A. Knowles, head of the U.S. Navy's Submarine Tracking Room, which depended heavily on Enigma solutions.

Some of the U.S. Navy personnel of OP-20-GI-2(A) who solved, translated, and evaluated Enigma intercepts. Among them are Erminnie Bartelmez, at extreme left; Marjorie Boynton, with blond hair, looking to her right; Knight McMahan, with hat at his feet; Bernard Roeder, commander of the unit, holding his hat; and Willard Van Orman Quine, standing behind seated William Lindsay.

A depth charge, dropped by a U.S. Navy torpedo-bomber during a U-boat refueling rendezvous, drenches the tanker U-117, whose bow emerges from the spray just before the U-66 dives.

An F4F-4 Wildcat from the aircraft carrier *Card* attacks the U-117, which circles in an effort to escape.

The U-117 races desperately through the sunlit sea as a depth charge explodes near her. Minutes later she was sunk.

toward her, foam peeling from their bows, flames bursting from their guns, struck fear into the crew. Some members recognized that the shells being fired were not real — they took them for warning shots — and thus not intended to sink their ship. Thinking at first that they might make a stand, they broke out small arms, mostly automatic pistols, from their grease-paper wrappings. But then the ludicrousness of this attempt overcame them, and they dropped the puny weapons on the mess table. Nor did they attempt to man the feeble deck weapons with which their vessel had been equipped: discretion was the better part of valor.

Gewald and all but two members of the crew climbed into the two lifeboats and quickly rowed as far away from the ship as they could. The two men left on board, including the mate, threw overboard the most precious item on the ship, the Enigma, and then stuffed documents into the coal-burning furnace of a boiler.

The *Tartar* ceased fire at 7:12 and sped toward the *Lauenburg*, coming alongside at almost 32 knots. The two men left aboard offered no resistance and willingly took the destroyer's lines. By then the order had been given, "Boarding party muster on forecastle."

The head of the boarding party was the ship's navigating officer, Lieutenant T. Hugh P. Wilson, nicknamed "Spider," a brown-eyed, bushy-browed, popular career officer. He was glad to be in the Royal Navy. Like the others in the Senior Service, he felt equal to anyone in the realm; their place in the hierarchy of the establishment assured them of this status, and as officers they were gentlemen. He had joined the *Tartar* at her builders' and on September 1, 1939, had been promoted to lieutenant, the basic naval rank, which meant that he could serve as officer of the watch on any ship. He had spent much of the war up to the Lofotens raid in tedious patrol duty on the destroyer. For work in the chart room, which was warm but drafty, and for the long hours on the open bridge, he had sewn a duffel skirt onto his duffel jacket and was thereafter called, whenever he wore it, "the Widow Twankey." Skipwith and the first lieutenant (the second in command) chose him to command the boarding party probably because they wanted a qualified officer and because he was the next in seniority.

As the *Tartar* and the *Lauenburg* rocked side by side in the slight swell, with the low sunlight diffusing through the haze, the great white wall of the ice gleaming in the distance, and the sounds of the gunfire still echoing in the Britishers' brains, Wilson looked down from the forecastle and saw that some of his boarding party, under Kelly, its second in command, were clambering over the guard rail onto the trawler. "Come along, Wilson," he said to himself. "You're supposed to be in charge of this lot." And he jumped down onto the trawler.

Unfortunately, the rising and falling of the ships in the swell caused him to misjudge the distance. His left foot struck the fish hold and was bent back against his shin, splitting his boot and pushing the toes back. In pain, he dragged himself up into the chart house and commanded the boarding party from there.

Some of its members checked the sea cocks and found them closed; no other men but the two first seen on deck were aboard. Kelly examined the ship and found her immaculate. The diesels were ticking smoothly: one of the ratings told Kelly they could have run forever. Her generators were running and her lights were on. The boarders found the handguns, still on their grease paper, abandoned on the mess table. There were some ashes in the boiler furnace, but all over the floor of the wheelhouse and chart house was paper. The boarders were wading in it.

Soon after the *Tartar*'s men boarded the *Lauenburg,* the other three warships arrived at the scene, and the *Jupiter* sent over a boat with G.C.&C.S.'s Allon Bacon. He appeared on board the trawler, saw the masses of paper lying about, and said to Wilson, "For God's sake, man, look at all this material. Pack it up!"

"What?" replied Wilson. "All this rubbish?"

But Bacon wanted it all, so Wilson told his men to get on with it, ordering Kelly to collect every piece of paper with writing on it. The sailors kept asking Wilson, "What do you want all this rubbish for?" As he perched on a stool in the chart house, they reported to him on the food they found in the refrigerator and the sealskins that were curing in barrels. Kelly told them not to turn on any other lights for fear of a booby trap. After about an hour on board, they had collected thirteen mail sacks full of documents, together with photographs of Hitler and Raeder. Kelly liberated the lamp from Captain Gewald's cabin. The three small deck guns were removed with their ammunition, as well as the small arms and radio equipment. Everything went back to the *Tartar.*

Admiral Burrough had decided not to bring the captured trawler back to Britain with him. He did not wish to immobilize a destroyer to escort her, and he feared that if a German aircraft sighted her with a destroyer or on a strange course, much of the value of the intelligence gained might be lost. The *Lauenburg*'s crew, the rest of whom had been picked up by the *Bedouin,* had been taken below at once so that they could not see what was happening to their ship. When Bacon said he was satisfied that the trawler had been thoroughly searched, Burrough ordered her sunk. The *Tartar* sent torpedomen aboard with scuttling charges. But they failed to explode, and the torpedomen's rivals, the gun crews, shouted their derision. Then it was their turn, and at a range of 500 yards Kelly's men slammed four semi-armor-piercing shells from B turret into the *Lauenburg* at the waterline. At 9 P.M., in thick fog, the ill-fated ship descended to a grave a thousand fathoms deep. Gewald was brought to the *Tartar* and put in a cabin over the propellers. Kelly gave him a light, and he lit up a cigar, greatly enjoying the first drag.

Bacon had the mail sacks brought to Captain Skipwith's main cabin, a room larger than his sea cabin and one that sometimes served as a surgeon's operating room. There Bacon sorted the captured documents and pieces of paper. Among the vast volume of charts and orders and gun manuals, he found what he was looking for: a table for the July home waters Enigma key, plus two sheets for the plugboard, one for July 1 to 15, one for July 16 to 31, and a sheet of internal settings.

The *Tartar* and the other ships arrived back at Scapa two days later. Bacon was taken to the *Dunluce Castle,* a forty-year-old passenger ship converted into a depot ship that was a regular stop for the ferry that made the hour-long trip across Pentland Firth to the railhead at Thurso on the Scottish mainland. From there, carrying his precious documents in a big canvas bag, he rode to Rosyth, the major naval base near Edinburgh, where a scrambler telephone enabled him to call Bletchley and tell the cryptanalysts what he had and when he would be arriving. He took the night train.

Hinsley and the naval cryptanalysts assembled, and early on Wednesday, July 2, Bacon came in with his canvas bag, flung it on the table, and opened it. "Here it is," he said. They all had a look, and within five minutes the cryptanalysts had taken the documents to Hut 8 next door. These papers would enable them to read July messages and so were immediately useful. At once the solution times fell. From about forty hours on July 1, to which they had risen when the *München*'s June keys had expired, they fell on the afternoon of July 2 to under three hours. Hinsley felt pleased that it had all worked out so well. But he couldn't allow himself to wallow in self-congratulation. He had work to do.

Fifteen

The Great Man Himself

THE CAPTURED DOCUMENTS from the U-110 and the two weather ships and the subsequent acceleration of solutions had no immediate direct effect on the Battle of the Atlantic. In June 1941, when solution times declined to three or four hours, roughly the same number of tons succumbed to U-boats as in May, when solution times ran three or four days. The same situation obtained in July and August, with their respectively fast and slow solution times. In fact, in the fast-solution months of June and July, U-boats sank almost exactly the same tonnage in the North Atlantic as in the slow-solution months of May and August. As these comparisons demonstrate, intelligence did not always rule in the war against the U-boats. Other factors outweighed it. The July–August loss of tonnage fell to under a third of the May–June figure for reasons unrelated to B.P. More escorts were available and were accompanying convoys uninterruptedly across the Atlantic. The escorts' experience made them more efficient. The minimum speed of ships sailing independently was raised from 13 to 15 knots. Air cover was increased. Also fewer U-boats were in the North Atlantic because some had been withdrawn to fight shipping to the Soviet Union, the new U-boat crews were less experienced, and Hitler was anxious to avoid clashes with American warships.

But in spite of the failure of codebreaking intelligence to contribute much to the Atlantic battle at that time, its potential to do so still seemed great. It might yet permit diverting convoys away from the U-boat wolfpacks that became ever more likely as the Germans built more and more submarines. So Hinsley, and Hut 8, continued their efforts.

And bit by bit they were rewarded. The insight gained into German naval communications procedures and the capture of the Short Signal Book from the U-110 enabled the Hut 8 cryptanalysts to concoct and test cribs more efficiently. They were aided by the growing number of kisses, especially in the Dockyard Cipher and in weather systems.

Conditions were further improved by an influx of men and machines. The number of bombes rose to eight by the end of June. All of this meant that after the first week in August, when cryptanalysis resumed, Hut 8 had mastered the Home Waters key. Its messages were at first not read currently, but after mid-August they were solved every day, most of them within thirty-six hours.

This success was made the sweeter by appreciatory visits to Bletchley Park. The first sea lord, Admiral Sir Dudley Pound, passed through on August 9, and a month later the great man himself, Prime Minister Churchill, appeared.

He had long been intensely interested in the results of codebreaking. It was into his hands that the Russian naval attaché had placed the *Magdeburg* codebook in October 1914, and he had witnessed the first successes it brought the Royal Navy. In November 1924, when he had just become chancellor of the exchequer following a Conservative landslide, he pleaded with the foreign secretary to be allowed to see the intercepts. "I have studied this information over a long period and more attentively than probably any other Minister has done," he wrote. ". . . I attach more importance to them as a means of forming a true judgement of public policy in these spheres than to any other source of knowledge at the disposal of the State." In September 1940, four months after he became prime minister, Churchill ordered that he be given "daily all Enigma messages." This proved impracticable, but by the summer of 1941 he was getting each day a selection of several dozen, together with reports on the progress of cryptanalyses, brought to him in a special dispatch box, buff-colored to distinguish it from the black boxes for other official papers. The box was to be unlocked only by Churchill, who carried the key on his key ring. Extremely watchful about access to these papers, he minuted once: "I am astounded at the vast congregation who are invited to study these matters," and he urged restrictions. This source of information was disguised at first under the codename BONIFACE, but later ULTRA came to be used as the collective cover name for the solutions of the Enigma intercepts. With those in the know, he used the solutions vigorously. He discussed them at his daily meetings with his chiefs of staff, fired off messages based on them to his field commanders, and in general used them to the maximum in running the war.

So on Saturday, September 6, 1941, as Churchill was driving to a friend's country estate for the weekend, he stopped off at Bletchley Park. Some thirty to forty of the higher-level workers gathered around him on the grass as he stood on the trunk of a felled tree near Hut 6 and said, in his incomparable tones, and with a mischievous twinkle in his eye, "You all look very innocent." The grateful and security-conscious prime minister praised them as the geese that laid the golden eggs and never cackled. He related a few stories of how their work had helped him and emphasized the great value of their accomplishments. Then he visited a few of the huts. In Naval Section, where a nervous Alan Turing was introduced to him, he was shown as a prize exhibit the Dockyard–Enigma kisses.

Gordon Welchman had, upon instructions, prepared a five-minute talk. He began, "I would like to make three points." He had completed only two when G.C.&C.S.'s second in command, Commander Edward Travis, interrupted: "That's enough, Welchman." Churchill winked at the speaker and said, "I think there was a third point, Welchman." Welchman presented John Herivel to Churchill as one of the solvers of Enigma. Herivel was thrilled.

Word of the visit raced through the Park. Those not present at the prime minister's speech heard that he had said "something great." The episode boosted morale. It was just as well that the Bletchleyites did not hear his remark to Sir Stewart Menzies, who as head of the Secret Intelligence Service was formally the director of G.C.&C.S., after viewing the unkempt crew of workers: "I know I told you to leave no stone unturned to find the necessary staff, but I didn't mean you to take me so literally!"

In addition to lifting spirits, the visit had a more significant effect. Back in April, the Kriegsmarine had slightly modified the Home Waters key for U-boats, probably to keep other German units from eavesdropping on submarine messages. This gave Hut 8 no trouble. In October, however, the navy set up a separate U-boat message cipher net called TRITON, which delayed the British solutions a little. The extra work entailed in solving the new settings perhaps contributed to the overworking of the punched-card section of Hut 8, compelling it to cut out night shifts. This delayed the recovery of any naval keys by at least twelve hours every day. To this serious problem were added others: failure to supply enough women to work on the bombes and insufficient personnel to decipher a Luftwaffe key for North Africa, which was providing data about General Erwin Rommel's air unit's order of battle, supplies, and tactical policy — all of great value as Britain was preparing an offensive. Yet no one seemed to be doing anything about these problems.

So around the middle of October, emboldened by Churchill's visit, Welchman, acting head of Hut 6, which solved German army and air force messages, gathered three other middle managers to discuss the possibility of appealing over Denniston's head to the prime minister himself. The others were Alan Turing, head of Hut 8; Hugh Alexander, Turing's deputy; and Stuart Milner-Barry, Welchman's deputy and an old and close chess-playing friend of Alexander's. They may have met first at the Shoulder of Mutton pub, where Milner-Barry and Alexander lived, but most of the subsequent discussions took place in Hut 6. All agreed with Welchman's plan, and Welchman, who spent much of his time writing powerful memoranda that he called "screeds," drafted the letter.

"Dear Prime Minister," it began. "Some weeks ago you paid us the honour of a visit, and we believe that you regard our work as important." The letter made plain that Travis, Denniston's deputy, was not to blame for the problems, pointing out that Travis had kept them well supplied with bombes and "has all along done his utmost."

> We think, however, that you ought to know that this work is being held up, and in some cases is not being done at all, principally because we cannot get sufficient staff to deal with it. Our reason for writing to you direct is that for months we have done everything that we possibly can through the normal channels, and that we despair of any early improvement without your intervention. No doubt in the long run these particular requirements will be met, but meanwhile still more precious months will have been wasted, and as our needs are continually expanding we see little hope of ever being adequately staffed. . . . as we are a very small section with numeri-

cally trivial requirements it is very difficult to bring home to the authorities finally responsible either the importance of what is done here or the urgent necessity of dealing promptly with our requests.

The letter then set out three areas where staff shortages were delaying work: recovery of naval Enigma keys, solution of Africa Luftwaffe keys, and bombe work. The four manager-cryptanalysts implied that Denniston could not solve these problems when they stated that "we have written this letter entirely on our own initiative" and concluded by saying that "if we are to do our job as well as it could and should be done, it is absolutely vital that our wants, small as they are, should be promptly attended to."

They dated the letter October 21, 1941 — the anniversary of the Battle of Trafalgar, when Nelson's defeat of the French fleet saved England from a Napoleonic invasion — a date that would not be lost on Churchill. To prevent the letter's being blocked in the bureaucratic hierarchy, they decided to deliver it personally to Churchill.

The job fell to Milner-Barry. On the twenty-first, he took the train to London. Scarcely believing what he was doing, he told a cab driver to take him to No. 10 Downing Street, the prime minister's residence and office. There he rang the bell, stated his business, was ushered inside, and was told to wait. Soon there appeared the shortish, dapper figure of Churchill's principal private secretary. Milner-Barry explained that he had come from a secret establishment and had an important letter to deliver to the prime minister in person. But the secretary knew nothing of G.C.&C.S. or of ULTRA, and Milner-Barry could not tell him, and the secretary quite naturally said that no one could see the prime minister without an appointment. Milner-Barry insisted, however, that the matters were of great importance but that he could not discuss them with anyone not authorized to know about them. He had no Foreign Office pass to prove his identity and nothing to show that he was on secret business. But he referred to Churchill's visit to Bletchley knowledgeably, showing that he had been present on that occasion, which the secretary knew about. This resolved the impasse, and the secretary promised to place the letter, unopened, before Churchill personally.

The very next day, Churchill wrote to the secretary of the Committee of Imperial Defence: "ACTION THIS DAY. Make sure they have all they want on extreme priority and report to me that this has been done." In less than a month, Menzies reported to Churchill that Bletchley's needs were rapidly being met. And though he criticized Welchman for having violated the chain of command, he appointed an independent investigator to look into the B.P. administration.

For the cryptanalysts' letter had revealed administrative stress. B.P.'s sevenfold expansion, from some 200 at the start of the war to 1,500 in early 1942, had rendered the creative anarchy of a small cryptanalytic bureau almost counterproductive. Services — housing, transport, and food — were faltering. B.P. also needed a stronger hand to fight the intelligence directorates on priorities and personnel. Several power struggles had already been resolved by outside authorities, but a new and more serious one — whether the army and air force or G.C.&C.S. should control production of the solutions and their evaluation — came to a head soon after the letter went to Churchill. (The Admiralty had resolved this problem by setting up a close liaison between the O.I.C. and Naval Section).

Many Bletchleyites blamed the chaos on G.C.&C.S.'s operating head. Alastair Denniston's noncombative personality made it difficult for him to demand the resources needed to overcome these problems. He was perhaps a defender but not an aggressor. If his subordinates said they needed twenty bombes, he would say, "Well, one, maybe two." Nigel de Grey, an assistant director of G.C.&C.S., as well as Frank Birch and others, agreed that Denniston simply could not cope. His era — one of a few eccentrics, of protecting his little domain from Whitehall's bureaucratic rules, even of the country-house spirit of the early days — had passed. He was not the man for the job.

Menzies's independent investigator reached the same conclusion, and in February 1942 a reorganization booted Denniston sideways. His title had always been deputy director; now another deputy directorship was created. An unhappy Denniston, removed from Bletchley entirely, became deputy director (C), handling commercial and diplomatic solutions from an office building in Berkeley Street, London. His deputy, Travis, a table thumper, a tough customer, a man whose ruddy face looked like "a carving in Spam," who had come up through the codemaking side, where he had worked since World War I, became deputy director (S), for the armed services, at Bletchley. Travis was a man who, when his cryptanalysts asked for twenty bombes, said he would get them — and did so. Bletchley now had a manager who could bring it into the modern era of cryptanalytic mass production.

Another change occurred that same year, but it was more gradual. The energetic chess champion, Hugh Alexander, took over more and more from Turing as head of Hut 8. He had the taste and the skills for administration — the attention to detail and the ability to deal well with people — that Turing lacked. Once, wishing to get rid of a particular woman as head of a shift, he reorganized the three shifts into a complicated arrangement of five, adding two women to head the new ones; after a while, claiming that the new system was not working, he reformed them back into the original three — dropping the woman he did not want. Turing never had that subtlety, and though he felt the loss of the headship, he recognized Alexander's superiority in it. Later in 1942, while Turing was in the United States, a form came to Hut 8 asking for the name of the head of the unit. "Well, I suppose I am," said Alexander, and thereafter he remained in smooth control of solving the naval Enigma.

The capture of the Short Weather Cipher from the *München* let B.P. steal kisses from weather messages. Hut 10 did the necessary preliminary work. Its head was George C. McVittie, a tall, thin mathematician-turned-weatherman. Professorial, unkempt, with a fine head of hair and a high voice, always jolly, never upset, good to his subordinates, and with a mind that absorbed everything quickly, McVittie and his section of less than a dozen people attacked German meteorological ciphers to get information about the weather in and around Europe that would be helpful to British air and sea operations.

Among the systems they worked on was the Kriegsmarine's weather cipher (not the same as the Short Weather Cipher). Messages in it were transmitted from various observation posts, including ships at sea, to a central point, sent from there to the great maritime radio station DAN in Norddeich, Germany, and broadcast on 150 kilocycles from the long, many-windowed building for the use of naval units all around Europe. The cipher was based on the International Meteorological Code. It represented such parameters as wind direction, precipitation, barometric pressure, and temperature by figures in a particular order. The German cipher grouped these figures in threes and replaced each triad with a three-digit codegroup. These equivalencies were listed in tables, of which the Germans used five at a time, each one for a different class of message (ground observation or ship report, for example); they changed these five tables five times a day. Hut 10 first cracked this cipher in February 1941. This solution, combined with the capture of the Short Weather Cipher, allowed Hut 8 to solve Enigma messages. It worked the two ciphers like a crossruff in bridge.

The German navy's high command had ordered U-boats to make weather reports. The submarines, like the weather ships, converted their observations into letters, using the Short Weather Cipher, and enciphered these letters with the Enigma. They radioed this cryptogram to Germany. Whichever radio station received it acknowledged receipt, stripped off the Enigma encipherment, and then forwarded it to a central meteorological station. Using the Short Weather Cipher, this center turned the letters back into meteorological data. Then, when it thought the information valuable, it enciphered these data in a German weather code and broadcast them to German ships at sea and posts ashore.

The British intercepted these broadcasts. Hut 10, having cracked the German weather codes, could reduce them to their meteorological plaintext version. It therefore had the same meteorological data that the U-boats were transmitting.

Now, using the Short Weather Cipher obtained from the *München*, Hut 10 could do what the U-boats had done: convert these data into letters, the plaintexts of the U-boats' Enigma weather messages. These served Hut 8 as cribs to the Enigma encipherments. A chief problem was identifying the U-boat message that eventuated in the broadcast, but Hut 10 was able to do that often enough. One of the cryptanalysts, the dark-haired, mustachioed Philip E. Archer, dealt so frequently in these matters with Hut 8 that the naval cryptanalysts called the meteorological kisses — in the Bletchley word-play tradition — "Archery."

When Bletchley solved intercepts about U-boats and passed them to the O.I.C., each sub was marked with a pin on the chart of the

Atlantic in the Submarine Tracking Room. As successive intercepts came in, revealing new positions, the watchkeepers moved
the pins. Sometimes the U-boats formed into wolfpacks; sometimes they stretched into long straggly patrol lines; sometimes they
coalesced into loose gatherings heading toward one general area.
The watchkeepers always viewed the sub pins in relation to the
pins representing the convoys, of which usually eight or nine were
crossing the Atlantic in each direction at any given time.

The United States was providing cargoes and convoy escorts to
Britain, and every day the Admiralty transmitted to the Navy Department in Washington its estimate of German submarine positions in the North Atlantic. The data came from sightings, engage-
ments, and torpedoings, from direction-finding, and — though this
was not made explicit — from solutions of the U-boats' own estimates of their positions. On the basis of this information, the Admiralty also sent the Navy Department proposed routes for forth-
coming convoys. One such route, sent on October 8, 1941, was for
convoy HX 155, scheduled to sail a week later from Halifax, Nova
Scotia.

HX 155's route was specified by a series of latitude and longitude points, each identified by a letter, through which the convoy
should pass. The time for the convoy to be at the mid-ocean meeting point, or MOMP, where American escorts transferred control
to British (and vice versa, for westbound convoys) was given in Z,
or Greenwich Mean Time, the point itself being designated by the
letter P. The Admiralty's message read: "HX 155 route recommended (1) D 47-00 north 51-00 west, E 54-00 38-00, F 58-50 30-
00, (2) 1000Z/25th October, (3) P 58-50 22-40, (4) Q 58-50 20-00,
R 59-50 07-00." A few hours after receiving the recommended
route, the U.S. Navy told the Admiralty it concurred.

On October 12, five American destroyers were designated as Task
Unit 4.1.7 and were ordered to "escort convoy HX 155 scheduled
depart Halifax October 16. Escort meet convoy on or to westward
of 55 meridian west and proceed via such route as may be prescribed by Opnav [Operations Division, Navy Department]." The
navy ordered the convoy to proceed at 8.8 knots. On Thursday,
October 16, the fifty-four ships of HX 155 steamed out of the entrance of Halifax harbor and assumed a sailing order of eleven
columns of four, five, or six ships each. The *City of Bath* was carrying copper and general cargo to Loch Ewe, Scotland. The *Mar-*

garita Chandris, heading for the same port, had grain in her hold. The *British Chemist* was taking fuel oil to the Clyde, Glasgow's river. Almost half the convoy was carrying some kind of oil — gasoline, aviation spirits, or other fuel.

At 12:55 A.M. on Saturday, the five destroyers of Task Unit 4.1.7 left Argentia, Newfoundland, where, two months before, President Franklin D. Roosevelt and Prime Minister Churchill had met and signed the Atlantic Charter, in which they proclaimed their high moral purposes in opposing fascism. At 9:30 that morning, the lead destroyer spotted the convoy off her port bow. Under high clouds, pushed by a gentle breeze and pitching to a swell from the west, the escort joined the merchantmen, and both headed due east into the Atlantic.

Around midnight, they turned a little northward. After about four hours, they swung still more toward the north until they were steaming northeast. They continued on this course through Sunday, passing through the first specified location, Point D.

In Britain, Submarine Tracking Room chief Rodger Winn and his subordinates continued to read the teletypes of solutions from Naval Section, some of which gave submarine locations. The direction-finding stations sent in bearings on which they had heard transmissions. Direction-finding head Peter Kemp plotted the bearings on his own chart and informed the duty officer at the main plot of the results. (Kemp's experience often enabled him to give the approximate location of a transmitter just by seeing the bearings sent in.) Winn pulled all of this together. From it emerged a U-boat estimate.

On the Thursday the convoy sailed, the report sent to the Americans estimated seven submarines in an area of the east central North Atlantic bounded by 53° and 57° north and 22° and 28° west. Four subs were thought to form a sparse line from Cape Farewell, at the southern tip of Greenland, southeast almost 300 miles. The next day, the seven U-boats had become "eight or nine" and their area had expanded north and west. The information was solid: eight ships from the unlucky convoy SC 48 from Sydney, Nova Scotia, had been torpedoed in that area. That convoy had been carefully rerouted past a U-boat concentration that Winn and his team had detected — but then had been spotted accidentally by a U-boat arriving to join a patrol line; among the ships attacked was the escorting American destroyer *Kearney.*

This news perhaps increased jitteriness among the escorts, for at 3:10 A.M. the next day, Sunday, the U.S.S. *Bainbridge* went to general quarters when it was reported that flashes, a searchlight, and possibly gunfire had been seen and heard broad on the port bow. But whatever these were, they proved to be a false alarm, and the destroyer secured from general quarters ten minutes later. The convoy continued northeast. The submarine report that day merely stated that U-boats were "probably" in the same area as before, and the report of the next day showed Winn's predictive abilities when it stated that "Admiralty presumes U-boats recently southeast of Greenland and those pursuing SC 48 about to take up new dispositions   Trend to westward thought likely."

Perhaps as a consequence of this report, the Admiralty recommended that HX 155 change its route to pass through two new points, H, at 50° 00′ north 46° 30′ west, and J, at 57° 30′ north 40° 00′ west. This would shift the convoy's march 165 miles to the west of the abandoned Point E, keeping it that much farther from the U-boat concentration. But HX 155 did not make this diversion until noon on Monday, October 20. Of course, the move sent the convoy closer to the U-boats that Winn had aligned southeast of Cape Farewell. But since there were only four of them, and their distance apart averaged 75 miles, far greater than the maximum visibility of 13 miles from the top of a conning tower, the danger seemed much smaller than that from the mass of U-boats that the Submarine Tracking Room was trying to avoid.

On that Monday, the submarine report said "5 or 6 subs between latitude 55/57 N west of longitude 15 W moving west" and — probably referring to the line of four — "Subs in Northern Atlantic appear to be proceeding west." It also located one U-boat at 55° north 42° west — right in the new projected path of the convoy. A message went out: "HX 155 to increase clearance from suspected U-boat area recommend change route from H to 56-00 north 42-30 west then to J." This would move the line of march even farther west. On Tuesday the convoy swung due north, moving at 8.8 knots under a cloudy sky with a moderate gale pushing it along from the starboard quarter. Early on Wednesday, the U-boat situation report declared that "10 have concentrated in area between 54 to 56 N 26 to 37 W," or west of the east central North Atlantic area where they had sunk so many ships of SC 48.

The convoy was scheduled to head east to aim once again for

Britain after its diversion, and the U.S. Navy radioed Task Unit 4.1.7 to recommend that "convoy proceed at utmost speed during next 48 hours." As the convoy turned northeast to pass north of the sub-infested area, it raised its speed to 10 knots. Over the next two uneventful days, it made a succession of turns to starboard until, on Friday, it was steaming due east. On Saturday, a few hours after a fog started to lift, the American escort met the British at the MOMP south of Iceland. The Americans departed for home. HX 155, having dodged the U-boats, continued on toward the British Isles. On November 3, the Admiralty messaged: "HX 155 met as arranged. All ships now arrived. No stragglers." The grain in the *Margarita Chandris,* the sugar in the *Coulberg,* the fuel oil in the *British Chemist,* the steel and copper and gasoline and tobacco had reached the island kingdom — thanks in part to the back-room boys, the boffins, of Hut 8.

Sixteen

When Sailors Look for Leaks

COMMUNICATIONS were essential to Dönitz's control of wolfpack warfare, and they ran smoothly. But those communications had to be secret, and this worried him.

From 1940 to 1943, his headquarters lay in three summer villas in Kerneval, a suburb of the port of Lorient on the southern coast of Brittany. Communications, under the effective Commander Hans Meckel, were centered in a bombproof bunker where the air always seemed bad.

Sending a message to a U-boat at sea began with Dönitz or a subordinate writing it out. A watch officer then took the message to a command transmissions officer, who time-stamped it and gave it to the radio watch officer for encipherment and transmission. The chief radio watch officer for much of the war was Lieutenant Helmut Kühne, who worked in the bunker, along with fifteen to twenty radiomen per shift.

Kühne handed the message to a radioman for enciphering on an Enigma. Radiomen handled both transmission and reception as well as ciphering, but Kühne, when he could, put those with better Morse touch and hearing on radios and those who typed better on Enigmas. Since only officers could prepare the machine's inner settings, which remained in force for two days, the radio officer on watch set all but one of the several Enigma machines with the new inner key before every other midnight; later in the war, this was done before every other noon. One Enigma was left set with the previous day's key to decipher late-arriving messages.

After the officer was finished, an enlisted radioman plugged in the jacks of the plugboard. The machine was thus ready for the radioman handling the message to establish the message key. When he had completed that intricate process, he turned the rotors to the key. As he finally did the easy part — pressing the letters of the plaintext on the keyboard — a colleague wrote on the message form the ciphertext letters as they appeared on the illuminable panel. The message was divided into four-letter groups. The two four-letter indicator groups at the beginning were copied at the end. The message was given a date-time number, a number indicating how many four-letter groups it had (excluding the repeated pair at the end), and a serial number.

But before the ciphertext was transmitted, it was given to another radioman, who, using only the indicators that it carried, determined the message key and deciphered the cryptogram as the radioman on a U-boat at sea would do. If he could not decipher it, the error was sought and corrected. Only when the cryptogram was successfully deciphered was it ready to be sent.

The radioman determined the operating area of the U-boat and whether it was attacking a convoy, which told him the traffic network, or circuit, to transmit on. Eventually U-boat Command had several geographical nets — Amerika A (northern area), Amerika B (southern area), Afrika 1 and 2, Ireland, and others — and two nets for submarines attacking convoys. One, named for the goddess of the hunt, was called DIANA; the other, named for the patron saint of hunters, was called HUBERTUS. Each geographical net had three radio frequencies, chosen to give the best reception in its area in the daytime, at night, and at twilight. HUBERTUS had six frequencies, among them 4601 kilocycles from midnight to 7 A.M., 7645 from 9 to 11, and 12950 from 1 P.M. to 8 P.M. Sometimes a wolfpack was given its own frequency.

The radioman in Kerneval chose the proper frequency, tuned his radio to it, and tapped out his dots and dashes. From the bunker, the pulses coursed by wire to radio towers in Lorient, whence they were pumped into the ether. They were received not only by U-boats but by the station of the then defunct French Colonial Office in Sainte Assise, a few miles southeast of Paris. This station repeated the cryptogram immediately with greater power to give the U-boats a second and better chance at hearing it. It also repeated the message two, six, twelve, and twenty-four hours later and, if very important, forty-eight hours later. On an average day, U-Boat Command sent some twenty to thirty messages this way. Each one took some fifteen to thirty minutes to transmit from the time the command transmissions officer got it.

Aboard each U-boat, one radioman was always standing watch, listening through his earphones for the ethereal chirping that linked him with home. Radio transmissions were received when the vessel was on the surface, nearly always when she was at periscope depth, and sometimes even when she was 40 feet down. The radioman wrote down all messages, whether or not they were addressed to his boat. The serial numbers told him whether he had missed any. Some radiomen missed no messages; some missed sixty on a cruise. The skipper determined whether missed messages meant that the radioman was negligent, in which case he would be arrested, or whether the messages were lost because the boat was frequently submerged.

When the radioman heard the peeps, he stored the first few letters in his memory as he put down his book or turned down the phonograph, then wrote them on a message form and began taking the rest of the text as it was transmitted. He replicated the complicated procedure that yielded the message key, turned his rotors to it, and deciphered the message. He then gave it to the skipper. If the message was addressed to his boat, the captain followed its orders; if it was not, he read it to know what was going on.

The captain drafted messages; his radiomen enciphered them and transmitted them to headquarters. U-boats used five main kinds of messages:

1. Convoy contact reports. These were usually encoded first in the Short Signal Book and then enciphered in Enigma. They were preceded by *dot dot dash dot dot* to clear the wavelength of less urgent signals; because that Morse symbol stood for the Greek letter alpha in German signals and a French accented *e* in the British, these messages were called alpha signals by the Germans and E-bar by the British.

2. Short transmissions of one to six groups, likewise encoded first in the Short Signal Book and then enciphered in Enigma. These reported, for example, a U-boat's position and fuel situation in answer to a query from headquarters. They were preceded by *dash dot dot dot dash,* beta in German Morse, called B-bar by the British because it added to the Morse symbol for *b* the dash for *t.*

3. Weather reports, encoded first in the Short Weather Cipher and then enciphered in Enigma.

4. Other messages, such as those dealing with rendezvous with refueler submarines, enciphered in Enigma.

5. The radio cipher conversation, in which headquarters and a U-boat established a key and used it for an exchange of messages, each picking up the encipherment from where the other left off. It was faster than setting up a new key for each party's successive messages.

Kerneval rebroadcast the U-boat messages it received both to acknowledge their receipt and to make sure that other boats heard them. Kühne's group deciphered the messages. But since the radiomen aboard ship did not always have the time or the desire to check their work by deciphering it before sending a message, and because their messages were harder to hear, unreadable cryptograms were more common in messages from U-boats than in those to them. To unscramble them, Kühne had a "puzzle group" whose members, he thought, were all but codebreakers.

The Enigma was, the navy said, "the main cipher method of the Kriegsmarine." All secret communications were to be enciphered with it, "except when the use of other cipher methods and systems is prescribed." It was considered superior to them, in speed as well as in strength. As a 1941 field report said, "Equipping with the Enigma all vessels that must send reports about the enemy quickly is viewed as absolutely necessary, since all other systems are too cumbersome." Moreover, many subordinate systems depended upon the Enigma for security, among them the Short Signal Book and the Short Weather Cipher.

Because Enigma protected the central element — control — of the central part — the U-boat offensive — of the naval war, the navy sought in a variety of ways to assure its security. Deciphering ciphertexts to make sure they were correct before transmitting them, for example, reduced the number of wrongly enciphered messages that had to be redone correctly, thus cutting the number of different cryptograms with identical plaintexts — a chink in a cipher's armor.

The navy monitored its own communications. When one of the monitoring posts spotted an error that could jeopardize cryptosecurity, even though it did not know whether the enemy had actually exploited it, the post notified the commands involved. In the spring of 1941, boat NS 25 off the Norwegian coast requested a weather report with the standard service abbreviation QOB. Because the enemy would know that the reply was a weather report and thus would have a crib, the monitoring post reported that this "made an answer impossible" and was "a serious violation." The culprit, Radioman Fourth Class Wilhelm Lemcke, was to be told of his error, restricted to quarters for three days, and sent to Stavanger in occupied Norway for additional instruction. The commands themselves sometimes blundered. At 8:29 P.M. on April 26, the headquarters at Stavanger radioed an Enigma message to the Admiral West Coast and to the ship *Seefalke*. The Admiral West Coast knew that the *Seefalke* had only the Dockyard Cipher, so, after deciphering the Enigma message, his headquarters reenciphered the text in the simpler Dockyard and at 8:56 transmitted it. This violated cryptographic security since solving the easier system would provide a kiss, as Bletchley called it, to the more difficult one.

The navy also minimized Enigma's physical exposure. In many cases, vessels undertaking operations that made them particularly susceptible to capture by the enemy, such as operating in shallow waters off the enemy coast, carried as few documents as possible. Thus when, on October 14, 1939, Lieutenant Gunther Prien's U-47 slipped between concrete-laden blockships into Scapa Flow to sink the battleship *Royal Oak* in one of the most daring escapades of the war, his sub carried no Enigma or Enigma keying documents, but only a hand cipher. And when, in December 1939, the pocket battleship *Admiral Graf Spee* sailed from Montevideo, Uruguay, to scuttle herself in shallow water before she could be sunk by three British cruisers awaiting her at the 3-mile limit, she left her Enigma with German diplomats on shore.

When a ship was lost where the British might be able to recover cryptographic material, either by salvage or by picking up flotsam, the German navy demanded a report. For example, when Submarine Hunter 173 was sunk by bombs on May 8, 1941, off the Norwegian west coast in 150 feet of water, her command detailed the destruction of the cryptographic material. At the time of the attack the regulations for use of the Enigma, the Dockyard Cipher, and cipher message sheets were in use. Also aboard were an Enigma, the general- and officer-grade keys for April and May, and the instructions for cue word PERSEUS for emergency change of Enigma settings. But, the report said, a bomb detonated under the radio shack, collapsing it, setting it on fire, and destroying the documents lying out. Radioman Koch smashed the Enigma machine. No papers would float. The report clearly implied that there was no danger of compromise, and reports of other events suggested the same thing.

Most important of all, the navy investigated situations in which the Enigma might have been compromised. Many of these probes were undertaken by Captain Ludwig Stummel, a career signals officer with a glass eye and a limp who was in effect chief of staff of the Naval Communications Service. He had joined the navy during World War I and later fervently supported Nazism, though his enthusiasm faded as the excesses of the regime increasingly offended his strong Catholicism. He hated sloppiness and required those under him to follow the book strictly. If a probe convinced him that corrective action was warranted, he ordered it.

Several events early in 1940 impelled Stummel to make his first investigation. Patrol Boat 805 was lost under obscure circumstances in the Heligoland Bight, off the northwestern coast of Germany. The U-33 was sunk in February in the Clyde estuary, whose waters were shallow enough for divers to reach the submarine. Four days later, the *Altmark,* a supply ship for the *Admiral Graf Spee* that was carrying British prisoners of war, was cornered in the neutral waters of a Norwegian fjord and boarded by the British, who, shouting "The navy's here!" freed the prisoners.

Though he did not conclude that a leak had occurred in any of these cases, Stummel, as a precaution, changed the indicator for weather messages, fake messages, and officer-grade messages to the indicator for general-grade messages; the German radiomen would see upon deciphering them what they were, but the enemy intercepters would not be able to differentiate and sort them out and so take even the first step toward solution. After several weeks of study, to which his cipher specialists contributed, Stummel reported comforting conclusions:

• The many components of the Enigma system offered security even if some components were lost to the enemy.

· Water-soluble ink protected most important documents.
· Solution could be achieved only through superimposition. But the frequent changes of keys — more frequent, he boasted, than in the enemy's systems — precluded this.

In April, Stummel investigated the British sinking of eight German destroyers near the end of a Norwegian fjord and concluded that "it cannot be thought" that a compromise occurred. Then, on June 17, Dönitz telephoned. The rendezvous point of some Allied convoys, against which some of his U-boats had been directed by radio, had been moved. Could this be attributed to British recovery of cipher documents from the U-13?

This time Stummel's superior, Admiral Eberhard Maertens, the head of the Naval Communications Service, mollified Dönitz. The enemy's reading of U-boat messages could be seen as likely only if all of four unlikely events had taken place: (1) the U-boat crew, threatened with capture, had not undone the Enigma machine's keys by changing the rotors, ring setting, and plugboard, (2) the water-soluble ink had not made the key list illegible, (3) the enemy could detect the difference between the actual settings and those the key list called for — this a consequence of the changes called for by the cue word, and (4) the enemy could solve the German messages and pick out and determine the meaning of those that ordered the submarines to the convoy rendezvous. Maertens said that individually these events were unlikely and together even more so.

The most serious fears about cipher security arose in 1941, triggering two major investigations.

The first followed the sinking of the *Bismarck*. That battleship, together with the heavy cruiser *Prinz Eugen,* had been assigned in May to disrupt as much British shipping as possible. To resupply the two ships on their three months of raids, the Naval War Command had dispatched five tankers and two supply ships to prearranged points in the empty wastes of the Atlantic; two scout ships also sailed to discover targets and warn of enemy warships. These vessels were at sea when the *Bismarck* was sunk and the *Prinz Eugen* escaped.

At the end of May, the British, who were reading Enigma messages with a delay of from three to two days, learned the support ships' locations and attacked them. On May 29, the Admiralty ordered its cruisers to search for an enemy supply ship in the area 57° to 59° north, 46° to 48° west. They found the *Belchen* on June 3, at 59° north, 47° west, and sank it. The British intercepted a message to the *Esso Hamburg*, which had refueled the *Prinz Eugen*, setting up a rendezvous with a supply ship for U-boats, the *Egerland*, to which she was to give torpedoes. On the evening of June 4, the Royal Navy cruiser *London* sank the *Esso Hamburg* and then, the next morning and in the same area, halfway between the bulges of Africa and South America, the *Egerland*. Other German ships were destroyed by British warships in other locations. The Admiralty had ordered that the tanker *Gedania* and the scout *Gonzenheim* be omitted from the plan of attack. It feared that if they were sunk, the Germans would conclude, correctly, that only codebreaking could have led to the loss of so many widely dispersed ships. But Royal Navy warships happened upon the *Gedania* and the *Gonzenheim* and, on June 4, destroyed both.

Thus, by June 21, all five tankers, the two supply ships, and one of the scouts had been sunk or captured, five of them on three successive days.

And what the British feared occurred. The losses, coming so close in time and so far apart in space, triggered German concerns about security. Admiral Kurt Fricke, chief of the Naval War Command, investigated the matter thoroughly. He advanced several theses to explain this improbable loss. One was coincidence: the ships could have been spotted accidentally, especially those in the busy area west of the Bay of Biscay. A spy could have betrayed the orders, though the frequent instructions radioed to the supply ships and tankers to go to new positions rendered this hypothesis a little thin. The British could have followed the ships' movements through direction-finding of their many signals. French agents could have tapped the navy's telephones. Perhaps British radar had a greater range than German. Or the enemy could have read the coded German messages.

Fricke gave this thesis his greatest attention. He presupposed that, even with an Enigma machine and all the rotors, solution was not possible without either parallel plaintext and ciphertext or all of the daily keys and the indicators. Could the enemy have obtained these? Fricke ruled out spying: the documents looked alike and underwent "daily, more than daily, monthly, or more than monthly changes, so the entire system is extraordinarily difficult, even for a man who has been well instructed in these things."

The orders for the destruction of cryptomaterial were clear and simple; the crews had been taught them, and in all previous cases the men had fulfilled their duty to guarantee security. The fundamental documents were in water-soluble ink and were kept separated: the indicators with the radiomen in the radio shack, the key lists with the radio officer elsewhere. A capture of one or the other would not suffice for solution; both would have to be seized, and this would be possible only if a British warship had, unnoticed, come alongside the German ship and a boarding party had surreptitiously entered her. Aside from the basic improbability of this scenario, Fricke maintained, his survey of the circumstances of the sinking of each German vessel showed that it seems not to have happened. He decided, without stating his ground, that "seizure of cryptomaterial is unlikely." He made the same determination in every case, either because — as with the tanker *Belchen* — the ship had been sunk by gunfire and the papers and machine went down with her, or because — as with the *Gonzenheim* — the crew had had enough time to destroy the material, or because — as with the *Esso Hamburg* — surprise entry was excluded.

What about pure cryptanalysis, unaided by booty? "After a renewed, very comprehensive examination," Fricke reported, "all specialists unanimously agreed that a reading [of German navy messages by the enemy through solution] is impossible." In the end, Fricke found "no palpable, unequivocal" cause of the roundup, though he tended to favor coincidence as the answer.

Despite his failure to reach a definite conclusion, the navy instituted a number of measures to restore or improve security. All orders were to be printed and charts marked in water-soluble ink. All radio messages pertaining to operations were to be top secret. Because documents recovered from the sea might have enabled the British to read German cryptograms for the period that the same keys remained in service, a new cue word — PERSEUS — put new and uncompromised keys into effect on June 22. In August Dönitz began addressing his submarines by the names of their captains instead of by their boat numbers.

The method of defining meeting points by latitude and longitude in the new Short Signal Book was regarded as compromised, so Dönitz sought to disguise their positions on the Kriegsmarine's grid of the oceans.

This grid was divided into quadrants 486 nautical miles on a side. Each was designated by a two-letter group; quadrants were designated from west to east in alphabetical order. Thus CA covered the East Coast of the United States from about Portsmouth, New Hampshire, south to Cape Fear, North Carolina, and from inland (though this was useless) to about the longitude of northeasternmost Maine; CB, adjoining it to the east, covered the Atlantic south of Nova Scotia; CC, CD, CE, and CF moved east across the ocean, putting CG on the coasts of Portugal, Spain, and North Africa, including the Strait of Gibraltar. South of the C row came the D row. Some quadrants were slightly irregular.

Each quadrant was divided into a nine-by-nine matrix of eighty-one smaller squares. Each of these was in turn divided into nine squares, and finally these again into nine. The squares of the first subdivision, represented by two digits, extended 54 nautical miles on a side; those of the fourth and final subdivision, represented by four digits, were only 6 miles on a side. A vessel could thus give its position with precision using two letters and four digits. For example AK 2799 marked the watery square at 57° 21' north latitude, 32° 00' west longitude, a spot in the middle of the North Atlantic where a U-boat might well be in wait for a convoy. The system saved enciphering and transmitting time.

Since the grid served the entire German navy, and since some high headquarters held the Home Waters U-boat Enigma key, these posts could follow the movements of the submarines. Dönitz feared that this situation endangered security. So he took yet another step to protect his U-boats: in addition to forbidding all but a few units to map U-boat locations, he ordered that these locations be disguised by replacing the grid digraphs for the North Atlantic with substitutes, known only to the U-boats and their commands, from Table B of the digraph substitution booklet FLUSS ("river"), also used to encipher indicator groups for the naval Enigma. The table consisted of a 26-by-26 square of letter pairs with single letters at the head of each column and row. This was modified for the grid encipherment. Atop each of the 26 columns the cipher clerk wrote one of the 26 most-used grid digraphs (omitting those for the Pacific, for example) in a sequence specified by U-Boat Command. The encipherer replaced the grid digraph with any one of the 26 digraphs under it. Thus grid digraph AL might become cipher KS, or LK, or OM, or any one of 23 other digraphs.

Dönitz enciphered these instructions in officer-grade Enigma and radioed them in six parts totaling 504 four-letter groups on September 10, 1941, to all U-boats. They went into effect immediately. And at the end of November the navy complicated the location system still more. Dönitz instituted the use of not one but many digraph tables, indicating each by a name and a street address, such as "Gottfried Becker, Bluecherplatz 30," which came into force at midnight, December 28. The number in the address was the key to the disguise of the four-digit location number. The 30, for example, meant that 3000 was to be added to the true number. Thus the grid digits 6268 would be enciphered as 9268 for transmission. Errors seemed to be rare, though one submarine was told with some asperity that according to its grid letters it was transmitting from the middle of the Andes.

In between these changes, on October 5, the high command segregated U-Boat Command communications from other users of the Home Waters key by modifying the settings. This new key net was called TRITON, after a sea demigod famed for sounding a conch shell as a horn. Not only would fewer people be able to read U-boat messages, but fewer messages would be sent in the basic daily key. This would reduce the chances of overlaps leading to superimposition solutions and of errors that would permit special-case solutions.

Four months after Fricke's investigation, however, a series of events led to another probe. One was an Admiralty announcement that the British had captured a U-boat all but undamaged at the end of August 1941. This was the U-570, which had unluckily surfaced south of Iceland at the very moment that a British patrol plane was passing overhead. The aircraft dropped four depth charges, which straddled the submarine, shook her severely, smashed many of her instruments, let in sea water, and persuaded the captain that the fight was over. When his men tried to climb out of the conning tower, the plane, to prevent them from manning guns, opened fire. The crew showed a white flag, and the airplane circled watchfully. Eventually a British destroyer arrived and took the U-boat in tow.

On October 18, Maertens opened his analysis of the security consequences of the capture by saying that "a current reading of our messages is not possible." On the next page, however, he conceded that if the enemy had found the Enigma undisturbed and all the key documents, a current reading was possible. But then he concluded that this was unlikely — that there was time to drench the documents, making their water-soluble ink unreadable — and in the end he left the impression that the British were not solving Enigma messages. Even if they were, the new keys that were to go into effect on November 1 would restore full security.

At about this time Dönitz sensed a trend that affected his tactics in the most fundamental way. He had come to suspect that his wolfpacks were finding convoys less often than individual U-boats were. The inference was that the British were steering the convoys away from the packs. Moreover, the Germans were finding it more difficult to locate the British supply ships. None of this, Stummel implied in a response to Dönitz, meant that the British were reading weak German ciphers. It could all be explained by Britain's full exploitation of her vast reconnaissance capabilities, including air reconnaissance of the supply route and of U-boat departure and arrival routes; possibly by airborne radar spotting that U-boats could not detect; and by extraordinary British direction-finding. In addition, a spy, a chatterbox, or laxness in locking up maps or cryptomaterial or other documents could not be ruled out. What could be ruled out was

> a current reading of our messages by the enemy. . . . Without any contradiction, all specialists, in particular those of the B-Dienst headquarters and of the most important specialists of the High Command of the Armed Forces, have determined, in comprehensive work, that the Enigma system is viewed as by far the most resistant of all known methods for secrecy in military communications.

Stummel may have consulted Captain Henno Lucan, the signals officer who in 1930 had proposed some useful improvements to the Enigma. The specialists in the High Command of the Armed Forces worked in the Chiffrierabteilung, or Cipher Branch, the descendant of the ChiStelle whose staff had, in the 1920s, adopted the Enigma for army use. The Cipher Branch's Desk IVa tested German cryptosystems. Dr. Karl Stein, the desk's head, a professor of mathematics, analyzed the Enigma theoretically, calculating limits of security and thereby complementing the pragmatic investigations of the B-Dienst cryptanalysts. Maertens summarized Stummel's report by saying, in his covering letter to Dönitz, that "despite great stresses, including, among others, losses, the resistance of the most important cryptosystems seems not to have been impaired."

The German cryptologists were not fools. Experience had taught them that cipher systems were usually broken because of laziness or errors on the part of cipher clerks or the capture of documents in wartime; they had not forgotten the *Magdeburg.* The system they had designed blocked both these avenues and at the same time rendered pure cryptanalysis all but impossible, they believed.

To prevent cipher clerks from choosing rotor settings that might lead to overlaps in the machine's cipher-alphabet sequence, which might permit solution, they prescribed the settings for a key net. And to nullify capture, they set up the system so that in most cases the capture of even three of the four elements — the machine, the machine-settings list, the indicators list, and the bigram tables — would still (they thought) preclude solution. The machine was assumed to be in enemy hands. But even if the British captured the machine-settings list and the indicators list, the cryptologists said, they would not be able to divine the indicator for a particular message because they did not have the bigram table that would link the unenciphered indicator to the enciphered one that was transmitted. Likewise, if the British had the indicators list and the bigram table, they would not know which rotors had been used in which order, nor their starting positions, nor the plugboard arrangement. Only if they seized the machine-settings list and the bigram table could they reconstruct the indicator and thus be able to read a message. But for this eventuality the Germans had devised the cue-word system. By immediately changing the rotor order and settings, the cue word rendered the captured machine-settings list useless. In addition, the Germans changed the bigram tables from time to time, and new machine-setting lists were issued each month. All these safeguards pretty much eliminated any dangers from captures and from cipherers' errors, they thought.

The cryptologists believed that trying to solve cryptograms on the basis of letter frequency was laughable: the Enigma generated far too many alphabets, and messages were kept too short, for this procedure to have any hope of working. The more promising method of the probable word, in which a presumed text was matched against a cryptogram, would founder on the vast number of possibilities that had to be tested, and the plugboard would make such a match even more difficult. Moreover, many messages had codewords from the Short Signal Book as their plaintext. And while solving one message would reveal the rotor order of other messages, it would not disclose rotor starting positions.

All in all, the German cryptologists had looked at the situation from both the theoretical and the practical points of view. They had evolved a system that apparently assured nearly perfect security for their messages, in which even a capture would give the enemy insight into German messages only for the brief and limited period before either new keys came into service or a cue word in effect created new keys immediately. Dönitz's directives to his U-boats, they assured him, were safe.

Nevertheless, the cryptologists did not rest on their laurels. They sought to further secure the system by facilitating the work of the encipherers and thus reducing human error. One measure sought to reduce the pressure — around 5 pounds — needed to depress one of the typewriter keys. The basic resistance came from the rubbing of the rotors against one another. Though this could not be cut down because it would have entailed too extensive changes in the machine's construction, other changes did lessen the pressure to about 4 pounds, which led to "a palpable lightening of operation." In another change, a larger illuminable panel was attached to make the letters more easily visible, particularly by the man who was writing them down. A third measure was to print the output, thereby eliminating this second man and his errors. The navy's first effort, a two-typewriter device called the MS, which weighed more than 100 pounds and cost 5,000 reichsmarks ($12,000 in 1991 dollars), failed. The manufacturers then sought to connect the Enigma to electric typewriters or punched teletype tape in a succession of "partial solutions" called the MZSB, MZSE, and MZSS devices. But metal shortages as the war went on had led the manufacturers to use plastic instead of metal in some parts, notably the indented thumb wheels for the hand turning of the rotors. This substitution required an increase in tolerances. And despite the Enigma's heavy construction and simple mechanics, the machine turned out to be extraordinarily sensitive to inaccuracies in manufacture. With an accidental accumulation of variations, the machine with a typewriter-printing attachment became unreliable. As a consequence, though some 700 machines were fitted with the tape printer, none of these "partial solutions" was deemed satisfactory, and the manufacturers, which now included a firm called Konski & Krüger and the Olympia typewriter company, took over the development. Delivery of their printing versions was to start in the fall of 1944.

In addition, the Kriegsmarine sought to reduce the number of machine breakdowns and to meet expanded communications demands by producing more Enigmas. With the original firm, Heimsoeth & Rinke, apparently producing at its maximum, the navy contracted with Olympia. On June 23, 1943, from its factory in Erfurt, southwest of Berlin, the typewriter firm delivered its first twenty basic Enigma machines. By December, it was delivering seventy-five a month.

Most important, the cryptologists also took steps to block the dangers from the constant increase in traffic. In 1939 radio messages averaged 192 a day; by 1942 volume had soared to six times that number, or 1,200 a day; in 1943 it was on its way to doubling again. The experts recognized that this volume gave enemy codebreakers more opportunities. As they put it in one case, "according to cryptanalytic knowledge the permitted limit of the daily total of radio messages had been overstepped."

One way to lessen the danger was to reduce the number of messages enciphered with the same rotor and ring positions by creating additional key nets. (The participants in each net shared the machine-setting list that specified these positions for each day.) TRITON, the Atlantic U-boat net, was one of these new key nets. Others were created throughout 1942, such as NEPTUN, for the operations of the main fleet, and MEDUSA, for the Mediterranean. By January 1, 1943, the Kriegsmarine was utilizing eleven key nets. As traffic grew, it kept adding others.

Another way to reduce the dangers of high traffic volume was to add another rotor to the machine. The advantages of a fourth rotor, which had been in development since 1940, were that it would raise the number of possibilities a cryptanalyst would have to test and would lower the likelihood of key overlaps that a cryptanalyst could exploit. But two serious practical difficulties blocked the implementation of the idea. First, adding another rotor would change the dimensions of the machine, requiring redesign of and retooling for parts of the machine not otherwise involved and making it impossible, on many ships, for the machine to fit into the space designed for the smaller version. Second, a fourth rotor would prevent communication with other branches of the service that used the three-rotor machine.

To get out of these difficulties, the navy came up with the idea of a thin rotor that could be fitted in next to a new, thinner reflector (the nonrevolving half-rotor that sent the current back through the three revolving rotors). The thin rotor would not revolve during encipherment because no stepping mechanism existed at the leftmost rotor. However, to create a key, the stationary thin rotor could be turned to any one of twenty-six positions. This multiplied by twenty-six the number of possible keys. And the fourth rotor could be wired so that in a certain position, it, with the new thin reflector, replicated the wiring of the old thick reflector, permitting communication with three-rotor machines. It took more than a year to resolve the problems of the extra rotor and to produce, test, and distribute the new machines. Finally, however, on February 1, 1942, the new model, called M4, went into service on the U-boats' TRITON key net. This was the most significant event in German cryptography during World War II.

If the advent of the M4 had been followed by a decrease in diversions of Allied convoys and an increase in sinkings in the mid-Atlantic, Dönitz might have guessed that the Enigma had earlier been penetrated. But the decline in Britain's cryptanalytic fortunes was concealed from him in part by American stupidities. The entry of the United States into the war against Germany on December 11, 1941, voided Hitler's concerns about sinking American vessels, and Dönitz sent his U-boats to the rich hunting grounds off the East Coast. Here freighters and tankers, trawlers and barges, marched individually up and down the coast, disdaining the lessons of convoy so painfully learned by the British over two world wars. And they did so before a blaze of city lights, foolishly kept burning by chambers of commerce afraid of losing business during the tourist season. As a consequence, for six months the U-boats enjoyed what they called a "happy time," sinking dozens of ships, sometimes within sight of crowds on shore, with barely a loss of their own. Finally, reason took over, convoying was introduced, and the U-boats quit the coast.

Then success kept Dönitz from seeing that the Allies had lost much of their U-boat intelligence. And later in the year, when the U-boats returned to the central Atlantic, he could attribute their increased sinkings, not to an Allied cryptanalytic failure, but to a German success: breaking Allied codes.

For the Kriegsmarine not only made codes, it sought to break them as well. The 900-man English-language section of the B-Dienst was headed by former radioman Wilhelm Tranow, who had been brought in to investigate the hermeticity of the Enigma. A tall, erect man, with firm features and a compelling way of talking, so bursting with energy that he seemed to skip instead of walk, he was that rarity in a bureaucracy: a man who both performed the technical aspects of his job in exemplary fashion and administered the men under him effectively. It has been said of him that "If one man in German intelligence ever held the keys to victory in World War II, it was Wilhelm Tranow." Tranow, who had cracked Royal Navy messages in World War I, achieved an important breakthrough in 1935.

He and his assistants had solved the Royal Navy's most widely used code, the five-digit Naval Code. But they had had less success with the more tightly held and more important Naval Cypher, which despite its name was a code; it used four-digit codegroups that were superenciphered to provide an extra layer of secrecy. The superencipherment consisted of adding to the four-digit code-groups random-seeming numbers from tables of 5,000 number groups. In the fall of 1935, a British naval squadron patrolling the Red Sea to keep watch on the Italian invasion of Abyssinia superenciphered its Naval Code messages, using, however, the Naval Cypher number tables. Since Tranow had solved the Naval Code, he could easily determine the superencipherment. He could then strip it from the Naval Cypher. His knowledge of the names of the ships and their movements cracked the bared Naval Cypher. And these systems were still in use when the war began.

The B-Dienst of that time employed 500 persons, some of them in its sixteen intercept posts, some at its headquarters in the main navy building, the brown sandstone structure at Tirpitzufer 72–76 in Berlin. By April of 1940, the B-Dienst was reading a third to a half of the messages it intercepted in Naval Cypher, which it called FRANKFURT. On August 20, 1940, however, the British replaced the Naval Code and Naval Cypher with new editions of each, reducing B-Dienst successes against them. In June of 1941, Naval Cypher No. 3 came into use for communications between the Royal and the United States navies. Many of the messages concerned convoys, stragglers, and the U-boat situation.

To strip the superencipherment from a message — the first step in solving it — required a "bite" of two or more messages with overlapping superenciphering numbers. This phenomenon was not at all uncommon. Indeed, in any one hundred messages the chances were better than half that two would not merely overlap, but would start at the same point in the number tables. Tranow's six tabulating machines prepared lists that discovered the overlaps. Like the British, the Germans exploited cribs. For example, the senior naval officer Newfoundland radioed a comprehensive convoy report for the North Atlantic at the same time every day that invariably began, "SNO Halifax BREAK GROUP Telegram in [a number of] parts FULL STOP Situation. . . ." Hut 8 would have recognized the technique.

With aids like these, the B-Dienst — by now totaling 5,000 persons, of whom 1,100 were in Berlin — mastered Naval Cypher No. 3 throughout most of 1942: by December it was reading 80 percent of the messages it intercepted. Dönitz planned nearly all his U-boat operations during this time on the information from these decrypts. On October 30, for example, the B-Dienst submitted a report that Convoy SC 107, then east of Cape Race, at the tip of Newfoundland, would steer 45°. At the same time, a U-boat sighted its exact position. Dönitz at once ordered his submarines to intercept it. "The timely arrival of the radio reconnaissance report on the route of the convoy," he later wrote in an appreciation to the B-Dienst, "made it possible to pull the U-boat formation together so narrowly that within a few hours of the first sighting several U-boats made contact." They sank fifteen steamers. Though this was an exceptionally striking case, the German cryptanalysts played an important role in U-boat attacks on convoys. Indeed, Dönitz estimated that 50 percent of his operational intelligence came from the B-Dienst.

Its romp slowed on December 15, when the British began enciphering their system indicators. But Tranow tripled the manpower working on the problem by shifting staff from other systems, and by February 1943 the B-Dienst was again solving a large proportion of the traffic, sometimes reading directives to convoys ten and twenty hours before the movements they ordered took place. Its information helped Dönitz position his U-boats for what turned out to be the greatest convoy battle of the war. During three days in March, the U-boats sank dozens of ships from convoys SC 122 and HX 229. The Admiralty despaired, thinking that the Germans had virtually cut Britain's lifeline to America. It was not until Naval Cypher No. 3 was replaced in June that the B-Dienst lost its grip on Allied communications.

Though these successes and failures tended to screen from Dönitz the Allies' varying fortunes in codebreaking, secrecy was so vital to the success of German naval operations that almost any suspicion of its loss demanded an investigation. Thus in March 1942, the loss of two German auxiliary cruisers — the disguised and armed merchant vessels that sailed the seas to harass and destroy enemy shipping — prompted Admiral Fricke to look once again at operational secrecy. He analyzed the evidence and found no leak from communications. The movements of enemy ships contradicted any suggestion that they were reading the messages radioed to the auxiliary cruisers, he said. Similarly, when the battleship *Tirpitz* sailed to Trondheim and the *Gneisenau, Scharnhorst,* and *Prinz Eugen* dashed through the English Channel and the Straits of Dover to haven in German waters, intercepts of British messages gave no hint that the British were reading German cryptograms. And there were no indications that British information on German U-boats came from codebreaking: the implication was that it came from direction-finding or air reconnaissance. Fricke said that the Enigma was sixty times better than the British system and concluded that it was "unimaginable" that the enemy could read it. At the time, for M4, he was right.

Seventeen

Blackout '42

A VARIETY OF CLUES told Naval Section starting in mid-1941 that the Germans were going to replace their three-rotor Enigma on the Atlantic U-boat net with a new, four-rotor machine. The captured U-570 had yielded up a machine lid with four windows for the rotor key letters. Solved intercepts referred to the new machine, which had sometimes been used in error. Indeed, in December 1941 one such message, combined with a repeat enciphered in the proper three-wheel mode, enabled Hut 8 to recover the wiring of the fourth rotor even before it officially went into service.

All this made the cryptanalysts very apprehensive. The new rotor would multiply their work by a factor of 26, and they were barely keeping up as it was. Their apprehensions were justified. With the introduction of the four-rotor Enigma on February 1, 1942, a virtual U-boat blackout descended upon Hut 8. No longer could it read messages to or from Atlantic submarines on patrol or attacking or ordered to attack convoys. The Submarine Tracking Room admitted in its first weekly U-boat situation report after M4 came into effect that "the picture of the Atlantic dispositions is by now out of focus." It grew increasingly indistinct.

Still, the situation was not quite as bad as during the no-Enigma-solution days preceding the captures of the *München* and the U-110 in mid-1941. Other sources of intelligence, such as aerial reconnaissance, were functioning better than before. The tracking room had built up considerable knowledge in the half year it had been reading combat U-boat messages. Those solutions had told the British such details as the U-boats' average speed of advance when proceeding to and from patrol and the endurance of the various types of submarines. Home Waters and Mediterranean Enigma and Dockyard messages, which continued to be solved at the astonishing combined rate of 14,000 per month, revealed the construction of new U-boats, their preparation and crew training in the Baltic, their addition to the fleet, their departures from their home ports. The Submarine Tracking Room thus knew the strength of the U-boat fleet and the number of boats at sea. It was further helped by radio fingerprinting, through which experienced intercept operators identified individual enemy radiomen by their distinctive methods of sending, or "fists," and by TINA, a device that recorded and displayed on long strips of paper radio transmission characteristics to identify individual transmitters. Though not very reliable, these techniques could at least distinguish supply and minelaying U-boats from combat boats. Rodger Winn put into effect his "working fiction," which maintained that the Submarine Tracking Room's best estimates should be treated as facts and acted on until proven wrong.

For information on the U-boats' locations in the Atlantic, the tracking room relied heavily during the M4 blackout on direction-finding. When a monitor in the big intercept rooms at Winchester or Scarborough heard a warship or a U-boat replying to the land station to which he or she was listening, the operator would yell out the frequency as loud as possible. At the far end of the room a controller would repeat it to the direction-finding stations on a direct landline.

The reported frequency went to the eight direction-finding stations from the Shetlands to Land's End. Each had several listening posts attached to it, as well as subordinate control centers. The control center attached to the DF post of Wick, outside the Scottish village of Bower, was an H-shaped building that included a dormitory. Bearings were taken in five 10-foot-square wooden huts isolated on the Caithness moors. Two were staffed by civilians and two by members of the Women's Reserve Naval Service, known as Wrens; the fifth was a spare. No roads led to the huts; the operators were driven as close as possible and then had to walk a mile or two across the boggy ground. In winter a sailor helped shovel paths through the snow. At all times the women yielded the paths to the menacing local cattle. If the weather was too bad, they stayed in the hut from one watch to the next, sleeping in the bunk, melt-ing snow for water, and heating cans of food in the kettle. But they preferred the trek back to the dormitory to staying in the hut and being jolted awake by the hut loudspeaker that announced a fre-quency on which a bearing had to be sought. None of the hard-ships fazed the young women. They felt that they were directly helping their men at sea and were proud to be doing the work.

Each operator sat at a desk listening to three telephone lines, one to the loudspeaker, one to each earphone. When the Wren heard the controller at Scarborough or another intercept post call out a frequency, she tuned the radio on her desk to that fre-quency. Early in the war, she would turn a wheel that rotated an antenna to reduce the signal to its lowest intensity; 90° from this was the source of the signal. Later she had a cathode-ray tube that scanned the horizon electronically. When it discovered the azi-muth at which the signal was strongest, a spot in the center of the 9-inch circular tube stretched itself out toward the circumference in both directions. The operator spun the movable glass plate within a metal ring marked in degrees until a wire embedded in the glass lay above the glowing green line. When she put the tube's cursor on the line, one half disappeared, so that it indicated a single di-rection — southwest, for example, rather than both northeast and southwest. The work had to be done very quickly, since many of the U-boat signals lasted mere seconds; sometimes the women got a bearing only on the last letter.

The operator noted the bearing in a log. When the control at Bower called on the intercom, she gave him the bearing; Bower would pass this to the Submarine Tracking Room's DF section, where the several bearings would be plotted on the chart that used the strings and pins.

During nearly all of 1942, Hut 8 solved only three TRITON keys: those for February 23 and 24 and March 14. The effect of this lack of ULTRA was becoming all too clear. In the last half of 1941, with Enigma solutions diverting Allied ships away from wolfpacks, U-boats sighted about one of every ten convoys. In the last half of 1942, with not very many more U-boats stationed on the North Atlantic routes, but with detours controlled only by direction-find-ing, U-boats sighted one of every three convoys. As a result, North

Atlantic sinkings, which totaled some 600,000 tons in the last half of 1941, more than quadrupled to 2,600,000 tons in the last half of 1942. And each of the nearly 500 ships sunk in those six months meant more freezing deaths in the middle of the ocean, more widows, more fatherless children, less food for some toddler, less ammunition for some soldier, less fuel for some plane — and the prospect of prolonging these miseries.

Of all this the cryptanalysts of Hut 8 were acutely aware. But they could find no workable cribs, and without these they could not test for keys. Moreover, the three-wheel bombes were inadequate for solving the four-rotor Enigma: the three solutions of February and March, based on kisses, had each taken seventeen days on six three-wheel bombes. High-speed bombes to attack M4 were designed and put under construction. Nevertheless, at the highest levels, fears grew that the lack of intelligence, combined with the growing numbers of U-boats, would sink more ships than could be built. The tonnage left would not suffice to maintain rations and sustain industry in the United Kingdom, much less bring over troops, supplies, weapons, and ammunition to carry the war to Hitler.

So, while doing everything they could to accelerate ship construction and protect existing vessels, the supreme commanders looked with growing impatience to B.P. for its contribution. On November 22, 1942, the O.I.C. urged B.P., with British understatement, to focus "a little more attention" on the four-rotor Enigma. The U-boat war was, it said in a silent scream, "the one campaign which Bletchley Park are not at present influencing to any marked extent — and it is the only one in which the war can be lost unless BP do help." Unbeknownst to the O.I.C., however, that help was already on the way.

Eighteen

The George Cross

IN SEPTEMBER 1941, Hitler ordered six U-boats to the Mediterranean. They were to sink Allied vessels transporting supplies to North Africa and so relieve pressure on Rommel. Dönitz objected. He wanted to pursue the fundamental goal of cutting Britain's supply lines. But Hitler told Dönitz that holding North Africa would keep Suez closed and force the British to go around the Cape of Good Hope, thus in effect costing them 3 to 4 million tons of shipping. In November he sent four more U-boats. They helped: Rommel, who had been driven back in 1941 almost to his starting position, was ready in January 1942 to launch an offensive. Eventually fifteen submarines, all of them with some of Dönitz's most experienced crews, prowled what Hitler now called the "decisive area for the prosecution of the war," the Mediterranean.

Among the more successful of these subs was the U-559. A standard Type VIIC submarine built by Blohm & Voss of Hamburg, she had had the same captain since her commissioning in February 1941. Lieutenant Hans Heidtmann, red-haired and bearded, was a solid, quiet man. He came from Lübeck, the ancient Hanseatic port of the Baltic, and was a typical north German: precise, orderly, no-nonsense. His first cruise, east of Greenland, resulted in no contact with the enemy but an unfortunate one with an iceberg, which damaged the periscope. His second likewise had good and bad aspects: the U-559 sank the 8,000-ton British freighter *Alva* northwest of Spain but was attacked by three British destroyers. Heidtmann and his crew rapidly learned what war was like: 180 depth charges exploded around them while they shivered 600 feet down; after twenty-four hours underwater, with the attackers apparently gone, they surfaced and returned to St. Nazaire.

Then the U-559 joined the submarines transferred to the Mediterranean, sliding through the Strait of Gibraltar on the strong current from the Atlantic. At first she was based at the Greek port of Salamis, which gave her young crew members both a rumor to wonder about and an insignia to laugh about. The rumor was that 25 percent of the U-boat sailors contracted venereal disease from the complaisant Greek girls and that many of the young men were executed for their carelessness. The insignia came from the belief that in Salamis donkey meat was used in the salami the sailors ate. For fun they painted a white donkey on their conning tower. It was German humor.

In cruise after cruise, submerging at first light and surfacing after dark, Heidtmann and his crew sought their prey. On November 27, 1941, they torpedoed a small Australian warship, the *Parramatta,* off Bardia on the coast of North Africa. And twenty-four action-filled hours began just after midnight of December 23, when they detected the shadowy apparent shape of a cruiser to the west and fired a spread of four torpedoes, all of which missed. They then lost contact, dived, were attacked by bombers, and surfaced. Sighting a two-freighter convoy, the U-559 fired three torpedoes as the ships overlapped in her line of vision. One torpedo sank, and the other two ran on the surface, striking the second freighter amidships and sinking it at once. Heidtmann and his men tried to attack the other steamer but could not approach because of its three escorts. They fired a torpedo at one of the destroyers, then saw it avoid the torpedo and turn and approach their submarine. They dived. They heard a weak detonation and then a very loud one that shook the boat. After sneaking away to the northwest, they heard weak propeller noise to the west and seven depth charges not very close; at 11:40 P.M., they surfaced and breathed deeply of the fresh salt air. Three days later, in the same area off the coast of Libya, where Hitler hoped to cut off British supplies to Tobruk, the U-559 sank a Polish steamer. Cruises like this earned Heidtmann the Knight's Cross and compliments from Dönitz such as "Decisively and well carried out operation."

At 4 P.M. on September 29, 1942, the U-559 sailed from the Sicilian port of Messina on her tenth cruise. She headed for grid square CP 3468, which covered part of the eastern Mediterranean just south of Turkey, close to the Syrian port of Latakia. Three days later U-Boat Command radioed Heidtmann's operational orders: "Free hunt off Palestine and Egyptian coast. Point of main effort: supply routes Alexandria–Port Said to Beirut, Haifa, Jaffa." Over the next several days, U-Boat Command passed on an agent's report that a British cruiser division in Haifa was expected to sail soon, listed the ships that were in the harbor at Beirut, and notified Heidtmann that a spy said two British steamers were sailing on October 10 from Port Said for the Turkish port of İskenderun, close to his operating area. On October 17, Dönitz moved Heidtmann's operating area south, to the west of Haifa, then farther west into the Mediterranean. But neither these moves nor the information that a German airplane had sighted a three-vessel convoy with escorts a few hundred miles to the southwest helped him sink any ships on this cruise. So, late in the evening of October 29, after asking him to report the weather if possible, Dönitz told Heidtmann to return to Messina after he had used up his fuel and armament. In the early morning hours of the thirtieth, the U-559, using its Short Weather Cipher, transmitted the requested meteorological report.

A little before dawn that same day, a Sunderland flying boat reported a radar contact, "possibly a submarine," in the eastern Mediterranean roughly halfway between Port Said, at the northern end of the Suez Canal, and Tel Aviv in Palestine. Four destroyers were ordered to search the area. Among them was H.M.S. *Petard*.

Built in Newcastle and launched into the brown waters of the River Tyne on a rainy day in March 1941, the *Petard* was one of eight P-class (for *Pakenham*) fleet destroyers. She had a handsome trawler bow, a single funnel, and a top speed of 32 knots, with great maneuverability at high speed and stability in bad seas. As her main battery she carried only four 4-inch guns, but she was otherwise well armed with eight torpedo tubes, one hundred depth charges, and two sets of depth-charge throwers. Her nine officers had individual cabins; the 211 ratings slept in hammocks.

By far the strongest personality aboard was the captain, a Royal Navy career officer, Lieutenant Commander Mark Thornton. He had come to the *Petard* after service aboard another destroyer, where he had won a Distinguished Service Cross for sinking a submarine.

Of medium height, with a square, muscular frame, a square head, closely cropped thick gray hair, and a face as battered as a boxer's, he struck terror into many. At the commissioning he promised to send back a trophy to show the shipyard the results of its efforts; his ferocious talk about destroying the king's enemies left some of the workmen shaking their heads with pity for his crew. His energy seemed barely contained. At Scapa Flow, he would sometimes leap up from the officers' mess, beat the after bulkhead with his fists until it boomed, and shout, "I must have action with the enemy now!" Earlier, during the evacuation of Dunkirk in 1940, many of his ship's inexperienced crew members had proved incapable of performing due to seasickness, strain, and lack of sleep, so on the *Petard* he was determined that events would not overwhelm the crew. He toughened his new men with relentless, almost merciless exercises. Once, just as the men were turning in from an exhausting day, he staged a false alarm: pretending the *Petard* had been torpedoed, he hosed them with icy sea water as they struggled to action stations. Gradually he whipped his crew into "a fully trained fighting machine."

Thornton's first lieutenant was Antony Fasson, a Scot from the border country. An experienced career officer, he exerted a firm discipline on his subordinates but also mixed easily with them. The ratings rarely took umbrage at his punishments; the junior officers found him a genial companion; those who fell short of the captain's difficult standards found Fasson understanding. And Thornton considered him an exceptionally fine leader.

During the summer of 1942, the *Petard* was sent around the Cape of Good Hope through the Suez Canal to join the Twelfth Destroyer Flotilla. During that long cruise Thornton and Fasson spent many an hour in the captain's cabin discussing the Mediterranean, an area Thornton knew very well. They formed a mutual determination to capture the confidential books from a U-boat: "Other destroyers might sink U-boats," Thornton said later, in ignorance of the U-110 exploit, "but we would capture one!" So they drilled a boarding team, and Fasson, who would lead it, wore gym shoes and his personal boarding gear day and night while at sea. He and Thornton, never doubting that an opportunity would come their way, discussed the boarding from every angle.

On September 22, as the U-559 rocked at her berth in Messina, the *Petard* was moored fore and aft to buoys at Port Said, almost abreast of the statue of the builder of the Suez Canal, Ferdinand de Lesseps. The next weeks were filled with antisubmarine practices and patrols and a sudden sortie to investigate a reported high-speed surface contact that ended in the *Petard*'s repelling three Junker 88s. It was difficult to keep the sailors from the off-limits bars and brothels of Port Said. Off Haifa, the stench of animal skins piled on the quays produced for the men aboard what one called "a night of unforgettable nausea." They spent seven days in Alexandria, where the crew, at sea on the night of October 23, saw the black sky to the southwest erupt with artillery flashes: the start of the battle of El Alamein! Thornton so itched for action that he repeated his bulkhead-beating performance. Then came the seaplane's report of a U-boat sighting as the *Petard* and other ships were sailing to Haifa. Being nearby, they were ordered to hunt the submarine.

The four destroyers reached the U-boat's suspected position a little after noon and began their sweep. The day was sunny, the wind light, the sea flat. The *Pakenham* obtained the first asdic contact, but the *Petard* attacked first, dropping five depth charges set to 250, 350, and 500 feet at 12:57 P.M. After the explosions, the *Petard*'s crew saw oil and heard a noise of escaping air — but saw no submarine. A moment later, the *Dulverton* dropped ten depth charges. As the *Petard* was heading in for her second attack, she and the other ships heard a heavy explosion apparently under her. But they saw no disturbance of the water, and the cause remained a mystery. The *Petard* dropped ten depth charges, and soon the asdic operator reported a hissing noise. This contact was held for fifty-five minutes but eventually proved not to be the submarine. Perhaps underwater bands of different density and temperature, aggravated by the fresh water from the Nile, were affecting the asdic.

The hunt continued for hours, with intermittent attacks. In the U-559 the men were naturally fearful, but none lost control. Heidtmann, with the calm that had won his men's admiration, repeatedly announced "Alarm!" in a quiet voice, so unlike the anxious, dramatic "Alaaaaarm!" of other skippers. As time went on, the air in the submarine, bad at the best of times with the smell of unwashed bodies, old cigarette smoke, toilets, garbage, diesel oil, diesel fumes, and cooking, grew even fouler.

The attacking destroyer was directed by a cross-bearing of asdic contacts by two other ships. Thornton seemed to have a sixth sense: when contact was lost, he conned the *Petard* back on target, constantly changing course and speed. Tension on the ship remained high. At slow speed, all hands topside scanned the sea for a periscope and torpedo tracks. When revolutions increased, men braced themselves against the thuds of the underwater explosions.

Darkness fell. The wind rose, and clouds covered the sky. A torpedoman aft sent Thornton word that he thought the submarine was below 500 feet — the maximum setting then on Royal Navy depth charges — but if he stuffed soap in the holes of the depth charges, the water pressure would build more slowly and the charges would sink deeper before going off. He was granted permission to do so, and at 6:42 the *Petard* loosed ten soaped-up charges. The wait for the explosion was longer than usual, then the crew members saw the shiver on the surface and felt the thumps on the hull. The trick worked: the sub moved and contact was regained. Over the next three and a quarter hours, three more attacks were made.

A little after 10 P.M., Thornton signaled to the *Dulverton* his intention to attack and, when the ship replied with ranges and bearings that matched the *Petard*'s, the ship's company felt that the hunt was nearly up; the sub must be close at hand. At 10:17 the *Petard* dropped depth charges. The heavy detonations and the fountains of water were followed by silence except for the noises of the ship and the sea. In Thornton's mind was only the lust to see the U-boat blown to the surface.

In the submarine, the crew counted 288 depth-bomb explosions; the last ones holed the bow and stove in plates on the starboard quarter. The air was intolerable: it seemed as if the oxygen had run out. Heidtmann ordered the ship up.

As the *Petard* nosed forward into the wind and the dark, a gun crew, the men on the bridge, and the gun director team suddenly and simultaneously smelled diesel fuel; a moment later, the asdic operators cried out that they could hear a submarine blowing its tanks. Guns were trained on the port bow bearing given by the asdic team; eyes strained to pierce the darkness. At 10:40, a patch of white water appeared on the black sea. The port signal lantern picked out a conning tower; a few moments later a 36-inch search-light brilliantly illuminated a submarine with a white donkey painted on her conning tower and a few white figures bursting from it, then crawling and skidding along the slippery deck into the sea.

Thornton ordered his guns to open fire. The pom-poms and one of the Oerlikons did so at once. At that range one of his forward 4-inchers could not be depressed enough to fire at the target, so Thornton turned the ship away long enough to give the gun crew a shot. With their one round the crew members hit the base of the conning tower. Many of the 114 pom-pom and 79 Oerlikon rounds struck the U-boat, but it rapidly became clear that she was stopped and being abandoned and that further gunfire damage would make it harder to save her. Fasson rang the cease-fire bells. Thornton issued orders to put his boarding plan into effect.

By this time, the *Petard* had stopped and the submarine was lying to port in the destroyer's lee, down by the bows in the roughening chop. Fasson was on the starboard side aft, starting to have the starboard boat lowered. Thornton roared at the gunnery control officer, Sub-lieutenant G. Gordon Connell, to dive over the side and swim to the U-boat. As Connell started to strip off his clothing, a young able-bodied seaman, Colin Grazier, joined him, shouting that he would swim across with him. Just then Fasson appeared. He told Connell to take charge of the whaler and bring it around the *Petard* to the U-boat. He himself was tearing off his uniform. Within moments he and Grazier had dived naked into the sea and were swimming to the U-boat. So was the fifteen-year-old canteen assistant, Tommy Brown, who had lied about his age to join the service. He dived into the sea before the canteen manager could stop him. A few moments later, the whaler, encumbered by German sailors clinging to it, reached the U-boat and made fast.

That vessel was in desperate shape. Its deck was awash, and waves broke over it continuously. The rigging and wireless aerials had been almost completely shot away. The top of the conning tower was a shambles; at its base was the hole made by the 4-inch shell; in the middle were two or three dozen punctures an inch in diameter, through which water sloshed. Plates on either side were stove in. The searchlight pinned the U-boat in its dazzle. The Germans in the water cried for help. In the darkness beyond, the *Petard*'s sister ships circled, listening for other U-boats.

Fasson and Grazier reached the submarine and climbed down into her control room. The U-boat's lights were on, and they could see two bodies there. Fasson shouted up that the submarine was holed forward. Then, using a machine gun, he smashed open cabinets in the captain's cabin and, finding some keys behind a door, opened a drawer. From it he took out some documents, apparently secret ones.

Tommy Brown had gone below to help Fasson and Grazier, water from the 4-incher's hole pouring onto his back as he went down the ladder. Now he carried these precious papers up the conning tower and gave them to the men in the whaler. Another sailor, K. Lacroix, at the top of the conning tower, pulled up some books with a line. Brown went down again to bring up more documents, managing to keep them dry despite the leaks and splashes. On his third trip, the water, which had been rising gradually, stood 2 feet deep on the submarine's inside deck.

Back in the control room, Fasson was trying to free a box containing some instrument — perhaps a radio or radar — from a bulkhead to which it was attached by wires. The water was getting deeper; outside, it was starting to cover the aft gun platform. Brown told the lieutenant that they were shouting on deck for them to come up. Fasson directed Brown to take up the next batch of papers. The teenager climbed the ladder with the documents and passed them into the whaler. Meanwhile, Fasson and Grazier had managed to break away the instrument box and tie it to a line to be lifted up. As the sailors hauled it out, Fasson called out that they were pulling too fast, that the instrument appeared delicate and important and that they should be careful with it.

By now the sea was over the afterdeck platform, and Connell told Brown not to go down again but to tell Fasson and Grazier to get out at once. Brown saw them at the bottom of the conning tower and shouted, "You had better come up!" twice. They had just started up when, unexpectedly and swiftly, the submarine sank. Brown jumped off; Lacroix, still on the conning tower, had to pull against the water pouring down as he climbed the last two rungs of the ladder. He swam away against the suction, and he and Brown were picked up by the whaler. But Fasson and Grazier had not been able to overcome the inrushing water. They went down with the submarine.

* * *

The whaler with its precious documents came alongside the *Petard* and was hoisted on the run as she and the *Dulverton,* their search-lights extinguished, moved at speed away from the possible danger of other U-boats. The euphoria of the crew members at having destroyed a hated enemy quickly turned to an inexpressible sorrow as they realized that they had lost a competent and well-liked officer and a regular serviceman who was an asset to the ship. The *Petard* continued to Haifa, where the valuable documents were given to naval intelligence officers. Thornton, true to his word that he would send a trophy to the ship's builders, sent a U-boat seaman's life jacket to Newcastle. After deciding that Fasson and Grazier could not be granted Britain's highest decoration for valor, the Victoria Cross, because they had not acted in the face of an enemy, the Admiralty posthumously awarded them Britain's second highest decoration for bravery, the George Cross.

The documents that had cost the lives of Fasson and Grazier included two that were most useful for G.C.&.C.S. in its stalled attack on the U-boat Enigma. One was the current edition of the Short Signal Book. But it was less immediately useful than the second edition of the Short Weather Cipher. That reached Bletchley Park — after the excessive delay of more than three weeks — on November 24. Once again Hut 8 could work the crossruff. It could turn Hut 10's solutions of broadcast weather messages back into the form the weather messages had when the U-boats enciphered them into Enigma, thus obtaining cribs. But because the second edition of the Short Weather Cipher, unlike the first, did not list the twenty-six rotor settings, each indicated by a letter, to be used in enciphering weather reports, the cryptanalysts thought that all four rotors were used to encipher weather messages. The tedious testing on the bombes of the possible weather kisses began.

On Sunday, December 13, 1942, Hut 8 struck pay dirt. One of the weather cribs that Archer had brought over yielded a key. It used the fourth rotor in the neutral position, making M4 equivalent to the three-rotor Enigma, the only kind the shore weather stations had. Shaun Wylie, on the night shift, was having breakfast in the canteen when somebody came in and said, "It's out!" Wylie left his food and went back to Hut 8, where he confirmed the work and telephoned a superior about it. Then he went to Hut 6, Hut 8's military counterpart. John Monroe was on duty, running the night shift. "It's come out in the zero position!" Wylie exulted. "Can I have six bombes?" Though Bletchley then had forty-nine bombes, they were in such demand that getting their allocation changed would almost require an act of Parliament, Monroe thought. But recognizing both the importance of the matter and the limitations of his power, he said yes, Wylie could have them — until the day shift came in. In fact, Hut 8 kept them longer.

The cryptanalysts learned that the four-letter indicators for regular U-boat messages were the same as the three-letter indicators for weather messages that same day except for an extra letter. Thus, once a daily key was found for a weather message, the fourth rotor had to be tested only in twenty-six positions to find the full four-letter key. This gave Hut 8 little difficulty. Later that Sunday, solutions of the four-rotor Enigma U-boat key, called SHARK by G.C.&C.S., started to emerge.

Late in the afternoon, Hut 8 telephoned the Submarine Tracking Room to report the break into SHARK. The call was taken by Winn's assistant, Reserve Lieutenant Patrick Beesly. The news thrilled him. In an hour the first intercept came off the teleprinter. It revealed the position of fifteen U-boats. Other intercepts arrived in an endless stream until the early hours of the next morning. Beesly began struggling with the difficult and confusing situation revealed by the intercepts. The night was exhausting but exciting. Gradually over the next weeks the situation clarified. The solutions again permitted evasive routing of the convoys, and sinkings were halved in January and February 1943 from the highs of the two previous months. And, as with the *Magdeburg*, the U-33, the U-110, the *Krebs*, and the weather ships, the precious papers that helped make this success possible had come from an enemy warship.

Nineteen

Enter the Americans

THE GERMAN NAVAL messages that were much of B.P.'s raison d'être were intercepted at two main posts: one on the cliffs near Scarborough on the North Sea coast, the other in the center of southern England, near Winchester. Some of the intercept operators, or monitors, were Royal Navy sailors; many others were Wrens.

Among the latter was Alice Axon, a prim and proper teenager who also did direction-finding. As a child in Gravesend, east of London, she had always been keen on signals: she had practiced semaphore as a Brownie and Morse code as a Sea Ranger. At seventeen, the slim young woman volunteered for the Wrens, hoping to be a wireless operator. She stood at the top of her class during the first three months of radio training in London and the second three months in the country. Axon and her fellow students were puzzled because they were taught only to receive Morse, at twenty-five words per minute, and not to send it.

The mystery was resolved when they were sent to the intercept station near Winchester, a large Royal Navy shore installation named as if it were a ship: H.M.S. Flowerdown. The main intercept building had places for about seventy-five monitors, all facing the controllers at one end of a big room. Work went on around the clock. The intercept operators lived in rows of one-story bungalows.

Each monitor listened through earphones to the peepings brought in by the radio set on a high bench in front of him or her. Each took down all the traffic — every schedule, in the intercept operators' term — on a single frequency. Axon, for example, copied primarily a frequency used by station DAN at Norddeich, which broadcast weather reports, and secondarily a frequency used by station LLA-bar, whose location she did not know. Some stations transmitted at regular times, others only when they had messages. When nothing was being transmitted, many of the women knitted.

But when a message began, the monitor immediately started to write it down in pencil on the topmost sheet of a pad of intercept forms. No carbon copies were made. He or she noted the time, the frequency, the signal strength, the addressee, and the sender, and wrote down the code groups in the little rectangles on the form's grid. The monitor was careful to write down only letters of which he or she was certain, omitting the others and indicating the omissions; guesses were not allowed, since a wrong letter was worse than a blank. But the German transmissions were very precise, very uniform; they reminded Axon of the goose step. When a transmission was completed, the monitor ripped the intercept form off the pad and held it up high. Often he or she was holding up one message while taking down another. A controller would take it to the teleprinter to be sent to the codebreakers.

The breaks into SHARK, the Atlantic U-boat key, of December 13, 1942, were followed by others. Not all keys could be recovered: in January 1943 no settings were recovered for a ten-day period, and none were found between February 10 and 17. Except for difficulties like these, however, SHARK solutions, early in 1943, rarely took longer than seventy-two hours and often less than twenty-four, making them of operational value.

Then disaster loomed. Hints appeared in the traffic that the Germans were going to replace the Short Weather Cipher that had just been recovered from the U-559. The new, unknown edition — the third — would cost Hut 8 its kisses. The first sea lord messaged the vice chief of the naval staff, then in Washington, that "U-boat Special Intelligence has received a severe setback. After 10th March it is unlikely that we shall obtain more than 2 to 3 pairs of days per month and these will not be current. After 2 to 3 months the situation should improve considerably."

The first sea lord was too pessimistic. When the new weather cipher went into effect, Hut 8 used the Short Signal Book taken from the U-559 to find cribs among the numerous short signals being emitted by the U-boats during the heavy convoy battles then going on. Like the weather code, this book used the Enigma in three-rotor mode, which speeded up the work of the bombes. Hut

8 fitted cribs to cryptograms by identifying U-boats through direction-finding, radio fingerprinting, and transmitter identification by TINA as well as through an index of the behavior and procedures of individual submarines and their skippers. As a consequence, of the 112 days from March 10 to the end of June, Hut 8 solved the SHARK keys for 90.

On July 1, however, yet another complication appeared: the Germans brought into service an alternative fourth rotor. Called gamma, it sometimes served in place of the original, called beta (no alpha rotor was ever recovered). Hut 8 reconstructed its wiring cryptanalytically within a few days. The cryptanalysts learned that the choice of rotors was made on the first of the month. This regularity simplified Hut 8's task: it was only when making the first break of a month that they had the extra task of determining which fourth rotor was being used.

As the convoy battles subsided and the supply of short signals dwindled, Hut 8 exploited the kisses between texts, such as general orders that were transmitted in three-rotor Enigma to surface forces and shore stations and in M4 to U-boats. These provided longer and more reliable cribs, but they took longer to test on the bombes than the short signals.

Bletchley's first bombe, AGNES, was installed on the grounds of the park itself. But to minimize damage from air raids, such as the one during the night of November 20–21, in which a direct hit destroyed a telephone exchange and a typists' room and a near miss burst six paces from Hut 4, the next bombes were sited elsewhere. A low, one-story brick utility building was constructed for them at Wavendon Manor, about 3 miles northeast of Bletchley. Still, by the spring of 1941, the codebreakers had only eight bombes and, by the end of 1941, only twelve. Huts 6 and 8 shared the bombes in those days of paucity. The question of who should have them was often difficult but only rarely resulted in fights — usually when Hut 6 was being pressed strongly to break an Afrika Korps key. One reason for this relative harmony was that the deputy heads of the huts at that time — Stuart Milner-Barry for 6 and Hugh Alexander for 8 — were good friends. Another was that Milner-Barry always believed, correctly, that losing the Battle of the Atlantic would mean losing the war; he often yielded his bombe time to the naval cryptanalysts, without, however, telling those who were pressing him for breaks.

Gradually the British Tabulating Machine Company increased the tempo of production at its main factory at Ignield Way in Letchworth, some 30 miles north of London. While the first machines took five weeks to construct, the later ones, built in batches of six, came off the assembly line at the rate of one a week. The bombes, about the size of three standing cupboards, were loaded onto ordinary trucks and, to maintain secrecy, given no special escort as they were driven to Crawley Grange and Gayhurst Manor, both stately homes near Bletchley, and Adstock, a village in Buckinghamshire. By August 1942, G.C.&C.S. had thirty bombes and had established a bombe station on London Road in Stanmore, a neighborhood in northwest London. The two parallel one-story brick buildings were divided into several big rooms, each with an office area and ten machines in two rows down the sides. The rooms smelled of oil, metal, and cement. The arrangement proved so successful that a similar facility was built 5 miles away between Eastcote Road and Lime Grove in Eastcote. To these were brought some of the bombes from the country. By March of 1943, sixty bombes were in operation and, by the end of the war, two hundred.

The bombes were black iron monsters 6 to 8 feet high, 10 to 12 feet wide, 3 feet deep. Each one was named. Those at Adstock were named after fighter planes, such as SPITFIRE. Those at Stanmore and Eastcote carried the names of towns in the United Kingdom and the British Commonwealth and of cities in Allied countries. On the face of the machine were rows of wheels, the analogues of the Enigma rotors, each 1½ inches thick and 5 inches in diameter, bearing a large number in the middle and the twenty-six letters of the alphabet around its circumference.

The bombes were tended by Wrens. Bletchley sent them a menu — the instructions for setting up a bombe, based on a crib and the loops derived from it. A Wren put on the rotors in the order specified by the menu, turned them to the menu starting positions, plugged in cables in the rear according to instructions, and turned on the machine. Then, sleeves rolled up, jackets and ties off, they would stand by, chatting over the whirring of the bombe and keeping an eye on it as it ran.

One bombe tender, Diane Payne, had joined the Wrens dreaming of the sea and with the romantic idea of marrying a sailor. At recruitment she was asked if she could keep a secret; she replied that she really didn't know because she had never tried. Despite this unsatisfactory answer, she was assigned to special duties. After basic training, she and the others were taken to a hut at Bletchley Park and told that their jobs would consist of shift work, with little hope of promotion, and the need for complete secrecy. Unreflecting patriotism led Payne and nearly all the others to accept — although the necessary silence about her work led some of her family and friends to consider her something of a failure in her war work. Another bombe tender, Marjory Mitchell, a Scott who, like all young women over eighteen had been called up for war work, was apparently assigned to the bombes because she had studied in Switzerland and learned four languages, although that had nothing to do with the work she eventually did. Unlike the Oxbridge cryptanalysts, who were never checked for possible subversion, she was carefully vetted, with police in her home towns of Fraserborough and Aberdeen asking friends and neighbors whether she had any connections with Germany. At Stanmore in 1942, after signing the Official Secrets Act, she was put into the D Watch of fifty young women and began working a three-shift system, 8 A.M. to 4 P.M. one week, 4 to midnight the next, then midnight to 8 A.M. the third week, with two days off between each shift change.

The change in hours didn't bother the women, who sometimes violated regulations by sneaking off to central London after a midnight-to-8 A.M. tour. But the 2,000 Wrens who eventually tended bombes took their work very seriously. From time to time B.P. would tell them that their work had led, say, to the sinking of a U-boat or the successful diversion of a convoy. "We felt the weight of responsibility that any mistake or time wasted could mean lives lost," Diane Payne said. Once a coworker turned white while taking tea with Payne and some relatives, remembering what she thought was a mistake while on duty. But she and Payne worked out the problem on a bit of paper and decided her work had been correct; then, frantic about security, they burned the paper in the sink. For some, the strain showed in upset stomachs, collapses, nightmares, going berserk on duty. For others the work was just boring. Marjory Mitchell, perhaps representative of others, did not think the work tedious; it was a job she had to do, it wasn't dirty, and she enjoyed the company of the other women.

The bombes broke down frequently; on average, one of the eight machines in D Watch's room would fail on a shift. The soldering joints on the cables in back were a particular source of trouble, frequently coming loose, and the wire brush contacts needed constant attention. Royal Air Force personnel would open the machine and brave its labyrinth of cables and gears to repair it. When a bombe functioned properly, however, the wheels in the top row all spun fast, those in the second row turned at one twenty-sixth the rate, and those in the bottom row seemed hardly to move at all. When the circuitry sensed a possible solution position, or "drop," the position of the spinning top rotors at that point was shown on an indicator; they were then slowed and stopped. The middle and bottom rotors were frozen in their positions. The Wren would report the settings of all the rotors, as well as the rotor order being run, to Hut 8. Because bombe time was so precious, she restarted the bombe while the cryptanalysts checked to see if the drop represented an actual key or merely a chance concatenation — what the cryptanalysts called a "legal contradiction." If the latter, they let the bombe run. If it was a key, they called to stop it. It took a bombe about 15 minutes to run one rotor order and so, with shifting rotors from one position to another and dealing with drops, some 100 to 150 days would be needed on one bombe to exhaust all 15,360 rotor orders possible on the menu from a single crib. The Wrens had little idea of what all this meant, but it was a thrill when the correct stop came from one's own machine.

When the bombes found a successful U-boat key, a half-dozen Hut 8 women assistants, using converted British rotor cipher machines resting on a shelf that ran around their room, transformed the intercepted messages into German on strips of gummed paper, which they glued onto full-sized sheets.

Messengers took them to the Hut 4 watch. Hut 4, like the other huts, had expanded and moved into a larger brick building, still separate from Hut 8. The translators sat around a long table in a double-sized room, and the messengers put the solved intercepts in a basket in front of the No. 2 on the watch. He sorted them according to urgency — an extremely responsible job — and distributed them to the four or five translators on the watch. They handwrote the English version of the German plaintext — usually only a line or two — on a separate sheet of paper. The abbreviations, which were numerous, often puzzled them. One translator, Leonard Forster, considered that they were specialists in the expansion of abbreviations. A separate team ascertained the meaning of the technical terms for newly invented devices — new mines, new torpedoes — and recorded these in a kind of dictionary for the translators.

They initialed their translations and gave them to the head of the watch, who vetted them and decided which should be sent to the Operational Intelligence Centre. One watch head, the prematurely balding A. A. Ernest E. Ettinghausen, considered that his job was chiefly to get the material out quickly and accurately and in the right order of priority. He did not have to motivate his men in this: there was a war on, and they sensed, if they did not know, that "to save an hour . . . was to gain an hour in which a U-boat gained six miles upon a convoy." He often picked up the direct telephone to the O.I.C. to alert them that an important message was coming through. The "teleprincesses" addressed the messages to O.I.C. to "I D 8 G," the I D for (Naval) Intelligence Division, the 8 for its Section 8, the O.I.C., the G for O.I.C.'s liaison with B.P. The sending teleprinters at B.P. made six carbon copies. These went to various sections of Hut 4, such as the unit dealing with U-boat technology. The teleprinters in the O.I.C. likewise made six copies, which were distributed to Denning, Winn, and others who needed that intelligence.

In Hut 4, a copy went as well to Harry Hinsley, who, seated in his smallish office, scanned them all. He could handle the volume of hundreds a day because most of the messages were so short and routine and took only a few seconds to read. He was looking for any variation from the ordinary patterns that might foretell some German activity. Once, for example, he realized that the U-boat addressed was under special orders because the frequency on which the message was sent was one not normally used by U-boats. Another message ordered a sub to rendezvous in an unusual position. Still another revealed that the group of subs was called GOEBEN, the name of a World War I German battle cruiser that achieved fame in the Mediterranean. All these clues gradually made clear to Hinsley in 1941 that submarines were to be sent from the Atlantic into the Mediterranean. And they were.

* * *

At the end of 1942, a U.S. Army contingent was sent to Britain to help B.P. Its three units — the 6811th, 6812th, and 6813th Signal Security Detachments — dealt respectively with interception, bombes, and cryptanalysis. The 6812th, with some two hundred men under the command of Captain Mortimer Stewart, a Texan and former I.B.M. employee, worked first at Stanmore and then at a bombe complex in the northern London suburb of Ruislip. Its work area was called UNITED STATES and each of its twelve bombes was named for an American city — among them Houston, for Stewart's hometown. The Americans were pleased to be working with the Wrens. One amazed lieutenant noted that the buildings at Stanmore "contained marvelous machines and many attractive ladies. The machines were made by the British Tabulating Machine Company and the ladies by God." The feeling was sometimes reciprocated: one tall, dark-haired Wren officer fell in love with blond Lieutenant Rolf Christiensen at first sight, to the envy of several of his compatriots.

Some of Stewart's men were also I.B.M.ers, and their practice of keeping records on the machines' performance delighted bombe maker Doc Keen, who used this information to make improvements. Stewart took pride in his unit's producing two to three times as many solutions as a comparable Wren unit, not because it ran the machines faster but because the men changed setups much more quickly. The 6812th began work on the U-boat cipher as soon as it arrived in Britain and continued to work a great deal on that prime target.

The role of the United States in breaking the naval Enigma eventually equaled Great Britain's. The cooperation between the two nations had started long before the American contingents arrived at Bletchley. Though British and American cryptanalysts had been in contact during World War I, a far more intimate relationship began in 1940 as part of a general exchange of scientific information. The Americans agreed to give the British their reconstruction of the main Japanese diplomatic cipher machine, which they called PURPLE, in return for British information about Enigma cryptanalysis. Four Americans were selected to accompany PURPLE to Bletchley Park and to learn about Enigma: two army reserve officers, Abraham Sinkov, a mathematical cryptanalyst, and

Leo Rosen, who had made an important breakthrough in solving PURPLE, and two navy officers, both communications intelligence specialists, lieutenants Prescott Currier and Robert Weeks. Flying was considered too risky, so the men were to travel on Britain's newest battleship, the *King George V*, which had brought over the new British ambassador.

The battlewagon anchored in Annapolis Roads on Friday, January 24, 1941. That same day government station wagons brought the four Americans, plus four wooden crates, each about 2 by 2 by 3 feet and containing the PURPLE machine and accompanying papers, from Washington to Annapolis. In a steady downpour the crates were manhandled into a liberty boat to be ferried with the men to the *King George V*. Rosen, in an open boat, oversaw the crates as they were lifted aboard in a cargo net and stowed in a strongroom below. The *KGV* sailed the next morning.

The trip across was uneventful except for occasional calls to action stations. The Royal Navy officers in the wardroom kept asking the Americans to explain the cartoons in *The New Yorker* and *Esquire*. At 2:32 P.M. on February 6 the ship anchored in Scapa Flow in a heavy snowstorm. The Americans and the crates transferred to a cruiser going to the Thames estuary. Steaming down the east coast of England, they saw the signs of war: ship after ship sunk in the shallow water, their masts and funnels visible. And they experienced the war as well: a German bomber attacked, its bombs exploding on the sea bottom and lifting the ship gently, as if by a hand. The crates, on deck, were peppered with machine-gun bullet ricochets but were not damaged.

The team was greeted at the end of its trip by the then No. 2 at B.P., Commander Travis, who took charge of the crates. The Americans were driven up to Bletchley, arriving at night. The big house was barely visible, with not a glimmer of light escaping through its blackout curtains. The men were led through the main doors, a blacked-out vestibule, and dimly lit hallways into Denniston's office. He and his senior staff were standing in a semicircle around his desk. In a memorable moment that marked the renewal of a fruitful cooperation, the Americans were introduced to each person in turn. After some pleasantries, they were driven off to Shenley Park, the country estate of an oil magnate; the next morning, they were fed a magnificent English breakfast just as if there were no rationing.

For the next five weeks, the American team not only spent time at Bletchley but visited the direction-finding network, the Admiralty's communications center, the O.I.C., the intercept stations at Scarborough and Flowerdown, and the radar at the underground command center beneath Dover Castle. At Bletchley, Rosen and Sinkov taught the British about PURPLE and took copious notes on the bombes and details of Enigma cryptanalysis. The British had few solutions to show, since up to the end of February Hut 8 had broken only eleven days of naval Enigma traffic, and the *Krebs* material arrived only five or six days before the Americans were to leave for home. But they did explain the attempts made to discover the machine settings, and they gave the Americans all the keys that had been recovered. And though the British never provided an Enigma, they did give Weeks a paper analogue. Sinkov and Rosen concluded in their official report: "We were invited to ask questions about anything we saw, no doors were closed to us and copies were furnished of any material which we considered of possible assistance to the United States."

By the time of Pearl Harbor the U.S. Navy was putting 20 percent of its interception effort and 3 percent of its cryptanalytic effort into German and Italian naval systems (all the rest of the work was going into Japanese naval and diplomatic codes and ciphers). For a year after the four Americans left B.P. in the spring of 1941, no Britons visited the U.S. Navy cryptanalysts, and no Americans went to B.P., though the two had been exchanging direction-finding bearings since May of that year. In April 1942, with the United States in the war, a conference in Washington between the communications intelligence specialists of the two nations led to increasing collaboration in the form of telecommunications, visits, and permanent liaison personnel. Winn, who had spent a year at Yale and a year at Harvard after graduating from Cambridge, persuaded the Americans to set up a system like his. Then, in the fall of 1942, Lieutenant Joseph Eachus, U.S. Naval Reserve, was sent to England.

A tall midwesterner, Eachus, who held a doctorate in mathematics from the University of Illinois, had taken a correspondence course in cryptology from the navy. After Pearl Harbor, he was called up and, on his first day, was sent to a large room in the Navy Department building. It was bustling with activity. One man was practicing Morse code by sending to himself. One was practicing Japanese by talking to himself. Another was trying to call himself on another telephone in the room — via Alaska. Said Eachus, when all of this was explained to him, "I'm going to like it here!" This was OP-20-G, the Navy's communications intelligence section: OP because it was a division of the office of the chief of naval operations, 20 the number of the communications division, and G for communications intelligence. When the section needed someone to go to England, Eachus could be spared, since he hadn't been there long enough to have an important job.

For months Eachus was the only American at B.P. He studied the British cryptanalysis, reported on it to OP-20-G, and assisted in codebreaking. When he came home for a while in the spring of 1943, he found that OP-20-G had moved into new quarters in a former girls' school, Mount Vernon Seminary, at 3801 Nebraska Avenue in northwest Washington. Here the cryptanalysts of OP-20-GY(A) — Y for the cryptanalysts, A for Atlantic — received intercepts from the posts scattered along the East Coast.

The codebreakers worked in what was called the "back room" but was actually three small rooms on the ground floor of what was called Building 2. One room was for the four women on each watch who sorted intercepts; both U-boat and U-boat Command messages could be intercepted on the East Coast. Another room housed the teletypewriters and cipher machines for communications with the intercept posts, G.C.&C.S., and the U.S. Navy's U-boat plot. The cryptanalysts worked on the Enigma intercepts in the third room. Headed by reserve Commander Howard Engstrom, a Yale mathematician, they cooked up cribs from such stereotypes as the standardized German beginnings of messages — "It's much easier to say the same thing the same way every day," observed one cryptanalyst — and a weather report put out daily for the Bay of Biscay, which the British intercepted and sent to Washington.

The cryptanalysts had other sources of cribs as well. Once an intelligence officer sent a memo to Engstrom:

The Star of Suez was torpedoed and sunk 15 December at 01 N 29-30 W. The sinking was claimed in the German broadcast of December 17. We have no message relative to the sinking, which was in the area being patrolled by [U-134 skipper Lieutenant Rudolf] Schendel. . . . A DF [fix] at 0019/17 [December] (TOO [time of origin] 2301) of 63 groups, fixed at 03-45 N 29 W, is the most likely message that reported the sinking of the Star of Suez, though it might be a report on the sinking of the East Wales, at 2025/16 at 00-24 N 31-27 W, also claimed in the same German broadcast. Possibly the names of these ships, or routes Trinidad to Capetown and Trinidad to Durban, respectively, with the skipper's name Schendel would afford a crib on the traffic for the 16th.

This crib may not have worked, for, as was later learned, a different U-boat had sunk both ships. But when one crib failed, the cryptanalysts tried different suppositions.

The codebreakers worked in close collaboration with Hut 8. The British forwarded messages that could not be intercepted in the United States, and the teams on both sides of the Atlantic sought cribs, dividing up the work by days. When the British found a crib, they transmitted the text of the intercept followed by the text of the crib; from this the Americans reconstructed the menu. If the Americans recovered a key, they would send it to Bletchley, where the British used it to decipher their intercepts. The two units communicated by radio and cable, the latter passing through the office of British Security Coordination in Rockefeller Center, New York. Secrecy was ensured by the CCM, the Combined Cipher Machine, which was not actually a single machine but, on the British side, the Type X cipher machine with an adapter that enabled it to decipher messages from the American machine, the ECM, or Electric Cipher Machine, and, on the American side, the ECM with an adapter for Type X cryptograms.

The menus that the Washington codebreakers made up were sent by pneumatic tube to the high-speed bombes on the first and second floors of a new building on the school's 35 acres. The American bombes, built by the National Cash Register Company in Dayton, Ohio, were designed to deal with the four-rotor Enigma. Each was the equivalent of six British three-rotor bombes. They ran much faster than the early British models. These monsters were about 7 feet tall, 10 feet wide, and 2 feet deep and weighed about 2½ tons. On their gray metal faces were two rows of black disks marked 00 to 25 around their circumference; centered within each was a rotatable brass pointer. Underneath ranged four rows of eight wheels each, the rotor analogues. The machines' vacuum tubes, relays, drive motor, clutch, brake, backup motor, and electrical losses generated so much heat that large air conditioners were needed every 10 feet, summer and winter. Once installed, the machines were operated twenty-four hours a day. They were tended by members of the navy's women's auxiliary — the WAVES (Women Accepted for Volunteer Emergency Service), the American counterpart of the Wrens. Trained mechanics installed and maintained the machines and made repairs — usually of broken carbon commutator brushes, of which there were hundreds on each machine.

When a WAVE received a menu, she would set up the bombe and start it running. If the crib was wrong, or if a rotor turnover occurred during it, the bombe would complete its run in as little as 10 or 15 minutes; some runs took longer. However, when a crib was right, a hit would occur, indicating that an electrical pathway had been found. The machine ran so fast that the connection merely activated a memory circuit, which recorded the position of the hit, turned off the power, and braked the drive shaft, then reversed the rotors until they returned to the hit position. A printer typed out the rotor positions. Then the machine started again — the hit might have been caused by a chance arrangement of the rotor wiring — and ran until another hit occurred or it reached the end of the run and stopped automatically.

The hit results, called "stories," were sent back up the pneumatic tube to the cryptanalysts, who would test each on a hand device that replicated the Enigma to see which one produced German text. To Lieutenant James T. Prendergrass, it was always a thrill to crack a cryptogram. "There's nothing like real blood," the cryptanalysts said to one another, referring to solving the life-or-death messages that the Germans were trying so hard to keep from them. The work, many of them felt, was exciting.

Recovered keys were turned over to the WAVES, who typed out the intercepts on Enigma analogues that turned out the plaintexts in long strings of letters. Yeomen carried these sheets of paper upstairs to the translators' office and dropped them into a wire basket. The translators (normally, two were on duty at a time) divided the strings of letters into words and converted them into English. One of the translators, a WAVE with a doctorate in German, Erminnie Bartelmez, a short, shy, vigorous woman, felt sad when she translated a message telling some U-boat sailor that his family had been killed in an air raid, even though they were the enemy. The flow of intercepts was intermittent, and during the quiet periods the translators checked over old messages for errors or gossiped, read, or knitted. Yeomen typed up their handwritten translations and carried them to the watch officers, who brought them to the intelligence section on the second floor.

Here, in a large office with windows on one side and a balcony on the other, filled with stenographers and littered with duplicating machines, the intercepts were turned into intelligence. Like the O.I.C., OP-20-GI-2(A) maintained a file on U-boat matters. It consisted of 5-by-8-inch cards in open-topped file boxes on three or four wide shelves, where it was easy to get to. Each card carried a solved intercept reproduced by a Ditto machine in its characteristic purple ink. Each message was copied on from two to eight cards, depending on its subject matter, and the cards filed under several categories. The master file was chronological, but files also existed on individual U-boats, on U-boat position reports, on assignments, on new equipment, weather reports, status reports, and so on. Though the files primarily served the translators and the watch officers answering questions about U-boats from the American Submarine Tracking Room, they were often used by the cryptanalysts for suggestions for cribs. Once a senior watch officer, reserve Lieutenant Knight McMahan, a Ph.D. in philosophy, whose duties included overseeing the files, found just the message needed by the cryptanalysts — who came upstairs a little later all smiles.

McMahan was stunned by the events he learned about. Fresh from academe, he had had no idea of the cruelty of the sinkings or of the secret war on, and he thought it was a horrible introduction to the real world. He empathized with the merchant seamen who were dying in the North Atlantic, and the images he formed of them, fed by the intercepts, motivated him in his work.

The watch officers read the day's intercepts as they came in, saw to it that the information from them was displayed on the large maps of the Atlantic that showed U-boats and convoys, added clarifications to the messages, and talked frequently on the telephone with the tracking room, whose staff needed to know, for example, where a U-boat had been or how much fuel it had left. Among the office's outputs was a daily report on the movement of the vessels of such neutrals as Spain and Portugal. But its main product was issued by Harvard logician and naval reserve Lieutenant Willard

Van Orman Quine. He had gotten into the work after a historian of science told him that a Harvard astronomer was recruiting for cryptanalysts; Quine met with him and signed up for the navy's correspondence course in codebreaking. Quine produced the daily U-boat summary, duplicated on paper with "Top Secret Ultra" in magenta at the head of each page.

By mid-1943, the U.S. and British cryptanalysts had developed such familiarity with the German naval signals organization that they rarely failed to find a crib, and they had enough high-speed bombes to try many cribs. From August of that year, naval Enigma was read regularly and rapidly without significant interruption for the rest of the war. This triumph, the result of hard work by brilliant people hidden in the shadows and the daring of men at sea, was the greatest extended intelligence exploit of all time.

Quine's U-boat situation report, as well as individual solved, translated, and annotated intercepts, were sent — sometimes in double-sealed envelopes by hand of an officer, sometimes by secure teleprinter — to a restricted group of individuals in the seventh wing of the third floor of Main Navy in Washington. This long low structure, on the Mall near the Lincoln Memorial facing Constitution Avenue, had been built as a temporary office building during World War I.

On December 27, 1942, a special unit, the so-called Secret Room, had been created to handle the intercepts. The unit formed a part of the thirty-man Combat Intelligence Section of the commander in chief, United States Fleet, Admiral Ernest J. King. (In another capacity, chief of naval operations, King was in charge of the much larger Office of Naval Intelligence, which dealt with long-range and strategic issues.) The Combat Intelligence Section and its commander were designated F-2; its Atlantic branch was F-21 and its Pacific, F-22. The quiet, boyish-looking Commander Kenneth A. Knowles, who had graduated 16th out of 579 in his Annapolis class of 1927 was F-21; he had quit his naval career because of nearsightedness but had been recalled after the outbreak of war. When, on May 20, 1943, King created the Tenth Fleet as an administrative body (it had no ships) to direct the antisubmarine war, he designated Knowles's unit as the intelligence staff for the Tenth Fleet as well as the U.S. Fleet.

F-21's Submarine Tracking Room, itself a confidential operation, was the only area through which the Secret Room could be entered. The Secret Room, F-211, was kept locked, and only the three men who worked in it, together with Knowles and a relief officer, had keys; no one else was admitted except a few higher-ups with special permission. In charge was a New York lawyer and naval reservist, Lieutenant John E. Parsons. As the intercepts came to the Secret Room, Parsons and his assistants entered the information on a daily location list of U-boats. From here it was transferred to one of three large wall maps — the North Atlantic map was 12 feet wide — on which the U-boats were represented by pins. Each one carried the bigram assigned by the Admiralty to that submarine, the skipper's name, the date of the position, and a colored tab to show whether it was a refueler, minelayer, cargo carrier, or combat sub. Other wall charts showed U-boats at the five Biscay bases, areas in which U-boats used particular frequencies (helpful in locating U-boats to which Dönitz sent messages), places where submarines had been sunk in the past month, and the results of OP-20-GI-2(A)'s special studies, such as one on areas that Dönitz considered especially dangerous because of aircraft. In addition, the Secret Room contained a card file of U-boats; logs of attacks on ships and on U-boats; a list of skippers; files of U-boat arrivals and departures, fuel, destroyed U-boats, and flotillas; and assessments of attacks on submarines. All of these depended on information that had been abstracted from the intercepts.

Intelligence moved out of the Secret Room in a variety of ways. Individuals, including King, viewed the charts and had the briefing officer in the room answer their questions. Every ten to fourteen days one of Parsons's assistants prepared a summary of trends in U-boat operations as well as of new tactics and equipment; this went to the officers who had access to F-211. Messages were sent to the Admiralty about U-boat identifications, which ones were involved in attacks, and similar matters. And the Secret Room staff gave the cryptanalysts information, using a special telephone for short items and notes for more complicated ones.

As head of Atlantic combat intelligence, Knowles was probably the chief consumer. His unit combined Parsons's ULTRA intelligence with intelligence from direction-finding, prisoners of war, action reports from Allied merchantmen and warships, reconnoitering airplanes, and other sources to figure out the U-boats' daily estimated positions. The Submarine Tracking Room had an officer and three enlisted men on watch at all times; the WAVES eventually replaced all the men except two officers not qualified physically for sea duty. (Captain Henri H. Smith-Hutton, who headed Combat Intelligence in 1943 and 1944, maintained that the plotting room ran better with the WAVES than it had earlier because the displaced men "were not as smart as these carefully selected WAVES.") Probably Knowles himself drafted or at least approved the daily U-boat situation estimate, with its forecast of where the submarines were going, that was transmitted to task forces at sea under the signature of the commander in chief, U.S. Fleet.

Knowles's detailed information went across the hall to the Tenth Fleet's Convoy and Routing Section, F 0. This body, the American version of the Admiralty's Trade Division's Movements Section, directed shipping in the U-boat-infested waters.

On a 40-foot-wide chart of the North Atlantic covering one wall of this room, U-boat positions were continually updated with pins. The section never knew that the submarine locations were furnished by codebreaking, though some suspected it; the cover story was that direction-finding provided this information. As the officers saw that "their" ships were about to encounter U-boats, they ordered diversions to detour them away from the submarine danger.

Among the convoys that twisted and turned in response to the section's orders was SC 127.

Twenty

SC 127

FOR HOURS on Friday, April 16, 1943, a few dozen ships furrowed the waters of the 10-mile channel to the sea from the bustling port of Halifax, Nova Scotia. They steamed between the red sand cliffs to starboard and the white granite hills to port that guarded the narrow entrance. Out on the ocean they arranged themselves into a convoy's customary broad-fronted formation. Convoy SC 127 had been born.

Its fifty-four ships, plus three that joined later from St. John's, were taking to Britain material both for the British war economy and for the eventual invasion of western Europe. The *Fort Howe* and the *Picotee* and the *Belgian Sailor* all carried tanks and grain. The *Keilhaven* and the *Mimosa* carried steel and lumber. No fewer than nine ships had explosives in their holds. Others were bringing over fuel oil, lubricating oil, sugar, and phosphates. The commodore's ship, the *Empire Franklin,* carried general cargo. Most were headed for Loch Ewe in northern Scotland; others for Glasgow, Belfast, Liverpool, Manchester, London.

The Atlantic into which they were heading was the theater of a battle in which the Germans seemed to be approaching victory. In 1942, the Germans had sunk more tonnage than the Allies had built. The daily average of U-boats in the Atlantic and Arctic rose from 92 in January 1943 to 111 in April. The number of Allied ships sunk almost doubled month by month: 29 in January, 50 in February, 95 in March. Indeed, March saw the greatest convoy battle of the war, when 45 submarines swarmed around convoys SC 122 and HX 229, sending dozens of ships to the bottom.

And this was happening at a time when, though it had become clear that Britain would not starve and her factories would not close down, severe shortages persisted. Stocks of food and goods had not yet recovered from having been drawn down during the previous year. Imports to Britain had in January reached their lowest level of the war. Beef and veal imports had begun their 1943 slide to 310,000 tons, about half the yearly prewar average. Rationing continued. Each individual was entitled to two ounces of tea per week and four ounces of bacon and ham. The cheese ration had been halved in February from the generous eight ounces of 1942.

The Ministry of Food sought to reduce the amount of wheat brought in, on which Britain was especially dependent: in 1939 she had produced 1,668,000 tons but had imported 8,519,000. The ministry considered raising the rate of extraction of flour from wheat from the customary average of 70 to 75 percent to 90 or 95 percent and diluting the flour with barley and oats, even though this would produce a darker, less palatable, and less digestible bread. But the barley could be obtained only by reducing beer production and closing the pubs two days a week. The committee in charge unanimously recoiled from this. It and the brewers finally agreed, however, that oats and dried potato bits would replace 10 percent of the barley used in brewing. The plan was put into effect, and 280,000 fewer tons of wheat had to be imported. Such were the contortions the British government went through to save shipping space.

At the same time, the euphoria of the Casablanca conference, at which Roosevelt and Churchill planned their next offensive and declared the war against the U-boats their priority, had all but worn off among the Allies' military chiefs. They had come to see that the shipping situation was far worse than their earlier vague, optimistic impressions. The War Office miscalculated the number of vehicles and therefore the amount of shipping space per man needed for the North African invasion. Also the number of troops for that operation constantly increased, and, owing to the unexpected strength of the enemy opposition, the date when the buildup would be complete continually receded. Instead of the thirty ships a month that maintenance of the North African offensive had been thought to require, ninety-two sailed in February, seventy-five in March, and thirty-eight in April. Meanwhile, Turkey demanded 150,000 tons of grain that had been promised to keep her from raiding her traditional enemy, Russia. So tight was shipping that, far from being able to mount the operations against Japan that the Allies had grandly planned at Casablanca, Britain's Ministry of War Transport was haggling over single ships on the routes to India and the Middle East. Famine loomed in Ceylon, where laborers were leaving the rubber plantations in search of food, and in East Africa, where Britain feared that the shortage of food would cause a breakdown in work at the main repair base of the Eastern Fleet in Mombasa. Ultimately, one and a half million people died of starvation or its diseases in British-ruled India.

All of this exerted extreme pressure on shipping, the shortage of which, the chief of the Imperial General Staff said, put "a stranglehold on all offensive operations." And though details were probably not known to the codebreakers of Hut 8 or OP-20-G, they certainly felt the great and relentless need to save as many Allied ships as possible.

Convoy SC 127 — codenamed for that series of convoys' original starting place, Sydney, Cape Breton Island, Nova Scotia — was a slow convoy, one that could not maintain a speed of 10 knots; a fast convoy was one that could maintain that speed. But since no convoy could steam faster than its slowest ship, slow convoys averaged 7 knots, fast, 9. SC 127's planned speed was 7.5 knots.

Because the British Isles are several hundred miles farther north than Nova Scotia, each convoy had to head north somewhere along its course. SC 127's course, established nine days before sailing, called for it to start by sailing to Point F, at 46° 30' north latitude, 46° 02' west longitude, slightly north and well east of Halifax. From there, it would swing more to the north for a long leg to point G, several hundred miles southeast of the tip of Greenland. Thence it would turn sharply eastward and then due east for the long run over the north of Ireland. If intelligence showed submarines lying along this route, it would be changed. And in fact, two days after it laid out the course, the Admiralty added some lettered points closer to Halifax, taking the convoy a bit south before it turned north.

The course changes were devised by Commander Richard Hall's Trade Movements Section to avoid U-boat packs. The section based its plans on the reports of Winn's Submarine Tracking Room, which depended heavily on the solutions put out by Hut 8 and OP-20-G. On April 16, when the convoy put to sea, the codebreakers were running three days behind in their solutions. But since this was the best available information, the two Submarine Tracking Rooms continued to issue their reports on the positions of enemy U-boats. The U.S. report for April 16 situated twenty to twenty-five U-boats in a rectangle bounded by 47° and 53° north and 44° to 37° west. The path of SC 127 that had been planned on April 7 ran right through this area. Hall would have to attend to that.

In the open sea SC 127 had formed itself into thirteen columns, of four or five ships, a pattern that reduced the number of shots a U-boat could get at the ships, compared to an arrangement with fewer but longer columns. The convoy's size, fifty-four ships, reflected a lesson learned from operational research. This new field applied mathematics and science to military and naval problems. Analysis of aerial attacks on U-boats had shown, for example, that many submarines were escaping damage because the depth bombs exploded too deeply; when the setting was reduced, the kill rate went up. The Admiralty's Operational Research Group had also calculated that a convoy twice as large as another one could be given the same protection with only one-third again as many escorts. In other words, a convoy of forty-eight ships could be as well protected with eight escort vessels as a convoy of twenty-four with six: in both cases the escort vessels would be 2 miles apart.

Five warships were to accompany SC 127, and by 1 P.M. on the day of sailing their leader, His Majesty's Canadian Ship *Dundas,* was steaming on the port side of the convoy on a course of 122°. Escort was needed from the start because U-boats had audaciously sunk ships not only in the shadow of the Canadian coast but within the Gulf of St. Lawrence itself. The convoy's commodore was a Royal Navy Reserve officer, W. van den Donker, master of the S.S. *Empire Franklin.* So SC 127 set out to bring her precious goods to Great Britain, heading southeast by east under a blue sky, on a calm sea, fanned by a gentle breeze from starboard, with visibility only 6 or 7 miles but with the barometer rising.

In Berlin, Hitler's staff increasingly recognized that Nazi Germany needed to make greater efforts if she was to win this war. The devastating defeat at Stalingrad had impelled propaganda minister Joseph Goebbels to ask of a clapping, shouting audience at Berlin's Sportpalast, "Do you want total war?" He got back a ringing "Ja!" The new armaments minister, Alfred Speer, increased war production. Authorities agreed that they had to cleanse the continent of subhumans; they put into effect the final solution of the Jewish people. And Dönitz, who on January 30 had been named commander in chief of the navy while retaining his post as commander of U-boats, and who now had more than four hundred submarines at his disposal, urged them to hurl themselves like wolves upon the enemy. On April 11, five days before SC 127 sailed, Dönitz told Hitler that his goal was to make the Allies bleed, to sink more ships than they could build.

Ahead of that convoy, perhaps half a dozen others were crossing the Atlantic in one direction or the other. To sink their ships Dönitz, had, on April 16, sixty-three boats operating in the Atlantic north of Halifax's latitude of 44° 38′ north. One of the convoys U-Boat Command was concentrating on was SC 127's predecessor, SC 126. A report by the B-Dienst told the command that four days previously SC 126 was located some 600 miles southeast of Cape Race, the southern tip of Newfoundland. The convoy had presumably passed the patrol line formed by a wolfpack codenamed TITMOUSE. But the submarines' surface speed was superior to that of most convoys (a U-boat could cover 320 miles in 24 hours, an average convoy 240), so in hope of catching the convoy, Dönitz stretched TITMOUSE into a 650-mile northwest–southeast line with the U-boats moving roughly northeast. The next day, however, he abandoned hope of catching SC 126, saying that it might have slipped through the patrol line because of poor visibility.

U-Boat Command knew the rhythm of the convoys, and it knew that they sought to go around the U-boat concentrations. So on the seventeenth, with visibility expected to improve, Dönitz added more submarines to TITMOUSE and, supposing that the next convoys from Nova Scotia would go north to avoid wolfpacks, ordered it to take up a new patrol line. Farther west than the previous line, it was intended to catch the Allied ships as they sailed parallel to the Labrador coast.

The next day, however, two U-boats not in TITMOUSE spotted a pair of convoys so far to the south that the TITMOUSE submarines could not find them. Despite these sightings, U-Boat Command clung to its view that the next convoys would take the northern route. Perhaps reinforcing its belief was a report of a submarine's sighting, to the north, a convoy that radio intelligence promptly identified as HX 234, from New York.

While U-Boat Command was mulling this over, SC 127 marched at about 7 knots along its predetermined course, passing points C, D, and E as it headed first southeast out of Halifax and then east. Upon reaching E, at 6 P.M. Sunday, the eighteenth, it turned onto a course of 66°, or east-northeast. The barometer was now falling and the sky had clouded over, but the sea remained smooth and the air calm. Allied cryptanalysts had solved that day U-Boat Command's long two-part message of the seventeenth establishing TIT-MOUSE, which ordered twenty-six submarines to form a patrol line as of 8 A.M. April 19, listing them in the order in which they were to take up position. Though the U-boats were identified only by their skippers' names, their numbers were known. The German naval grid positions for the five points through which the line was to run were enciphered, but the cryptanalysts had determined the true meanings of many of the enciphered grid bigrams as well as of the disguised grid four-digit groups. They had learned, for example, that VD 0798 (the northwesternmost point) stood for AJ 5798, or 53° 45′ north, 46° 15′ west and that BU 8641 (the southeasternmost point) was BC 3641, or 49° 45′ north, 39° 55′ west. The solution revealed that the U-boats were to stay 15 miles apart and were to maintain radio silence "except for reports of tactical importance." And, in a warning ominous to the Allies, it stated: "A convoy headed northeast is expected from that time on" — meaning from the time of the setting up of TITMOUSE.

The watch officers transmitted the first part of the solved, translated, and edited intercept to F-21, the Atlantic intelligence section of the headquarters of the U.S. Fleet, at 9:55 P.M. on Sunday, April 18, and the second part eight hours later, at 5:50 A.M. the next morning. Later on Monday Cominch — the commander in chief, U.S. Fleet — issued his submarine estimate for April 19. It named sightings, attacks, and direction-finding as sources; cryptanalysis was not cited, though much of the report was based on Enigma solutions. But Cominch blurred the precision that cryptanalysis provided, in part to conceal it as a source but in part because the U-boats might have moved since they received the intercepted orders and might have erred in their own positions and because Cominch did not want convoys and escorts not in the immediate area to relax their guard.

Part 3 of the estimate's six geographical parts dealt with the North Atlantic. It began: "Twenty to thirty [U-boats] estimated patrolling general area 49-00 to 54-00 [north] and 38-00 to 48-00 [west] from light DF activity." This was clearly based on the solution of the long message of April 17. It drew a rectangle based on the patrol line as its diagonal and fudged the number of U-boats. The rest of Part 3 gave details about other subs.

All day Monday, SC 127 followed the same northeast course in cloudy but calm weather. During the morning a patrolling Catalina seaplane made a welcome appearance overhead.

In Washington and Bletchley, the cryptanalysts hit a snag. They were unable to find any cribs, unable to create any usable menus, and so unable to recover the naval Enigma keys for that day. No messages enciphered with the keys of April 19 could be read. As a consequence, the U-boat situation report for Tuesday, April 20, merely repeated the most critical information from the nineteenth: the large rectangle containing the U-boats remained the same, though the number of U-boats reported in it came into focus: twenty-five. Other details changed slightly. For example, the "Four [in] general area 60-00 24-00" of the April 19 report became "About four within 150 miles of 59-00 from numerous DFs" in the April 20 report. This information was available to the Tenth Fleet's Convoy and Routing Section, which digested it.

Germany's naval codebreakers were more successful at that moment than the Allies'. They solved a message Tuesday that revealed that on Saturday convoy HX 234, then south of Cape Race, had been rerouted sharply to the north, probably to avoid a concentration of submarines. To counter this, U-Boat Command on Tuesday ordered TITMOUSE to move a second time: to the north and slightly west, to block the likely new route of HX 234.

The B-Dienst also solved an intercept dealing with SC 127. This convoy had been placidly plowing the calm western Atlantic on its east-northeast course, and continued to do so on Tuesday, when, at 9:55 A.M., a British escort relieved the Canadians. The German solution placed the convoy southeast of Cape Race at 5 P.M. Tuesday. "Since this position lies relatively far to the south," U-Boat

Command stated, "it is assumed that the convoy, contrary to earlier experience, will keep on the previously steered easterly course." The command detached four boats from TITMOUSE to set up a short north-south patrol line, to be expanded by submarines coming from the east. The position of the line showed that the Germans expected SC 127 to steam south of the concentration of U-boats they knew the Allies knew about.

That Tuesday, April 20, Adolf Hitler celebrated his fifty-fourth birthday. Before and after it he received the leaders of his cobelligerents in Klessheim castle in Salzburg. On the battlefronts, little of note was happening. Army Group Africa, squeezed into a corner of Tunisia, struck out with a counterattack to throw British preparations for an assault off balance. In the air, the British bombed Stettin, a Baltic port, with 304 planes; the Soviets likewise attacked Tilsit, farther east. The Jews in the Warsaw ghetto were in the second day of their heroic uprising. In Germany, people were talking about the discovery of the mass grave in Katyn of more than 10,000 Polish officers murdered by the Soviets. Some saw it as an example of what awaited the Germans if the Russians won the war; others said the Germans had no right to criticize since they had killed Jews and Poles in much greater numbers. Of the war situation, Germans said realistically that they were powerless in the air and that a German Dunkirk was approaching in Tunisia. Some wanted Hitler to show himself more, at least in newspaper photos and newsreels, to prove that his hair had not turned white. But any despair they felt was not translated into a slowdown at work: production of guns, planes, U-boats climbed.

In the United States, the baseball season opened. Since President Roosevelt was away — meeting the president of Mexico in Monterrey and pledging to beat the Axis so that the Good Neighbor policy could be extended throughout the world — the first ball was thrown out by Paul V. McNutt, the manpower commissioner. A crowd sprinkled with khaki and blue watched the Washington Senators beat the Philadelphia Athletics, 7–5. New York Mayor Fiorello La Guardia announced that 625 summonses had been served on retail food stores for violating food price ceilings and rationing regulations. In Tampa eight men and a cat came ashore in a life raft after their ship sank in the Gulf of Mexico.

And in the huge room of the Tenth Fleet's Convoy and Routing Section in Washington, and in the staff rooms of the U-Boat Command in Berlin, men in blue uniforms pored over their vast lined charts of the North Atlantic, playing their deadly games of nautical chess, seeking, with the help of the totality of their knowledge, to outthink the other side and moving their vessels to destroy as many of the enemy's or save as many of their own as possible. On April 20, the naval officers in Washington, including blond Lieutenant Commander Rollo N. Norgaard, who shared responsibility for SC 127, outthought — either by luck or by design — the officers in Berlin. They sent SC 127 not to the south of the big rectangle in the west central Atlantic that had held the TITMOUSE submarines, as U-Boat Command expected, but west and north of it. At 1539 hours Greenwich mean time, they released the first part and, five minutes later, the second part of a message to the warships escorting SC 127.

The convoy was then heading east-northeast to Point F, where it was to turn northeast to Point G — a route that would have taken it directly through the concentration of U-boats. The message told it to head instead for a new point, WL, at 50° north, 50° west. After that it was to steer due north to WM, at 55° north, 50° west, and then east-northeast to WN, east-southeast of Cape Farewell, the southern tip of Greenland. This diversion would take it around the U-boats, leaving them to the east and south. When it received this message, the convoy had passed the 50th meridian; to get to WL, it had to backtrack a little. At 1850 Greenwich mean time, the commodore, van den Donker, altered course. The officers of Convoy and Routing had made an important move in the game.

U-Boat Command continued to seek the convoy to the south. On Wednesday, April 21, it ordered the formation of a new wolfpack, WOODPECKER, for the boats detached from TITMOUSE and for more than a dozen others recently refueled by the tanker U-487. By noon the next day, WOODPECKER was to stretch some 300 miles north and south. The convoy was expected a few hours before the formation was complete, but surfaced U-boats could easily catch the convoy even if it arrived early. To prevent the Allies from learning of WOODPECKER and so possibly diverting SC 127, the U-boats were instructed to maintain radio silence until contact reports had to be made.

While WOODPECKER was forming, one of TITMOUSE's northernmost boats, the U-306, spotted the New York convoy HX 234. At 1:55 A.M. on Thursday, the U-306 torpedoed a 10,000-ton Danish freighter, the *Amerika*. Soon seven and eventually twenty-one TITMOUSE boats were operating against HX 234. This drew them away from SC 127, whose new route would have taken it almost through the center of the TITMOUSE patrol line.

SC 127 was, however, having troubles of its own. On Wednesday morning, the third ship in the fifth column reported seeing a periscope between herself and the sixth column. The escort leader attacked with a pattern of fourteen depth charges what he thought was "a very doubtful contact"; he concluded that it was a false alarm. Immediately thereafter, the convoy, on its new, backtracking northwest course, spotted ice. One of the escorts thought the convoy could get through the loose pack and bergs and accompanied it; the escort commander followed a lead in another direction but could see no open water. He finally asked van den Donker to steer due east to work around the ice. The convoy had to turn around in a 4- to 6-mile gap in the ice, which the commodore and the other masters accomplished with great skill.

But the escort commander, Lieutenant Commander C. E. Bridgeman, Royal Naval Reserve, could see that heading east would send the convoy right toward the area that the new course was intended to avoid. Instructed to head north, not east, he wanted to gain ground to the north by going northeast, and felt that the bright moon and good visibility would limit the danger from the ice. So after several hours of steaming east, he altered to the northeasterly course, sending one of the escorts ahead as an ice patrol; it stood by one berg with dimmed lights as the convoy paraded slowly by. During the night, the growlers and bergs thinned out, and early in the morning of Thursday the twenty-second, Bridgeman thought it safe to return to the original northwest course, which the convoy soon did.

By then the Allies had resumed solving German U-boat messages. But they were not quite current: messages of the twentieth and the twenty-first were being sent to Knowles's Submarine Tracking Room on the twenty-second. One of the solutions perhaps elicited some satisfaction among Norgaard and the others who had diverted SC 127. U-Boat Command had told WOOD-

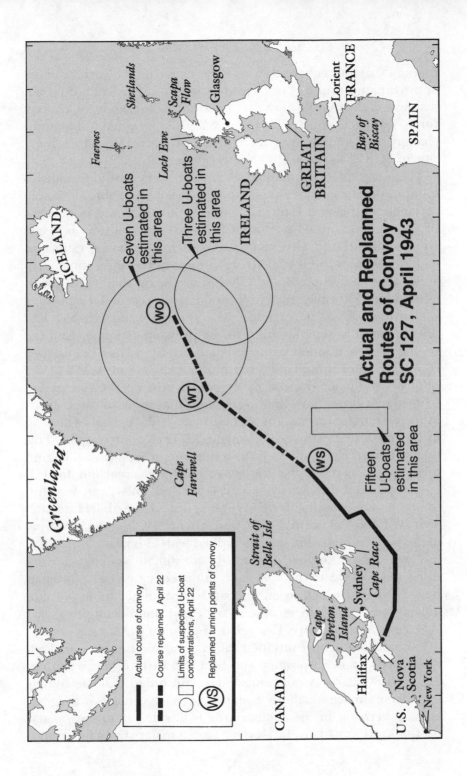

Actual and Replanned Routes of Convoy SC 127, April 1943

Seven U-boats estimated in this area

Three U-boats estimated in this area

Fifteen U-boats estimated in this area

Legend:
- Actual course of convoy
- Course replanned April 22
- ⬜ Limits of suspected U-boat concentrations, April 22
- ⓌⓈ Replanned turning points of convoy

Greenland

ICELAND

Shetlands

Faeroes

Scapa Flow

Loch Ewe

Glasgow

Lorient

FRANCE

Bay of Biscay

SPAIN

GREAT BRITAIN

IRELAND

Cape Farewell

Strait of Belle Isle

CANADA

Cape Breton Island

Sydney

Cape Race

Halifax

Nova Scotia

New York

U.S.

PECKER that an eastbound convoy was expected on April 22 in the approximate latitude of naval grid square BC 69, which would put it almost in the middle of the WOODPECKER line, an ideal location for a wolfpack attack. This was SC 127's original route, now changed; the solution confirmed that Convoy and Routing's diversion of SC 127 to the north had been wise.

The intercepted German messages were reflected in Cominch's U-boat estimates. The estimate for the twenty-first shrank the big rectangle in the west central Atlantic both in size and in number of U-boats and added two other infested areas halfway between Newfoundland and Greenland: "About ten [U-boats] estimated within 150 miles 56-00 46-00 from numerous DFs indicating probability that both HX 234 and ON 178 are being shadowed X Several within 150 miles of 54-00 50-00 from recent DFs possibly shadowing ONS 3." The ten were the TITMOUSE boats, which had not appeared as separate units in the previous estimate. And the second area mentioned lay directly athwart SC 127's new planned route: its center was 60 miles south of SC 127's Point WM.

That would not do, but other routes also entailed risks. On Thursday, Convoy and Routing, noting that some of the U-boats in the rectangle were, as the sub estimate said, "probably moving to the north or northwest," changed SC 127's course again. This time it moved the course south so the convoy would pass behind these boats and those of TITMOUSE, which were reaching for HX 234. It ordered the convoy to omit Points WL, WM, and WN and to "alter course forthwith for (WS) 050 deg 31' north 044 deg 02' west (WT) 56–58 north 34–57 west, thence (WO)." Point WS lay in the big rectangle that had been filled with U-boats, but that day the area did not appear in the U-boat estimate, its boats having dispersed. WT lay to the northeast, at the edge of a circle as big as New Mexico in which seven U-boats were thought to be present, moving west or southwest; the risk seemed small enough to take. WO, east-northeast of WT, was likewise within the circle.

U-Boat Command continued the cat and mouse game. It kept WOODPECKER in its position south of TITMOUSE, but when the expected SC 127 was not contacted, it concluded that the convoy had taken a more northerly route. To ensure contact, it assigned U-boats arriving in the combat area to form, by Sunday, a new wolfpack: BLACKBIRD. Its eleven boats were to patrol a line trending north-northwest–south-southeast and moving westward. But its location was south of the new route for SC 127, and although the boats began to appear in the submarine estimate for April 23, Good Friday, as "about four within 200 miles of 56-00 27-00 moving westward," the convoy's course was not altered for BLACK-BIRD.

One reason for not changing course was that well over a dozen submarines had clamped onto HX 234. And they were sinking ships. The U-306 torpedoed a 7,000-ton American freighter on Good Friday, and an hour later the U-954 sent a 5,000-ton British vessel to a watery grave 1,500 fathoms deep.

Subsequently, however, Cominch adjusted SC 127's course again and again in response to perceived threats. On Saturday, for example, it replaced Point WT with WP, to the east-northeast. On Easter Sunday, the convoy having passed into the area of British control, the commander in chief Western Approaches in Liverpool ordered the convoy escort to report "if you consider you are being shadowed." No reply was received, so it seemed that the escort believed that the convoy was not being followed. And U-Boat Command appeared to have abandoned its attempts to grapple with SC 127. Its order to BLACKBIRD to take up its patrol line and direction of movement meant, it noted, that BLACKBIRD's "advance toward the SC convoy is at present no longer possible." Nevertheless, Western Approaches twice ordered slight changes in SC 127's course on Monday, April 26, as the convoy steamed southeast of Cape Farewell and began to approach Iceland.

That same day, a Liberator arrived in the morning to give air cover: the convoy had successfully traversed the dreaded Greenland air gap, the "black hole" in the middle of the North Atlantic that could not be patrolled with the airplanes then available. On Tuesday a Liberator and a Catalina provided air cover throughout the day.

Also on Tuesday, the solutions of two week-old messages dealing with SC 127 arrived in U-boat headquarters. They reported the locations of the convoy on the twentieth and the twenty-first and the courses it was given. The command observed that "It swung to the north quite early, probably to go around an assumed U-boat concentration."

On Wednesday, SC 127's escort obtained an asdic bearing on a possible submarine; the escort searched the area with no result. On Thursday, the five ships destined for Iceland were detached, together with SC 127's only straggler, which blamed bad coal for its frequently being 4 to 5 miles behind. The convoy escort messaged Western Approaches: "Do not consider SC 127 seriously threatened by U-boats at present." Air cover was provided throughout that day and the next. At 6 A.M. on Saturday, May 1, the seventeen ships headed for Loch Ewe were detached. The rest of the convoy arrived off Scotland's Oversay at 6 P.M. on Sunday. And later there arrived in Convoy and Routing that most welcome of telegrams from the Admiralty, this one putting the seal of success on the transatlantic crossing of SC 127: "All arrived."

Twenty-One

The Cavity Magnetron Clue

SC 127 eluded U-boats at one of the most difficult times in the Battle of the Atlantic. The ocean was so full of U-boats that the first sea lord feared that "We can no longer rely on evading the U-boat packs and, hence, we shall have to fight the convoys through them." In addition, the B-Dienst was at the height of its powers, solving 5 to 10 percent of its intercepts in time for Dönitz to use them in tactical decisions. Early information sometimes enabled him to move his U-boats so that a convoy would encounter the middle of the pack, enabling more boats to attack than if the convoy met only one wing of the patrol line.

But the first signs of German weakness had begun to appear. Stronger Allied defenses — more escorts, more airplanes — kept the U-boats from attacking with the vigor and daring of the previous years. Dönitz's exhortations grew shriller, complaining that anyone who failed to engage the enemy closely was "no true U-boat man." The rate of success declined. The great convoy battle of March 1943, during which U-boats sank Allied ships at twice the rate at which they were being built, was followed in April by a fight that brought poorer results: the Germans sank twelve merchant vessels, but at a cost of seven U-boats. The situation worsened the following month.

"In the Atlantic in May," wrote Dönitz in his war diary, "the sinking of 10,000 tons was paid for with the loss of one U-boat, while not very long before that time one boat was lost for the sinking of about 100,000 tons." He called such losses "unbearable," and on May 24 he pulled the seventeen submarines on the North Atlantic convoy routes out and sent them to what he thought was a "less air-endangered area" to the south. From there they could operate against the convoys between the United States and the Strait of Gibraltar, through which supplies for the American forces in North Africa had to pass. But this was not the vital traffic whose loss would defeat Britain and keep the Allies from mounting an assault against *Festung Europa*. The move marked a major defeat for the Germans in the vital Battle of the Atlantic.

The success of Allied convoy diversions in January and February 1943 had again raised Dönitz's suspicions about the security of his ciphers. For two and a half weeks in January, U-boat sweeps had discovered no convoys along the North Atlantic routes to Britain; for the first time since the United States entered the war, merchant ship losses in all Atlantic areas fell below one a day. In February, the few convoys that were not sighted by chance were spotted only by single boats at the ends of patrol lines, suggesting that the convoys were going around the wolf packs. Dönitz's concern was intensified when Allied destroyers came upon the U-459 as it was refueling an Italian U-boat some 300 miles east of St. Paul's Rock, the desolate traditional division between the North and the South Atlantic, far from any destroyer bases and far from the normal convoy lanes. And the B-Dienst's solutions of Allied U-boat situation reports raised suspicions. On April 18, for example, an intercept of an Allied submarine situation report showed that the Americans suspected the presence of twenty submarines in the rectangle running from 48° to 54° north latitude and from 38° to 45° west longitude. And the report was correct: TITMOUSE was in the area with eighteen boats.

Dönitz asked Maertens, the head of the Naval Communications Service, to investigate, as he had done in 1941. Again Maertens exculpated Enigma. The British U-boat situation reports themselves stated that the Allies' information on submarine locations was coming from direction-finding, he said. Documents found in a French Resistance agent's radio station showed that the Allies were obtaining information from the Resistance on departure times for U-boats and on whether they were headed for the North or the South Atlantic, enabling the foe, Maertens said, to estimate submarine movements with some accuracy. The British information about the wolfpacks DOLPHIN and FALCON was vague; if the information had come from cryptanalysis, it would have been exact. At worst, capture, perhaps of a cue word, which — contrary to all regulations — would have to have been written down, might have given the Allies insight into some messages. The chief of the Naval War Staff conceded that a capture was possible, and he approved Maertens's plan to establish separate regional key nets.

Maertens was supported in his position by the coincidental discovery on February 2, in a British bomber downed at Rotterdam, of a new type of radar. It was based on the cavity magnetron, a block of copper with eight cylindrical holes bored in it parallel to and around a central axis. These hollows enabled the radar to operate on a wavelength of 9.7 centimeters, much shorter than the earlier 1.5 meters. Because its wavelength was measured in centimeters, the device was called "centimetric radar." It gave the British two advantages: it depicted objects — coastlines, buildings — on the radar screen, which the older radar could not do, and the U-boats' radar warning receivers, which were tuned to the longer wavelength, could not detect it. With centimetric radar, British airplanes could thus locate surfaced U-boats from a distance without alerting the submarines and could attack them by surprise. The Royal Air Force Coastal Command had begun doing just this with some success against U-boats traversing the Bay of Biscay. Though Dönitz had as yet no evidence that centimetric radar was being used in the Battle of the Atlantic, the use of this powerful new weapon could not be excluded.

So Dönitz accepted Maertens's view that Kriegsmarine ciphers were secure and that the leaks were elsewhere. "With the exception of two or three doubtful cases," he confided to his war diary, "enemy information about the position of our U-boats appears to have been obtained mainly from extensive use of airborne radar, and the resultant plotting of these positions has enabled him [the enemy] to organize effective diversion of convoy traffic." And when SC 127 circumvented a wolfpack, he gave as the most probable reason that "the enemy has an extraordinary location device, usable from airplanes, whose effect cannot be observed by our boats."

Nevertheless, suspicion that the Allies were solving naval Enigma messages would not die. Dönitz tried to reconcile his concern with Maertens's reassurances, but he was not always able to. On April 27, as SC 127 was slogging across the ocean, the Allies, in a U-boat situation report that the B-Dienst solved, reported five U-boats within a 150-mile radius of 50° north, 34° west. "For some time resupplying has been carried out here," Dönitz noted. "It remains disquieting that they were suspected precisely in the area in which no radioing had been done for several days."

A few days later, Dönitz, for reasons that went beyond his fears about cryptosecurity, fired Maertens, sending him to Kiel to run a shipyard. He replaced him with the glass-eyed Stummel, Maertens's chief of staff, promoting him to rear admiral. Stummel maintained, as always, that Enigma "had, on the basis of repeated and thorough investigations, proved itself up to the present as unbreakable and militarily resistant." Dönitz apparently believed him, for in June he was telling the Japanese ambassador that U-boat losses were due to a new Allied direction-finding system.

Despite his claims, Stummel began in 1944 to prepare a measure that would carry the Kriegsmarine's basic cryptosecurity principle to its logical conclusion. By subdividing the navy's cryptosystem into as many key nets as necessary, Stummel sought to reduce the number of messages in a common key. As the volume of traffic grew, Enigma key nets had expanded from one in the early 1930s to separate home and foreign key nets and to the addition of a U-boat net and many others by 1943, when traffic averaged 2,563 radio messages a day. Now Stummel proposed to give each U-boat its own key.

Individual keys were issued to some submarines shortly after D-Day, June 6, 1944; they began to be widely used in November, and by February 1945 they were carrying practically all the operational traffic of the U-Boat Command. In that month, Dönitz told Hitler that Allied knowledge of wolfpacks came from radar and betrayal. By then Stummel had also been ousted, but his program of individual keys justified his faith in Enigma: G.C.&C.S. solved only three keys for brief periods. Perhaps not coincidentally, sinkings rose steadily from November 1944 to April 1945 in the North Atlantic and North Sea, although the absolute number remained small. Solution of these individual keys would have required a great increase in personnel and in bombes, but G.C.&C.S. felt confident that it would have been able to do it. Germany's surrender saved it from this test.

Long before that happened, Dönitz mourned the loss of the source of information that he said gave him half of his intelligence: the

B-Dienst. He had feasted on it for so long in part because the Germans had no monopoly on cryptographic failure. In this respect the British were just as illogical as the Germans. The surprise of the North African invasion confirmed the Admiralty's belief that its cryptosystems were secure, just as Fricke had argued that the operations of British ships gave no indication that the British were reading German messages. And G.C.&C.S. retained confidence in its superencipherment (even though it had solved similar systems before the war) because it was encountering increasing difficulty in solving high-grade Italian codes after the summer of 1940 and fewer problems with nonnaval Enigma; this logic resembles the Kriegsmarine's argument that Enigma must be secure because it was unable to break the American naval cipher machine.

The cherished beliefs of the British were wrong. In December 1942, they learned from their Enigma solutions that the Germans were reading Naval Cypher No. 3, the main cryptosystem for convoy arrangements in the North Atlantic. And in Washington, in March 1943, Lieutenant McMahan of OP-20-G saw a German intercept that canceled an order by Dönitz of a few hours earlier and directed a radical change of course. McMahan thought that only a German solution of a message diverting an Allied convoy could have caused Dönitz to react like that. He went downtown to Convoy and Routing in Main Navy and, after some difficulty, persuaded them to let him see the messages to Allied convoys. His discovery of the very message that had ordered the detour brought together compartmentalized elements and confirmed the Allies' recognition that the Germans were reading their traffic.

In June, when Naval Cypher No. 5 replaced Nos. 3 and 4, the B-Dienst made no real progress against it. Concerns about the security in heavy traffic of the superencipherment, called the long subtractor system, had been raised as early as 1940; G.C.&C.S. devised a replacement — the stencil subtractor — by 1941, but the services did not decide to adopt it until after extensive trials that ended in March of 1942. Design and production of the devices and printing of the tables took the rest of the year, distribution for the Royal Navy until the middle of 1943, and distribution within the U.S. Navy until January 1, 1944 — a record of cryptographic negligence that compares favorably with Germany's. Still, from the middle of June 1943, the B-Dienst was effectively shut out from its vital Anglo-American intelligence. In May 1944, Hitler asked his naval codebreakers which English systems could be broken. They had to confess that although they were solving a number of secondary systems and a convoy system for stragglers, "The two main English systems cannot be read, the one [the main warship cryptosystem] since the start of 1944 and the other [the convoy system] since the start of June 1943."

This admission unwittingly confirmed the Allied victory in cryptology. In August 1943, the British and the Americans had begun reading Enigma messages nearly always currently. The capture of the U-505 by an American task force on June 4, 1944, provided a copy of the *Adressbuch* that provided the keys for disguising grid positions; from then on the Allies read them as easily as the Germans did.

But solving German messages did not always mean the successful diversion of convoys. It is true that in January and February 1943, when solutions were almost uninterrupted, the Allies suffered far fewer losses than in March, when for days no solutions were achieved. On the other hand, two convoys out of three escaped detection in August and September 1942, during the ULTRA blackout, while less than half avoided being spotted in the first five months of 1943, when solutions were frequent. The totality of other factors eclipsed ULTRA: the number of U-boats on patrol, the quantity of very long range aircraft the Allies had, centimetric radar, shipboard direction-finding, operational research, the arrival of escort aircraft carriers, the increase in escort vessels. But when ULTRA worked with these new Allied strengths, particularly after Dönitz withdrew his U-boats from the North Atlantic on May 24, the results could be spectacular. On September 21, 1943, Churchill announced to the Commons that, in the third of a year just ending, not one merchant ship had been lost to enemy action in the North Atlantic. The House erupted in cheers.

Twenty-Two
The U-Tankers

THE EXTENSION of the U-boat war to the American coast in January 1942 created a problem for Dönitz. Because it took his submarines substantially more time to get to and from their rich target areas off New York or Virginia or Florida than it took to reach patrol lines off Newfoundland or Nova Scotia, their combat time was reduced. To prolong their battle period as much as possible, he resupplied the U-boats at sea, using special submarine tankers. These "milch cows," twice as big as the standard Type VII combat submarines, carried 400 tons of fuel oil, 50 tons of provisions, a workshop, a physician, and personnel to replace injured or sick combat-sub crewmen. When the first U-tanker began work in March 1942, a U-boat averaged 41 days at sea. With one resupply, this time was extended to an average of 62 days and, with two, to a maximum of 81. Even for the more northerly operations, refueling was essential for efficiency. Experience showed that submarines had to spend from three to five weeks in the operational area before encountering a convoy in a favorable position. This meant that to make success likely, Type VIIC boats had to be refueled twice. After twelve months, by May of 1943, the U-tankers had completed 390 refuelings.

It became clear to the Allies that sinking one milch cow would reduce the effectiveness of many combat U-boats. They were unable to plan such an attack during the codebreaking blackout of 1942 because they could not read the instructions for the refueling rendezvous, and U-Boat Command had taken care to have the submarines meet in remote locations, far from the convoy tracks and out of the range of Allied airplanes. The U-tankers maintained radio silence. Instructions were enciphered in the special officer-grade keys and then reenciphered in the general key; the grid encipherment disguised positions. In 1943, however, with codebreaking restored, it became possible for the Allies to attack tankers. The solved messages sometimes disclosed the date and place of a refueling rendezvous; when these specifics were not available, the O.I.C.'s knowledge of the departures and movements of the supply submarines and of favorite refueling areas could guide ships and airplanes to likely hunting grounds.

But three factors saved the supply submarines for a while: the inability of Allied aircraft to reach the rendezvous, the need for surface forces to stay close to convoys, and the adamant refusal of the British to attack the isolated refueling points for fear that the Germans would guess that their cipher system had been solved. This refusal stemmed originally from the anxiety the British had experienced after the 1941 roundup of *Bismarck* supply ships, when two that were to be left alone so as not to raise German suspicions were accidentally attacked. Their decision was hardened by leakages that could be traced to Enigma solutions, by four cases in which Enigma solutions were repeated almost verbatim in British messages, and by a scare in March 1943.

The Kriegsmarine, an intercept showed, had grown suspicious about British warships sighted in an area where they would have encountered a German convoy bringing supplies to North Africa had the convoy not been delayed. The first sea lord reprimanded the Mediterranean commander in chief, and Churchill threatened to withhold Enigma intelligence, or ULTRA, unless it was "used only on great occasions or when thoroughly camouflaged." At the same time, the first sea lord emphasized in a personal message about ULTRA to his American counterpart, Admiral King, his anxious desire that "we should not risk what is so invaluable to us." The next month he resisted American proposals for using Enigma U-boat solutions to attack U-tankers at their supply rendezvous, arguing that "if our Z [ULTRA] information failed us at the present time it would, I am sure, result in our shipping losses going up by anything from 50 to 100%."

But this risk declined late in May, when Dönitz pulled his submarines out of the North Atlantic. And a few weeks later an event showed how Enigma information, while still used with great care for its security, could greatly enhance the new offensive strength of the Allies at sea. This new strength consisted of the Americans' introduction of task forces centered on small, "escort" aircraft carriers. These could bring airplanes to within striking distance of a refueling rendezvous. On June 12 the escort carrier *Bogue*, using information from both Enigma decrypts and direction-finding, sent out airplanes that, shortly after noon, spotted the 1,700-ton converted minelayer U-118 cruising placidly on the surface. The planes bombed and strafed her, drove her under, and, when she resurfaced, sank her. Her loss forced U-Boat Command to recall some submarines and delayed other combat boats in reaching their target areas. These disruptions, mentioned in Enigma intercepts, showed the Allies the value of attacking the U-tankers — a demonstration that was reinforced in a negative sense when the tanker U-488 refueled twenty-two boats to overcome the emergency. As a consequence, the Americans pressed to use Enigma information against the supply subs. By this time the British fears of the loss of ULTRA were allayed because using aircraft to spot the submarines covered their reliance on cryptanalytic intelligence, so Britain concurred in the American proposal. Enigma solutions now enabled the escort carriers to carry the war to the enemy. For the first time, the Allies attacked U-boats not just defensively, as in fighting off wolfpacks, or fortuitously, as when a plane spotted a submarine, but actively — aggressively seeking out subs and hitting them. Enigma decrypts had changed from a shield to a sword.

Among the targets of these machete chops was the U-117, a sister ship of the U-118. She had taken her crew of fifty-odd on three supply cruises when, on July 22, 1943, she sailed from France under the command of Lieutenant Commander Hans-Werner Neumann as one of five supply submarines that Dönitz sent to sea in the last third of July. Three of these were sunk while crossing the Bay of Biscay before the end of the month; a fourth was destroyed west of the Faeroes. This put additional pressure on the U-117 to meet and refuel combat submarines that otherwise might not have been able to return home.

One of these was the U-66, a veteran boat that had completed nine patrols in areas ranging from Cape Hatteras to the Mediterranean, had landed a saboteur on the northwest African coast, claimed to have sunk 200,000 tons of shipping, and had provided each of her two commanders with a Knight's Cross to the Iron Cross. On this cruise she had been at sea the extremely long time of three months, during which time she had sunk two American tankers. On July 27, U-Boat Command ordered her to square CD 50, about halfway between Washington, D.C., and Lisbon, Portugal, to rendezvous with the U-117 for reprovisioning.

The message was intercepted. But it had not yet been solved when the cryptanalysts read a message giving a new rendezvous for 8 P.M. August 3. The solution gave the location as "square 6755 of the large square west of" another square, which was disguised by the grid encipherment but which the cryptanalysts thought was CE. This would put little square 6755 in large square CD, making it 37° 57' north latitude, or roughly east of Washington, D.C., and 38° 30' west longitude, or north of the bulge of Brazil.

At 1:05 P.M. Eastern War Time, August 1, 1943, the U.S. Navy's codebreaking unit on Nebraska Avenue in Washington, D.C., teletyped a solved intercept to F-21, the Atlantic section of the Combat Intelligence section of Cominch, where the Submarine Tracking Room was located.

The message was about twelve hours old, the time it took for Commander Engstrom's back-room boys to crack it and the translators and evaluators to append to each U-boat commander's name the number of his submarine and the latitude and longitude of its naval grid references. They put these insertions in double parentheses to show that they were not part of the original message. The first part of the text directed two submarines not to refuel but to proceed home. The second and more interesting portion, however, dealt with the U-117: "Neumann ((117)) head for Nav Sq 67 ((probably CD 67 = 37.57 N − 38.30 W))."

Fifteen minutes later, the teletypewriter tapped out another solved German message. Sent ten hours after the first, it instructed the U-66's captain, Lieutenant Friedrich Markworth, where and when to get supplies: "Beginning 3 August 15 2000B Markworth ((66)) will provision from Neumann ((117)) in Sq 6755 ((probably CD 6755 = 37.57 N − 38.30 W)). . . . After execution Markworth report affirmative, Neumann wait in that area."

The day after these messages went to F-21, Cominch headquarters radioed the information to units at sea that could use it. It was included in the U-boat report for August 2. Not giving the source of the intelligence, the report stated: "Several [U-boats] area 3800 [north] 3830 [west]." The data were repeated in the next day's report, with a cover source: "Several vicinity 3800 3830 by recent DFs suggesting refueling operations X."

One of the recipients was the U.S. Navy's Combat Task Group 21.14, a convoy support group consisting of the escort carrier *Card* and three old destroyers. The U-boat situation reports told its commander, Captain Arnold J. (Buster) Isbell, where to look for subs to sink. He knew that if refueling, they could be caught at a particularly vulnerable moment — moving slowly on the surface, joined by a fuel hose — and that one of them would be a particularly valuable target. He headed toward the reported U-boat concentration while his planes scouted ahead and to the sides.

Late in the afternoon of August 3, as the *Card* was perhaps 150 miles from that area, two of his pilots, reserve Lieutenant (j.g.) Richard L. Cormier, in a Grumman TBF-1 Avenger torpedo-bomber, and his wingman, reserve Ensign Arne S. Paulson, in a Grumman F4F-4 Wildcat fighter, making a routine submarine search, were flying southwest at 5,000 feet in clear skies when Cormier, with his binoculars, spotted a grayish white submarine off to port about 11 miles away. She was fully surfaced, cruising so slowly that no bow wave or wake was noticeable. It was the U-66.

Paulson, on Cormier's orders to strafe the submarine, gave his fighter full throttle and, 100 feet above the waves, raced directly at the U-boat. At 500 yards, he began firing and saw his bullets strike the conning tower, kicking up puffs of rust. He saw nobody; on the U-boat, however, a machinist who was topside smoking was wounded in both thighs. Cormier then swept in to depth-charge the U-boat, but the charges failed to release. As he circled to attack again, Paulson made another run. It was met at this time with inaccurate antiaircraft fire from the six or eight men now topside. The attack had, however, killed the submarine's second watch officer and panicked the men in the conning tower into ringing the diving alarm. But Markworth, demonstrating anew why he had won the Knight's Cross, bulled his way up the ladder, belayed the command to dive, and held his men to their guns.

In his torpedo-bomber, Cormier sped toward the U-boat, skimming the water. He pressed his electrical bomb release and immediately pulled the emergency release. This time his acoustic torpedo and both depth charges dropped. Within seconds, while making a climbing turn, he saw a shock wave centered about 25 feet from the submarine's starboard side and just forward of her conning tower. It swept to her port side and appeared to lift her from below and make her list to port. Then a heavy column of water about 100 feet high obscured the U-boat. When she reappeared, she was turning to starboard. Paulson attacked again. He saw half a dozen figures, some inert, on the conning tower. His shots killed one sailor who had kept firing despite several wounds, wounded another in the chest, and slightly injured six others. No further fire was returned. Cormier strafed, seriously wounding Markworth in the abdomen. Then it became clear to the men on the submarine that the planes had no more bombs and that it was therefore safe to dive, so the first watch officer gave the order. The bodies of the officer and the seaman had to be left where they were. Slowly at first, and then more rapidly, at an angle of 50 degrees, the U-boat submerged. Just as she was disappearing, Paulson made a final run, firing at the underside of the stern.

Cormier dropped a marker and circled over the spot for forty-five minutes. Though neither he nor the pilots of the other planes that the *Card* sent saw any debris, oil, or air bubbles, the squadron commander claimed a sinking. He was wrong. Though the U-66 had two fatalities, several seamen wounded, and a captain suffering from a bullet in his guts, and though her ballast and fuel tanks were leaking, she had escaped.

But she still had not met the U-117. She limped east toward home, with not enough fuel to make it and only two days' worth of provisions. The next day, after midnight, she surfaced. Though the sailor's body had washed overboard, the second watch officer's body was, ghoulishly enough, still on the lower machine-gun stand. It and the body of a sailor who had died from his wounds were buried at sea.

Meanwhile, Buster Isbell on the *Card* was being further tantalized by F-21's U-boat situation reports to his carrier task group telling of combat and tanker submarines nearby. On August 6, for example, he was told, "One probably refueler locality 3915 3730 by DFs 052330 and 052350 probably moving NE." By 2 P.M., he was steering for that area.

* * *

That same day, the U-66 proposed a new rendezvous with the U-117 for that noon, some 54 miles north and 12 miles east of the August 1 meeting place. Dönitz acquiesced a few hours later. The Allied cryptanalysts could not read these messages as promptly as the others, and they remained a closed book. But the Tenth Fleet's ULTRA-based knowledge of the rendezvous attempts, together with its background information that on July 30 the U-117 had been ordered to stand by within 100 miles of 38° 50′ north, 37° 20′ west, a circle within which the August 1 rendezvous was to have been effected, made it worthwhile to keep the *Card* in the vicinity.

Shortly before noon on Friday, the U-117 and the U-66 finally met. After dark the combat submarine took aboard some provisions and a physician to treat Markworth. But, unable to refuel at night, the pair waited for morning. With daylight, the U-66 began to take on oil. At just about the same time, 6:49 A.M. Saturday, the *Card* flew off the same kind of airplane pairing as had attacked the U-66, an Avenger and a Wildcat. An hour into the patrol, however, the Wildcat had to return to the carrier because of engine trouble. The Avenger, piloted by reserve Lieutenant (j.g.) Asbury H. Sallenger, continued its routine submarine search. At 9:46, while flying west-northwest at 4,500 feet in a cloudless sky, Sallenger spotted a large white object 15 miles off his starboard bow. He thought at first it was a merchantman, but he soon realized that it was two submarines, painted white, close together, fully surfaced and proceeding very slowly southwest, with neither bow waves nor wakes. The refueling was still in progress.

Sallenger radioed the *Card*, 82 miles away, and maneuvered to attack. Selecting the U-boat nearest him, which was slightly behind the other, he approached from the port quarter at 220 knots, out of the sun. "This is it!" he told his crew. The U-66, spotting him, shoved the throttles of both diesels to full speed ahead. When Sallenger was about 400 yards from the subs, both opened fire with their 20-millimeter guns. These filled the sky with white puffs, but Sallenger bored in and, from about 125 feet, dropped two depth charges, set to explode at 25 feet. They straddled the U-117. Three seconds later the explosions raised two columns of water on the starboard side, one about 10 feet out, the other some 20 feet out, cutting the refueling hose. Sallenger banked to the left and climbed. The submarine spurted flame from its stern, and dense gray smoke rolled out. The TBF's turret gunner, Ammunition Mate Third Class

James H. O'Hagan, Jr., sprayed the deck with his .50-caliber machine gun, then concentrated his fire around the machine guns on the conning tower. He saw about twenty men. The radioman took pictures, which would be used to improve tactics.

The U-boat began maneuvering erratically, as if her steering apparatus had been damaged. She started to trail a heavy oil slick. The U-66 was following her, seemingly trying to help. After about fifteen minutes, the undamaged U-66 started to submerge, apparently in an attempt to save at least herself. While she was thus vulnerable, Sallenger, who had been watching from 6,500 feet, dove to attack. As he flew along her track at 130 knots in level flight, 200 feet up, the U-117 threw intense antiaircraft fire at him. O'Hagan fired back. Sallenger dropped his acoustic torpedo on the last seen course of the submerged U-boat, 150 yards ahead of the diving swirl and 50 yards to starboard some forty seconds after she disappeared. Sun glare prevented him or his crew from observing any results. But the U-66 escaped.

His armament exhausted, Sallenger soared to 6,400 feet to vector in the other planes. As he circled, the damaged U-tanker tried to dive. For a moment, Sallenger thought she was gone, but she surfaced almost immediately. At 10:33 A.M., twenty minutes after his second attack, two Avengers and two Wildcats arrived from the *Card*. On command, one of the fighters made a strafing run. He fired a test burst from 2 miles away, but the bullets fell short, and he held his fire until he was in range. During his run, gun flashes from the 20-millimeters at the base of the conning tower winked at him, and he concentrated his fire on this area, though he saw no gunners; apparently they were well protected. He swooped around and attacked from the other side. But the U-boat continued her heavy antiaircraft fire, which forced the lead Avenger, flown by Lieutenant Charles R. Stapler, to weave as it bored in. In a shallow dive, Stapler released two depth charges at 185 feet. They fell close aboard the port side just ahead of the conning tower, and the explosion drenched the submarine. As Stapler pulled up, his gunner strafed the vessel. The first fighter again attacked, and so did the second, just before the second Avenger, coming from the U-boat's stern, dropped its two depth charges 20 to 25 feet from the submarine on her starboard quarter. Spray covered her. The fighters zoomed down to strafe some more, finally silencing the antiaircraft fire.

As the two Avengers circled, the crippled U-117 turned to starboard, apparently trying to dive but instead only mushing down, stern first. Then she did go under, and the Avengers turned to attack with their acoustic torpedoes. But they pulled up when the bow and conning tower broke water and the submarine, now barely moving, struggled to surface. Quantities of oil leaked from her. After five minutes, she lost the fight. She began to settle. Her stern went down, her bow rose slightly; the conning tower slipped under, then the bow, and she was gone. Now the Avengers could use their acoustic torpedoes. Stapler dropped his 200 feet ahead of the oil slick and 100 feet to starboard of the U-boat's last track. Ten seconds later, the other Avenger dropped its 400 feet ahead and to port of where the pilot had last seen the submarine. Some distance away, the crew of the U-66, still submerged, heard detonations, some sharp, some muffled.

The Avengers circled. A patch of oil 200 feet in diameter where the submarine had last been seen seemed to grow. The radioman of the second Avenger reported seeing a shock wave in the water forward and to starboard of the same point. The U-66 heard crackling noises, and finally sounds that the crew interpreted as those of a boat sinking. The airmen saw a very light blue area that seemed to be caused by small bubbles aerating the water. This persisted for many minutes. Nothing else was seen. At 11:26 the four planes were recalled to the *Card*. They were relieved by three Avengers which, however, saw neither submarine. Though Isbell claimed that one submarine had been "definitely sunk" and the other "probably sunk," he was only half right. The U-66 had escaped. But the U-117 had made her last dive. She had gone down about 17 miles north and 40 miles west of where the August 6 U-boat situation report had told Isbell that "probably refueler" would be found. In the vast wastes of the ocean, that was practically pinpointing the target.

Reporting the episode early Sunday morning, the U-66 did not tell U-Boat Command about the detonations she had heard. U-Boat Command, assuming that the U-117 had survived, gave both submarines a new rendezvous for noon. Later the command observed that with the loss of another milch cow, the last fuel reserve for boats coming from the south had been exhausted, and all fourteen had to refuel now from the U-117. But when the U-66 reported on Wednesday that it had waited two days in vain for the U-117, and when the tanker failed to respond to orders to report, the command concluded that she had been lost during the attack. The critical supply situation forced U-Boat Command into complicated maneuvers: some combat submarines had to give fuel to other boats, then return home using fuel as sparingly as possible. The U-66 made it. The loss of the tankers, Dönitz complained, forced him to end operations in the mid-Atlantic earlier than planned.

Between June and August, American carrier planes, aided by ULTRA, sank five milch cows and reserve tankers. The British lost all reservations about using Enigma intelligence in these operations. On October 2 the Admiralty asked the U.S. Navy whether it could send a task force against a refueling to take place north of the Azores; Navy planes found four U-boats on the surface and sank the milch cow U-460. A similar request less than a week later ended in the sinking of the combat boat U-220. By the end of October, of the ten milch cows that Dönitz had had in service in the spring only one remained. The effect on U-boat operations was severe. Because resupply by U-tankers was so dangerous, Dönitz avoided it, compelling his U-boats to break off their operations correspondingly early and destroying his hopes for a formidable offensive in distant waters, far from Allied air cover. In November he abandoned the convoy routes as a theater of operations.

But he returned to the fray the following month. When a patrol line failed to find any ships, he broke it up into subgroups of three boats each in the hope that they would spot targets. It didn't work. Between mid-December 1943 and the middle of January, they sighted not one of the ten convoys that sailed close to them, and they sank only one merchant ship. At the end of February, Dönitz formed what would be the last wolfpack worthy of the name. PRUSSIA's sixteen submarines sank two small British warships — at a cost of seven U-boats. On March 22 Dönitz ordered another withdrawal. In the first three months of 1944, his U-boats sank only 3 merchantmen in convoy out of 3,360 — at a cost of thirty-six submarines. He persisted with his "wonder weapons" — the acoustic torpedo and the snorkel, a valved tube to the surface that enabled a submarine to run on its diesels while under water, increasing its submerged speed and range. But he concentrated now on sinking shipping around the British Isles for the expected invasion of western Europe.

ULTRA had little effect on this. The few U-boats dotting the Atlantic posed little threat. The vast convoys, sometimes of hundreds of ships stretching from horizon to horizon, proceeded majestically across the broad expanse of the Atlantic, guarded by sea and by air, bringing the men and materiel that would drive a stake through the heart of the wickedest regime the world had ever seen. With the help of ULTRA, the Battle of the Atlantic had been won.

Twenty-Three

The Reckoning

ULTRA WAS the greatest secret of World War II after the atom bomb. With the exception of knowledge about that weapon and the probable exception of the time and place of major operations, such as the Normandy invasion, no information was held more tightly. Churchill's anxiety about the secrecy of ULTRA was constant; rules in all of the armed forces forbade any action to be taken on the basis of Enigma intercepts unless some cover, such as air reconnaissance, was provided. The security implies ULTRA's significance. ULTRA furnished intelligence better than any in the whole long history of humankind. It was more precise, more trustworthy, more voluminous, more continuous, longer lasting, and available faster, at a higher level, and from more commands than any other form of intelligence — spies or scouts or aerial reconnaissance or prisoner interrogations. It thus fulfilled better than ever before intelligence's ultimate purposes, one in the psychological component of war, one in the physical. It improved command, and it magnified strength.

It improved command by reducing much of the uncertainty surrounding the enemy. As one scholar has written, "ULTRA created in senior staffs and at the political summit a state of mind which transformed the taking of decisions. To feel that you know your enemy is a vastly comforting feeling. It grows imperceptibly over time if you regularly and intimately observe his thoughts and ways and habits and actions. Knowledge of this kind makes your own planning less tentative and more assured, less harrowing and more buoyant." This benefit of Enigma solutions was intangible but real.

ULTRA magnified strength in the sea war in several ways. It enabled the Allies to steer the escort-carrier hunter-killer groups toward their prey instead of having to search a large area for them. In sixty days in July and August 1943, when a daily average of fourteen U-boats dotted an area the size of the United States west of the Mississippi, those task forces made forty attacks, sinking thirteen submarines. Since with each attack the task force had found a few U-boats in an oceanic waste the size of Texas, it was doing work that without ULTRA would have required many more task forces. Likewise, a U-boat whose location had been revealed by ULTRA within the previous five days was three times more likely to be sunk than one not so compromised. Thus did ULTRA focus the anti-U-boat efforts and so greatly increase their efficiency.

Defensively, ULTRA magnified strength relative to the enemy by depriving him of his powers. Steering a convoy around a wolfpack meant that the U-boats could not attack it, thus in effect adding convoy escorts and retaining ships that it would otherwise have lost. Though the value of ULTRA as convoy defense cannot be quantified as precisely as with the offensive operations, some conclusions can be drawn.

When naval ULTRA was current, U-boats contacted only two-thirds as many convoys as during a blacked-out period. And the rate of sinking of merchant ships in an operational area when ULTRA was current declined to one-sixth of that during a blacked-out period. A comparison on a different basis between ULTRA and non-ULTRA periods concluded that Enigma solutions saved between 1.5 and 2 million tons of shipping in the last half of 1941 and more than 650,000 tons in the first five months of 1943.

So, did ULTRA win the war?

Some writers claim that it did. But even as hyperbole this is nonsense. The Allies would have won without it — though at a much greater cost in men and materiel. Some historians argue that "Without ULTRA . . . the Allies could not have won the Battle of the Atlantic." This too exaggerates. So does the view that ULTRA stands "at the top" of the factors that influenced the outcome of the Atlantic battle. The most important factor was the construction of an unbelievable number of vessels by American shipyards — so many so fast that even the total effort of all Dönitz's U-boats was doomed to ineffectuality. Also more important than ULTRA was air cover, which drove the U-boats under water and thereby slowed them so that they could not keep up with the convoys.

What effect, then, did ULTRA have? Can it at least be estimated how many months of war the solving of the naval Enigma saved?

Any answer must be hypothetical, and similar calculations could be made about any wartime activity. Nevertheless, it is illuminating to suggest a figure. Without the shipping saved by ULTRA, forces would have been withdrawn from the Pacific to attempt to keep to the timetables for the invasions of Sicily and Italy and, above all, of Normandy. Calculations of ship production and of logistic problems suggest that these invasions would have been delayed by about three months. In particular, the great assault on Normandy might have taken place, not in June 1944, but in the fall, or possibly not until the spring of 1945. During this delay, Hitler's V-weapons would have caused far greater devastation. The additional submarines that would have come into service would have made crossing the Atlantic and supplying the Soviet Union even more costly in ships and men. The Allied offensives would have come later and perhaps less strongly. The war in Europe might have been prolonged for one year, and because of the withdrawal of forces and supplies from the Pacific to the European theater, the entire conflict might not have ended until 1947. So, taken in isolation, it may be concluded that ULTRA saved the world two years of war, billions of dollars, and millions of lives.

But events do not occur in isolation. Even if the codebreakers of Hut 8 and OP-20-G had been totally ineffective, even if the war had been prolonged three months or even more because of their inability, something entirely external to them would have taken control of events: the atom bomb. If Germany had continued fighting into the summer of 1945, the first nuclear weapon would probably have exploded not over Hiroshima but over Berlin. And the war would have ended then, no matter what the codebreakers had done, or had not.

To anyone who looks back at the German navy's use of the Enigma machine, one question screams out: if the Germans feared that the Enigma was being solved, why didn't they change to another cipher machine? The answer, upon reflection, is simple. They didn't have another machine. Should they have prepared one? With hindsight, one can say yes. But several factors stopped them. The rotor principle offered the most secure practical cipher system then known. No other mechanism matched it. The Germans could have adopted a machine similar to the rotor devices of Britain and America, which used five or even ten rotors at a time, and which stepped them in a far more complex motion than the Enigma's odometer-like regularity. They failed to adopt such a machine for two reasons.

First, they did not face the reality that Enigma could be broken. The Enigma was an excellent machine, and it was embedded in an excellent web of safeguards against loss, error, and cryptanalysis. The German communications security specialists saw no way that it could be broken. Though they certainly realized that cribs could be used to test for keys, they believed that the vast number of keys defeated this method in practice. They failed to imagine that scores of speedy, brute-force codebreaking machines might be used; their own few cryptanalytic mechanisms were much more primitive. Though the chief judge of the machine's invulnerability, cryptanalyst Wilhelm Tranow, was not biased in its favor (he had once even urged abandoning the Enigma in favor of a codebook and superencipherment), the officers who did support it would have found it difficult to admit to themselves, to Dönitz, and to Hitler that the system was not invulnerable, as they had repeatedly said it was, and that a new one would have to be created. Finally, because the Germans never had irrefutable evidence of the enemy's success in cryptanalysis, they never had to concede that the Enigma was broken. That documents were taken from the weather ships never crossed their minds. With the modifications made to accommodate the growing traffic, they viewed the machine as secure. A new machine was not necessary. Indeed, during the entire war, the Germans never even changed the wiring of the Enigma rotors.

The second reason for not abandoning the Enigma in favor of a new machine was that they had invested too much in the older one. They had bought many machines, distributed them widely, and trained many men in their use. To invent a new system, design a mechanism for it, test a breadboard model, produce thousands of copies, get them to ships (some of them on long patrols), and to shore stations, teach men to use them, and then put them all into service simultaneously, with the inevitable blunders that would call down the wrath of fighting admirals and generals — this was unthinkable.

Thus the Germans stayed with the Enigma. But explaining why they did so does not tell why the Allies proved superior to the Germans in codebreaking.

Perhaps the most important reason was that the Allies, as Poland was before the war, were on the defensive at first. And the defense requires intelligence. Clausewitz defined the characteristic feature of defense as "awaiting the blow." An army awaits a blow only if it believes that a blow is planned, and such a belief exists only through information about the enemy. The offense, on the other hand, is "complete in itself," Clausewitz said. An attacking army need not even know where the enemy force is: it can march about, imposing its will, until it meets its foe. An aggressor nation will put more of its energy into men, tanks, ships, planes, and guns and less into intelligence, one form of which is codebreaking.

A nation that believes it will be attacked will learn what it can about the enemy's intention. Thus Poland's fear in the 1920s of German revanche, touching Poland's very existence as a state, spurred her efforts to solve the Enigma. She established courses in cryptology. Rejewski, perhaps driven by the same patriotic concern, exerted the extra effort that produced his magnificent solution. This is what the Pole Langer meant when, seeking to ease the embarrassment of Bertrand, who had to admit that France had not been able to crack Enigma, he said courteously, "You don't have the same motivation as we do."

The same defensive concerns compelled the Allies to put better men into cryptology than the offense-minded Germans did. In Poland, the Biuro Szyfrów, looking far down the road of cryptanalytic need, hired mathematicians. In Britain, Cambridge students and graduates were the cream of the nation, and G.C.&C.S. took the cream of that cream. In the United States, the draftees who scored the highest on an IQ test were proposed for cryptologic work. But in Germany, no such recruiting seems to have taken place; the Germans, on a blitzkrieg of conquest, seemed not to feel that they needed codebreakers badly. With one or two exceptions, they brought in mathematicians for cryptanalysis only later, during the war. So their agencies, despite individually bright men, did not perform as well as did the Allied units.

The leaders of Britain and Germany personified these differing behaviors. Churchill eagerly read the intercepts and encouraged his cryptanalysts to continue laying their golden eggs. Hitler, although he accepted intercepts, never visited any of his cryptanalytic agencies, never thanked them, and never showed any special interest in their output. In part this difference stemmed from the two nations' different immediate needs: for a long time, Churchill had little more than intelligence, while Hitler was conquering Europe. In part it was a matter of background: Churchill had for decades dealt intimately with the results of codebreaking, Hitler had never done so. And in part it reflected long-standing national policies. Britain's maintenance of the balance of power is a reactive or defensive technique that requires intelligence to succeed. Germany utilized the strategic offensive to resolve her problems of indefensible borders and severe domestic tensions. But this does not call for intelligence, and so her leaders interested themselves in it less than Britain's leaders did.

Another basic reason for the superiority of Allied cryptanalysis lay in the rule of law. This proved more efficient than a dictator's whims. Agreement on impersonal norms permitted both Britain's and America's high commanders to centralize and rationalize their cryptologic efforts instead of competing for the power that knowledge confers. At Bletchley, the concentration of effort let the various huts share knowledge and bombes and find kisses. In Washington, the army and navy, despite some friction, divided up their work. In Germany, on the other hand, seven major codebreaking agencies continued to work separately at least in part because the organizations of which they were part — among them the army, the Armed Forces High Command, the Foreign Office — were fighting for access to Hitler. He wanted that arrangement because it remitted power to him. But this fragmentation spread cryptanalytic manpower very thin and deprived the agencies of the benefits of cooperation. Parliamentary authority, more rational, prevented such a situation from arising in Britain or the United States.

Two other reasons, of a far less fundamental nature, also conduced to Allied superiority. First, since Germany used a single cryptosystem very extensively, the Allies could concentrate more manpower on it, had more intercepts in it to work on, and looked forward to greater rewards from solving it than if they had to work on many systems of several nations, as the Germans did. Second, the Allies ruled the sea. They thus could seize documents from enemy ships. The Germans captured only a few Royal Navy cryptographic documents.

One day during the war, a can of Spam appeared on the table of Leonard Forster, a translator in Hut 4. "Look," said his wife, "here's this new thing that's come from America." When he saw the can, Forster felt a great swelling of pride. For he had had a hand in getting that food to Britain.

ULTRA had helped bring food to his table and to millions of others in Britain. It was one of the great intellectual achievements of the century, no less remarkable because it was achieved against a secret produced by men rather than one of nature. The unraveling of the Enigma was the equivalent of those endeavors that are awarded Nobel prizes. And, like those, it benefited humankind.

By bringing peace closer, ULTRA shortened the time that fathers were separated from their children, husbands from wives. And it spared an untold number of people — men in the cargo ships and their escorts; men at the fighting fronts; men, women, and children under the bombs in the cities of the home fronts. That was ULTRA's greatest gift: it saved lives. Not only British and American lives, but German lives as well. That is the debt the world owes the Bletchley codebreakers; that is the crowning human value of their triumphs.

APPENDIX

NOTES

BIBLIOGRAPHY

INDEX

PHOTO CREDITS

Appendix:
Enciphering with Naval Enigma

Preparing to encipher a message in naval Enigma was a complicated and multistep procedure. It required an indicators book, which listed groups of three letters by key net (such as Home Waters), that month's machine-setting list, which gave each day's settings, tables to encipher pairs of letters into other pairs, and other papers.

The first steps, preparing the so-called "inner settings," could be done only by an officer. He would do the following:

1. Select from the eight rotors available the three that the machine-setting list specified for that day.
2. On each rotor, turn the alphabet ring to the position prescribed in the machine-setting list and lock it in place with the pin.
3. Assemble the rotors on their shaft in the order prescribed by the machine-setting list and insert them into the machine.

The radioman would then prepare the outer settings. He would:

1. Turn the rotors until the three letters specified in the machine-setting list appeared in the windows of the machine's closed lid.
2. Insert the plugs at both ends of the plugboard cables into the proper sockets of the plugboard to connect the pairs of letters prescribed by the machine-setting list.

The radioman next readied the message key. He would:

1. Determine the key net on which the message is to be set.
2. In the distribution list in force, find the numbers of the columns in the indicators book assigned to that key net.
3. From one of those columns, pick out at random a three-letter indicator.
4. Write this key-net indicator in the last three cells of the first line of the encipherment form's book-group column (perhaps called that because for some years the German plaintext was encoded in the *Allgemeines Funkspruchbuch* before being enciphered in Enigma).
5. Make up a dummy letter at random (a null) and write it in the first cell.

6. In the indicators book, pick out at random any three-letter indicator.
7. Write it in the first three cells of the second line of the encipherment form's book-group column.
8. Make up a null at random and write it in the last cell of that line.
9. Determine the bigram table in force from the key list.
10. Combine the letters of the first cells in the first two lines into a vertical pair.
11. Look up the vertical pair in the bigram table and replace it with its cipher pair.
12. Write the two letters of this cipher pair horizontally into the first two cells of the first line of the radio-group column of the encipherment form.
13. Repeat this process with the three remaining vertical pairs in the book-group column, writing them horizontally into the first two lines of the radio-group column.
14. Press, on the Enigma keyboard, the three letters of the original, unenciphered key-net indicator and write down at the top of the message form the letters lit up on the illuminable panel (this becomes the message key).
15. Turn the rotors until the letters of the message key show in the lid windows.

The cipher clerk would then write the plaintext into the book-group columns of the cipher form without word breaks but with *x* or *y* to separate sentences. He replaced the common letter-pairs *ch* and *ck* with *q*. Priority indications, such as SSD (for *sehr sehr dringend,* very very urgent), would be replaced by a variety of words, such as *Wespe.* Ready at last for the actual encipherment, he would summon a colleague. As he pressed the successive letters of the plaintext on the typewriter keyboard, his co-worker would write down in the radio-group columns of the form the letters that lit up on the illuminable panel — the letters of the crypto-

---

A naval Enigma encipherment worksheet. The cipher clerk would write the plaintext in the right-hand column under the heading *Bedeutung* (meaning). The first word, *Wespe,* is a priority indicator. The message begins, *"Leipzig an Flotte. Köln Standort Norderney Leuchtturm . . ."* (*Leipzig* to the fleet: *Cologne* location Norderney lighthouse . . .). The clerk would then follow the instructions for choosing and enciphering the indicators and finally for enciphering the plaintext. Translations, beginning at the left-hand column: *Anfangskenngruppen,* beginning indicator groups; *Verschlüsselt mit Schlüssel M,* enciphered by Enigma; *Endkenngruppen,* final indicators groups; *Uhrzeitgruppe,* time group; *Gruppenzahl,* number of groups; *Funkgruppen,* radio groups; *Buchgruppen,* book groups; *Spruchschlüssel,* message key; *gültig für 3.8.,* valid for August 3; *Schlüsselkenngruppe,* key-net indicator; *Verfahrenkenngruppe,* message-grade indicator (but actually a random group).

| Uhrzeitgruppe 1053 | Spruchschlüssel: s p l |
| Gruppenzahl 35 | gültig für 3. 8. |

	Kenngruppe	Buchgruppen	Bedeutung
Anfangskenngruppen			
1	b_1m o_2g	x_1 h_2 y_3 u_4	Schlüsselkenngruppe
2	p_3y u_4d	y f n h	Verfahrenkenngruppe
Verschlüsselt mit Schlüssel M			
3	f j i a	w e s p	Wespe
4	t z w r	e l e i	
5	l h s c	p z i g	Leipzig
6	q f d x	a n a n	an
7	n o a p	f l o t	Flotte
8	a s w l	e y k o	
9	r p g i	l n x s	Köln
10	e m k n	t a n d	Standort
11	w a k k	o r t n	
12	y z r z	o r d e	Norderney
13	e v i b	r n e y	
14	c m k e	l c t r	Leuchtturm
15	s k e a	m i n e	in
16	l q u d	i n s s	1
17	y f v x	e c s n	6
18	p m b o	u l g r	0
19	o m g l	a d d r	Grab
20	q s o h	e i s m	3 sm
21	y r h q	a b x g	ab
22	r q d e	e a m i	gehe mit
23	h j f u	t t t t	T
24	n c x m	e i n s	1
25	d p k l	f u n f	5
26	s b i j	d r e i	3
27	g x t g	n a c q	nach □
28	f u c n	u n e u	9
29	p h z t	n f u a	5
30	t o w v	f f u n	5
31	u d j b	f e i n	1
32	v c y b	a l i n	links
33	j i n g	k o b n	oben
Endkenngruppen			
34	b m o g	— — — —	
35	p y u d	— — — —	

121	122	123	124	125	126	127	128
1 JAO	QGH	KAK	VXX	OJW	DML	HYH	UDY
2 PİZ	EVK	RMO	ZNO	WUZ	KİA	JTİ	DXS
3 MNN	BNN	OİQ	DAL	LGA	ANO	CSU	QBO
4 TUR	SİZ	XVE	İİA	QYY	GHP	POD	KRA
5 VQA	WQD	USA	RQW	MMR	NJC	LİF	GTİ
6 AWW	DKİ	CND	XJE	AFT	BGB	SXR	MFF
7 FKD	HXG	ZUU	GMZ	EXV	FOZ	YZZ	XAD
8 YLC	NUY	FTF	UTD	STJ	QWD	ERW	BPT
9 RZQ	GDJ	İKH	PYY.	NCG	WRR	VFX	JER
10 DOK	AAS	WPJ	YSG	VHH	TSE	NEA	SWH
11 LFM	JYR	EQC	NVC	ZOX	İYİ	AMC	YQQ

Part of a page of a *Kennbuch,* or indicators book, showing the random three-letter groups that form part of the Enigma key. A deciphering portion has the indicators in alphabetical order with their column numbers next to them.

Tafel **E.** Verschlüsseln.

———— Zweiter Buchstabe des Buchstabenpaares ⟫————→

	a	b	c	d	e	f	g	h	i	j	k	l	m	
a	bq	ap	gg	pt	dh	sk	*l*x	wi	fm	ry	eb	og	go	a
b	ip	ga	na	ka	qa	cm	yd	fa	as	nk	ŭy	sd	ao	b
c	ŭi	im	ea	vt	ia	yi	kn	ra	ko	ws	dn	kx	oq	c
d	fj	ce	rn	ta	ay	in	et	qq	tc	bv	wŭ	xt	*l*g	d
e	qh	yw	fs	mo	ox	*l*v	yv	nq	gp	xb	mp	vk	xc	e
f	eo	kg	wb	jŭ	ŭa	cy	ma	wt	va	hd	zc	do	fb	f
g	*l*e	aq	pŭ	nw	nb	tb	bk	ek	nc	aa	op	wz	ca	g

A portion of a bigram table, which serves to encipher part of the Enigma key.

Datum	Innere Einstellung Walzenl.	Ringstellg.	Ausseneinstellung f.Admiralsverkehr 0000-1159	1200-2359
1.10.	I III II	H L D Z	R H K O	L Y E F
2.10.	I II III	I Y M A	H B L Q	R W A Z
3.10.	III I II	W V L T	Z X Q P	W H X X
4.10.	I III II	I T R U	U T E Y	R Q C P
5.10.	I II III	Q W K T	K N W V	X Y D Z
6.10.	III II I	G W Y I	T P F I	B A H L
7.10.	II III I	P H Z Y	K L T M	T V N W
8.10.	II I III	T X R S	R I K H	Y C R E
9.10.	III I II	D S T P	Y P S P	E A F X
10.10.	III II I	U M K G	S V Q V	A R F R
11.10.	II I III	H Z P Q	K O T K	V U Z K
12.10.	II III I	Y S P K	X R X U	X C A R
13.10.	II I III	T C S C	K A Z B	Z T Q F
14.10.	I III II	Y H Y H	N O F K	R L E E
15.10.	I II III	R X M N	K G U P	S Y D S

A portion of a key list for the commercial Enigma used by German forces in the Spanish civil war. For each day it shows, under *Innere Einstellung* (inner setting), the positions for the three removable rotors in roman numerals and the alphabet ring settings for the three removable rotors and the reversing rotor. Under *Ausseneinstellung* (outer setting), it gives the rotor positions for the start of encipherment of each message sent during two periods of the day.

Zuteilungsliste für Kenngruppen
zum K. Buch — M. Dv. Nr. 98.

Teil B.

Schlüsselkenngruppe	Verfahrenkenngruppe	
	Schlüssel M	R. H. B.
Spalte	Spalte	Spalte
1—30 M Neptun (M Nep)	1—733 Allgemein	1—290 Offizier
31—80 Schiffssonderschlüssel*) (MS)		291—733 Allgemein
81—140 M Triton (M Tri)		

A distribution list for the indicators book. It shows, for example, that the three-letter indicators in columns 81 to 140 of the book are to serve as key-net indicators for the TRITON key net, used by Atlantic U-boats. Indicators from other columns specify other key nets.

gram, the secret message that was to be sent. The cipher clerk would cross out the book-group column to avoid its being transmitted by mistake. He would transmit the enciphered indicators before the enciphered message.

At the other end, the recipient would decipher the indicators, recover the message key, and translate the message.

The system was enormously complex. But it was formidably strong.

In addition, two kinds of messages were encoded for brevity before being enciphered in Enigma. U-boat sightings and other reports were condensed into four-letter groups by the Short Signal Book. Weather reports converted measurements into single letters using tables in the Short Weather Cipher. Thus, in Table 3 of the edition in use in 1941, atmospheric pressure of 971.1–973.0 millibars was represented by N, 973.1–975.0 by M. In Table 6, cirrus cloud cover of 1/10–5/10 became E. Using the Short Weather Cipher, the observer aboard ship converted his measurements into letters in a prescribed order. For example, a surface observation from 68° north latitude, 20° west longitude (northwest of Iceland) reporting atmospheric pressure of 972 millibars, temperature of minus 5° Celsius, wind from the northwest with force 6 on the Beaufort scale (a strong breeze of 25 to 31 miles per hour), 3/10 cirrus cloud cover, and visibility up to 5 nautical miles, would become MZNFPED. To this would be appended the two-letter signature of the reporting ship.

I. Operationsabſichten.

a) Angriff.

aaaa Beabſichtige gemeldete Feindſtreitkräfte anzugreifen
aabb Beabſichtige gemeldete Feindſtreitkräfte anzugreifen in ☐ . . .
aacc Beabſichtige gemeldete Feindſtreitkräfte anzugreifen am . . . um . . . Uhr
aaee Beabſichtige Durchführung Unternehmung wie vorgeſehen
aaff Beabſichtige Durchführung Unternehmung mit vollem Einſatz
aagg Beabſichtige Durchführung Unternehmung unter Vermeidung vollen Einſatzes
aahh Beabſichtige Unternehmung auszudehnen nach ☐ . . .
aaii Beabſichtige Unternehmung auszudehnen nach Seegebiet . . .
aajj ....
aakk ....

Part of a page of the Short Signal Cipher of 1941. This page deals with plans
for attacking. Each four-letter group replaces a phrase. Thus *aabb* stands for
"Intend to attack reported enemy forces in naval square . . ." The encoding
shortens the message to be enciphered and provides an extra layer of secrecy.

T

Tafel 11.

T = Lufttemperatur in ganzen Celsius-Graden.

+ 28°[1]) C = a	+ 15° C = n	+ 3° C = a	− 10° C = n
+ 27° = b	+ 14° = o	+ 2° = b	− 11° = o
+ 26° = c	+ 13° = p	+ 1° = c	− 12° = p
+ 25° = d	+ 12° = q	0° = d	− 13° = q
+ 24° = e	+ 11° = r	− 1° = e	− 14° = r
+ 23° = f	+ 10° = s	− 2° = f	− 15° = s
+ 22° = g	+ 9° = t	− 3° = g	− 16° = t
+ 21° = h	+ 8° = u	− 4° = h	− 17° = u
+ 20° = i	+ 7° = v	− 5° = i	− 18° = v
+ 19° = j	+ 6° = w	− 6° = j	− 19° = w
+ 18° = k	+ 5° = y	− 7° = k	− 20° = y
+ 17° = l	+ 4° = z	− 8° = l	− 21°[2]) = z
+ 16° = m		− 9° = m	

Temperatur wegen Schadens am Meßgerät nicht meßbar: x

[1]) oder mehr.   [2]) oder weniger.

Anmerkung: Bis 0,4° nach unten, von 0,5° an nach oben abrunden.

Beiſpiele: Abgelesene Temperatur + 7,4° = + 7° = v
                                              + 7,5° = + 8° = u

Part of a page of the 1942 edition of the Short Weather Cipher, the edition
captured from the U-559. In each table a letter replaces a meteorological
observation. In Table 11, air temperature in whole degrees centigrade, 21°
becomes *h* in the sequence of letters to be enciphered. Table 12 lists differ-
ences between air and water temperatures, and Table 12A the time of the
weather observation.

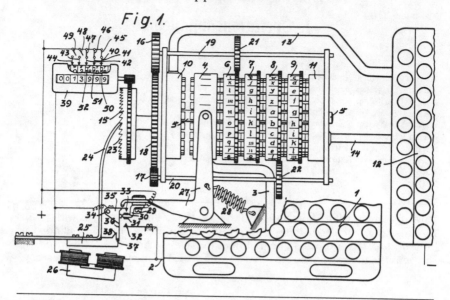

A drawing from Arthur Scherbius's U.S. initial patent for the Enigma. Figure 1 shows the typewriter keyboard (1), the input plate (4), the rotors (6, 7, 8, 9), and the output (12), here a perforator for a teletypewriter paper tape. There is no reversing rotor; the current goes through the rotor sequence only once.

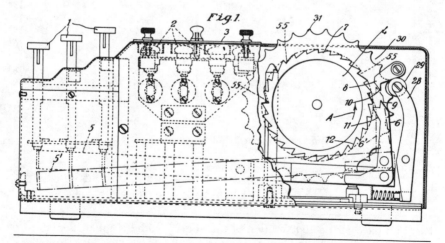

A side elevation of an Enigma machine, from Willi Korn's patent for adding notches to each rotor's alphabet ring to vary the advancing of the adjacent rotors.

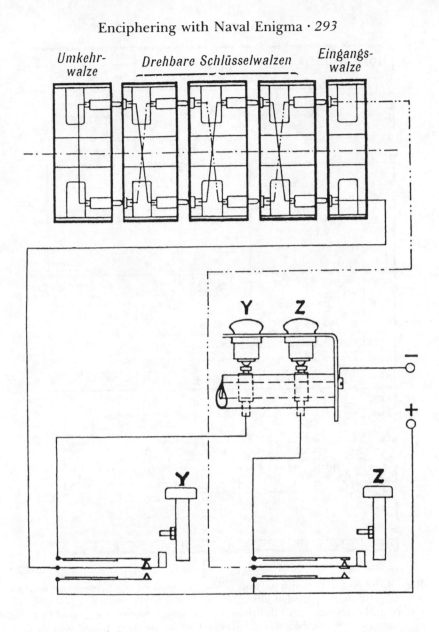

The route of the electrical current in the Enigma, as shown in a German navy manual. *Umkehrwalze*, reversing rotor; *Drehbare Schlüsselwalzen*, turnable rotors; *Eingangswalze*, entry rotor.

Part of the North Atlantic portion of the German navy's grid of the world's oceans. The chart is divided into approximate squares designated by pairs of letters, and each square is subdivided into smaller squares designated by pairs of numbers. The numbered squares could be further subdivided into smaller numbered squares for greater precision in location.

Notes

The following abbreviations are used in the notes:

ADM	Admiralty series, PRO
CLKE	Clarke Papers, Churchill College, Cambridge
DEFE	German naval intercepts, PRO
DENN	Denniston Papers, Churchill College, Cambridge
FO	Foreign Office Papers, PRO
MA	Militärarchiv, Freiburg-im-Breisgau
M.Dv.	Marinedienstvorschrift (naval regulation)
NA	National Archives, Washington, D.C.
PG	German naval documents captured by the British
PRO	Public Record Office, London
RG	Record Group, NA
RM	Naval documents, MA
WK	Wehrkreis (army documents), MA

Data on times of solution come from DEFE 3, which gives for each intercept the date and time of interception and the date and time of its dispatch to the Operational Intelligence Centre. The difference is called the solution time, which includes translation.

Figures for tonnage sunk come from Roskill, *War at Sea*, 1:615–16, 2:485–86, 3:388–89; Morison, 1:410–411, 10:365; and Rohwer, *Axis Submarine Successes*. All are in gross tons (sometimes called gross register tons), not deadweight tons or displacement tons.

1. A Staff School Memory

Unless otherwise specified, all information in this chapter comes from ADM 1/11133; PG 30106; Roskill, *Secret Surrender;* and interviews with Baker-Cresswell, Balme, and Wilde.

PAGE

1   James Roosevelt: *New York Times*, May 10, 1941.
2   OB series: Rohwer, *Axis Submarine Successes*, 321.

3   asdic: Hackmann.
4   radar errors: Kemp interview; RM 7/104:87; MacLachlan, 112; Rohwer, "La radiotélégraphie."
5   less than 70 days: Hinsley, 1:163, 337.
5   two days before the attack: DEFE 3:1:2TP368.
5   126,000, 249,000: Roskill, *War at Sea*, 1:616.
5   rationing hurting, thinking with stomachs: Leonard Mosley, *Back to the Wall: The Heroic Story of the People of London During World War II* (New York: Random House, 1971), 225.
5   meat, cheese rations: Great Britain, Ministry of Food, *How Britain Was Fed in War Time*, 58.
5   31 million tons: Winston S. Churchill, *Secret Session Speeches*, ed. Charles Eade (New York: Simon and Schuster, 1946), 38, 49–50.
6   28 million tons: Schoenfeld, 126.
14   "Is there a chance": Baker-Cresswell interview.

2. *The Wreck of the* Magdeburg

All details about the *Magdeburg* grounding, salvaging attempts, and codebook jettisoning are from Assessor Tolki's report of Sept. 17, 1914, in PG 64859; Makela; Germany, Marine-Archiv, *Ostsee*, 1:76–85. Details of bringing the codebook to Britain are from Count Constantine Benckendorff, *Half a Life: The Reminiscences of a Russian Gentleman* (London: Richards, 1954); ADM 53/62801; FO 371/2095:490–509; Hammant.

15   *Magdeburg* specifications: Gröner, 1:172, 175.
19   fourth lay hidden: The accounts in Tolki's report in PG 64859 mention only three codebooks aboard the *Magdeburg* — those in the steering room and radio shack and on the bridge. All were said to have been burned or jettisoned. Makela, p. 49, lists the serial numbers of three codebooks: 145, 151, and 974. Both sources thus imply that only three books were aboard the cruiser. But the book sent to the British, 151, now in the Public Record Office as ADM 136/4156, shows no signs of immersion. It thus could not have been one of the three mentioned in PG 64859. The *Magdeburg* therefore had to have had four codebooks. Why is the fourth not mentioned in the sources? Because the crew members did not know about it, forgot it, or suppressed their knowledge of its existence in their testimony, while the serial number of one of the other three was not recorded or was lost. This seems to me more likely than the only other explanation that would account for No. 151 being captured dry: that it was left in the steering room, on the bridge, or in the radio room by Bender or Szillat or Neuhaus, who then, to avoid punishment, lied about throwing it overboard or burning it, while Galibin, to brag, lied about finding the codebook in the captain's cabin, it really having been found elsewhere by him or another Russian. Makela's statement, p. 49, that

the codebook on the bridge was not destroyed is contradicted by the statement on the next page that that codebook was jettisoned.

21 codebook in cabin: PG 64859:11. Aug. 1915, the report of an interrogation of Galibin after his capture by the Germans. Makela, p. 78, and Hammant, p. 18, concur, though other details differ. N. B. Pavlovich, *The Fleet in the First World War,* 1: *Operations of the Russian Fleet* ([Moscow: Ministry of Defense, 1964], trans. for Smithsonian Institution and National Science Foundation [New Delhi: Amerind, 1979]), 76, states that the Russians found in the captain's cabin the cipher key to the codebook and gave it to the British. For some reason, the British never received it, for Rotter had to solve it. Yankovich, "The Origins of Russian Navy Communications Intelligence," trans. Thomas B. Hammant, *Cryptologia* 8 (July 1984), 193–202, adds little to these accounts.

21 "most secure means": Winston Churchill, *The World Crisis* (New York: Scribner's, 1923), 1:503.

22 Ewing: Beesly, *Room 40,* 10; A. W. Ewing, *The Man of Room 40: The Life of Sir Alfred Ewing* (London: Hutchinson, 1939), passim; R. V. Jones, "Alfred Ewing and 'Room 40,'" *Notes and Records of the Royal Society of London* 34 (July 1979), 65–90; Andrew, *Secret Service,* 86. For a different view of Ewing's early work, see Hiley.

23 Denniston: Beesly, *Room 40,* 12; *Dictionary of National Biography, 1961–1970,* 286–87; R. A. Denniston, passim; David Wallechinsky, *The Complete Book of the Olympics* (New York: Penguin, 1984), under "Field Hockey," where the name is erroneously given as "Andrew Dennistoun."

23 "singularly ignorant": DENN 1/3, p. 4.

23 Rotter: DENN 1/4, p. 5; CLKE 3, chap. 4, pp. 2–3.

23 seized from a merchantman, method for disguising: Australian Archives, Navy Office, Accession MP 1049/1, Items 1914/0351 and 1914/0444; Australian War Memorial, Donated Records List, No. 586 (2nd ser.); ADM 137/4388.

24 "their folly": DENN 1/3, p. 5.

24 third major codebook, S-119: Jones, "Alfred Ewing," 75; Beesly, *Room 40,* 27, 6–7; Germany, Marine-Archiv, *Nordsee,* 2:191–96; ADM 137/4374.

24 "never wise": Jones, "Alfred Ewing," 75.

25 divers, Miller: Grant, 34–40. I am grateful to Dr. Grant for letting me see this manuscript.

25 Knox: Fitzgerald, passim; R. F. Harrod, *The Life of John Maynard Keynes* (New York: Harcourt, Brace, 1951), 40, for "He has got," and 65; *Who Was Who, 1941–1950; Herodas,* notes by Walter Headlam, ed. A. D. Knox (Cambridge: Cambridge University Press, 1922, reissued 1966), lxi.

26 Birch: Fitzgerald, 93, 138; Beesly, *Very Special Intelligence,* 124; *Who Was Who, 1956–1960; Times,* Feb. 16, 1956, p. 12; Morris and Mavis Batey interviews.

27 "in the same way," new codebook, mechanical: PG 64839:22. Feb 1915.

27 "the *Handelsschiffsverkehrsbuch*": RM 47/N.259:19.Nov.1914. The British found no codebook aboard the *Ophelia* (ADM 137/2081, p. 385). The indications by which the Reich Naval Staff concluded that the *HVB* had been compromised remain a mystery.

28 superencipherment keys: Kleikamp, 34.

28 cases of British steaming out: Kleikamp, 34.

29 range, frequency, call signs: Bonatz, *Deutsche Marine-Funkaufklärung*, 13; Tranow interview.

30 regulations forbade: Kleikamp, 8.

30 Roubaix: Hermann Stützel, "Geheimschrift und Entzifferung im ersten Weltkrieg," *Truppenpraxis* 7 (July 1969), 541–45.

30 Neumünster, Braune: Tranow interview; Kahn, *Hitler's Spies*, 38; Walle.

30 improvements: Kleikamp, 33–35; DENN 1/3.

3. The Man, the Machine, the Choice

Details of Scherbius's offer and his correspondence with the naval authorities are in MA:Fasz. 5708:II.8–12. The evolution of the Enigma system and discussions of the hand systems may be traced in PG 48934, 48795, 80609, 34455F, 34466.

31 three other men: Kahn, *Codebreakers*, 410–24.

34 October 20, businessman, Oberrealschule: Niedersachsiches Hauptstaatsarchiv (Hannover): Hann. 146A: Matrikelbücher der Technische Hochschule Hannover: Nr. 110: Matrikel Nr. 903 (folio 427).

34 jobs, inventions: "A. Scherbius," *Elektrotechnische Zeitschrift* (May 23, 1929), 774; "Arthur Scherbius," *Zeitschrift des Vereins Deutscher Ingenieure* 73 (June 15, 1929); his articles and letters in *Elektrotechnische Zeitschrift*, 1921, 1923, 1924, 1927; German patents 465,557, 465,638, 457,181, 457,740.

35 patents: Türkel, 45–46.

36 best ideas, musical: Helmuth Heimsoeth letter.

36 Chiffriermaschinen Aktien-Gesellschaft: *Handbuch der Deutschen Aktien-Gesellschaften, 1925*, 2:2888.
articles: in *Radio News* 5 (January 1924), 878, 997–98; *Elektrotechnische Zeitschrift* (1923), 1035–36; *Zeitschrift für Fernmeldetechnik, Werk- und Gerätebau* 7 (1923), 70–74; *Der Radio-Amateur* (November 1923), 76–78; *Umschau* 27 (August 25, 1923), 552–54; *Das Echo* 42 (1923), 3168.

36 "Glow Lamp": Türkel, 85–88, Table O.

37 rotors removable, movable ring, reflector: U.S. patents 1,705,641, 1,938,028, 1,733,886; German patent 411,126.

38 Fisher: *Memories* (London: Hodder and Stoughton, 1919), 108–9.

39 "At the beginning": Winston Churchill, *The World Crisis* (New York: Scribner's, 1923), 1:503. The book was published in German in 1924. Churchill, incidentally, obtained official permission to publish his information about Room 40 (FO 371/179:33–35; Great Britain, Parliament, House of Commons, *Parliamentary Debates,* 5th. ser., vol. 163 (London, His Majesty's Stationery Office, 1923), col. 435.

39 "the German fleet": Germany, Marine-Archiv, *Nordsee,* 4:149.

40 by 1925: my supposition, based on the belief that the machines went into service early in 1926, based in turn on the date of February 9, 1926, on *Der Funkschlüssel C,* the official naval manual for the machine. The 1928 date given in Erich Raeder, *My Life* (Annapolis: United States Naval Institute, 1960), 204–5, may be in error. I searched through all the indexes to the German naval records in the U.S. National Archives and examined all likely pre-1926 files provided by the Militärarchiv (PG 49061–49069, 48934, 15389, 15390, RM 8/28, 8/47, 20/305, and 20/306), but I did not find any memoranda urging the adoption of the Enigma, any correspondence or contracts with Scherbius or his firm, any purchase orders or copies of receipts for machines, any orders for the institution of the Enigma as the naval cipher machine, or any papers dealing with the training of radiomen (who handled the ciphering) on the Enigma or with distribution of the machine. Werther provides no data on this question.

40 naval machine: *Der Funkschlüssel C.*

40 only officers: PG 34456:13 Feb. 1930, p. 2.

40 superimposition: implied in M.Dv.Nr. 32/1, p. 43, and in RM 7/108, p. 44. For an explanation, see Kahn, *Codebreakers,* 236–37.

41 Schmidt: he was then signing the intercept reports of the Chiffrierstelle (Militärarchiv: OKW 2298); Militärarchiv: Sammlung Krug: MSg 109/2373.

41 July 15, 1928: my presumption, inferred from the fact that the Poles intercepted the first German army messages in Enigma on that date (Rejewski, "Enigma 1930–1940," unpublished).

41 couple of hundred: my assumption, based on the fact that a list of the Baltic Naval Station for May 28, 1938, shows 49 sets of keys for the Enigma distributed to 32 ships or units (PG 34456:367–68). That station was one of the navy's four major commands, along with the North Sea Naval Station, the fleet command, and navy headquarters.

41 horse-drawn wagon: Helmuth Heimsoeth letter.

41 May 13, 1929: "A. Scherbius," *Elektrotechnische Zeitschrift;* "Arthur Scherbius," *Zeitschrift des Vereins Deutscher Ingenieure.*

41 plugboard: NA: RG 165: Military Intelligence Division, Correspondence 1917–41: MID4131-754:2 July 1931.

43 navy plugboard: M.Dv.Nr.21g.

45 "During a change": Der Reichswehrminister, Jahresverfügung 1933/34, Betrifft: Spionageabwehr in der Wehrmacht, 15. Oktober 1934, p. 8 (copy in WK VII/2530).

45   Bress: PG 34441:17.Feb. 1934.
45   1916 case: RM 47/N.264:25.Nov.1916.
46   "should not have," "multiple": PG 48908:222.
46   Kunert: OKM 20/15390:138–41, 157.
47   "It is assumed": PG 34534:138. Similar in PG 34456:394.
47   water-soluble ink: PG 34455F:4.Dez.1939.
47   cue word system: PG 34455F:18.Sept.1939.
47   keying system: M.Dv.Nr. 32/1.
48   "because our cipher systems": PG 34455F:4.Nov.1939.
48   group tactics: Bauer, 109–10; Rohwer, "Die Funkführung," 324;
      Jeschke, 38, 64.

4. The Codebreaker and the Spy

The solutions of the 1920s are from Ribadeau-Dumas, 30; MA: OKW 2288–2318; A. G. Denniston, 54–55; Herbert O. Yardley, *The American Black Chamber* (Indianapolis: Bobbs-Merrill, 1931), 332.

The material on Kowalewski is from Listowel and Jedrzejewicz interviews; Listowel, 21–39; Ziaja. Details of Polish cryptanalysis during the Russo-Polish War come from Sciezynski (Kasparek trans.) and in the 1920s from Kozaczuk. Personal information about Rejewski is from Schaerf and Birnbaum interviews; and Kozaczuk, passim. Details of his solution are from Kozaczuk and the appendixes therein and from discussions with Deavours.

Bertrand's life story is from Bertrand interview. Details about Schmidt and his spying are from Paillole; Bertrand; and Bloch, all passim; from his Nazi party membership card in the Berlin Document Center; and from David Kahn, "The Spy Who Most Affected World War II," *Kahn on Codes* (New York: Macmillan, 1983), 76–88.

51   February 1921: League of Nations, *Treaty Series* 18 (February 19, 1921),
      12, 13.
56   October 30, 1930: Bertrand, 18.
64   theorem: The formal theorem is set out in Garrett Birkhoff and
      Saunders MacLane, *A Survey of Modern Algebra* (New York: Macmil-
      lan, 1965), 135. Deavours calls this "the theorem that won World
      War II."
65   "The very first trial": Rejewski in Kozaczuk, 258.
66   "To this day": Rejewski, "How Polish Mathematicians," 221.
67   lacked mathematical cryptanalysts: Deavours interview; Rejewski let-
      ter, December 7, 1975.
67   "renunciation": *Mein Kampf* (Munich: Eher, 1932), 154.
67   merit of Pokorny and Ciężki: The great American cryptanalyst Wil-
      liam F. Friedman shares this merit. In 1931, he hired two mathema-
      ticians (Solomon Kullback and Abraham Sinkov) as cryptanalysts in
      the Army Signal Corps. In addition, in the 1920s, Friedman solved a
      simpler rotor machine (Deavours and Kruh, chap. 2).

5. Racing German Changes

Details of the continuing solutions are from Kozaczuk and the appendixes therein; Gaj, passim; Deavours, *Breakthrough '32*, passim. Details about Schmidt are from Paillole, passim; and Bertrand, passim.

72 Pyry: Zygalski interview; Kozaczuk, 44.
74 "Ah! Those departures": Bertrand, 24–25.
75 paid in reichsmarks, ticket: Navarre, 55.
76 none reached the codebreakers: Rejewski, "Remarks on Appendix 1," 77.
77 new indicators method: WK XIII/69:1938/47:17. and 19. August 1938.
78 "all support": Great Britain, Foreign Office, *Documents on British Foreign Policy 1919–1939*, 3rd ser., 4: 546.
79 "null and void": Germany, Auswärtiges Amt, *Documents on German Foreign Policy 1918–1945*, ser. D, 6:347–51.
79 France promised: France, Ministère des Affaires étrangères, *Documents diplomatiques français 1932–1939*, 2nd ser., 16:461–62.
79 July 24: Bertrand, 59–60; Garlinski, 42–45; Beesly, "Who Was the Third Man at Pyry?"
81 Dunderdale: Brown, 207–8; Dunderdale interview.
81 "Accueil triomphal": Bertrand, 60–61.

6. Failure at Broadway Buildings

Details of the formation of G.C. & C.S. are from ADM I/8637/55; Ferris, 56–58, 89; A. G. Denniston, 49; Andrew, *Secret Service,* 260; Clarke, 55, 57; Jeffery and Sharp, 106–7; Curzon, passim.

85 Fetterlein: Andrew, *Secret Service,* 261–62; A. G. Denniston, 50, 53–54; Filby.
85 deliberate exposure: Christopher Andrew, "The British Secret Service and Anglo-Soviet Relations in the 1920s. I: From the Trade Negotiations to the Zinoviev Letter," *Historical Journal* 20 (1977), 673–706; Christopher Andrew, "British Intelligence and the Breach with Russia in 1927," *Historical Journal* 25 (1982), 957–64; A. G. Denniston, 55.
85 Germany: Clarke, 221, 223; A. G. Denniston, 54, 56, 59, 60, 61; Ferris, 72; Hinsley, 1:54.
86 "because of the delightful": A. G. Denniston, 59.
86 Knox attack on Italian Enigma: Fitzgerald, 254; Denniston, 60.
87 Knox and *la méthode des bâtons:* implied in photo 12 in Kozaczuk. See also Deavours, "La Méthode des Bâtons."
87 1937 success: Hinsley, 1:54.
87 plugboard; A. G. Denniston, 60.
88 creation of O.I.C.: Beesly, *Very Special Intelligence,* 9–23; Hinsley, 12–13; Denning, 270–72.

88 first time since 1928: CLKE 3, no. 40.
88 German subsection: Hinsley, 1:55.
88 Bletchley Park: R. A. Denniston, 114; D. C. Low, *The History of Bletchley Park and Mansion* (n.p., 1963). For Leon: *Debrett's Peerage and Baronetage* (1985), B536.
89 *Schleswig-Holstein:* Germany, Auswärtiges Amt, *Documents on German Foreign Policy 1918–1945,* ser. D, 6:471–72, 807; 7:195–96; Bertil Stjernfelt and Klaus-Richard Böhme, *Westerplatte 1939,* Einzelschriften zur militärischen Geschichte des Zweiten Weltkrieges, 23 (Freiburg: Rombach, 1979), 79.

7. *Phantoms*

The material on Turing is from Andrew Hodges, passim, and from Good, 3–4, 5. Information on the Turing bombe is from Andrew Hodges, 176–85; Deavours and Ellison interviews; Deavours and Kruh, "Turing Bombe"; and Gaj, 148–60. Material on the bombes is from various interviews. Material on the diagonal board is from Welchman, *Hut Six Story,* 81–83, 295–309, and Deavours and Ellison interviews. Information on Welchman is from Milner-Barry and Tischler interviews; on de Grey, from Filby, 275; on Adcock, from Morris interview and *Dictionary of National Biography, 1961–1970,* 6–7; on Alexander, from Milner-Barry interview, Milner-Barry, "C.H. O'D. Alexander," and Good, 3, 5–6; on Milner-Barry, from Milner-Barry interview and *Who's Who, 1990;* on Forster, from Forster interview and *Who's Who, 1990.*

90 Polish evacuation: Kozaczuk, 69–80; Watt, 7–9.
94 bright ideas: Twinn interview.
94 "then there is": "On Computable Numbers, with an Application to the Entscheidungsproblem" (1937), reprinted in Martin Davis, *The Undecidable* (Hewlett, N.Y.: Raven Press, 1965), 148.
100 first bombe: Hinsley, 1:184, says August, but 1:494 says May; Welchman, "From Polish Bomba," 107, says September; Welchman, *Hut Six Story,* 147, for "Agnes"; Monroe interview.
100 Hut 8: Wylie, Good interviews.
100 ISK: Lewin, 118–19.

8. *The Rotors*

All the information in this chapter is from PG 30030, ADM 199/123; Rottmann and Masanek interviews; and Becker letter.

9. *Royal Flags Wave Kings Above*

Information on the Polish cryptanalysts in Algeria and southern France is from Bertrand, 107, 117, 140–42; and Braquenié interview in Kozaczuk, *Geheimoperation Wicher,* trans. Theodor Fuchs, ed. Jürgen Rohwer (Koblenz: Bernard & Graefe, 1989), 322. Enciphering the solutions in Enigma is from Kozaczuk, *Enigma,* 87; and R. A. Denniston, 114. Information on the threats to the security of Enigma solutions is from Bertrand, 156–58, 184–85; and Kozaczuk, *Geheimoperation Wicher,* 203–6, 210, 216–17, and 334–37.

All details of the capture of April 26, 1940, are from ADM 199/476. I believe this is the Vorpostenboot VP2623 mentioned in Hinsley, 1:163, 336. The Kriegsmarine did not have a Vorpostenbootflotille 26, and no patrol boat number VP2623. Though a contemporary document refers to VP2623 as the source of cryptographic documents — probably Hinsley's source — the Royal Navy's War Diary for Home Commands (ADM 199/2203) for April 26, 1940, mentions only the trawlers and says nothing about patrol boats. Moreover, Hinsley says that VP2623 had been looted, as was the *Polares.* Nothing was found about any captures or sinkings of ships on the date in question in the following German navy war diaries: Commanding Admiral Norway, Admiral of Norwegian West Coast, Admiral of Norwegian North Coast, Admiral of Norwegian Polar Coast, Wehrmacht Command South Coast Norway, Coastal Commander Denmark, Commandant in Section West Coast Denmark.

On the *Glorious,* the antecedent events, and the effects of its loss: Beesly, *Very Special Intelligence,* 37–38; Hinsley, 1:141; Winton, *Carrier Glorious,* 165–82; Roskill, *War at Sea,* 1:194–96; Hinsley interviews. Ian Fleming's idea of seizing an Enigma from a German air rescue ship and the ensuing events are from ADM 223/463:38–39 and Wilson.

Material on Hinsley is from Hinsley interview and from Andrew, "F. H. Hinsley"; on Haines, from Hinsley, 1:274; Beesly, *Very Special Admiral,* 169, 193; CLKE 3, p. 5; and Wylie interview.

112   rotors VI and VII: Hinsley, 3:2:957. He states at 1:336 that three rotors were captured from the U-33, but that one of those captured may already have been known.

113   Herivel tip: Herivel interview; Welchman, *Hut Six Story,* 98–99; Welchman, "From Polish Bomba," 99, 107.

114   "Royal Flags Wave Kings Above": Monroe interview.

114   May 22, 1940: Hinsley, 1:109, 144.

114   83 percent: Rejewski, "Remarks on Appendix 1," 81.

115   hundred keys: Hinsley, 1:493; Bertrand, 79.

115   "Concerning directive": Bertrand, 285.

116   encouraged Naval Section: Hinsley interview.

118   Radio Cipher H, Dockyard: Morris, 115–16; M.Dv. Nr. 103.

126   "the recent recrudescence": Winston S. Churchill, *Blood, Sweat, and Tears* (New York: Putnam's, 1941), 411.

126   atmosphere not disheartened but industrious: Wylie and Hinsley interviews.

10. *In the Locked Drawer of the* Krebs

Information on the Tribal class destroyers and the *Somali* is from Brice, 7, 15–18, 228–34; Peter Hodges, 6–7, 10, 53; Wellings, 47, 53, 57, 58, 60. All details of the raid on Norway are from DEFE 2/142, which includes some information deleted from Tovey; MA:M815/47219:4.3. [1941]:1435; interviews with Warmington, Stuart-Menteth, Low, and Harper-Gow; and Roskill, *War at Sea,* 1:341–342. On Warmington: Warmington interview; *Who's Who, 1990; Burke's Peerage and Baronetage* 103 (1963), 2505.

11. *Kisses*

Information about Wylie, Good, Brett-Smith, and Lever and on life at Bletchley is from Good, 7; and from interviews with Good, Hilary Hinsley, Barbara Eachus, and Mavis Batey. Details about banburismus, other Hut 8 cryptanalysis, and cribs are from Andrew Hodges, 197; Morris, 112–15; and interviews with Hinsley, Good, and Monroe. Direction-finding details are from Kemp interview. Information on Thring, Winn, and the Submarine Tracking Room is from MacLachlan, 102, 107–9; Beesly, *Very Special Intelligence,* 55–58, 158, 165–66, and passim.

143 Hut 4 handled non-Enigma: Hinsley interview.
144 "Gardening," "special planting," "Squares BF2927": AIR 4/797:26A, 28A, and DEFE 3:27:ZTG/9880.
148 "who go out": Winston S. Churchill, *The Unrelenting Struggle: War Speeches* (Boston: Little, Brown, 1942), 98.

12. *A Trawler Surprised*

Information on German weather ships is primarily from PG 36742 and, on their sailings, from PG 34814–34837. Details of the planning of the attack on the *München* are from Hinsley interview. Details of the attack are from ADM 199/447; ADM 53/114202; and interviews with Warmington, Low, Wiggeshof, and Rebelein. Bremerhaven, where the *München* was worked on, was then called Wesermünde.

150 "augmented weather report": MA: M/19/36742:4.9.40.
150 U-Boat Command objected: Godt letter; Hessler, 145; Dönitz, 148.
150 October 24, *Adolf Vinnen:* PG 47109.
150 *München: Lloyd's Register of Shipping,* No. 11470.
151 Wetterkurzschlüssel: M.Dv.Nr. 443.
155 three-page report: Hinsley, 1:565–69 (original is three pages long).
156 Holland: Ludovic Kennedy, *Pursuit: The Chase and Sinking of the Bismarck* (New York: Viking, 1974), 62; Ernie Bradford, *The Mighty Hood* (London: Hodder & Stoughton, 1959), 173.
157 "Werde gejagt": PG 34833:7.5.41; DEFE 3:ZTP384.

159 "One of our patrols": *Times* (May 10, 1941), p. 4, col. 6; PG 34832:10.5.41.
160 Hitler and Raeder discussed: Germany, Oberkommando der Kriegsmarine, *Lagevorträge*, 229, 231–38.

13. *The Staff School Memory*

The references are the same as those for Chapter 1.

14. *"All This Rubbish?"*

I am grateful to Captain Hugh Wilson and Chief Gunner's Mate Thomas Kelly for reading a draft of this chapter and making extremely valuable comments and corrections.

Details of the capture of the *Lauenburg*, unless otherwise specified, are from ADM 199/430; ADM 53/14797; Kelly, diary; and interviews with Wilson, Kelly, Kennedy, Braun and Klarman. Information on Gewald is from Buhr, Gratz interviews and Mohr, passim. On Bacon, from Forster, Hinsley interviews. On Skipwith, from Wilson, Kelly interviews.

170 cryptanalysts would face delays: Hinsley interview.
170 *Lauenburg: Lloyd's Register of Shipping*, No. 10301.
175 "You don't know": Brice, 251.
182 Hinsley pleased: Hinsley interview.

15. *The Great Man Himself*

Churchill's passion for solved intercepts is detailed in "Churchill Pleads for the Intercepts," ed. David Kahn, *Cryptologia* 6 (January 1982), 47–49; Hinsley, 1:295; Gilbert, *Finest Hour*, 611–13, 814, 848–49. Aspects of his visit to Bletchley are from *Finest Hour*, 1185; Malcolm Kennedy, 439; Andrew Hodges, 205; Brown, 398; and interviews with Good, Milner-Barry, John and Mavis Batey, and Herivel.

The cryptanalysts' problems, their letter, and Denniston's removal come from Hinsley, 2:25–28, 655–57, 272–74, 279, 286, 289–90; Milner-Barry, "Action This Day," 272–76; R. A. Denniston, 116–17, 122–24; Filby, 275–76; Malcolm Kennedy, 440; Brown, 401–2; Milner-Barry, Monroe interviews. Travis is described in *Who Was Who, 1950–1959;* Malcolm Kennedy, 442; Welchman, *Hut Six Story*, 274; Brown, 397; Andrew Hodges, 177–78, 204; interviews with Milner-Barry, Twinn, and Davidson.

The story of convoy HX 155 was assembled from U.S. Navy, Navy Historical Branch, Operational Archives, Tenth Fleet Files, Convoy and Routing Section, Folder for HX 155; that archive's World War II Action Report, Commander Destroyer Division 62 (Commander Task Unit 4.1.7), Escort of Convoys HX 155 and ON 31; RG 24, Logbooks of U.S.S. *Sturdevant* and U.S.S. *Bainbridge;* BdU, KTB, 1.–30.Oktober 1941; SRMN-

033, 4–30 October 1941; Hinsley, 2:174; Rohwer, " 'Special Intelligence,' " 719; Rohwer, "Ultra and the Battle of the Atlantic," 422.

183 solution times: The solution time was calculated for each intercept in DEFE from May to August 1941 and averaged for each month.

183 reasons for July–August tonnage loss decline: Macintyre, 87, 88, 91.

184 eight bombes: Hinsley, 1:338; Welchman, *Hut Six Story,* 139.

184 Pound: Malcolm Kennedy, 439.

184 BONIFACE, ULTRA: Gilbert, *Finest Hour,* 612.

186 TRITON: Erskine, "Naval Enigma: Breaking of Heimisch and Triton," 180. Some writers use TRITON to mean the four-rotor Enigma, but this is wrong. TRITON carried U-boat messages enciphered in three-rotor Enigma well before the four-rotor machine came into service on February 1, 1942 (see, for example, PG 32137:203 and M.Dv.Nr.443g, p. 4, of 1941).

189 Alexander takes over: Good, 5–6; Andrew Hodges, 204, 227–28.

189 McVittie: Filby and Howse interviews.

190 Kriegsmarine weather cipher: BJ 5/288.

190 Archer: Howse and Wylie interviews.

191 Admiralty transmitted to Washington: copies in U.S. Navy's Operational Archives.

16. When Sailors Look for Leaks

Details of U-boat communications are from interviews with Meckel, Kuhne, and Wilde; NA:RG 165: Box 727, Folder U-118, Interrogation of Josef Hoeller, Oberfunkmaat, pp. 9, 10, 12, 17–19; SRGN 15993; SRMN-032, 98–99; Hirschfeld, 141–44; Dönitz (trans.), 231, 246.

The several investigations into German cipher security may be found in RM 7/103 at 38–39, 42, 62 (Stummel's investigations), PG 34534 (Fricke's first investigation), RM 7/121:57–61 (his second), and PG 32137 (Maertens's investigation). Measures to restore or improve security are given in PG 34534 at 143–44, 153, and in MA:M797/47357:47.

The naval grid and its encipherment are described in Erskine, unpublished study; BdU, KTB, 1.–15.September 1941, Anlage; Hinsley, 2:681; ADM 223/3:259–60.

The proposals to improve the Enigma are in MA: III M 1006/6:51–55; RM 7/108:45. For the fourth rotor and the thin reflector, see Erskine and Weierud. On the B-Dienst and its successes: Tranow interview; MacLachlan, 77; Bonatz, *Deutsche Marine-Funkaufklärung,* 80, 86, 103, 105, 174; Bonatz, *Seekrieg,* 29, 32, 33, 36; Hinsley, 2:634–36; Kahn, *Hitler's Spies,* 212–22; Dönitz letter, January 27, 1970.

198 "main cipher method": M.Dv.Nr.32/3 (1941), 2.

198 "Equipping with the Enigma": PG 47006:Bericht über den Nachrichtendienst am 4.3.41.

198 Navy monitored, required reports: PG 34455F:19.Januar 1939, 28.November 1939; MA:M797/47357:50–51, 8. Mai 1941; Kleikamp, 15; PG 47364:26.Mai 1941 and 29.April 1941.

199 Prien, *Graf Spee:* RM 7/103:36, 41.

205 5 October 1941: Erskine, "Naval Enigma: Breaking of Heimisch and Triton," 180.

205 U-570: ADM 199/2058:38. BdU, KTB, 5 November 1941, on the surrender of the U-570, has nothing about ciphers.

207 Desk IVa: Kahn, *Codebreakers,* 456, 458.

207 "despite great stresses": PG 32137:186.

209 rise in traffic volume: Rohwer, "Ultra and the Battle of the Atlantic," 429, 432.

209 January 1, 1943: Rohwer and Jäckel, 125.

210 February 1, 1942: Hinsley, 2:179.

213 sixty times better, "unimaginable": RM 7/121:60.

17. *Blackout '42*

214 recover the wiring of the 4th rotor: Hinsley, 2:747.

214 cryptanalysts apprehensive: Wylie interview.

214 "the picture": Hinsley, 2:230.

214 considerable knowledge: Beesly, 111–12.

215 14,000 per month: Hinsley, 2:29.

215 radio fingerprinting, TINA: SRH-368, 10.

215 "working fiction": Beesly, 113.

215 direction-finding: Mitchell interview.

216 three TRITON keys: Hinsley, 2:228.

216 one of ten, one of three: Rohwer, "Ultra and the Battle of the Atlantic," 432, 435.

217 600,000, 2,600,000: Roskill, *War at Sea,* 1:618, 2:486.

217 seventeen days: Hinsley, 2:228.

217 fears grew: Hinsley, 2:168–69, 548.

217 "a little more," "the one campaign": Hinsley, 2:548.

18. *The George Cross*

Details of the U-559, its cruises, and its captain are from PG 30594; Rohwer, *Axis Submarine Successes;* NA:RG 165:G-2 Captured Personnel and Material Branch: Enemy POW Interrogation File (NIS-Y): German Prisoners at Byron Hot Springs: Albert Müller, 23881. Details of the *Petard,* its captain and crew, and the attack on the U-559 are from ADM 199/ 2060:44–45; ADM 1/14526; Connell, passim, esp. 65–71; Thornton (unpublished), passim. In a letter of October 8, 1989, Connell wrote that he and several other members of the crew of the *Petard* to whom he has shown this file agreed that some statements in it, made several weeks or months after the sinking of the U-559, confuse this incident with the similar boarding of the Italian submarine *Uarsciek*. The *Petard* came along-side the *Uarsciek* but stayed perhaps a hundred yards away from the U-559. I have therefore eliminated from my account all references to the U-559's closing with the *Petard*.

218   U-boats to Mediterranean: Dönitz, 158, 199; Germany, Oberkommando der Kriegsmarine, *Lagevorträge*, 409.

218   "decisive area": Germany, Oberkommando, 302.

226   "It's out": Wylie interview.

227   "It's come out": Monroe interview.

227   four-letter indicators: Hinsley, 2:750.

227   Beesly thrilled: Beesly, *Very Special Intelligence,* 152.

227   position of fifteen U-boats: DEFE 3:705:ZTPGU 1; Erskine, "Naval Enigma: The Breaking of Heimisch and Triton," 120.

227   sinkings halved: Roskill, *War at Sea*, 2:486.

19. Enter the Americans

Details about interception and direction-finding come from Mitchell interview. Information about the Bletchley bombes is from interviews with Herd, Milner-Barry, Monroe, and Stewart; Payne, 9–16; "Breaking Enigma"; Hinsley, 1:338, 2:748, 750; Welchman, *Hut Six Story,* 141, 144, 147. Details about Hut 8 and cribs are from interviews with Wylie, Amys, and Hinsley; Deavours and Kruh, "Turing Bombe." Information about the Hut 4 watches are from interviews with Forster, Ettinghausen, and Eytan.

The background to the British-American exchange of cryptanalytic information may be found in Hall and Wrigley, 358–63, 375–81; Hinsley, 2:55; Ronald W. Clark, *Tizard* (Cambridge, Mass.: M.I.T. Press, 1965), 248–71. Cryptanalysis is specifically mentioned in NA:RG 165: War Plans Division 4340: September 9, 1940. The story of the trip of the four American cryptanalysts comes from Rosen interview; Currier, untitled memoir; Weeks letter; SRH-145, 002–004; ADM 199/447:Operation Parcel; ADM 53/114501:January 24–February 6, 1941.

The operation of the American naval cryptanalysis and its cooperation with the British come from interviews with Joseph Eachus, W. V. Quine and Marjorie Quine, Prendergrass, McMahan, and Bartelmez; Hinsley, 2:56; Beesly, *Very Special Intelligence,* 108–10; "U.S. Navy Communication Intelligence Organization Liaison and Collaboration 1941–1945," SRH 197 (October 8, 1945), reprinted in *NCVA* [Naval Cryptologic Veterans Association] *Cryptolog* 5 (Winter 1984), 5–11.

235   U.S. Army contingent: Parrish, 106.

235   6812th, two to three times as many solutions, U-boat cipher: Stewart interview.

237   20 percent, 3 percent: Safford, 12.

237   exchanging direction-finding: Safford, 4.

238 former girls' school: "Rochefort Affair: Admiral Stone Comments," *NCVA Cryptolog* 6 (Fall 1984), 6.
238 "The Star of Suez": SRMN-032,001.
239 high-speed bombes; Atha, 332–36.
242 daily U-boat summary: W. V. Quine interview.
242 naval Enigma read to end of war: Hinsley, 2:751–52, 552. The date of May 24, 1943, at 2:667 should be May 24, 1945 (Hinsley).
242 solutions to Knowles: Knowles, 445.
243 Secret Room: SRMN-038.
244 "were not as smart": Smith-Hutton, 396–97.
244 Convoy & Routing chart: Norgaard interview.

20. SC 127

Information on the convoy's composition, escorts, and routing is from U.S. Navy, Naval Historical Center, Operational Archives, Tenth Fleet Files, Convoy & Routing Section, Convoy Folder SC 127, and from ADM 199/580, supplemented by National Archives of Canada, Record Group 24, Vol. 11335, File C-8280, SC 127. All Allied estimates of submarine locations come from SRMN-033. All U.S. solutions of German naval messages come from SRGN. All information about German intelligence and activity comes from BdU, KTB, under the appropriate dates. Weather conditions are from the log of H.C.M.S. *Dundas*.

Food and shipping problems are from Behrens, 201, 312, 328, 331, 334, 342, 345–46; Hammond, 1:261–68, 2:792; Great Britain, Ministry of Food, *How Britain Was Fed in War Time*, 58–59.

245 April 16 sailing details: National Archives of Canada, Record Group 24, vols. 12015, 12042.
245 92, 111, 29, 50, 95: Morison, 1:410.
248 three days behind: DEFE 3.
248 U.S. report for April 16: SRMN-033:2074.
248 operational research: Blackett; Waddington; Schofield, 161.
249 63 boats operating: BdU, KTB, April 16, 1943.
250 grid bigrams: comparison of SRGN 15945 and DEFE 3:716:131, in which the British message gives the enciphered coordinates and the American message the solved ones.
251 no messages solved for Monday: SRGN 16029 is a message of April 18, SRGN 16030 is a message of April 20.
251 "Since this position": BdU, KTB, April 18, 1943.
252 Katyn, a German Dunkirk, white hair: [Germany], Reichssicherheitshauptamt, Amt III, *Meldungen aus dem Reich*, ed. Heinz Boberach (Neuwied: Luchterhand, 1965), Nr. 377.
252 In the United States: *New York Times*, April 21, 1943.
257 HX234: Hinsley, 2:568.

21. The Cavity Magnetron Clue

259   "We can no longer rely": Hinsley, 2:563.

259   5 to 10 percent: Rohwer, "Einfluss," 359.

259   "In the Atlantic": BdU, KTB, May 24, 1943.

260   no convoys: Hessler, §301.

260   April 18: BdU, KTB, April 18, 1943.

260   Maertens exculpated Enigma: RM 7/107

261   regional key nets; RM 7/108:44; BdU, KTB, February 3, 1943.

261   new type of radar: Reuter, 113–14.

261   "With the exception" BdU, KTB, March 5, 1943.

261   "the enemy has": BdU, KTB, April 27, 1943.

262   "For some time": BdU, KTB, April 27, 1943.

262   Maertens, Stummel: Walter Lohmann and Hans H. Hildebrand, *Die Deutsche Kriegsmarine 1939–1945: Gliederung, Einsatz, Stellenbesetzung* (Bad Neuheim: Podzun, 1956), 3:320, 386.

262   "had, on the basis": MA: III M 1006/4:147.

262   telling the Japanese ambassador: NA:RG 457:Diplomatic "Magic" Summaries: 24 September 1943:2.

262   basic cryptosecurity principle: MA: III M 1006-/4:147.

263   Naval Cypher No. 5: Hinsley, 2:636–38.

264   "The two main": MA: III M 1006/6:169.

264   Adressbuch: Hinsley, 2:552, 681–82.

264   less than half avoided: Hinsley, 2:555.

22. The U-Tankers

Information on the attacks on the U-66 and U-117 comes from U.S. Navy, Naval Historical Center, Operational Archives, World War II Action Report, Commander in Chief, U.S. Atlantic Fleet, Hunter-Killer Operations, Serial 001020, Report Nos. 1-43 and 2-43, Task Group 21.14. Other details come from SRGN; SRMN-033; PG 30063; BdU, KTB; the deck log of the U.S.S. *Card;* and Lundeberg.

265   milch cows: Werner Rahn, "Weiträumige deutsche U-Boot-Operationen 1942/43 und ihre logistische Unterstützung durch U-Tanker," unpublished paper.

266   adamant refusal: Hinsley, 3:1:212–13.

266   "we should not risk": Hinsley, 2:549.

266   "if our Z information": Hinsley, 2:549.

267   U-118: Y'Blood, 55–59.

23. The Reckoning

Calculations of the value of codebreaking are from SRH 368 and Rohwer, "Einfluss," 359–61.

Bibliography

Books and Articles

Allason, Rupert [Nigel West]. *The Sigint Secrets: The Signals Intelligence War, 1900 to Today, Including the Persecution of Gordon Welchman*. New York: Morrow, 1988.

Andrew, Christopher. "F. H. Hinsley and the Cambridge Moles: Two Patterns of Intelligence Recruitment." In *Diplomacy and Intelligence During the Second World War: Essays in Honour of F. H. Hinsley,* ed. Richard Langhorne, pp. 22–40. Cambridge: Cambridge University Press, 1985.

―――. *Secret Service: The Making of the British Intelligence Community*. London: Heinemann, 1985.

Andrew, Christopher, and Jeremy Noakes, eds. *Intelligence and International Relations 1900–1945*. Exeter Studies in History, 15. Exeter: University of Exeter, 1987.

Arnold, Philip M. "A German Code Book." *Cryptologia* 3 (October 1979), 243–45.

Atha, Robert I. "Bombe! I Could Hardly Believe It!" *Cryptologia* 9 (October 1985), 332–36.

Bauer, [Hermann]. *Das Unterseeboot: Seine Bedeutung als Teil eine Flotte — Seine Stellung im Völkerrecht — Seine Kriegsverwendung — Seine Zukunft*. Berlin: Mittler & Sohn, 1931.

Beesly, Patrick. "Das Operational Intelligence Centre der britischen Admiralität und die Schlacht im Atlantik." In Rohwer and Jäckel, pp. 133–47.

―――. *Room 40: British Naval Intelligence 1914–18*. London: Hamish Hamilton, 1982.

―――. "Special Intelligence and the Battle of the Atlantic: The British View." In Love, ed., pp. 413–19.

―――. *Very Special Admiral: The Life of Admiral J. H. Godfrey, CB*. London: Hamish Hamilton, 1980.

―――. *Very Special Intelligence: The Story of the Admirality's Operational Intelligence Centre, 1939–1945*. London: Hamish Hamilton, 1971.

———. "Who Was the Third Man at Pyry?" *Cryptologia* 11 (April 1987), 78–80.

Behrens, C[atherine] B. A. *Merchant Shipping and the Demands of War.* History of the Second World War: United Kingdom Civil Series. London: Her Majesty's Stationery Office, 1955.

Bertrand, Gustave. *Enigma, ou la plus grande énigme de la guerre 1939–1945.* Paris: Plon, 1973.

Blackett, P. M. S. "Operational Research: Recollections of Problems Studied, 1940–1945." In *Brassey's Annual: The Armed Forces Year-Book, 1953,* pp. 88–106. London: Clowes, n.d.

Bloch, Gilbert, *Enigma avant Ultra (1930–1940).* Texte définitif. Paris: privately printed, 1988. C. A. Deavours translated an earlier version as "Enigma Before Ultra," *Cryptologia* 11 (July 1987), 142–55, and (October 1987), 227–34.

Böddeker, Gunter. *Die Boote im Netz: Der dramatische Bericht über Karl Dönitz und das Schicksal der deutschen U-Boot-Waffe.* Bergisch Gladbach: Gustav Lubbe, 1981.

Bonatz, Heinz. *Die Deutsche Marine-Funkaufklärung 1914–1945.* Beiträge zur Wehrforschung, XX/XXI (Arbeitskreis für Wehrforschung). Darmstadt: Wehr and Wissen, 1970.

———. *Seekrieg im Äther: Die Leistungen der Marine-Funkaufklärung 1939–1945.* Arbeitskreis für Wehrforschung und Bibliothek für Zeitgeschichte. Herford: Mittler, 1981.

Branicki, Oscar. "Wetterdienstunternehmungen während des Zweiten Weltkrieges." *Truppenpraxis* 27 (August 1983), 594–97.

"Breaking Enigma." *After the Battle* no. 37 (1982), 1–8.

Brennecke, Jochen. *Die Wende im U-Boot-Krieg: Ursachen und Folgen 1939–1943.* Herford: Koehler, 1984.

Brice, Martin H. *The Tribals: Biography of a Destroyer Class.* Shepperton, Surrey: Ian Allan, 1971.

Brown, Anthony Cave. *"C": The Secret Life of Sir Stewart Graham Menzies, Spymaster to Winston Churchill.* New York: Macmillan, 1987.

Calvocoressi, Peter. *Top Secret Ultra.* New York: Pantheon, 1980.

Churchill, Randolph, then Martin Gilbert. *Winston S. Churchill.* 8 vols. plus documentary vols. Boston: Houghton Mifflin, 1966–1988. Vol. 6, *Finest Hour, 1939–1941* (1983); vol. 7, *Road to Victory, 1941–1945* (1986).

Clarke, William F. "Government Code and Cypher School." I: "Its Foundation and Development with Special Reference to Its Naval Side," *Cryptologia* 11 (October 1987), 219–26; II: "The Years Between," *Cryptologia* 12 (January 1988), 52–58; III: "Bletchley Park 1941–1945" (April 1988), 90–97.

Clössner. "Die Meteorologie im Weltkriege." *Velhagen & Klasings Monatsheft* 32 (February 1918), 154–63.

Connell, G. G. *Fighting Destroyer: The Story of HMS Petard.* London: William Kimber, 1976.

[Curzon of Kedleston, Marquess.] "The Government Code and Cypher

School: A Memorandum by Lord Curzon," ed. Keith Jeffrey. *Intelligence and National Security* 1 (September 1986), 454–58.

Deavours, C. A. "The Black Chamber: How the British Broke Enigma." *Cryptologia* 4 (July 1980), 129–32.

———. "The Black Chamber: La Méthode des Bâtons." *Cryptologia* 4 (October 1980), 240–47.

———. *Breakthrough '32: The Polish Solution of the Enigma.* Laguna Hills, Calif.: Aegean Park Press, 1988.

Deavours, Cipher A., and Louis Kruh. *Machine Cryptography and Modern Cryptanalysis.* Dedham, Mass.: Artech House, 1985.

———. "The Turing Bombe: Was It Enough?" *Cryptologia* 14 (October 1990), 331–49.

Deavours, Cipher A., and James Reeds. "The Enigma. Part I: Historical Perspectives." *Cryptologia* 1 (October 1977), 381–91. (No Part II was published.)

Denning, Norman. "Erfolge und Misserfolge bei der Nutzung von Aufklärungserkenntnissen: Beispiele aus meiner Erfahrung." In Rohwer and Jäckel, pp. 265–99.

Denniston, A. G. "The Government Code and Cypher School Between the Wars." *Intelligence and National Security* 1 (January 1986), 48–70.

Denniston, R[obin] A. "The Professional Career of A. G. Denniston." In *British and American Approaches to Intelligence,* ed. K. G. Robertson, pp. 104–29. London: Macmillan, 1987.

Dönitz, Karl. *Zehn Jahre und Zwanzig Tage.* Frankfurt am Main: Bernard & Graefe, 1957. English translation: *Memoirs: Ten Years and Twenty Days,* trans. R. H. Stevens. Cleveland: World, 1959.

Douglas, W. A. B., and Jürgen Rohwer. " 'The Most Thankless Task' Revisited: Convoys, Escorts, and Radio Intelligence in the Western Atlantic, 1941–1943." In *The RCN in Retrospect, 1910–1968,* ed. James A. Boutilier, pp. 187–234. Vancouver: University of British Columbia Press, 1982.

Erskine, Ralph. "Naval Enigma: The Breaking of Heimisch and Triton." *Intelligence and National Security* 3 (January 1988), 162–83.

———. "Naval Enigma: A Missing Link." *International Journal of Intelligence and Counterintelligence* 3 (Winter 1989), 493–508.

———. "U-Boats, Homing Signals and HFDF." *Intelligence and National Security* 2 (April 1987), 324–30.

———, ed. "From the Archives: GC and CS Mobilizes 'Men of the Professor Type.' " *Cryptologia* 10 (January 1986), 50–59.

———, ed. "U-Boat HF WT Signalling." *Intelligence and National Security* 2 (April 1987), 324–30.

Erskine, Ralph, and Gilbert Bloch. "Enigma: The Dropping of the Double Encipherment." *Cryptologia* 10 (July 1986), 134–41.

Erskine, Ralph, and Frode Weierud. "Naval Enigma: M4 and Its Rotors." *Cryptologia* 11 (October 1987), 235–44.

Farago, Ladislas. *The Tenth Fleet.* New York: Ivan Obolensky, 1962.

Ferris, John. "Whitehall's Black Chamber: British Cryptology and the

Government Code and Cypher School, 1919–1929." *Intelligence and National Security* 2 (January 1987), 54–91.

Filby, P. William. "Bletchley Park and Berkeley Street." *Intelligence and National Security* 3 (April 1988), 272–84.

Fischer, Gerald J. *A Statistical Summary of Shipbuilding Under the U.S. Maritime Commission During World War II.* Historical Reports of War Administration: United States Maritime Commission, no. 2. N.p., 1949.

Fitzgerald, Penelope. *The Knox Brothers.* New York: Coward, McCann & Geoghegan, 1977.

Gaj, Krzysztof. *Szyfr Enigmy: Metody Złamania.* Warsaw: Wydawnictwa Komunikacji i Lacznosci, 1989. Portions translated by Christopher Kasparek.

Garlinski, Jozef. *The Enigma War.* New York: Scribner's, 1979.

[Germany] Marine-Archiv. *Der Krieg zur See,* ed. E. v. Mantey. Berlin: Mittler, 1929–1964. Subseries *Der Krieg in der Nordsee,* vols. 2 (1922), 3 (1923), 4 (1924), by O. Groos; vol. 7 (1964) by Walter Gladisch. Subseries *Der Krieg in der Ostsee,* vol. 1 (1922) by Rudolph Firle.

[Germany] Oberkommando der Kriegsmarine. *Lagevorträge des Oberbefehlshabers der Kriegsmarine vor Hitler.* Arbeitskreis für Wehrforschung. Ed. Gerhard Wagner. Munich: Lehmann, 1972.

Giessler, Helmuth. *Der Marine-Nachrichten- und -Ortungsdienst: Technische Entwicklung und Kriegserfahrungen.* Wissenschaftliche Berichte (Arbeitskreis für Wehrforschung), 10. Munich: Lehmann, 1971.

Gilbert, Martin. See Churchill, Randolph.

Good, I. J. "Early Work on Computers at Bletchley." NPL Report Com Sci 82, September 1976. N.p.: National Physical Laboratory, Division of Computer Science, 1976.

[Great Britain] Central Statistical Office. *Statistical Digest of the War.* London: His Majesty's Stationery Office, 1951.

[Great Britain: Ministry of Food.] *How Britain Was Fed in War Time: Food Control, 1939–1945.* London: His Majesty's Stationery Office, 1946.

Gröner, Erich. *Die deutschen Kriegsschiffe 1815–1945.* 2 vols. Munich: Lehmanns, 1966–1968.

Hackmann, Willem. *Seek & Strike: Sonar, Anti-Submarine Warfare and the Royal Navy, 1914–1954.* London: Her Majesty's Stationery Office, 1984.

Hall, H[essel] Duncan. *North American Supply.* History of the Second World War: United Kingdom Civil Series. London: Her Majesty's Stationery Office, 1955.

Hall, H[essel] Duncan, and C. C. Wrigley. *Studies of Overseas Supply.* History of the Second World War: United Kingdom Civil Series. London: Her Majesty's Stationery Office, 1956.

Hammant, Thomas. "The *Magdeburg* Incident: Russian Intercept and Cryptanalytic Efforts in World War I." *Cryptologia* 8 (April 1984), 18–21.

Hammond, R[ichard] J[ames]. *Food.* History of the Second World War:

United Kingdom Civil Series. 3 vols. London: His Majesty's Stationery Office, 1951–1962.

Hepp, Leo. "Die Chiffriermaschine 'ENIGMA.' " *F-Flagge* (1978), 13–23.

[Hessler, Günter.] Ministry of Defence (Navy). *German Naval History: The U-Boat War in the Atlantic, 1939–1945*. Facsimile ed., introduction by Andrew J. Withers. 3 vols. in 1. London: Her Majesty's Stationery Office, 1989.

Hiley, Nicholas. "The Strategic Origins of Room 40." *Intelligence and National Security* 2 (April 1987), 245–73.

Hillgruber, Andreas, and Gerhard Hümmelchen. *Chronik des Zweiten Weltkrieges*. Arbeitskreis für Wehrforschung. Frankfurt am Main: Bernard & Graefe, 1966.

Hinsley, F. H., with E. E. Thomas, C. F. G. Ransom, and R. C. Knight. *British Intelligence in the Second World War: Its Influence on Strategy and Operations*. 3 vols. in 4 parts. Cambridge: Cambridge University Press, 1979–1988.

Hirschfeld, Wolfgang. *Feindfahrten: Das Logbuch eines U-Boot-Funkers*. Munich: Heyne, 1982.

Hodges, Andrew. *Alan Turing: The Enigma*. New York: Simon and Schuster, 1983.

Hodges, Peter. *Tribal Class Destroyers: Royal Navy and Commonwealth*. London: Almark, 1971.

Holzapfel, Rupert. "Deutsche Polarforschung 1939/45." *Polarforschung* 3 (1951–55), 85–97.

Howarth, Patrick. *Intelligence Chief Extraordinary: The Life of the Ninth Duke of Portland*. London: Bodley Head, 1986.

Jeffery, Keith, and Alan Sharp. "Lord Curzon and Secret Intelligence." In Andrew and Noakes, 103–26.

Jeschke, Hubert. *U-Boottaktik: Zur deutschen U-boottaktik 1900–1945*. Einzelschriften zur militärischen Geschichte des Zweiten Weltkrieges, 9. Freiburg: Rombach, 1972.

Kahn, David. *The Codebreakers: The Story of Secret Writing*. New York: Macmillan, 1967.

———. *Hitler's Spies: German Military Intelligence in World War II*. New York: Macmillan, 1978.

Kennedy, Ludovic. *Sub-Lieutenant: A Personal Record of the War at Sea*. London: Batsford, 1942.

[Kennedy, Malcolm D.] "From Broadway House to Bletchley Park: The Diary of Captain Malcolm Kennedy, 1934–1946," ed. John Ferris. *Intelligence and National Security* 4 (July 1989), 421–50.

Kleikamp, [Gustav]. *Der Einfluss der Funkaufklärung auf die Seekriegsführung in der Nordsee, 1914–1918*. Kiel: Leitung der Führergehilfeausbildung der Marine, 1934.

Knowles, Kenneth A. "Ultra and the Battle of the Atlantic: The American View." In Love, ed., pp. 444–49.

Korbel, Josef. *Poland Between East and West: Soviet and German Diplomacy*

Toward Poland, 1919–1933. Princeton: Princeton University Press, 1963.

Kozaczuk, Wladyslaw. *Enigma: How the German Cipher Machine Was Broken, and How It Was Read by the Allies in World War II.* Ed. and trans. Christopher Kasparek. Frederick, Md.: University Publications of America, 1984.

Kruh, Louis. "Why Was Safford Pessimistic about Breaking the German Enigma Cipher Machine in 1942?" *Cryptologia* 14 (July 1990), 253–57.

Lenton, H. T. *German Submarines.* Navies of the Second World War. 2 vols. Garden City, N.Y.: Doubleday, 1965.

Levine, Jack. *United States Cryptographic Patents, 1861–1981.* Terre Haute, Ind.: Cryptologia, 1983.

Lewin, Ronald. *Ultra Goes to War: The First Account of World War II's Greatest Secret Based on Official Documents.* New York: McGraw-Hill, 1978.

Lewis, R. P. W. "The Use by the Meteorological Office of Deciphered German Meteorological Data During the Second World War." *The Meteorological Magazine* 114 (April 1983), 113–18.

Listowel, Judith, Countess of. *Crusader in the Secret War.* London: Christopher John, 1952.

Lloyd's Register of Shipping, July 1, 1939 –June 30, 1940. London, 1939.

Love, Robert William, Jr., ed. *Changing Interpretations and New Sources in Naval History: Papers from the Third United States Naval Academy History Symposium.* New York: Garland, 1980.

Macintyre, Donald. *The Battle of the Atlantic.* New York: Macmillan, 1961.

MacLachlan, Donald. *Room 39: Naval Intelligence in Action, 1939–1945.* London: Weidenfeld and Nicolson, 1968.

Mäkelä, Matti E. *Das Geheimnis der "Magdeburg"; Die Geschichte des Kleinen Kreuzers und die Bedeutung seiner Signalbuch im Ersten Weltkrieg.* Koblenz: Bernard & Graefe, 1984.

Mallmann Showell J[ak] P. *U-Boats Under the Swastika: An Introduction to German Submarines 1935–1945.* New York: Arco, 1974.

March, Edgar J. *British Destroyers: A History of Development, 1892–1953.* London: Seelkey Service, 1961.

Meckel, Hans. "Die Funkführung der deutschen U-Boote und die Rolle des xB-Dienstes (deutscher Marine-Funkentzifferungsdienst)." In Rohwer und Jäckel, pp. 121–32.

Middlebrook, Martin. *Convoy: The Battle for Convoys SC 122 and HX 229.* London: Allen Lane, 1976.

Milner-Barry, Stuart. " 'Action This Day': The Letter from Bletchley Park Cryptanalysts to the Prime Minister, 21 October 1941." *Intelligence and National Security* 1 (May 1986), 272–76.

———. "C. H. O'D. Alexander — A Personal Memoir." In *The Best Games of C. H. O'D. Alexander,* ed. Harry Golombek and Bill Hertston, pp. 1–9. Oxford: Oxford University Press, 1976.

Mohr, Adrian. *Fischfang ist Not: Freuden und Leiden der deutschen Hochsee-fischerei.* Leipzig: Koehler & Amelang, 1926.

Monsarrat, Nicholas. *The Cruel Sea.* New York: Knopf, 1952.

Morison, Samuel Eliot. *History of United States Naval Operations in World War II.* 15 vols. Boston: Little, Brown, 1947–1962. Vol. 1, *The Battle of the Atlantic, September 1939–May 1943* (1947); vol. 10, *The Atlantic Battle Won, May 1943–May 1945* (1956).

Morris, Christopher. "Ultra's Poor Relations." *Intelligence and National Security* 1 (January 1986), 111–22.

Muggeridge, Malcolm. *Chronicles of Wasted Time. Chronicle 2: The Infernal Grove.* New York: Morrow, 1974.

Mulligan, Timothy. "The German Navy Evaluates Its Cryptographic Security, October 1941." *Military Affairs* 49 (April 1985), 75–79.

———, ed. *Records Relating to U-Boat Warfare, 1939–1945.* Guides to the Microfilmed Records of the German Navy, 1850–1945, 2. Washington: National Archives and Records Administration, 1985.

Navarre, Henri, et al. *Le Service de Renseignements 1871–1944.* Paris: Plon, 1978.

Padfield, Peter. *Dönitz: The Last Führer — Portrait of a Nazi War Leader.* London: Gollancz, 1984.

Paillole, Paul. *Notre Espion Chez Hitler.* Collection "Vécu." Paris: Laffont, 1985.

Parrish, Thomas. *The Ultra Americans: The U.S. Role in Breaking the Nazi Codes.* New York: Stein & Day, 1986.

Pate, Elbert W. "Weather and the War in Europe." *United States Naval Institute Proceedings* 68 (March 1942), 327–32.

Payne, Diana. "My Secret Life with Ultra." *After the Battle* no. 37 (1982), 9–16.

Payton-Smith, D[erek] J[oseph]. *Oil: A Study of War-time Policy and Administration.* History of the Second World War: United Kingdom Civil Series. London: Her Majesty's Stationery Office, 1971.

Price, Alfred. *Aircraft versus Submarine: The Evolution of the Anti-Submarine Aircraft, 1912–1980.* 2d ed. London: Jane's, 1980.

———. *Instruments of Darkness: The History of Electronic Warfare.* New ed. London: Macdonald and Jane's, 1977.

Quine, W. V. *The Time of My Life: An Autobiography.* Cambridge, Mass.: MIT Press, 1985.

Rejewski, Marian. "How Polish Mathematicians Deciphered the Enigma." *Annals of the History of Computing* 3 (July 1981), 213–34.

———. "The Mathematical Solution of the Enigma Cipher." In Kozaczuk, pp. 272–91.

———. "Remarks on Appendix 1 to *British Intelligence in the Second World War* by F. H. Hinsley." Trans. Christopher Kasparek. *Cryptologia* 6 (January 1982), 75–83.

———. "Summary of Our Methods for Reconstructing Enigma and Reconstructing Daily Keys, and of German Efforts to Frustrate Those Methods." In Kozaczuk, pp. 241–45.

Renauld, P. "La Machine à chiffrer 'Enigma.'" *Bulletin Trimestriel de l'Association des Amis de l'École supérieure de guerre* no. 78 (1978), 41–60.

Reuter, Frank. *Funkmess: Die Entwicklung und der Einsatz des RADAR-Verfahrs in Deutschland bis zum Ende des Zweiten Weltkrieges.* Wissenschaftliche Abhandlungen der Arbeitsgemeinschaft für Forschung des Landes Nordrhein-Westfalen, 42. Opladen: Westdeutscher Verlag, 1971.

Ribadeau-Dumas, L[ouis]. "Essai historique du chiffre. 4e partie (1919–1939)," *Bulletin de l'Association des Réservistes du chiffre* no. 3, n.s. (1975), 19–33; "5e partie (La Guerre 1939–1945)," *Bulletin* no. 4, n.s. (1976), 33–47.

———. "La Machine à chiffrer Enigma (suite)." *Bulletin Trimestriel de l'Association des Amis de l'École supérieure de guerre* no. 82 (1979), 33–37.

Rohwer, Jürgen. "Die Auswirkungen der deutschen und britischen Funkaufklärung auf die Geleitzugoperationen im Nordatlantik." In Rohwer and Jäckel, pp. 167–200.

———. *Axis Submarine Successes 1939–1945.* Introductory material trans. John A. Broadwin. Annapolis: Naval Institute Press, 1983.

———. *The Critical Convoy Battles of March 1943: The Battle for HX229/SC122.* London: Ian Allan, 1977.

———. "Der Einfluss der alliierten Funkaufklärung auf den Verlauf des zweiten Weltkrieges." *Vierteljahrshefte für Zeitgeschichte* 27 (1979), 325–69.

———. "Die Funkführung der deutschen U-Boote im zweiten Weltkrieg. I: Land-Peilung und Bordradar," *Wehrtechnik* (September 1969), 324–28; "II: Funkpeilung von Bord" (Oktober 1969), 360–62, 364.

———. "The Operational Use of 'Ultra' in the Battle of the Atlantic." In Andrew and Noakes, pp. 275–92.

———. "Radio Intelligence in the Battle of the Atlantic." In *Clio Goes Spying: Eight Essays on the History of Intelligence,* ed. Wilhelm Agrell and Bo Huldt, pp. 85–107. Lund Studies in International History, 17. Malmö: Scandinavian University Books, 1983.

———. "La radiotélégraphie, auxiliaire du Commandement dans la guerre sous-marine." *Revue d'Histoire de la Deuxième Guerre Mondiale* 18 (January 1968), 41–66.

———. " 'Special Intelligence' und die Geleitzugsteuerung im Herbst 1941." *Marine-Rundschau* 75 (November 1978), 711–19.

———. "Ultra and the Battle of the Atlantic: the German View." In Love, ed., 420–43.

———. " 'Ultra,' xB-Dienst, und 'Magic.' " *Marine-Rundschau* 76 (October 1979), 637–48.

Rohwer, Jürgen, and G. Hümmelchen. *Chronology of the War at Sea, 1939–1945.* 2 vols. Trans. Derek Masters. New York: Arco, 1972–1974.

Rohwer, Jürgen, and Eberhard Jäckel, eds. *Die Funkaufklärung und ihre*

Rolle im Zweiten Weltkrieg. Eine internationale Tagung in Bonn-Bad Godesberg und Stuttgart vom 15.–18. November 1978. Stuttgart: Motorbuch, 1979.

Roskill, S. W. *The Secret Surrender.* London: Collins, 1959.

———. *The War at Sea 1939–1945.* History of the Second World War: United Kingdom Military Series. 3 vols. in 4 parts. London: Her Majesty's Stationery Office, 1954–1961.

Safford, Laurance F. "A Brief History of Communications Intelligence in the United States." In *Listening to the Enemy: Key Documents on the Role of Communications Intelligence in the War with Japan,* ed. Ronald H. Spector, pp. 3–12. Wilmington, Del.: Scholarly Resources, 1988.

Schoenfeld, Max. "Winston Churchill as War Manager: The Battle of the Atlantic Committee, 1941." *Military Affairs* 52 (July 1988), 122–27.

Schofield, B[rian] B. "The Defeat of the U-Boats during World War II." *Journal of Contemporary History* 16 (January 1981), 119–29.

———. "Die Rolle der Trade Division der Admiralität und die Gründe für die Wende in der Schlacht im Atlantik im Frühjahr 1943." In Rohwer und Jäckel, pp. 152–66.

Sciezynski, Mieczyslaw. *Radjotelegrafja: Jako Zrodlo Wiadomosci o Nieprzyjacielu* [Radiotelegraphy as a Source of Intelligence on the Enemy]. Trans. in part by Christopher Kasparek. Przemysl: Army Corps District No. 10, 1928.

Stagg, J. M. *Forecast for Overlord: June 6, 1944.* New York: Norton, 1971.

Steinhardt, Jacinto. "The Role of Operations Research in the Navy." *United States Naval Institute Proceedings* 72 (May 1946), 649–55.

Stengers, Jean. "Enigma, the French, the Poles and the British, 1931–1940." In *The Missing Dimension: Governments and Intelligence Communities in the Twentieth Century,* ed. Christopher Andrew and David Dilks, pp.126–37. London: Macmillan, 1984.

Syrett, David. "German Meteorological Intelligence from the Arctic and North Atlantic, 1940–1945." *Mariners Mirror* 71 (August 1985), 325–33.

Terraine, John. *Business in Great Waters: The U-Boat Wars 1916–1945.* London: Leo Cooper, 1989.

Tovey, Jack C. "Raid on Military and Economic Objectives in the Lofoten Islands." *Supplement to The London Gazette of Tuesday, the 22nd of June 1948* (June 23, 1948), 3683–692.

Trenkle, Fritz. *Die deutschen Funkpeil- und Horch-Verfahren bis 1945.* Frankfurt am Main: AEG-Telefunken-Aktiengesellschaft, 1982.

Türkel, Siegfried. *Chiffrieren mit Geräten und Maschinen: Eine Einführung in die Kryptographie.* Graz: Mosers, 1927.

van der Vat, Dan. *The Atlantic Campaign: The Great Struggle at Sea 1939–1945.* London: Hodder & Stoughton, 1988.

Waddington, D. H. *O.R. in World War 2: Operational Research Against the U-Boat.* London: Elek Science, 1973.

Walle, Heinrich. "Die Anwendung der Funktelegraphie beim Einsatz deutscher U-Boote im Ersten Weltkrieg." *Revue Internationale d'Histoire Militaire* no. 53 (1985), 111–39.

Wandycz, Piotr S. *France and Her Eastern Allies, 1919–1925: French-Czechoslovak-Polish Relations from the Paris Peace Conference to Locarno.* Minneapolis: University of Minnesota Press, 1962.

———. *The Twilight of French Eastern Alliances, 1926–1936: French-Czechoslovak-Polish Relations from Locarno to the Remilitarization of the Rhineland.* Princeton: Princeton University Press, 1988.

Wark, Wesley K. *The Ultimate Enemy: British Intelligence and Nazi Germany, 1933–1939.* Cornell Studies in Security Affairs. Ithaca: Cornell University Press, 1985.

Welchman, Gordon. *The Hut Six Story: Breaking the Enigma Codes.* New York: McGraw-Hill, 1982.

———. "From Polish Bomba to British Bombe: The Birth of Ultra." *Intelligence and National Security* 1 (January 1986), 71–110.

Wellings, Joseph H. *On His Majesty's Service: Observations of the British Home Fleet from the Diary, Reports, and Letters of Joseph H. Wellings, Assistant Naval Attaché, London 1940–41,* ed. John B. Hattendorf. Naval War College, Historical Monograph Series, No. 5. Newport: Naval War College Press, 1983.

Werther, Waldemar. "Die Entwicklung der deutschen Funkschlüsselmaschinen: Die 'Enigma.' " In Rohwer and Jäckel, pp. 50–65.

Wilson, H. J. "What Should We Do with a Captured Heinkel?" *MHQ: The Quarterly Journal of Military History* 2 (Summer 1990), 22–33.

Winton, John. *Carrier Glorious: The Life and Death of an Aircraft Carrier.* London: Leo Cooper in association with Secker & Warburg, 1986.

———. *Ultra at Sea.* London: Leo Cooper, 1988.

Woytak, Richard. *On the Border of War and Peace: Polish Intelligence and Diplomacy in 1937–1939 and the Origins of the Ultra Secret.* East European Monographs, 49. Boulder, Colo.: East European Quarterly, 1979.

Y'Blood, William T. *Hunter-Killer: U.S. Escort Carriers in the Battle of the Atlantic.* Annapolis: Naval Institute Press, 1983.

Ziaja, Leon. "Kowalewski, Jan." Trans. Christopher Kasparek. *Polski Słownik Biograficzny* 14 (1968–69), 524–25.

Unpublished Works

Babbage, Dennis W. "Sillies." August 1982.

Behrens, C. E. "Evaluation of the Role of Decryption Intelligence in the Operational Phase of the Battle of the Atlantic." U.S. Navy OEG Report No. 68, 1952. SRH-368.

Colpys, G. E. "Admiralty Use of Special Intelligence in Naval Operations." In ADM 223/88.

Currier, Prescott. Untitled memoir of visit to Bletchley Park and British radio intelligence units. January 10, 1984.

Grant, Robert N. "Antisubmarine Warfare 1914–1918." Unpublished manuscript, 1987.

Habermehl, R. "Die Entwicklung des militärischen Wetterdienstes in Deutschland." Speech at Air Force Academy, Colorado, January 1961.

"History of German Met. Operations in the Arctic, 1940–1945." Naval Section, G.C.&C.S., July 17, 1945. In ADM 223/6.

Lundeberg, Philip L. "American Anti Submarine Operations in the Atlantic, May 1943–May 1945." In Naval Historical Center, Operational Archives.

Mayer, S. A. "The Breaking Up of the German Ciphering Machine 'Enigma' by the Cryptological Section in the 2nd Department of the Polish Armed Forces General Staff." May 31, 1974.

———. "Supplement to the Paper of 31.5.74: 'The Breaking Up of the German Ciphering Machine Enigma.'" December 4, 1974.

McVittie, G. C. Excerpt from memoirs and diary. 1979.

Morgan, C[harles]. "NID 9 and NID 17." In ADM 223/463.

Outerbridge, Richard. "The Role of 'Z' Intelligence in the Battle of the North Atlantic, May 1941–May 1943." Term paper, University of Toronto, Fall 1982.

Parker, Alexander. "The Impact of Special Intelligence on Atlantic Convoys SC 7, OG 65 and HX 239, October 1940 to May 1943." Senior thesis, Yale University, April 18, 1988.

"A Preliminary Analysis of the Role of Decryption Intelligence in the Operational Phase of the Battle of the Atlantic." U.S. Navy OEG [Operations Evaluation Group], Report No. 66. August 20, 1951. SRH-367.

[Rejewski, Marian.] "Enigma 1930–1940. Metodi i historia rozwiazania niemieckiego syfru maszynowego (w zarysie)" [The method and history of solving the German machine cipher (an outline)]. Portions trans. Alfred Piechowiak. n.d.

Russell, Jerry C. "Ultra and the Campaigns Against the U-Boats in World War II." U.S. Army War College, Carlisle Barracks, Pa. May 20, 1980. SRH-142.

Thornton, Mark. "U-559." n.d.

[U.S. Navy.] "Allied Communications Intelligence and the Battle of the Atlantic." 2 vols. SRH-007 and SRH-008.

Interviews

Some of these interviews were in person, some by telephone. Some persons were interviewed for earlier books.

Amys, W. Robert, Hut 8 cryptanalyst.
Babbage, Dennis, Hut 6 cryptanalyst.
Baker-Cresswell, A. Joseph, captain of the *Bulldog*.
Balme, David, head of boarding party on the U-110.
Bartelmez, Erminnie, analyst in OP-20-G.
Batey, John Keith, and Batey, Mavis Lever, British cryptanalysts.
Beesly, Patrick, officer in Submarine Tracking Room.

Bertrand, Gustave, head of French cryptologic espionage.

Birnbaum, Z. William, Polish mathematician who knew Rejewski.

Braun, Kurt, crew member of the *Lauenburg*.

Buhr, Sophie de, and Gratz, Hinrich, daughter and grandson of captain of the *Lauenburg*.

Campaigne, Howard, American cryptanalyst at Bletchley Park.

Charton, Peter, crew member of the U-110.

Davidson, John C. F., World War I Royal Navy cryptographer, subordinate of Edward Travis.

Deavours, Cipher A., Enigma historian and mathematician.

Denning, Norman, head of German intelligence in Operational Intelligence Centre.

Doniach, Nakdimon Shabbethay, Hut 10 cryptanalyst.

Dönitz, Karl, commander of U-boats.

Dunderdale, Wilfred, Paris representative of British Secret Intelligence Service.

Eachus, Joseph, U.S. cryptanalytic liaison to Hut 8.

Eachus, Barbara, administrative assistant at Bletchley Park.

Ellison, Carl, student of rotors.

Emery, Valerie, daughter of Edward Travis; worked in captured naval documents section of Bletchley Park.

Ettinghausen, A.A.E.E., Hut 4 watch head.

Eytan, Walter, head of Hut 4 watches.

Filby, William, British weather and diplomatic cryptanalyst.

Forster, Leonard, Hut 4 translator.

Good, I. Jack, Hut 8 cryptanalyst.

Harper-Gow, Leonard M., Norwegian translator on Lofotens raid.

Herd, Marjory, bombe Wren.

Herivel, John, Hut 6 cryptanalyst.

Hinsley, F. Harry, Hut 4 analyst.

Hinsley, Hilary, Hut 8 cryptanalyst.

Howse, Philip P., Hut 10 cryptanalyst.

Jedrzejewicz, Waclaw, Polish intelligence officer in 1920s.

Kelly, Thomas R., chief gunner's mate on the *Tartar*.

Kemp, Peter, head of British radio direction-finding.

Kennedy, Ludovic, sub-lieutenant on the *Tartar*.

Klarman, Georg, crew member of the *Lauenburg*.

Krailsheimer, Alban John, British field cryptanalyst.

Kühne, Helmut, chief of U-Boat Command radio room.

Lisicki, Tadeusz, Polish signals officer.

Listowel, Judith, Countess of, author of book on Jan Kowalewski.

Low, Maurice G., physician aboard the *Somali*.

Masanek, Ernst, crew member of the U-33.

McMahan, Knight, OP-20-G analyst.

Meckel, Hans, head of U-boat communications.

Milner-Barry, Stuart, deputy head of Hut 3.

Mitchell, Alice, interceptor of German naval messages.
Monroe, John, Hut 6 cryptanalyst.
Morris, Christopher, Dockyard Cipher cryptanalyst.
Norgaard, Rollo N., U.S. naval convoy and routing officer.
Quine, Willard Van Orman, and Quine, Marjorie Boynton, head analyst and assistant in OP-20-G.
Prendergrass, James T., OP-20-G cryptanalyst.
Rebelein, Fritz, crew member of the *München*.
Rosen, Leo, accompanied PURPLE machine to Britain.
Rottmann, Heinz, officer on the U-33.
Schaerf, Henry M., Polish mathematician who knew Rejewski.
Scherer, Helmut, radioman on weather ship *Sachsen*.
Stewart, Mortimer, head of U.S. Army bombe unit at Bletchley Park.
Stuart-Menteth, Henry A., officer on the *Somali*.
Tischler, Rosamond, Gordon Welchman's daughter.
Tranow, Wilhelm, head cryptanalyst for the German navy.
Twinn, Peter, British cryptanalyst.
Warmington, Sir Marshall, boarded the *Krebs* and the *München*.
Welchman, Gordon, head of Hut 6.
White, David, U.S. naval direction finder.
Wiggeshof, Heinrich (Henry), radioman on the *München*.
Wilde, Heinz, radioman of the U-110.
Wilson, T. Hugh P., head of party boarding the *Lauenburg*.
Wylie, Shaun, Hut 8 cryptanalyst.
Zygalski, Henry, Polish cryptanalyst.

Author's Correspondence

Becker, Johannes, officer on U-33.
Budde, Wilhelm, German naval radio intelligence officer.
Connell, G. G., officer on the *Petard*, author of *Fighting Destroyer*.
Currier, Prescott H., accompanied PURPLE machine to Britain.
Dresky, Hans-Wilhelm von, nephew of captain of the U-33.
Erskine, Ralph, historian of naval Enigma.
Gewald, Carl-Heinz, son of *Lauenburg* captain.
Good, I. Jack, Hut 8 cryptanalyst.
Godt, Eberhardt, deputy to Admiral Dönitz.
Hawker, Pat, British radio interceptor.
Heimsoeth, Dr. Heinz, cousin of Arthur Scherbius, younger brother of Rudolph Heimsoeth.
Heimsoeth, Dr. Helmuth, son of Heinz Heimsoeth.
Hepp, Leo, German army signals officer.
Rejewski, Marian, solver of the Enigma.
Ribadeau-Dumas, Louis, French cryptologist.
Ridder, Karl-Heinz, crew member of the U-559.
Rohwer, Jürgen, naval historian.

Szameitat, Bernhard, crew member of the U-559.
Tyner, Clarence, owner of a commercial Enigma.
Weeks, Robert H., accompanied PURPLE machine to Britain.

German Cryptographic Manuals and Keys

ARMY. HEERESDIENSTVORSCHRIFTEN (H.DV.) BERLIN

H.Dv.g.13. *Gebrauchsanleitung für die Schlüsselmaschine Enigma.* Vom
12.1.1937. Berlin: Reichsdrückerei, 1937.
H.Dv.g.14. *Schlüsselanleitung für die Schlüsselmaschine Enigma.* 8.VI.1937.
Berlin: Reichsdrückerei, 1937.

NAVY. MARINEDIENSTVORSCHRIFTEN (M.DV.) BERLIN

[No M.Dv. number]. *Der Funkschlüssel C.* 1926.
M.Dv.Nr.21. *Der Funkschlüssel C. (Vorschrift).* 1933.
M.Dv.Nr.32. *Der Funkschlüssel M. (Vorschrift).* 1934.
M.Dv.Nr.32/1. *Der Schlüssel M. Verfahren M Allgemein.* 1940.
M.Dv.Nr.32/2. *Der Schlüssel M. Verfahren M Offizier und M Stab.* 1941.
M.Dv.Nr.32/3. *Der Schlüssel M. Allgemeine Bestimmungen.* 1941.
M.Dv.Nr.42. *Schlüssel H. (Sonderschlüssel für Handelsschiffe).* Ausgabe 1938.
1938.
M.Dv.Nr.82. *Geheime Marinefunknamenliste.* Berlin, 1943.
M.Dv.Nr.96. *Kurzsignalheft 1941.* (Nachdruck vom 25.2.1944). Berlin, 1941;
Kurzsignalheft 1944, II: Buchgruppenheft. Berlin, 1944; *Flottenkurzsig-
nalheft — Kennwort: Feodor.* Berlin, 1940.
Zu M.Dv.96. *Kenngruppenheft Nr. 2 zum Kurzsignalheft 1941.* Berlin, 1941.
M.Dv.Nr.98. *Kenngruppenbuch.* Berlin, 1929, 1939, 1941.
[No separate M.Dv. number; belongs to M.Dv.98]. *Schlüsselheft für Kenn-
gruppen — Kennwort: Sturm.* Berlin, 1939; ——— *Kennwort: Glanz.*
Berlin, 1939; *Zuteilungsliste für Kenngruppen — Kennwort: Forelle.* No
date; ——— *Kennwort: Hering.* No date.
M.Dv.Nr.103. *Schlüsselheft Nr. 47 zum Werftschlüssel.* Berlin, 1941.
M.Dv.Nr.136. *Geheimer Wetter- und Seeschlüssel der Kriegsmarine. Teil 3: Wet-
termeldungen für Handelsschiffe.* (7. Ausgabe.) Berlin, 1941.
M.Dv.Nr.150. *Signalbuch der Kriegsmarine.* Berlin, 1940.
M.Dv.Nr.212. *Geheimer Wetter- und Seeschlüssel der Kriegsmarine.* Berlin, 1938.
Zu M.Dv.Nr.212. *Wettertauschtafeln.* Berlin, 1938.
M.Dv.Nr.299. *U-Boots-Kurzsignalheft.* Berlin, 1940.
M.Dv.Nr.434. *Sammelmappe für Schlüsselmittel.* Berlin, 1939.
M.Dv.Nr.443. *Wetterkurzschlüssel.* (Ausgabe 1940.) Berlin, 1940; (2. Auf-
lage.) Berlin, 1941; (3. Auflage.) Berlin, 1942.
M.Dv. Nr.929/1. *Reservehandverfahren Offizier.* Berlin, 1940.
M.Dv.949. *Bestimmungen zur Wahrung der Schlüsselsicherheit bei Verlusten von
Schlüsselmitteln.* Berlin, 1943.

Unpublished Documents

The files listed here consist of ship's logs, reports of proceedings, memoranda, war diaries, and reminiscences.

PUBLIC RECORD OFFICE, LONDON

DEFE 3 [solved and translated intercepts of German naval messages; dates as given in notes or text].
DEFE 2/142; ADM 1/8637/55; ADM 1/11133; ADM 1/14256; ADM 53/113712; ADM 53/113713; ADM 53/113714; ADM 53/114202; ADM 53/114203; ADM 53/114500; ADM 53/114501; ADM 53/114161; ADM 53/114624; ADM 53/114797; ADM 137/4156; ADM 137/4374; ADM 137/4388; ADM 137/4500; ADM 199/123; ADM 199/430; ADM 199/447; ADM 199/476; ADM 199/626; ADM 199/1080; ADM 199/1082; ADM 199/1083; ADM 199/1084; ADM 199/1085; ADM 199/1086; ADM 199/1091; ADM 199/1101; ADM 199/1942; ADM 199/1963; ADM 199/2047; ADM 199/2053; ADM 199/2057; ADM 199/2203; ADM 199/2227; ADM 199/2228; ADM 199/2060; ADM 205/10; ADM 223/2; ADM 223/3; ADM 223/6; ADM 223/78; ADM 223/191; BJ 5/288.

MILITÄRARCHIV, FREIBURG-IM-BREISGAU

German naval files have a variety of signatures because the Militärarchiv is reclassifying them and because some were seen at the U.S. National Archives on microfilm, which retains the old PG numbers assigned by the Admiralty after World War II ("PG" is said to stand for "pinched from the Germans").

Oberkommando der Kriegsmarine, 1. Seekriegsleitung, Kriegstagebuch. Teil A. Dates as given in notes or text (cited as OKM, KTB).
Befehlshaber der Unterseeboote, Kriegstagebuch, dates as given in notes or text (cited as BdU, KTB).
Fasz. 5708 II 8–12; PG 15389; PG 30030; 30063; PG 30106; PG 30110; PG 30547; PG 30594; PG 30692; PG 30882; PG 33270; PG 34455F; PG 34456; PG 34466; PG 34529; PG 34530; PG 34534; PG 34814–PG 34837; PG 35185; PG 36742; PG 46635; PG 46656; PG 46676; PG 46853b; PG 46864; PG 46869; PG 46873; PG 46877; PG 46965; PG 46985; PG 47006; PG 47092; PG 47109; PG 47325; PG 47326; PG 47347; PG 47364; PG 48795; PG 48802; PG 48908; PG 49066; PG 64859; PG 78130; PG 80609; M/815/47218; M/815/47219; M/816/47264; M/816/47357; RM 7/85; RM 7/103–RM 7/108; RM 7/121; RM 7/127; RM 8/28; RM 8/47; RM 12 II/161; RM 20/306; RM 20/305; RM 47/v.259; RM 47/v.264; III M 1006/6; OKW 2228–OKW 2318; AOK [Armeeoberkommando] 2:19902/122; AOK 10:p1483/b; WK [Wehrkreis] VII/2530; WK XIII/69; WK XII/73; Sammlung Krug: MSg 109/2373.

NATIONAL ARCHIVES, WASHINGTON

Record group 24.
Deck log of U.S.S. *Card*, July 1–December 31, 1943.
Record group 457

SRGN + number (solved and translated intercepts of German naval messages; dates or serial numbers as given in notes or text).
SRH-145; SRH-236; SRMN-030; SRMN-032; SRMN-033; SRMN-035; SRMN-038; SRMN-048; SRMN-049; SRMN-051; SRS-548.

OPERATIONAL ARCHIVES, NAVAL HISTORICAL CENTER, WASHINGTON

[Sebald, William J.] "The Reminiscences of Ambassador Wm. J. Sebald (Capt. USNR Ret.)." Annapolis: U.S. Naval Institute, 1979.
[Smedberg, William R., III.] "The Reminiscences of Vice Admiral William R. Smedberg, III, U.S. Navy (Retired)." Annapolis: U. S. Naval Institute, 1979.
[Smith-Hutton, Henri.] "The Reminiscences of Captain Henri Smith-Hutton, U.S. Navy (Retired)." Annapolis: U. S. Naval Institute, 1976.
Task Forces 21.13–21.15. Box 105.
    Folder Task Group 21.13. Action Report. Hunter/Killer Group Operations, Report of. December 5, 1943.
    Folder Task Group 21.14. Action Report. Hunter/Killer Group Operations, Report of. November 9, 1943.
Tenth Fleet Files. Convoy and Routing Section. Folders for Convoys HX 155, ON 179, SC 127, ONS 4.
World War II Action Report. Commander Destroyer Division 52 (Commander Task Unit 4.1.7). Escort of Convoys HX 155 and ON 31, October 18–November 15, 1941, November 24, 1941.
World War II Action Report. Commander in Chief, U.S. Atlantic Fleet. Hunter-Killer Group Operations. September 25, 1943.

NAVAL HISTORICAL BRANCH, LONDON

[Godfrey, John H.] "The Naval Memoirs of J. H. Godfrey." 8 vols., mimeographed. N.p., n.d.
Home Fleet Narrative. 1941.

BERLIN DOCUMENT CENTER

Hans-Thilo Schmidt, party no. 738736 (1.12.1931)
Rudolf Heimsoeth, party no. 3739694 (1.4.1936)

CHURCHILL COLLEGE, CAMBRIDGE

Clarke Papers: CLKE 2, 3.
Denniston Papers: DENN 1/2, 1/3, 1/4.
MacLachlan-Beesly Papers: MLBE 1/5, 1/13, 2/8, 2/11, 2/14, 2/30, 3/25, 5/1.

Index

Photo Credits

Enigma machine sequence: National Security Agency
The *Magdeburg:* Bundesarchiv
Scherbius: Heinz Heimsoeth
Schmidt: Berlin Document Center
Knox: Oliver Knox
Rejewski: Wladislaw Kozaczuk
The U-33, Hitler greeting crew: Ernst Masanek
Lofotens raid: Ludovic Kennedy and Imperial War Museum
The *Krebs:* Maurice Low
The U-110: Heinz Wilde
Balme: David Balme
Wilde: Heinz Wilde
Travis: Valery Emery
Hinsley: Harry Hinsley
Welchman: Rosamond Tischler
Alexander: Stuart Milner-Barry
Playing rounders, watching a match: Barbara Eachus
Lauenburg capture sequence: Ludovic Kennedy and Imperial War
    Museum
U-559, Antony Fasson: G. G. Connell
Dönitz: Bibliothek für Zeitgeschichte
Wall plot: Imperial War Museum
U.S. Navy bombe: National Security Agency
Knowles: National Archives
OP-20-G personnel: Erminnie Bartelmez
U-boat attacks: National Archives

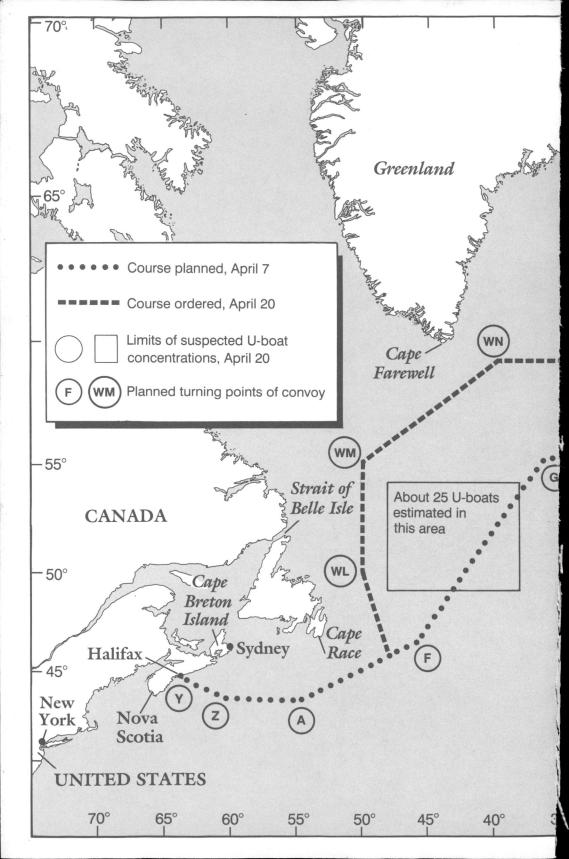

70°

65°

Greenland

• • • • • Course planned, April 7

━ ━ ━ ━ Course ordered, April 20

◯ ☐ Limits of suspected U-boat concentrations, April 20

(F) (WM) Planned turning points of convoy

Cape Farewell

(WN)

55°

Strait of Belle Isle

CANADA

(WM)

(G)

About 25 U-boats estimated in this area

50°

(WL)

Cape Breton Island

• Sydney

Cape Race

Halifax

45°

(Y)

(F)

New York

(Z)

(A)

Nova Scotia

UNITED STATES

70°   65°   60°   55°   50°   45°   40°   3